AFFECTIVE IMAGES

AFFECTIVE IMAGES

POST-APARTHEID DOCUMENTARY PERSPECTIVES

MARIETTA KESTING

SUNY
PRESS

Cover image courtesy of the author.

Published by State University of New York Press, Albany

Printed in the United States of America

For information, contact State University of New York Press, Albany, NY
www.sunypress.edu

Production, Eileen Nizer
Marketing, Fran Keneston

Library of Congress Cataloging-in-Publication Data

Names Kesting, Marietta.
Title: Affective images: Post-apartheid Documentary Perspectives / Marietta Kesting.
Description: Albany : State University of New York Press, [2017] | Includes bibliographical references and index.
Identifiers: ISBN 9781438467856 (hardcover : alk. paper) | ISBN 9781438467849 (pbk. : alk. paper) | ISBN 9781438467863 (ebook)
Further information is available at the Library of Congress.

10 9 8 7 6 5 4 3 2 1

Contents

List of Illustrations vii

Acknowledgments xiii

Introduction 1

Chapter 1 Mapping Context and Place 17

Chapter 2 Affective Images 29
- 2.1. Photographs of Black Suffering and Violence 29
- 2.2. Affective Images in the "New" South Africa 55

Chapter 3 Burning Questions 79
- 3.1. The "Burning Man" 79
- 3.2. The Afterlife of Nhamuave's Photograph 97

photo gallery follows page 118

Chapter 4 Photographic Speech Acts 119
- 4.1. Migrant Life and the Image 119
- 4.2. Documentary Participatory Photography and Politics 134

Chapter 5 In/Visibilities and Reenactments 143
- 5.1. De-identification and Multiplication? 143
- 5.2. From Documentary to Fiction—and Back: *District 9* 162

Chapter 6 Conclusion: Affective Images of Belonging 183

Notes 203

Glossary 245

Bibliography 249

Filmography 269

Index 273

List of Illustrations

Introduction

0.1	A "pass burning" demonstration, Soweto, SA, 1961, Magnum Photos, Ian Berry.	1

Chapter 1

1.1	Reenactment of Great Trek, "Piet Retief's Manifesto, a float in the 1952 Jan van Riebeeck Festival," Courtesy of the Cape Times.	19
1.2	Still from Lionel Rogosin's *Come Back, Africa*, street scene in Johannesburg 1959.	23
1.3	*Drum* Cover from June 1951, Bailey History Archive (in gallery).	
1.4	Still from the music video "Got Till It's Gone" (in gallery).	
1.5	Still from the music video "Got Till It's Gone" (in gallery).	

Chapter 2

2.1.1	Ernest Cole, Handcuffed Black Men 1967, *House of Bondage*. The Ernest Cole Family Trust and the Hasselblad Foundation.	31
2.1.2	Poster to end the conscription campaign of the SADF 1985, SAHA.	33

2.1.3 Hector Pietersen shot by police, carried by Mbuyisa Makhubo, on the left his sister, 1976. Photograph by Sam Nzima. 37

2.1.4 Poster by the Student Union for Christian Action 1985, SAHA. 41

2.1.5 Greg Marinovich, Inhlazane, Soweto, September 15 1990 (original in color). 46

2.1.6 Still from the music video "I ain't gonna play Sun City" (in gallery).

2.1.7 Still from the music video "I ain't gonna play Sun City" (in gallery).

2.2.1 Still of female witness in tears at TRC hearing, *Facing the Truth*, 1995, by Gail Pellett, gailpellettproductions.com; last accessed 8/9/2014 (original in color). 58

2.2.2 Fatima's testimony in tears, still from *Conversations* (original in color). 63

2.2.3 Martiné's daughter, still from *Martiné and Thandeka* (original in color). 67

2.2.4 Martiné's daughter inside the tent, still from *Martiné and Thandeka*. 70

2.2.5 A single tear from Martiné's daughter, still from *Martiné and Thandeka*. 71

2.2.6 Silent female protestors during Zuma's speech at the ROC 2016. 73

2.2.7 Fatima refuses the conversation (still from *Conversations*). 75

Chapter 3

3.1.1 "The Burning Man," Photographer Simphiwe Nkwali, March 2008 (original in color). 83

3.2.1 The portrait photo of Ernesto Nhamuave, which was widely published after his death, still from *The Burning Man* (original in color). 98

3.2.2 Newspapers of the event, still from the film *The Burning Man*. 99

3.2.3 The filmmaker Adze Ugah, still from the film *The Burning Man.* 100

3.2.4 Road and landscape in Vuca, still from *The Burning Man.* 101

3.2.5 Ernesto's son seen from behind, still from *The Burning Man.* 102

3.2.6 Striking a match, still from *Man on Ground* (in gallery).

3.2.7 The statement "Too many foreigners," still from *Man on Ground* (in gallery).

3.2.8 Car burning with Femi inside, still from *Man on Ground* (in gallery).

3.2.9 Shack burning, still from *Man on Ground* (in gallery).

3.2.10 Stills from music video "Powa" by Tumi Molekane, South Africa 2011. 115

3.2.11 Stills from music video "Powa." 116

Chapter 4

4.1.1 Boarded-up door with signs in Hillbrow, 2011, Marietta Kesting. 119

4.1.2 Example of a correct South African passport photo, source Passport Agency Website. 122

4.1.3 Nelson Mandela burning his pass, photo by Eli Weinberg 1960. University of the Western Cape, Robben Island Mayibuye Archives. 125

4.1.4 Zimbabwean Nationals waiting at Home Affairs in Johannesburg, photographer Believe Nyakadjara 2011 (in gallery).

4.1.5 Flyer of the IOM and SACTAP Campaign Against Trafficking (original in color). 128

4.1.6 Poster for exhibit by Médecins Sans Frontières, 2011 (original in color). 129

4.1.7 Poster by the Black Women Studies Group, 1982, SAHA (original in color). 131

4.1.8 Example of the self-labeling as a foreigner. The author is wearing the "Kwerekwere" campaign T-shirt, Marietta Kesting. 133

4.2.1 Self-portrait and text of Patience produced at *Hotel Yeoville* (in gallery) © Terry Kurgan & Hotel Yeoville.

4.2.2 Self-portrait and text taken in the photo booth at *Hotel Yeoville* (in gallery) © Terry Kurgan & Hotel Yeoville.

4.2.3 *Working the City,* poster presentation of Mimi. African Centre for Migration & Society (ACMS), the Market Photo Workshop (MPW) and, the Sisonke Sex Worker Movement (in gallery).

Chapter 5

5.1.1 Stills from *We Are Nowhere* (original in color). 146

5.1.2 Simon's ID Photo (reenactment), Marietta Kesting. 148

5.1.3 At Lindela Detention Center, women hiding—a still from *Conversations.* 151

5.1.4 At Lindela Detention Center, women lying on the floor and hiding—a still from *Conversations.* 151

5.1.5 Stills from *Border Farm* (in gallery).

5.1.6 Still from *Border Farm,* crossing of the Limpopo River, reenacted (in gallery).

5.1.7 Still from *Border Farm,* crossing of the Limpopo River, reenacted (in gallery).

5.1.8 A staged demonstration, still from *Conversations.* 157

5.1.9 A staged demonstration, still from *Conversations.* 158

5.2.1 The aliens on Earth, and the camps that they have to stay in, stills from *District 9* (original in color). 164

5.2.2 Staged news cast, still from *D9.* 167

5.2.3 Staged news cast, still from *D9.* 168

5.2.4 Poster *District 9* (original in color). 172

5.2.5 Poster by the APF "Stop Xenophobia," 2008, SAHA (original in color). 173

5.2.6 Spaceship over Johannesburg, stills from *D9*. 175

Conclusion

6.1 Still from *Nando's* "Diversity Clip" (original in color). 184

6.2 Still from *Nando's* "Diversity Clip." 185

6.3 Still from Michelle Monareng's *Removal to Radium*. 187

6.4 Still from Michelle Monareng's *Removal to Radium*. 188

6.5 Still from Michelle Monareng's *Removal to Radium*. 188

6.6 Still from Michelle Monareng's *Removal to Radium*. 189

Acknowledgments

Preparation of this book was undertaken while I was part of the research group "Gender as a Category of Knowledge" at Humboldt-University, Berlin, and it would not have been possible without the support and resources I found there.

In the final phase Beth Boulokos and Rafael Chaiken of SUNY Press have advised me on all issues ranging from the practical to the conceptual, and I am deeply thankful for that.

Moreover, three anonymous peer reviewers have read my manuscript and offered detailed and thoughtful suggestions for changes and edits that the book benefited from immensely and that widened its scope.

A big thank you to the Hasselblad Foundation and the Ernest Cole Family Fund as well as the South African History Archive, UWC Robben Island Museum Mayibuye Archive, and to all other photographers and filmmakers, who have allowed me to publish their work.

While it is impossible to name all of those who have helped me with their discussions and insights or by their reading more or less developed drafts of this book, I want to thank particularly Christina von Braun, Gabriele Dietze, Claudia Bruns, Alisa Lebow, Julia Schoen, Katrin Köppert, Kirstin Mertlitsch, Nana Adusei-Poku, Todd Sekuler, Käthe von Bose, Aljoscha Weskott, Ole Graf, Thenjiwe Niki Nkosi, Pamela Phatsimo Sunstrom, Rangoato Hlasane, Darryl Els, Ulrike Kistner, Steven Brimelow, Avital Nates, Terry Kurgan, Michelle Monareng, Caroline Kihato, Loren Landau, Martin Ebner, Nanna Heidenreich, Diedrich Diederichsen, Daniel Hendrickson, Henriette Gunkel, Ulrike Auga, and Sophia Kunze.

In addition, Helga Kesting-Rathmann, Herwig Rathmann, Frank Dörwaldt and Dagmar Weiß, Gerhard and Anne Weiß, and Wolfgang Kesting have provided support in innumerable ways.

Parts of chapter 4 have been published in the essay "Photographic Portraits of Migrants in South Africa" in *Social Dynamics. A Journal African Studies*, vol. 40, (Cape Town: Taylor and Francis) 2014, 471–494, and are reprinted with permission.

Introduction

A Burning Lens Magnifying Burning Pass Books

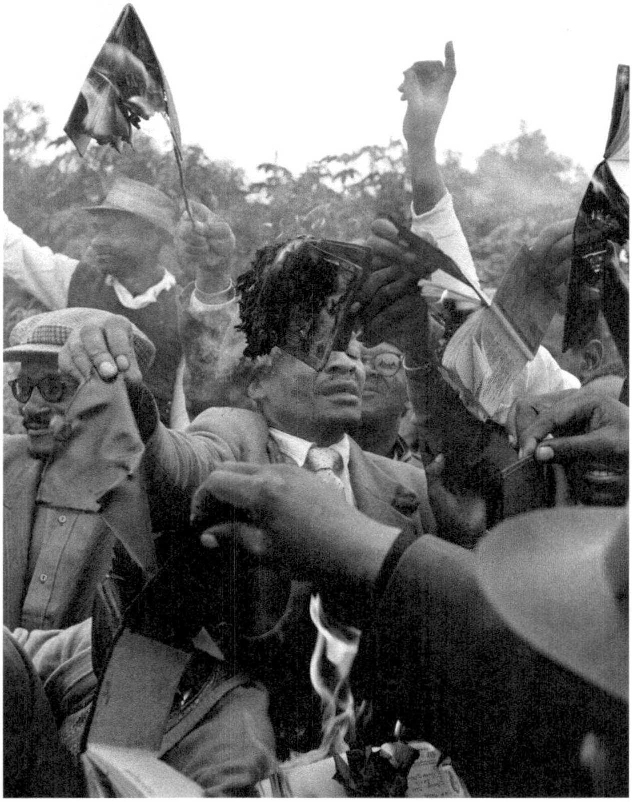

Figure 0.1. A "pass burning" demonstration, Soweto, SA, 1961, Magnum Photos, Ian Berry.

Looking at a black-and-white photograph from 1961 in the Magnum Photos Archive. It shows the scene of a pass-burning demonstration in Soweto, South Africa.[1] Black South Africans were demonstrating against the apartheid pass laws, which treated them as "foreigners" in their own land. When "traveling" the 20 km from Soweto to their workplace in the city of Johannesburg, black South Africans were obliged to present pass books even though they were not crossing any international or national borders on that route.[2] To protest the pass laws, they were destroying these documents of identification in public as acts of defiance.[3] The white British photojournalist Ian Berry took this photograph.[4] Only black men are visible in it, dressed formally in shirts and ties. The image is confusing at first glance, as hands holding half or completely burnt pass books protrude into the photo from all sides, often blocking out parts of the men's faces.

The photographer composed the image in such a way that in its very center a dramatically charcoaled and frayed piece of a pass book is visible, thereby making this object the main focus of attention for the viewer. The photograph is in vertical format; this is uncommon for photographing events like a demonstration, which are usually shown in landscape format. Here it may have been used to concentrate the action and underline the vertical lines of the hands and fingers, one of which is pointing up to the sky. This visual composition adds force to the scene, it looks like a theatrical staging. Wafting smoke from the burning passes further obscures the image, and flames are visible in the lower part. The men hold the pass books gingerly, as if not wanting to burn their hands, and also because the pass books were hated, despised objects.[5] The hands in the air and the smiling faces of some of the men lend the setting an almost festive atmosphere or make it look like a choreographed dance. The man in the center of the image was caught with his eyes closed, radiating serenity and commitment. The photograph has little focus depth and looks compressed, this is indicative that a telephoto objective, also called a burning lens, was used to take the image from farther away on a bright day with a small aperture setting. It leads to the impression that everything is happening in a very condensed and crowded space that seems to be in the "middle of nowhere," a barren area outside of the city, as was common for the township locations under apartheid, without any urban qualities or other features of a particular place visible in the background. The photograph's affective index brings across the action of resistance and intensity, bundling energy through the upstretched hands, arms, passes, and finger and transmits a feeling of hope, community, and men acting together. They may have called out "phambili"—"forward," as was common at protests. This documentary photo and similar images by Magnum photographers Abbas and Chris Steele-Perkins were my first exposure to the specific documentary tradition of image production in South Africa amplified by the fight against apartheid, in which images of injustice were used as weapons against the oppressive government.[6]

The photograph taken with a burning lens acts as a magnifying glass, by focusing on four relevant and problematic issues this study is concerned with. First, when official identity documents with passport photos are obliterated, racialized subjects render themselves unidentifiable, severing the connection between a body and a document, which had restricted this body's very movement and opportunities in life.

Second, the act of destroying an official photo, which is at the same time a self-portrait, is a reflective political act, since it is an effective and affective performance. As image theorist W. T. J. Mitchell has argued, images may become imbued with a particular agency "not merely as sentient creatures that can feel pain and pleasure but as responsible and responsive social beings. Images of this sort seem to look back at us, to speak to us, even to be capable of suffering harm or of magically transmitting harm when violence is done to them."[7]

Third, it is striking that a privileged white male photographer has captured this image of the marginalized black others while they are in the process of becoming officially invisible or undocumented, highlighting the inherent contradictions in the discourse of in/visibilities and (political) self-representation. The white skin of the photographer also seems to render him invisible and unmarked in his privileged male subjectivity and to make him immune to apartheid police persecution.[8] And yet, one must assume that the presence of the white photographer was welcomed by the pass-burners, since the documentation of their action advanced the publicity and was useful for further mobilization.

Fourth, neither is the photographer female nor are there any other women in front of the lens, which points to a blind spot or missing image, since female black South Africans were equal if not the prime protagonists in the protests against the pass laws.[9] These are four conflicting and ambiguous conditions that have to be negotiated when analyzing affective images of post-apartheid. I want to examine and foreground the connection between politics and affect that are prevalent when making documentary films and photography about injustice, violence, and resistance.

As South African historian Patricia Hayes has demonstrated, progressive documentary photography and the discipline of social history or a "History from Below" developed in South Africa hand in hand. Both disciplines naturalized similar conventions: "the one to end silence, and the other to end invisibility."[10] This thought may have been inspired by Roland Barthes, who had linked the invention of photography to the emergence of history as a discipline.[11] The documentation of the life and "reality" of the disenfranchised African majority was therefore imbued with the concept of empowerment and progressive, leftist political aims. Hence, politics and ethics have always been inextricably linked with the production, presentation, and viewing of photography and film in South Africa.[12]

In the current age that is both disillusioned with politics, media, and activism and at the same time is seeing the rise of new social movements and protests worldwide, I want to analyze and historicize how the "political" is evoked with the means of affective (documentary) images today. These images are involved in many different public scenarios, in which claims and contestations need to be visualized as in "awareness" campaigns, court scenarios, and lobbying. I use the term "political" following Jacques Rancière as viable sites where various orderings and social relations become "sensible."[13] These public and political realms are structured by perceptions and affect. This study examines how they are mediated through documentary media, meaning what becomes visible and which affective responses are prevalent.

Approaches, Places, and Material

While the aim of documenting injustice seemed "right" and convincing until the official end of apartheid in 1994, in post-apartheid times the feasibility of the "socially concerned" documentary photography, of which Magnum photographers were always some of the strongest global representatives, became more and more complicated and dubious. These questions and doubts, however, never led to the documentary project being given up as a whole, even though feminist film critic Trinh T. Minh-ha had already claimed in the 1990s that: "There is no such thing as documentary . . . despite the very visible existence of a documentary tradition."[14] This is the inherent contradiction and ambivalence of documentary film and photography. In a similar vein Abigail Solomon-Godeau fleshed out the current critique of documentary photography, noting that "the category "documentary" remains in service as a workable, although untheorized, rubric."[15] But she highlighted: "between the apparently unmediated (but still highly mediated) images of the electronic surveillance camera . . . and for example, the emphatically personal and "expressive" photographs of postrevolutionary Iran taken by Gilles Peress, lies a very large and very gray area."[16] Minh-ha on the other hand emphasized that documentary film always has intrinsic aspects of construction and fiction and no privileged access to real life or 'true reality': "A documentary aware of its own artifice is one that remains sensitive to the flow between fact and fiction. It does not work to conceal or exclude what is normalized as 'nonfactual' for it understands the mutual dependence of realism and 'artificiality' in the process of filmmaking."[17]

This study examines documents of visual culture as a whole—the pioneer of this approach was Aby Warburg. I am following the diverse but related works by Christina von Braun, Roland Barthes, and W. J. T. Mitchell who all include visual material from newspapers, websites, documentary art projects, documentary film, and advertisement images in their insightful analyses.[18] Accordingly, I argue that in the visual sphere there exists something akin to intertextuality, which I will call "intervisuality." At the same time there occur cross-references and dialogues between the verbal and the iconic realms. I am treating (documentary) images as a separate discourse that is nevertheless connected with textual discourse, yet without being completely absorbed by it. In addition, referring to film scholar Linda Williams and her study *Playing the Racecard*, there is a melodramatic impact of documentary footage.[19] Williams proved that seemingly factual information conveyed through documentary footage is viewed or organized by viewers into familiar narratives and viewing patterns, as for example the melodrama.

By taking up a perspective from the outside and looking at documentary images of post-apartheid affect through the lens of migration, I write not "about" images of African migrants in South Africa but write *alongside* or rather *close-by* these sites of image productions but also the blind spots, omissions and misrepresentations. This approach is informed by Minh-ha and her criticism of the ethnographic approach, who discussed the inherent power constellations of the term of "the real," and who called for a practice of "speaking nearby" as opposed to "speaking about."[20]

Foreigners Don't Leave Us with the Tourists!

In 2008 perceived foreigners from other African countries were assaulted, heavily injured, or killed in most urban areas in South Africa and their peripheries.[21] The violent excesses were called "xenophobic attacks" and included the looting of shops, burning of homesteads, and the injuring and killing of people. In the course of the attacks about sixty-two people were murdered, and several hundred injured. In the aftermath tens of thousands of displaced people lived temporarily in police stations and later in refugee camps.[22] In response the pan-African cultural magazine *Chimurenga* instigated various activities. It devoted one of their editions to the topic, and put up signs all over Johannesburg, saying for example: "We are all Nigerians."[23] In addition, some of the slogans were printed on T-shirts, as, for example: "FOREIGNERS PLEASE DON'T LEAVE US WITH THE TOURISTS."[24] Needless to say, also the Western artist or image producer stands in the footsteps of "missionary, ethnographer and adventurer," yet while acknowledging this heritage, one should not let it overdetermine the present. I am a white European female foreigner in Johannesburg, but I want to take *Chimurenga*'s campaign seriously and report from Johannesburg as an outsider, albeit one who is deeply engaged with the local politics and people, since I have worked and temporarily lived in Johannesburg off and on for at least some time each year for the last nine years. I was involved both in practical and documentary work including filmmaking and photography, an art exhibition and film screenings, and as an academic, doing research in archives, attending conferences and community events, and giving papers.

And yet, these are overlapping spheres since I analyze visual culture and argue for a perspective that is informed by knowledge on the technicalities and practices of image making. Often meaningful conversations have taken place also at a gallery reception, waiting in line at the cinema, preparing for filming on a car drive or walk, sometimes in a parking lot. I took visual notes in the form of photographs or video footage and collected flyers, books, and artists' films that were not yet released on DVD. All of this material forms the backdrop of my study and augmented this manuscript.

The Lens of Migration

It is meaningful to "revisit . . . South African social science through migration and displacement" looking at the contestations over mobility as a "metanarrative,"[25] as Johannesburg-based social scientist Loren Landau has argued. By the same token Rory Bester affirmed: "Any examination of contemporary South African responses to 'foreigners' is bound to overlap with a history of 'strangeness that extends to banishment, Bantustans, ethnicity, forced removals, migrant labor, and pass laws.' "[26] I am using the "lens of migration" to reconsider documentary image politics and affect. Similarly, but not analogously, Mitchell, who imbues images with their own agency, has even tried to equate migrating images with people who migrate: "To what extent . . . are images like migrants: homeless, stateless, displaced persons, exiles, or hopeful aspirants to 'a new location' where they might find a home? We live in a world in which many persons are without passports, without states, dislocated. Are images like that?"[27] Beyond a too simple equation between visual travelers and human travelers I want to point instead to the processes of complex mutual influences, but it seems valid to see images as part of a larger network of living and non-living actors, affect, modes of transmission and viewing that are partly determined by technical constraints and possibilities.

Affective images reflected political changes, but also got restaged under changed auspices. I learned about current productions of documentary photographs and film in South Africa by artists and filmmakers like Thenjiwe Nkosi, Khalo Matabane, and the Center for Historical Reenactments and valued them for their experimental and innovative approaches.[28] These experimental formats were often a response to highly pressing issues, like the "xenophobic attacks" in May 2008. The perpetrators of the xenophobic attacks were black South African men and women, the victims were "perceived others"—mostly black African immigrants. Foreigners were singled out by pseudo-ethnic markers—shades of skin color, since South African Blacks consider themselves to be lighter than, for example, Zimbabweans, and also by language tests—to see if they understood *isiZulu*, one of the dominant "ethnic" language groups of South Africa.

The xenophobic attacks from 2008 are treated as a caesura in this study, because they started a meta-reflexive process within and about the "new" South Africa and sparked many (documentary) image productions. They created strong affective responses since they seemed to shatter the myth of the "peaceful rainbow nation" that South Africa had been celebrated for since 1994.[29] These changes in documentary practices are traced and interpreted from very immediate responses to more problematizing approaches of image and film production. Most of the analyzed works originate in and around the megacity Johannesburg, since this place operates as a hub both for sub-Saharan African migration as well as for the South African documentary photography and film scene, where new practices emerge and experiments are attempted and discussed as to their impacts and implications. The relationship between looking and differentiating is both spelled out and critiqued, which hints at the complicity of visual media as such in seemingly producing knowledge about the other.

The admittance to space is very regulated and controlled even in post-apartheid times due to high crime and the partial persistence of apartheid practices, for example in the police force or in private security companies.[30] Identity documents must be presented on a daily basis when entering "official, professional" spaces like a university, government agency or another institution, but also when entering a private, secluded and upper-class space like a gated community. Of course this is not the same as the urban zoning or pass-book system for black South African migrant workers during apartheid, yet some of these exclusionary practices seem uncannily familiar. A visual regime of who looks as if he or she belongs to a certain place and therefore may have a right to be there or not is constantly reenacted and performed.[31]

Documentary works always had inherent blind spots and omissions, especially in photojournalism. On this matter South African photographer Santu Mofokeng has stated that photographs are tools of "world-making" and "language" since by making something visible, it becomes discussable, and it can be turned into a political agenda. Accordingly, he noted "there is no vocabulary for the non-photographed of apartheid."[32] Mofokeng tried in his own practice located in between art and social photography to counteract this invisibility by collecting photographs from black subjects and exhibiting them as the "Black Photo Album/Look at Me 1890–1950."[33]

A documentary, which is considered to offer "factual" visibility and comprehensiveness, simultaneously renders other aspects invisible. This tension needs to be addressed on several levels. On the one hand, I hold the position that one needs to look beyond the shocking images from news media in "sophisticated" documentary works, and also include ordinary images, for instance, of socioeconomic inequality in order to understand the xenophobic attacks. On the other hand, I want to emphasize the necessity of exposing oneself to the shocking images and of not looking away, but of letting oneself be moved by them. This complex of visualizations produces a set of psychic relations that Sigmund Freud described as "a group of interdependent ideational elements cathected with affect."[34]

Images of Crises from the Xenophobic Attacks

The "xenophobic" attacks in South Africa 2008 were seen across the world through the documentary images that they produced, which made the front pages of newspapers and online portals. This event crystallized in the documentary photograph of the "Burning Man," which documented the communal killing of a Mozambican man named Ernesto Alfabeto Nhamuave, who had been set on fire by a mob.[35] This photograph was a singular image that hurts to look at, and which had countless repercussions in the visual, political, and emotional realm. It produced shock mixed with pain, sadness, speechlessness, and anger. Once I had seen it, I could not get it out of my head. At the scene of the burning, shouting and laughing bystanders, police, and photographers were all present, but only the police tried to extinguish the flames and save him. It was too late.[36] Shortly after the photograph was taken, Nhamuave died from his injuries.[37] The photograph of Ernesto Nhamuave became an important documentary icon that signified the totality and ruthlessness of the widespread violence on perceived foreigners from other African countries.

This image can be identified as what Rancière has called "intolerable," one that cannot be viewed without "pain or indignation."[38] In addition, Rancière emphasizes: "What it shows is deemed too real, too intolerably real to be offered in the form of an image. This is not a simple matter of respect for personal dignity."[39] Instead the collusion of images is exposed since they are part of the same "regime of visibility" that they should criticize. In spite of this complicity Luc Boltanski has pointed out that viewing suffering can induce action on the side of the audience. He proposes: "Faced with the spectacle of an unfortunate suffering far away, what can a morally receptive spectator do when he is condemned, at least for the moment, to inaction?" He can become *indignant.*"[40] This study does not solely focus on shocking images to unravel and discuss (documentary) strategies of visualizing migration and migrants, a few particular intolerable photographs need to be examined in depth. Rancière, however, like Judith Butler and others, reminds us that a second question is bound up with the affect that we immediately feel when viewing such an "intolerable image:" "Is it acceptable to make such images and exhibit them to others?"[41] This analysis is therefore always in conjunction with an inquiry about the ethics and politics of documentary images both on the side of the image viewers as well as the image producers.

> I was aware that that there were incidences . . . it was pretty much the Sunday before Ernesto—the Mozambican was *burnt* . . . I understood the historical importance of it immediately but also just like the need to be there—to *witness* you know—I don't know—I hate the word—like witness but there is something within that.[42]

The motivation of the photographers, who were present at the scene of the xenophobic attacks in 2008 was to witness, as is indicated by the quote above from white South African photographer Nadine Hutton. The role of the photographer, as Ariella Azoulay has analyzed, consists of: "gathering testimonies . . . even if they strike him as disturbing or meaningless."[43]

The bloodshed in May 2008 led to a new urgency to understand precarious citizenship, migration and migrant life in its vulnerability.[44] Some of the most imperative questions were: What factors and incidents had led to this violence and "xenophobic" hatred? What was the trigger for the attacks at that particular time? What policies protected the aggressors and exposed the victims to attacks? Why were people who had worked and lived in South Africa for many years suddenly perceived as foreigners? And why was the violence only targeted against a specific group of immigrants—that is, poor black Africans—and not against the hundreds of thousands of white Europeans?[45]

The (audio-)visual documents that I refer to not only criticize South African society and nationhood, but also reflect on the role of visual media itself. As Christina von Braun reminds us, the terms "cliché" and "stereotype" come from the technical vocabulary for the printing press and are therefore inherently connected to visual media.[46] This study attempts to take up the question: Can unjust and stereotypical images of the other be "set right," balanced or "healed" by offering counter images? Or are conscious acts of complicating, fictionalizing and thus making less unequivocal and more ambiguous documentary images the key to use them more effectively as activist photography and political documentary? Several answers will be explored throughout the study, showing that while a case can always be made for remaining "invisible," documentary image productions can, however, also produce non-normative images.

Affect and Documentary

Different modes of (audio-)visual address are always connected with a simultaneous invocation of different modes of affect that initially register as "intensity" and subsequently get translated or interpreted into *feelings* as shock, dismay, shame, compassion, and sadness. "Affect" is derived from the Latin term *affectus*, which translates as "condition, disposition, passion, emotion, and feeling" or the verb *afficere* "to cause, afflict, move," indicating both an active as well as a passive or involuntary force.[47] Throughout this study the term *affect* refers to its usage by Gilles Deleuze and Felix Guattari's concept, who adapted it from Baruch de Spinoza's *Ethics*.[48] I follow them in distinguishing between "affect" and "feelings." As "emotions" are understood as something that people own, "affect" always possesses a surplus value, something that "escapes confinement."[49] Feelings are expressions of affect, but feelings are always already interpreted, whereas affect lies before interpretation.[50]

Feminist theory and gender studies have, however, always been concerned with the body, perceptions, feelings, and the unconscious, and thus the phenomena, which have been excluded from the seemingly "pure" sphere of knowledge or the "mind."[51] These theoretical approaches have explored ways to break down the body-mind dichotomy, rather than trying to bridge these areas, similar to what the "affective turn" seems to promise nowadays. Therefore, one could argue that feminist thought practiced "affect studies" *avant la lettre*.[52] I also want to note that the separation between "affect" and "feeling" is an artificial divide for analytical purposes and may not always be established in as clear-cut a manner as one would wish, since this study is primarily concerned with images and their affective relations and effects on viewers, who translate affect into subjective feelings.

How is affect now invoked or transferred when viewing documentary photographs or films? What is the ineluctable relationship between image, affect, and the political? Viewing documentary materials is always a relational experience that engages the spectator with cognitive and affective processes that may involve identification, memory, and sometimes (secondary) trauma.[53] One can imagine a chain of re/action as an event takes place, for instance, a forced removal of migrant people, leading to intense affect and protest, *infecting* bystanders who start taking sides, and this event may be recorded—immediately, as it happens or later as a scene of aftermath—by a filmmaker.[54] She may have been moved to do so by feeling empathically with the people losing their places to live, yet she also crafts a certain perspective on the events by choosing camera angle, framing the shots, recording or not recording live sound, and thus she also adds a layer of analysis or interpretation. In turn, the final product may act contagiously when being screened to audiences who may be compelled to change their perspective after seeing the film, feeling both immediately affected and at the same time starting a reflective process.[55] This chain of affect and thought can both be broken apart or picked up again at each station.

I consider "affect" therefore to be an inherent but undertheorized dimension of producing and viewing documentary films and photographs, and I am arguing for a way of embodied seeing that cannot be separated from a purely analytical gaze.[56] Brian Massumi follows Deleuze and Guattari and theorizes affect as pure intensity that opens a short interval of undecidedness into which direction an action or event may lead. Thereby one can locate a possibility for change exactly there. Massumi even euphemistically or provokingly called affect "hope" in the sense of a step forward or sideward, or rather that something is happening, starting, moving—into an unknown future.[57]

I can see artists and image-makers work on strategies to include a meta-reflective dimension into their documentary works, which activates and stimulates intellectual debate while also moving the viewer affectively.

This is necessarily related to Judith Butler and her idea of "affective frames," and who can be mourned in what context.[58] Linking the "affective frame" with the Deleuzian notion of "blocs" of affect, initiated through perceptions/percepts, one can re-think the societal framework beyond the individual person and the reproduction of the subject.[59] Deleuze and Guattari defined this "bloc" as follows:

> What is preserved—the thing or the work of art—is *a bloc of sensations, that is to say, a compound of percepts and affects*. Percepts are no longer perceptions; they are independent of a state of those who experience them. Affects are no longer feelings or affections; they go beyond the strength of those who undergo them. Sensations, percepts, and affects are *beings* whose validity lies in themselves and exceeds any lived.[60]

Minoritarian or excluded elements of society—both individuals or groups—may thus be able to start a movement of the whole bloc of affect, for example the movement against apartheid that was supported by many different members of South African society, temporally united in the pursuit of justice for black South Africans. As I argue throughout this study, images play a key role in the distribution and intensification of affect and may become political. Thereby I consider the visual realm always inseparably entwined with the political and affective realm.

"Affect" can theorize the potential of these images to "move" and to "hurt," and to explain their status as "open wounds" or "painful evidence," and attest to both their "eventfulness" (*Ereignishaftigkeit*) and their ability to trigger reactions in the viewers. Furthermore, affect has the potential to de-center the subject or the atomized viewer, who is often thought of as passive. Thus affect in the Spinozian understanding can create collectivities connected by intensities and is useful for theorizing our referentiality or relatedness with others—both persons and things and the constant exchange of intensity, feelings, and knowledge.[61] Affect may establish community without unity, but at the same time I understand every subjectivity—following Butler and Levinas—to exist only with and in relation to or *through* the others.[62] Similarly, sociologist Serhat Karakayalı, who refers back to Deleuze's reading of Spinoza, put it:

> Following Spinoza (but also Ahmed), feelings do not describe the inner state of a subject, but instead are connected with social interaction and thereby a function of power. This makes sense

> since ideas are not opposed to feelings or derived from them. They do not represent a thing outside of the mind, but rather every idea is already connected with an affect. . . .[63]

Affective responses may even be used strategically and calculatedly to induce reflection and critical thought in a secondary process that is different from, yet acknowledges being moved on the grounds of what gets interpreted as feelings. Affect may thus prepare the ground for the deeper engagement with topics that necessarily need to be in a reflective mode that connects to critiques of representation, and not in a simple flow of affect. Deleuze and Guattari propose, that "[a]ffects are becomings."[64] They instigate processes and changes in space and time without a clearly identifiable beginning or end.

How are affective visual politics intertwined with—and operant in—the production of political perspectives on "reality" when viewing and producing documentary images? Related questions are concerned with visibility and having a voice both in the concrete and the symbolic realm within society. However, these questions are always already connected with the question of bodily politics, sexuality, and modes of othering. South African migration researcher Ingrid Palmary described migrant visibility as being constituted at the intersections of *race* and gender.[65]

Each of these features—in/visibility, voice, and gender—involved in documentary practices are tied to political struggles, and they need to be discussed and connected to post-colonial critiques from Frantz Fanon and Achille Mbembe but also read in the light of recent arguments on the topic of the so-called othering by cultural and gender theorists Pumla Gqola, Gabriele Dietze, and Judith Butler.[66] Categories of gender and race are always linked to the question of visibility and have gained a new urgency due to a conservative framing of the topic of migration in the nation-state. According to Judith Butler: "Xenophobic exclusion operates through the production of racialized *others*, and those whose 'natures' are considered less rational by virtue of their appointed task in the process of laboring to reproduce the conditions of private life. This domain of the less than rational human bounds the figure of human reason, producing that 'man' "[67]

~

Throughout this study I will highlight meaningful historical incidents and political frameworks in the context of migration and racism and the images they produced. Giving a historical outline necessarily leads to selecting certain events and developments and thus remains fragmentary. This study begins by contextualizing documentary photographs of black and white migration during apartheid and then focusses on post-1994 documentary works. The 2008 attacks function as a "zooming in" for documentary photographs and films dealing with the image of the other, and hence migration, since the violent events were a "call to action" and thus added a new urgency and immediacy to the work of documentary photographers, filmmakers, and artists in South Africa. As the *Filmmakers Against Racism* collective proclaimed: "We fought a long hard battle to overcome the brutal forces of racism in South Africa—we cannot let racism defeat us again."[68] The statement is evidence of the recognition of the special historical situation of South Africa, being a country that had recently overcome a racist regime. This concern culminated in many new works being produced that explicitly or implicitly dealt with the attacks and their aftermath but that also cited South Africa's promise for a post-racial society. Furthermore, there were meta-discursive aspects in the works searching for responsible image production of the other and trying to discern why the 2008 attacks on alleged foreigners happened.

Therefore this text will at times follow an oscillating movement between past and present, linking current visual documents to previous ones and showing their connection, since the present is always and already informed and coded by the historical events that have filtered through. This movement will also capture how the future is partly controlled by the past through the unconscious that expresses itself in the reenactment of apartheid visual icons. Even though it is important to emphasize that the construction of normative narratives and restaging of visual documents is not a closed system, there are possibilities of re-telling past and present events in a reflective way or of imagining the present and future differently.

Current documentary images are always pervaded by historical quotations and re-stagings. Following Maurice Halbwachs I am arguing that individual and collective memories are interwoven, constantly transforming each other.[69] Halbwachs identified individual and collective "frames" (Fr. *cadres*) as a prerequisite for remembering and forgetting. Without social frames of reference, the individual as well as collectivities cannot construct memory/ies.[70] The notion of "framing" in this project refers both to Halbwachs's frames of memory as well as to Judith Butler's notion of "frames" as a prerequisite for understanding public visibility of certain bodies versus the invisibility of others.[71]

As Christina von Braun has argued, however, Halbwachs neglected the role of media in the construction of memory.[72] This study therefore specifically looks at the (audio-)visual archives and the staging and restaging of visual documents and extends Halbwachs's notion of "frames of reference" with U.S.-American media scholar Alison Landsberg's findings on "prosthetic memory," which specifically focuses on the role of mediated memories.[73] Landsberg proposes that: "Taking on prosthetic memories of traumatic events and the disenfranchisement and loss of privilege that such an experience often necessitates can have a profound effect on our politics."[74] If one follows this line of thought, one can come to understand political effects and affective involvement both on the part of the audience of documentary film and photography, as well as on the part of the producers of these works. In South Africa the black South Africans' experience of life under apartheid has only become a "worthwhile" and national memory through the dissemination of (audio-)visual documents after the official end of apartheid in 1994.

1

Mapping Context and Place

South Africa's Visual History of Migration

> Essentially Mozambique borders on Zululand . . . like these are artificial borders. Xenophobia doesn't make sense. . . . the idea of the foreigner doesn't make sense . . . essentially it's all down to the Berlin Conference you know—scramble for Africa. . . .[1]

White South African photographer Nadine Hutton (self-)consciously explores some of the contradictions of the South African nation, as well as the question of who is considered a "foreigner" and who is a "citizen." Her quote evokes images of maps and the drawing and re-drawing of borders on the African continent with a ruler by the colonial powers at the Berlin conference in 1914. "South Africa" itself was invented by the colonial empires and thus had a 350-year history of European and therefore white domination that was foreshadowed by the landing of Vasco da Gama and his men in South Africa in 1497 en route to India. In 1652 Jan van Riebeeck established a permanent settlement of Europeans at the Cape.

Yet, it is important to remember that the European borders were also highly contested and artificial constructs and that any idea of "natural" borders is only indicative of a desire for a romanticized primal state, which never existed, either in Africa or in Europe.[2] Rather, the Berlin conference marks the entangled histories of Europe and Africa and thus is an event of modern global history. At the same time history was locally defined and constructed in the territory that is today South Africa. To return to photographer Hutton's quote, she claims that the "idea of the foreigner" makes no sense since the black people, who live across the border area in South Africa and Mozambique speak the same language—Xitsonga, also known as Tsonga or Shangaan. Hutton, however, does not reflect that she herself may be considered a "foreigner" in South Africa by some people and does not question her own history of her European ancestors migrating to South Africa. The most prominent event of white migration within South Africa started in 1830—the "Great Trek" of mostly Dutch, German and French settlers from the Cape up north toward the inner parts of South Africa. Thus there were white European migration movements to Africa and there were black African migration patterns without equating the two—one being a clearly colonial endeavor of conquest and domination and the other dependent upon survival, labor, and other factors that may not have been researched thoroughly—I suggest, however, that they are both part of the visual history archive of migration within South Africa.

This study is not an attempt to write yet another "history of South Africa;" it is therefore beyond its scope to give a thorough account of history and politics, but instead it only cross-maps the interconnection of the historical visualization of black and white migration, by looking at some selected visual examples—film stills, maps, and posters to analyze how concepts or conceptions of a history of migration and at the same time belonging in South Africa can be "excavated" in the Benjaminian sense.[3] As Walter Benjamin has exemplified in a short text—which he called a "Denk-Bild"—a reflective image with the programmatic title "Excavation and Memory," the work of remembering, memory, and understanding the past is akin to the work of an archaeologist, who digs into layer after layer of the ground to unearth what is hidden beneath.[4] Benjamin emphasized that while doing so, one must not be afraid to come back to the very same subject again and again, comparing it to someone digging up the soil and breaking it up, scattering it, and rooting it around all over again. Similarly, this study will again and again return to historical "crosscuts" (as in the mining industry) from the past that pierce through and puncture the present and may get restaged and reenacted.

White Migration—"The Great Trek"

A photograph from 1952 documented the reenactment of a historical event of the *Great Trek* of the white Dutch settler (Boers); it was broadcast on the weekly newsreels in the cinemas throughout South Africa. The year 1952 marked exactly 300 years after the arrival of the Dutch Jan van Riebeeck with three ships at the Cape of Good Hope on April 6, 1652, whereas the *Great Trek* originally had taken place between 1830 and 1840, and therefore no photographic image exists from it.[5] In the photograph of the reenactment a float is visible, symbolizing a ship (from van Riebeeck's fleet), draped in white linen with white women and men onboard, grouped around a giant wheel of an ox wagon. The women are all wearing pure white clothes, the men are half naked, underlining their athletic bodies.

This iconography immediately calls up registers of both Leni Riefenstahl and fascist visuality as well as the western frontier that both combine "aestheticized leadership and segregation."[6] This event of festive reenactment was remarkable in several ways—first of all it combined two historical dates that were far removed from each other but were both imbued with special ideological meaning for the apartheid regime. Second, the "great trek" of white migration was staged as a heroic, visual spectacle, thus highlighting the construction of history by visual means; this was called "'n Fees vir die Oog"—a feast for the eye.[7] This draws attention to the inherent relationship of visual media as recording and storing devices and the question of a national archive. The ANC and other anti-apartheid organizations protested against the festivities, and called instead for a "People Protest Day," thus contesting who "the people" of South Africa are and whose history should be remembered.

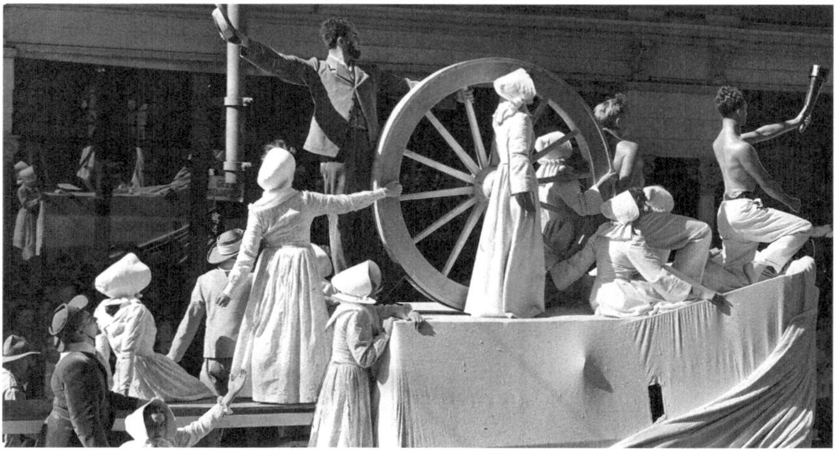

Figure 1.1. Reenactment of Great Trek, "Piet Retief's Manifesto, a float in the 1952 Jan van Riebeeck Festival," Courtesy of the Cape Times.

In British-ruled colonial Africa the spheres of "custom" and law were disjoined at the basis of a system of "indirect rule" that did not extend full citizenship rights to the African population.[8] In the seventeenth and eighteenth centuries, the white Afrikaans leaders, who were discontented with British rule, crafted the myth of South Africa as "an empty land" awaiting its occupation and cultivation by white settlers. This notion culminated in the "Great Trek" of the "Voortrekkers"—a self-given name of the settlers and farmers of mostly Dutch, German, and French decent.[9] The Voortrekkers went north and eastward during the 1830s and 1840s, away from the British control of the Cape Colony. As postcolonial and gender theorist Anne McClintock has stated: "In the voluminous Afrikaner historiography, the history of the 'volk' is organized around a male national narrative figured as an imperial journey into empty lands."[10] However, African people already populated the Southern part of the African continent. In order to integrate this contradiction into the Afrikaans historical narrative, a conflict around the merit of *civilization* had to be staged. Therefore, "the colonial journey is figured as proceeding forward in geographical space, but backward in racial and gender time, to a prehistoric zone of linguistic, racial and gender degeneration. At the heart of the continent, a historic agon is staged as degenerate Africans 'falsely' claim entitlement to the land."[11]

"Native Reserves," "White Cities," and "Homelands"

> Awaking on Friday morning, June 20, 1913, the South African native found himself, not actually a slave, but a pariah in the land of his birth. . . .[12]

The Native Land Act 1913 (No. 27 of 1913) was passed by the parliament of South Africa in order to regulate the acquisition of land by black people.[13] It was also known as the "Black Land Act," and was passed because of pressure by whites to prevent blacks from settling in white areas. This law incorporated territorial segregation into legislation for the first time since the founding of the Union of South Africa in 1910; it made it illegal for blacks to buy land from whites.[14] It gave whites control over the majority of the land, displacing blacks and forcing them to live in only 7.3 percent of the country that was allocated as "native reserves." It also made it illegal for blacks to stay on the land of whites unless they were so-called *bona fide* employees. This created even more unequal power relations and modes of dependence between black workers and white employers and intensified the migrant labor system.

The apartheid government's enforcement of material separation in space needs to be connected with the segregation of the affective imaginary realm in order to divide and control people's desires and aspirations. Different visual regimes were created for people classified as white and as black; this meant that there were separate film productions for white and black audiences, who were also not allowed to watch films together.[15] These divisions and control of the audio-visual sphere had a political impact and determined who was depicted and whether or not these images showed people in "despair" or positions of "victimhood" versus having a "good life," and more generally who becomes visible in the first place and therefore is part of the national cultural archive.

The white South African parliament passed the Entertainment Act of 1931 that established censorship clearance of films before public screening and prohibited scenes that showed "intermingling of Europeans and Non-Europeans." In 1934 an amendment was added that further restricted film societies, especially with "native members," to show films that included "communist propaganda."[16] Film censorship was thusly connected to apartheid visual segregation, restricting the visual, political, and affective realm. The amendment from 1934 shows that the regime was also afraid of the affective impact of images to *move* the population politically—and especially the population classified as black since they were constructed as childlike and "naïve."

When apartheid was set into place, the whole African (black) population was perceived as foreigners belonging only to their ahistorical, assigned homelands, depending on their (constructed) ethnicity. So while black men were forced into becoming migrant workers, the right to reunite with their families was denied to them, as black women and children were kept immobile in the "native location." Black women, however, did not let the state take away their right to move; they organized the first anti-pass campaign 1913 in Bloemfontein.[17] The fight against the pass laws, which came to symbolize oppression as a whole, continued over the next decade.[18] The right-wing general and later Prime Minister Jan Smuts, who supported racial segregation and white minority rule, argued in 1944, ". . . it is this migration of the native family, of the females and children, to the farms and towns which should be prevented. As soon as this migration is permitted the process commences which ends in the urbanized detribalized native and the disappearance of the native organization."[19]

Moreover, Jan Smuts's statement shines a light on the ambivalent meanings that have been conferred to "migration" in the South African context and especially to the migration of the *othered* and raced parts of the population—a motor of modern urbanity, a necessity, a threat, a frequently denied choice of living and working circumstances, as well as a promise for a different (often imagined better) life. As Mamdani proposed: "The migrant worker needs to be seen as the locus of all major social contradictions in such a context. Besides articulating the tensions generated by a market economy—those of class, gender, and age—migrant labor also came to be the focus of differences reinforced by the mode of rule that was decentralized despotism: the interethnic and the urban-rural."[20] African women's status in the urban areas was even more precarious than African men's, since by the apartheid government they were regarded only as African men's "superfluous appendages" and even more firmly controlled and regularly imprisoned and sent back to the "homelands."[21] Female African workers often stayed in a type of rudimentary servants' quarter on the property of their white employees, working the lowest-paid jobs in childcare, cooking, and cleaning.[22] What knowledge and which results can be gained from the historicization of visual documents of migrant labor in South Africa and how can this be reconnected to the later analysis of African migrant workers in South Africa today? This question can be addressed through the film *Come Back Africa*, one of the few sources that presented the African migrant worker as a main character. This film is an important precursor to post-apartheid productions.

Come Back, Africa—Intersections of Documentary and Staged Images

Documentary work in South Africa during apartheid was a struggling endeavor, since the regime tried to control the act of filming and the circulation of certain images, particularly of the black population. This also implies that state-sanctioned documentary photographs and film could never be completely trusted or be taken at face value.

The first documentary-fiction hybrid from South Africa that found international acclaim and shaped the perception of a world audience of what black South Africans had to endure under apartheid was *Come Back, Africa* from 1959. The American Lionel Rogosin, who directed the film, had to pretend that he was making a commercial music documentary in order to avoid censorship. The film was partly improvised and filmed as a documentary-fiction hybrid, using many non-actors.[23] It narrates the story of a black migrant worker and was filmed in 1959 with a small crew in and around Johannesburg. The main character Zachariah (Zacharia Mgabi) comes to Johannesburg to work in the goldmines, but loses his job there. Subsequently he tries his luck as a domestic worker, failing due to his unfair female white boss. Finally he works at a car garage. The story line invokes the already established literary and cinematic trope of the "Jim Comes to Jo'burg" story, but as a drama, the injustice of the system makes life impossible for him. He is caught in the political turmoil, between the "stay away" protests and violence.[24]

While the film portrays the individual fate of one black man, it was exemplary of the lives of many black South Africans who shared this type of life in its essential features. A migrant African workforce was needed in the white cities mostly for the mining industry, as well as domestic workers like gardeners, nannies, cooks, and cleaning staff for white households. Hence, the presence of black workers was mandatory, while at the same time, the apartheid system wanted to eradicate any black person living in a white area. The migrant workers were recruited both from the homelands as well as from Botswana and other neighboring African states. *Come Back, Africa* has a prominent scene in a *shebeen*, where black male intellectuals—among them journalists from *Drum* magazine Lewis Nkosi, Can Thema, and Bloke Modisane—discuss Alan Paton's novel "Cry Beloved Country."[25] While the men talk, South African Miriam Makeba sings, presenting the

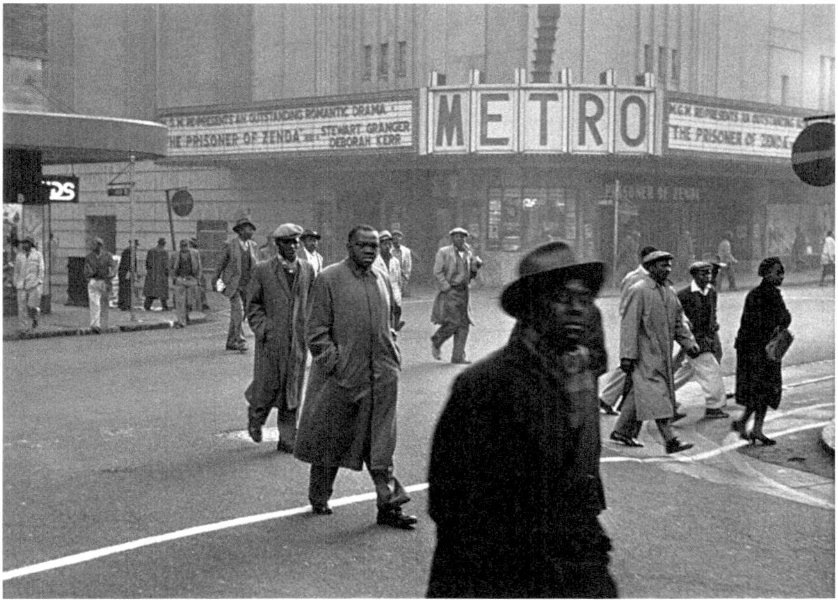

Figure 1.2. Still from Lionel Rogosin's *Come Back, Africa*, street scene in Johannesburg 1959.

stereotypical view of gendered roles.[26] *Drum* writer Lewis Nkosi who had participated in the script writing of *Come Back, Africa* as well as appearing before the camera in the *shebeen* scene, commented later: "The film is not great by any standard. There are too many technical weaknesses in the development of the story. However, with all these faults, the story emerges as a powerful document of social truth such as no other producer's camera has unfolded in this country."[27] Could Nkosi mean that the "visual excess," the everyday details that were captured and life intervening into the shooting process managed to convey the specific atmosphere of living as a black South African during apartheid? Furthermore the film captured an inherent "black melancholia" that can be connected to the difficult work and life situations under apartheid, but it also used these sad scenes strategically to reproach the injustice of the system.

Similarly, South African film curator Darryl Els summed it up: "Lionel Rogosin critically reflects on both the mining industry and the migrant labour system it fostered, two fundamental elements in understanding South Africa's entry into modernity and the subsequent formation of *apartheid ideology*."[28] At the same time the film serves as a counter-history that challenges national and hegemonic myths by highlighting the history of the suppressed African majority of South Africa, providing rare documentary footage of the *Drum* magazine writers, as well as with the singer Miriam Makeba, who are all "playing themselves." Lewis Nkosi, Can Themba, and Miriam Makeba went into exile shortly after the film was completed, and only returned to South Africa in post-apartheid times. Rogosin helped with Makeba's international career start.

"Rogosin's depiction of blackness and dispossession creates a contrary narrative of the black South African urban experience of the 1950s."[29] Thereby the film also created a visual archive of the black South African presence, giving visibility to black bodies as modern subjects in the cities, imagined as white and counteracting ". . . a world predetermined by BLACKNESS as ABSENCE"[30] as Frank Wilderson III termed it. When simply looking at the film still from *Come Back, Africa* without reading the caption, one could assume that one is seeing a street scene from Harlem, New York, or from another African metropolis, alluding to a global realm of internationality circulating images and to a shared visual realm of modern urbanity, connected to desires and modes of subjectification.

At the same time, this visual document, however, never reached its intended audience, as it was banned in South Africa right after it was released, while the director was accused of being a communist in the United States, thus creating many difficulties for the distribution of his film there.[31]

In this regard, the film can be said to have had a similar diasporic life to the subject it depicts, only being screened in South Africa for the first time in 1988.[32] A film that is not projected and seen remains to some extent unrealized, invisible, and incomplete. *Come Back, Africa* was never widely distributed, even though it made a "career" at left-wing off-space screenings, in churches and educational spaces, as well as in the "small" but politically active cinemas in Europe and the United States as a filmic document against apartheid oppression. In 2014, when the film was presented in Berlin as part of the *Visionary Archive* series, some of the visiting South African artists saw it for the first time then and there in an equally migrant setting of terms, far away from home.[33]

While films like *Come back, Africa* were almost inaccessible in South Africa, in an remarkable twist, cinema with its roots in popular fairs and low-brow mass entertainment was also one of the first places to relax strict segregation, allowing mixed audiences to watch films together. Besides, economic interests were inextricably accorded in this foray against apartheid division, as "in 1985 Ster-Kinekor [one of South Africa's largest cinema chains] acknowledged that they hoped that their application to open all cinemas and drive-ins to mixed audiences would reduce the threat of the cultural boycott."[34] Thereby, cinemas aligned themselves with apartheid ideology by not showing certain films and at the same did not align with practices of segregation for economic reasons.

Portraying Black South African Lives—*Drum* Magazine

The editorial team of the *Drum* magazine played a significant role in *Come Back, Africa* in which black intellectuals acted both in front of the camera and behind it, in the writing of the script and the production. *Drum* magazine was an important publication that was founded in the 1950s by Jim Bailey, a white British man, but included black and white writers on staff. They created new representations of blackness and offered intellectual discussion. It was the most significant and widely read output for the photographs of black culture on the margins of the apartheid city and thereby constructed a precarious archive of black South African's everyday urban life during apartheid.[35] *Drum* was modeled after illustrated magazines such as *Life* or *Picture Post*. Its picture pages presented and promoted glamorous and hopeful images of black South African lives (see figure 1.3 in the color gallery). The magazine was produced in Johannesburg and edited by the previously mentioned Jim Bailey, but had black and white photographers such as Jürgen Schadeberg, Peter Magubane, and Alfred Khumalo on staff.[36] In its self-positioning *Drum* claimed to be a magazine "of Africa for Africa," emphasizing its focus on local stories and people.

Working conditions of black photographers were more restricted and difficult than those of their white colleagues. The black photographer Peter Magubane, for example, was repeatedly arrested, banned, and spent over a year in solitary confinement. Often black photographers were also not as well-connected to the European and American news agencies, who paid for the photographer's gear and assignments. At the same time *Drum*, in its working environment, as well as the reportages it presented, attested to the fact that while the apartheid system was brutal, its control was never total. Despite the social exclusion, economic injustice, and political oppression, black South Africans were able to share and take part in a global culture and remained open to international cultural influences, especially in the early years of apartheid before Sharpeville in 1976.[37] *Drum* was not just a popular culture magazine, instead it became more politicized and later included acclaimed political documentary reportages as well, presenting undercover stories from the apartheid prisons and revealed the mistreatment of black workers on white farms.[38]

African-American artist Janet Jackson created a memorial to the history of *Drum* 1997 in the music video "Got 'Till It's Gone," set in apartheid South Africa.[39] The song featured the rapper Q-Tip and a line from folk singer Joni Mitchell's song *Big Yellow Taxi*. The video depicts black people free and living a good life within the narrow limits of apartheid South Africa. The visual language is inspired by a blend of '60s and '70s African and African-American culture and fashion, including the work of noted Malian photographer Malick Sidibé (see figures 1.4 and 1.5 in the color gallery).[40] At the same time it keeps a solemn and meditative feel and shows evidence of apartheid segregation like African people holding up pass documents. The final image shows a typical apartheid-era sign, saying in English "For Europeans Only" and in Afrikaans "Slegs Blankes." A bottle is thrown against the sign, breaking as it hits, spilling foamy liquid.

The video borrows ambivalently the middle-class notion of a nostalgic longing for better times in the past, as Joni Mitchell's lyrics went:

> Don't it always seem to go
> That you don't know what you've got
> 'Till it's gone.
> They paved paradise
> And put up a parking lot.

While for black people the apartheid past was usually nothing to be nostalgic about, in personal memories and family photographs, however, they can be remembered as more ambivalent times: South African historian Jacob Dlamini has pointed out that several South Africans—including himself—also feel nostalgic about growing up in a township. He suggests that "This phenomenon makes sense only if one understands that not everything we did in townships was a reaction to white oppression. Townships were (and are) dynamic places. . . ."[41] The video testifies to yet another form of restaging of apartheid images, in this case concentrating on the positive aspects of black life and culture and using it in a popular music format.

Black and White "Veils" during Apartheid—Double-Concisousness and Moments of Passing

The cover of *Drum* magazine from July 1965 screamed: "BLACKMAN HAS WHITE PARENTS."[42] The absurdity of the apartheid classification system was thus shown by cases of people who were first classified into a certain group and managed to contest and change their assigned status, for example a "Colored" changing to become a "White."[43] In another prominent case even siblings were classified in different sections, demonstrating the arbitrariness of the process, and yet the impetus to "classify" and separate people into different groups persists in racial stereotypes and prejudices also in post-1994 South Africa.

W. E. B. Du Bois had described black subjectivity shaped by slavery and racism in the United States at the beginning of the twentieth century as an experience of being disguised and having a double consciousness: "The Negro is a sort of seventh son, born with a veil, and gifted with second-sight in this American world—a world which yields no true self-consciousness, but only lets him see himself through the revelation of the other world."[44] A vivid account of the performance of whiteness and blackness in everyday life, again using the metaphor of the veil and including the transgression of the color line can be found in the writing of white South African author Ivan Vladislavić. He describes the experience of a young white man growing up in the apartheid state and taking on a manual job, working outside in a parking lot—a type of work that usually only black people would do:

> I was a solitary actor on a stage: a white boy playing a black man. In a small way, I was a spectacle. Yet I felt invisible. I savoured the veil that fell between my sweaty self and the

> perfumed women sliding in and out of their cars. I flitted across the lenses of their dark glasses like a spy.[45]

This description manages to convey the dialectical relationship of in/visibility in South African society. The main character, a young white man, feels *invisible* as he is performing the work that a black man would usually be doing, but at the very same time it is not lost on him that he is also a spectacle by doing something that does not quite fit into the rigid prescribed norms apartheid society had set. He feels like a *spy* in someone else's life, this perception resonates with how very little knowledge many white South Africans had about the daily lives of the black South Africans.[46]

The sunglasses that the white (and they can only be white, as they are "perfumed" and "sliding in and out of their cars," marking class and status) women are wearing, here act like a double screen—both mirroring and projecting his own image, as well as screening the wearers from the bright light which could imply both "seeing reality for what it is" as well as being blinded by the sun and, accordingly, not able to see anything anymore in the glare of brightness: the sunglasses darken their views by nuances. Yet it also shows that there were small possibilities of transgressions of the color line.

2

Affective Images

2.1 Photographs of Black Suffering and Violence

> Affects are not individuated like people and things, but nevertheless they do not blend into the indifference of the world. They have singularities, which enter into virtual conjunction and each time constitute a complex entity. It is like points of melting, of boiling, of condensation, of coagulation, etc.[1]

Documentary Style

During apartheid the documentary style came to prominence, predominantly in news photography to visually attack the injustices of the system by showing the violence and oppressive mechanisms to which the African majority of the population were being subjected. Most of the famous photographs, for instance those of the Sharpeville massacre that will be discussed in this chapter, were black-and-white images, because color film was more expensive and it only became more widely used in South Africa in the late 1980s. In addition, there were technical reasons for this, since the first color film stock from Kodak was optimized for calibrating white skin tones, meaning African people's skin was rendered too dark and without any details.[2]

Furthermore there exists an uneasy correlation between black-and-white photographs and people classified as *black* and *white*. The question of the other and the concept of race are historically connected to the invention of photography and to ethnology and imperialism, and emphasizes visual media's impetus to expose, compare, and stereotype.[3] Since black-and-white photographs diminish the subtleties and often display high contrast that translates each color into a shade of grey, they tend to simplify, abstract, and aestheticize their subjects. Christina von Braun has argued in the context of filmic records from WWII that documentary material in general may aestheticize and thereby render abstract and artificial what is being shown.[4] No simple connection exists between the photograph of an event and the event itself, instead there is a visual excess of images, which nevertheless conveys traces and induces affective responses in viewers. Black-and-white photography may also translate into a certain sincerity or seriousness of a subject. These technical and aesthetic aspects complicate and influence the affective intensities being formed. It is impossible to divorce an image's composition from what it depicts, therefore aesthetic, technical modalities and content are always inextricably linked, both within the perceptive and the affective realm. Certain iconic historical photographs are revisited in this chapter to give a background to visualizing both migration and the restriction of movement.

African Migrant Workers and Pass Laws—*Violent versus Violating Images*

In South Africa there exists a long history of violence during apartheid and the violent or rather *violating* photographic images that were produced in response to it. I use the term "violence" following Arendt and Butler.[5] I build on Hannah Arendt's definition of violence that spells out its dialectical qualities in connection with affect, justice, and rationality.[6] By "violating" I am speaking of photographs that are transgressive and violating both to the eyes of the spectator and to the depicted person(s). The focus lies on the visual presentation of black bodies in pain and constrainment, paradigmatically exploring the affective image archive of black South African lives. These images are violent since they show the aftermath of infliction of pain and injuries on black bodies.

At the same time it is these very images that evoked strong affective reactions that were not necessarily only perceived as negative—at least not from the perspective of the photographers who were part of this tradition and reproduced it. Consequently, we have to look at who was behind the lens and what the production settings were. There is to an extent irresolvable tension between a shocking image, the photographer who took it, the demands it seems to make on viewers, and the question of affect as well as conflicts around attention economies, visual censorship, and the reproach of voyeurism; the different strands will be laid out in detail without privileging one side.[7]

The beginning marks a photograph that Ernest Cole took in the 1960s that does not show spectacular violence but rather a form of "quiet" violence.[8] My selection of photographs as such tries to suspend the logics of sensationalism whenever possible while it does not mask the openly shocking photographs. Cole was one of the first black South African photographers; he went into exile to the United States at the age of twenty-six. In the United States his book "House of Bondage" was published in 1967, earning him international acclaim. In South Africa his book was immediately banned. The title made a drastic comparison that immediately alludes to the history of slavery.[9] Cole's photograph shows two enchained hands, belonging to two separate men, who were arrested for being in a white area illegally, and thereby disobeying the pass laws that severely restricted the mobility, visibility, and aspirations of black South Africans. As a central topic "the pass," with all its different implications of "passing," and "burning passes," will emerge repeatedly throughout this study.[10]

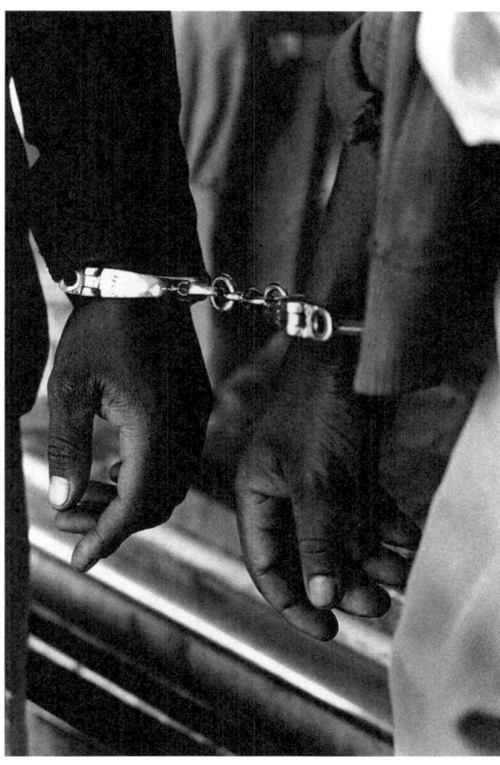

Figure 2.1.1. Ernest Cole, Handcuffed Black Men 1967, *House of Bondage.* The Ernest Cole Family Trust and the Hasselblad Foundation.

Let us take a closer look at the photograph by Ernest Cole. It is a close-up of two hands, belonging to separate black men, their hands are chained together as if they were criminals. The photograph can be held up against the very first image this study showed of the pass-burning demonstration in Soweto, giving the justification for that protest. The formerly free hands burning the pass-books are now chained together, unable for any further action. One man is wearing a dark jacket, the other seems to have his sleeve rolled up, which looks torn, maybe hinting at the fact that he is a manual laborer; also his hand looks like it has a lot of strength. Diagonal lines are visible in the background, linking the two hands, perhaps the lines belong to a police vehicle onto which the men would be loaded and taken to prison, incarcerating them until a family member or white employer would vouch for them. Both men's hands are in the same relaxed gesture, half open, there is no resistance visible, no clenched fists. The photograph presents calmness and submission. Apparently the photographed men knew the protocol—this was a standard routine to them, they did not fight the measure.

The apartheid pass laws criminalized the majority of the population of South Africa and severely restricted their movement, especially in the cities. "Presumably over seventeen and a half million black persons were prosecuted under the pass laws between 1916 and 1981."[11] There is no visual evidence of these enormous numbers, except maybe the pass photos themselves that every person classified as African was required to take and carry at all times in his or her pass book. These pass photos could be considered *ex negativo* as a visual memorial of the mass imprisonments.[12]

The apartheid regime tried to prohibit pictures, like the one of Cole, of black South Africans being punished; it did not want the shameful images to be visible to the gaze of the larger international community. Producing images was therefore almost automatically a political act, even though it cannot solely be defined in political terms. Often, photographers had to defy the South African government, became imprisoned, or went into exile. It was not easy to take pictures, which can sometimes be deduced from the resulting photographs: they were often taken from behind, far away, or at awkward angles. The black South African photographer Alfred Khumalo recalls how he had to hide his camera "concealed in milk cartons or loaves of bread."[13] Using the camera was thereby an act of provocation during apartheid, as Nigerian photo historian and curator Okwui Enwezor stated: "No form of testimony frightened the regime more than photography did, with its powerful testimony that could be used to expose and counteract the sanitized, propagandistic images working in the government's favor, or to fashion an oppositional artistic practice of self-representation."[14]

Excursion: Borders and Militarized Citizenship

In the South African History Archive, sifting through visual documents of the history of the struggle against apartheid, I came across a complexly and carefully constructed poster of the "End Conscription Campaign" (ECC), which acted as a media intervention and political critique of the status quo (see figure below). This poster brings together several thematic strands that are meaningful for the visual history of borders, migration, violence, and

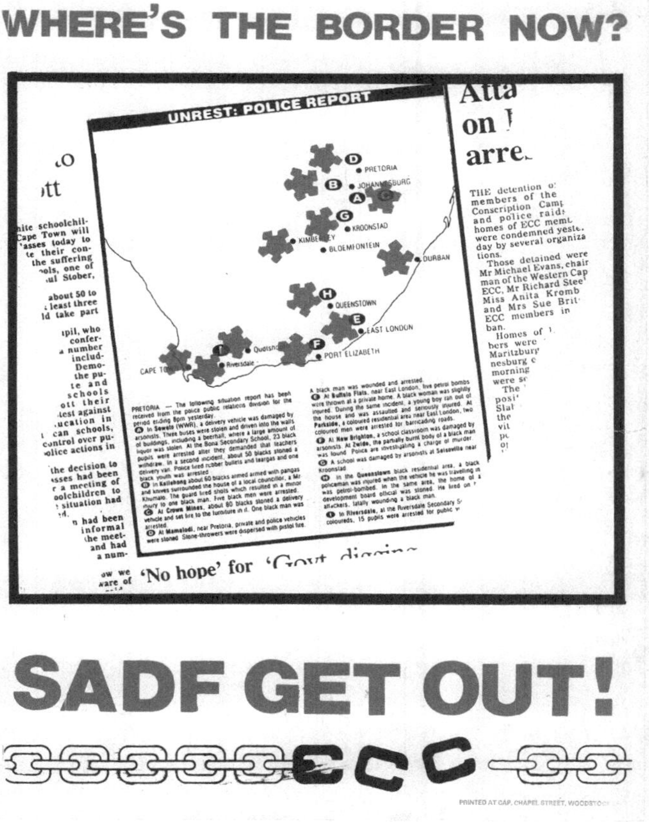

Figure 2.1.2. Poster to end the conscription campaign of the SADF 1985, source: SAHA.

militarized citizenship, consisting of an affectively loaded text and images, and inciting action while at the same time offering a meta-perspective.

On the poster a collage technique of text *and* images and text *as* image is used. This was a common conjunction in activist iconography, in part inspired by Soviet constructivism. A newspaper has been cut into the shape of the South African territory. One could pose that this map of South Africa already includes its own deconstruction, as the depiction of the South African territory is overwritten by words, meanings, and incidents. This technique reflects critically on the general usage of maps as production sites of evidence and means of control.[15] It is a map with a metanarrative. The headlines visible on the poster read: "Unrest: Police Report" and "No hope for (Govt digging . . .)." The negation of hope introduces a strong affective tone here, even if only as an "ugly" feeling of despair or as a mobilizing rage against the status quo. The words on the edge can be assumed to be "Attack on" and "arrest." Inside the cut-out the shape is doubled by a smaller partial map, showing South Africa once again, giving the names of larger cities and townships and red crosses or stars that indicate troubled hotspots or so-called "areas of unrest," which are detailed in the text below it. These fragmented words construct an "affective assemblage" of South Africa as a place of terror, threat, and fighting. An assemblage in the Deleuzian sense is a "coming together" or combination of affect, desires, percepts, images, and things.[16] In addition, the title question—"Where is the Border Now?"—shifts the attention to the unclear status of the South African external and internal borders, indicating that the civil war in the townships draws new borders within South African territory, separating "safe" white areas of living and "unsafe" black South Africans' living spaces. The newspaper map was very likely fashioned after a real newspaper from the 1980s, documenting the violence and acts of defiance occurring mostly in the townships. Similar headlines from the archive of the *Weekly Mail* from 1985 read, for example, "Twenty-one hanged in seventy-two hours"[17] or in 1988 "Soweto Ungoverned,"[18] attesting to the omnipresence of violence and death, especially in black South Africans' lives.

If one zooms into the picture, one can read each report, e.g., it says: "Soweto: A delivery van was damaged by arsonists, three busses were stolen and driven into walls, including a beer hall where a large amount of liquor was stolen. At the Bona Secondary School 23 black pupils were arrested after they demanded that teachers withdraw. In a second incident about 50 blacks stoned a delivery van. Police fired rubber bullets and teargas and one youth was arrested." These news-texts attest to the civil-war-like situation, interrupting everyday life of black South Africans and affecting everyone living in the townships. The townships were contested scenes in an unequal fight between the well-equipped white army (SADF) and the black "freedom fighters" from the militant ANC section "Umkonte we Sizwe" who were actively supported by black youths from the townships.[19] In the news the political nature of the actions was occluded to make them appear as simple "crimes." Often political activists were imprisoned, banned, or even sentenced to death for criminal actions. The United Democratic Front (UDF) issued a statement in 1987 stating: "It is apartheid that is the violent system. It is apartheid that eventually begets responsive violence from its victims. . . ."[20]

Apartheid South Africa had aggressively attempted to expand its national territory during 1966–1986. These raids into neighboring countries were the so-called "border wars," which the South African Defense Force (SADF) fought in Namibia and Angola against the South West Africa People's Organization (SWAPO).[21] There had been a general conscription of all white men into the South African Defense Force for two compulsory years since August 4, 1967. This created a militarized white masculinity and citizenship.[22] In 1983 opposition began against the "border wars" and the ECC was started, the aim of which was to stop the general and mandatory conscription of all white South African men into the South African army. During these border wars, the homelands, where the African population was supposed to live, were often used as a "buffer" and thus a protection for the borders between South Africa and the other African states surrounding it. As an example, the homeland of "Bophutatswana" was located at the South African-Botswanan border and military from the homeland was allocated to guard it. At the same time the white SADF troops were deployed to fight the "inner" war in South Africa's townships against the black South African population and the "terrorists" of the ANC.[23] The SADF was instrumental in upholding the apartheid regime. In 1988 the apartheid government banned the ECC along with many other civil organizations. The length of conscription was shortened in 1989, however, it finally ended only in 1993.

But let us take a second look at the ECC poster. There is more to see below the doubled contours of the South African map where a tough chain is visible, blocking the lower part of the poster; then the chain is broken, and the broken links read ECC for *End Conscription Campaign*, illustrating the claim that the if general conscription is ended, one is closer to "freedom," breaking free from the vicious cycle of violence and counter-violence. In 1985 the ECC held a rally called "Troops out of Townships." Black South Africans in the townships were fighting informally against the white South African army and police force. But conversely, to the white soldiers and police, black South African men and women were forbidden to carry weapons. "So while aiming to constitute a *white* militarized masculinity the apartheid regime, at the same time, constituted masculinity in general as militarized—inside and outside the institutionalized initiation framework of the army. Masculinity, more generally, was hence contested through male bonding in the moment of violence."[24] Black masculinity was constructed in the white imaginary as both hyper-masculine and thus a threat to the white race as embodied in white women, as well as infantile, feminine, and irrational. These contradictory discourses, however, denied black South Africans in general access to full citizenship rights. They organized informally in self-defense units in the townships in response to the violence of the white South African army. The collateral damage of this asymmetrical conflict resulted in gruesome photographs of black injured bodies, as will be discussed in detail in the next section. In addition, film documents that will be analyzed in later chapters will refer to both white and black masculinity, uniting in moments of violence again, linking up to the historical struggles and a "tradition of violence" but also starting new conflicts.

The Photograph of Hector Pieterson—*The South African Pietà*

One of the most iconic photographs from the struggle against apartheid in South Africa shows a dying black boy—the pupil Hector Pietersen, who was shot by the police during the Soweto Uprising in 1976. On June 16, 1976, he and other school children protested in the "Soweto Uprising" against the implementation of Afrikaans and English as the dual medium of instruction in secondary schools. This policy was applied to all schools for black children throughout South Africa regardless of the languages spoken locally.[25] Pupils and students gathered to peacefully demonstrate, but then they clashed with the police force. The armed policemen started shooting into the crowd, killing twenty children. Hector Pietersen was shot at the age of twelve.

The well-known photograph shows an older boy, Mbuyisa Makhubo, carrying Hector after the bullet had struck him. Running next to him is Antoinette Sithole, Hector's sister.[26] It is winter in South Africa, and it must have been around midday because the sunlight is shining from straight overhead, making short shadows. An older woman, dressed in a bright dress, intently looks at the group from behind. Other children are seen running and looking backward in the background of the image.[27] Antoinette Sithole is wearing her school uniform. Her eyes are pinched tight, her mouth is open, and she seems to be crying out. The facial expressions

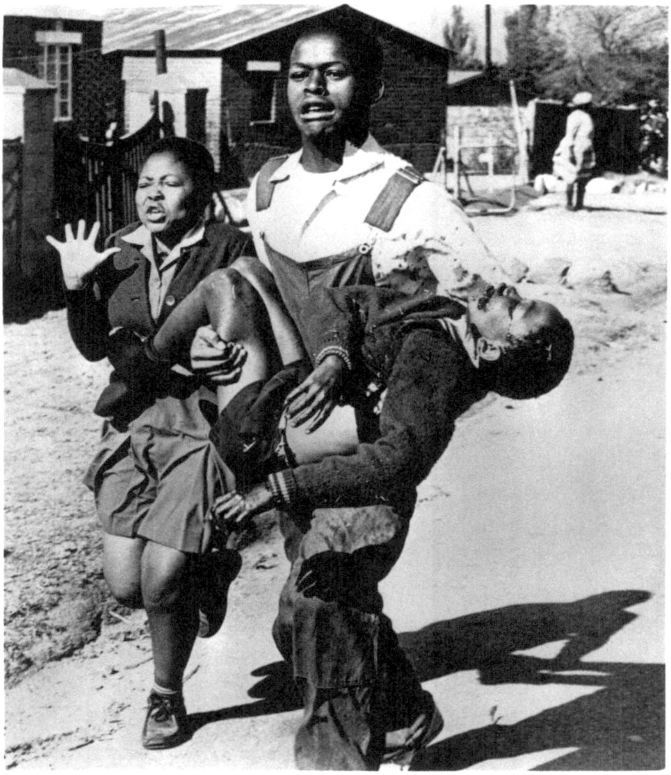

Figure 2.1.3. Hector Pietersen shot by police, carried by Mbuyisa Makhubo, on the left his sister, 1976. Photograph by Sam Nzima.

of both Makhubo and Sithole show anguish and pain. Hector's right arm looks stiff and his pullover has been hiked up or was maybe pulled up to check on his injuries, exposing his ribs. His left shoe is missing, showing his black sock. There are traces of blood on the side of his mouth. The sister is holding her hand in front of her shoulder in a both protective and defensive gesture. The photograph offers a frozen moment, which nevertheless conveys motion, the sister and Mbuyisa are almost running. In the far background groups of youths are visible, no clear motion can be detected, just turmoil. Hector's lost shoe furthermore attests to moments of chaos and panic, probably lost in his attempt to run away, then falling.

The image of one person holding or carrying another is the classical iconic figure of "rescue." More importantly though, the activities in this image of rescuing are not carried out by trained professionals, who are experienced in limiting the extent of injury, but instead the rescuer is an inexperienced boy. As Azoulay has argued, "the child as rescuer is the epitome . . ." of this category of photographs of unprofessional rescue operations.[28] The photograph is also over-determined because the rescue is in vain; it shows a dying child. As Belinda Smaill has pointed out: "Non-fiction representations frequently co-opt the child into a politics of hopefulness and futurity."[29] The photograph of Hector Pietersen dying profoundly destroys the viewers' hopes for the future life of this child and negates all the affective attachments usually connected to the image of a child. Consequently, this photograph can be identified as belonging to the Rancièran category of "intolerable images," it is painful to look at, and it constitutes an open wound.[30] In the photograph, even though it is silent—as all photographs are—the visible screams almost become audible. The affective excess of this photograph is one of the significant reasons why it became a successful visual icon of anti-apartheid protest, moving people into action. Like no other image it stood as a symbol of the brutality of the apartheid government and was used to mobilize resistance. The photograph was printed on posters and T-shirts, in films, and on banners all around the world. As such it was able to bundle sympathy and outrage both nationally and internationally. Another formal reason the image became so prominent may be that it fits a Christian iconography of the religious image of the Pietà, showing a child in the position of the dead Jesus. The Pietà is a famous subject in Christian art depicting Mary cradling the dead body of Jesus after the crucifixion, most often found in sculpture.

The photograph of the dying Hector Pietersen made the loss of a young black boy's life visible and mournable, and thus seems to illustrate the equation of documentary photographs as important weapons in fighting apartheid. Photographs like this one became political by disturbing what was visible in the national framings of apartheid South Africa. As Judith Butler argued, s/he who can be grieved officially in a society is determined by politics and state control, and she therefore asks, "Why is it that governments so often seek to regulate and control who will be publicly grievable and who will not?"[31] Despite its religious connotations of sacrifice and martyrdom, globally in documentary visual media on conflict and war, "images of suffering children are constantly universalized to emphasize human vulnerability and frequently they also suggest that not only a subjective, but also a collective future is in jeopardy."[32] They thus become symbols of a suffering collective or nation.[33] After 1994 a Hector Pietersen Memorial has been established in

Soweto. It includes a museum, on whose walls large photographs are featured that of course include the iconic photograph.[34]

There is, however, never a straightforward translation of an affective image into the affect of the audience and into political action, but in this case a photograph of pain was able to intensify the affective responses that were translated into empathy for the victim and justified indignation about his pain. Mourning and outrage was further channeled into agency of a collective of viewers. The movement against apartheid gained momentum in the years following Sharpeville 1960, and reached its peak in the early 1980s earning a lot of international support. In the same year the UN endorsed a resolution of cultural boycott against South Africa.[35]

With Kylie Thomas I consider photographs of black bodies in pain foremost as "wounding apertures" that produce affective excess, as immaterial wounds that are constantly updated and adjusted, as they reiterate historical pain and injustice.[36] For a photographer the word "aperture" is familiar as it designates the opening or hole through which the light travels in the optic lens of the camera before rendering the image on the light-sensitive film or digital sensor. In the human eye the pupil is the aperture, widening when it is dark and becoming small when it is very bright. The aperture of a camera can be changed from large to small, thereby controlling how much light is passing through and how these rays of lights are focused. If the aperture is small, the resulting image will have a wide depth of field, if it is large, the image will only be in focus in a certain area, the rest will be blurry. Thomas's notion of calling images "wounding apertures" thus reminds one of the optical processes of image creation both in cameras and in human eyes.

Thomas locates a potential in the "wounding aperture" that hurts to look at, but at the same time "opens a space for affective engagement with both the violence of the past and the present."[37] Similarly, I want to argue that photographs like the one of Hector Pietersen present us with instances of "wounding apertures," "opening us to a consideration of what apartheid did to those marked for elimination and who were subject to violence and atrocity, and also to engage with the enduring effects of such violence."[38] Thus the photograph prompts those of us who live in the time after apartheid's legislative end to engage with the painful past and reflect on what those events of violence mean for us in the present.

Black Pain and Melodramatic Overtones?

Film theorist Linda Williams stated about the visual materials, which the American abolition movement yielded, that there was an equation of "black suffering with the more conventionalized and familiar suffering of innocent (white) children, which was already a cliché of Victorian sentimental fiction and melodrama."[39] This melodramatic coding of images was not only recognizable in fiction films but, as Williams has shown through her analysis of the visual news media as for example of the O. J. Simpson case, it also became salient in the documentary realm. Ernest Cole's photograph of the black handcuffed men may also remind one of a global visual archive of black suffering with melodramatic overtones; it is similar to the images from the anti-slavery movement in the United States, showing black injured and suffering bodies as, for example, the famous porcelain placard from the potter Josiah Wedgwood with the inscription "Am I not a Man and a brother?"[40] The photograph of Hector Pieterson killed could also be read in a sentimental narration. Paul Gilroy stated that "[t]he sentimentality that is perceived to underpin this position has been under attack for decades. In politics, it has been judged to be a corrosive and antidemocratic force, and in art and literature it is associated above all with kitsch."[41] Yet Gilroy, together with Luc Boltanski, has equally argued that these sentiments were instrumental in creating an affective politics that envisioned black citizenship and humanity.[42]

Although South Africa and the United States have different histories and had different systems of racism and oppression, similar conventions ruled the visual perceptions of equating Africans with children or less "advanced" or educated people. Yet at the same time there was also a discourse of fear concerning a presupposed hyper-sexuality and virility of black masculinity. The images of black men as injured or constrained victims seemed at the same time to erase and to confirm this stereotype of black masculinity as "dangerous." The next photographic example of this study serves as an example of both; it registers melodramatic pity and victimhood and the affective reactions it provoked. Furthermore the questions of melodramatic traces in documentary scenes will be taken up again in the second part of "affective images" on visualizing tears.

Strategic Usage of Images of Suffering

How did activist organizations take up the visual politics of images like the one from Hector Pieterson and how did they integrate documentary photographs into their poster compositions as means of mobilization? The potential of these photographs was widely recognized, as is evidence by an exemplary poster, produced at the height of the protest against apartheid (see figure on opposite page) with the tag line: "People in Pain: How long

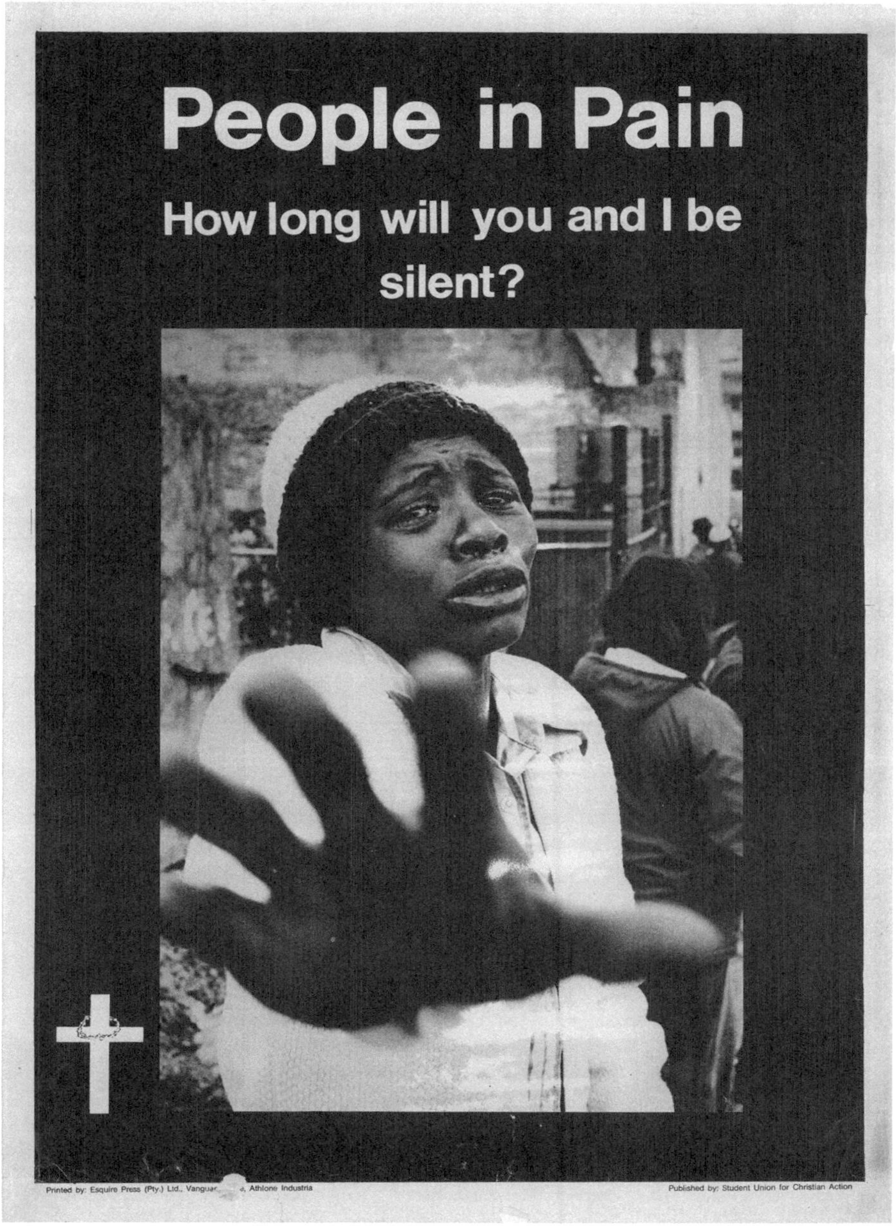

Figure 2.1.4. Poster by the Student Union for Christian Action 1985.

will you and I be silent?" It was published by the Student Union for Christian Action (SUCA). SUCA was not only a religious, but also a political union established in 1979 in South Africa. Previously, in 1977 the most popular organizations had been banned by the apartheid government. New organizations like SUCA hat to be extremely careful not to oppose the system too openly. The overall aim of the union was as such formulated to "uphold Christian and Civilized Standards." Most of the posters by SUCA commented on the social impact of forced removals due to the homeland system and criticized the segregated zoning in the cities. The poster "People in Pain" was produced using offset lithography print, which was an inexpensive method of producing a large number of posters. It is black and white, with a black background, lending it a sober atmosphere and at the same time better readability by using white lettering. There is also a white cross with a small crown of thorns in the lower left corner, signifying the religious context of the poster makers, but also—possibly inadvertently—making the poster look like an obituary in the newspaper. The central part of the poster, however, gives prominence to a photograph since "a picture is worth a thousand words."[43] The photographer's name is not given on the poster, nor are the names of the photographed subjects known.

The content of the image is rather ambiguous. The photograph is dominated by black-and-white contrasts, since the person is wearing light-colored overalls, rendering the outstretched hand clearly visible and letting it appear dark; in addition the person is wearing a white wool hat with a black rim. In the background, on the righthand side, a person clad in dark clothes is visible, turning his or her back toward the photographer, so that the main focus is on the central figure. A person, presumably a woman, in the middle of the frame is visibly moved and upset. Tears are welling up in her eyes. The left eye is already obscured behind a glossy barrier of lachrymal fluid. The face is twisted in grief. Her hand is outstretched, reaching out of the picture directly toward the photographer and thus us, the viewers, who may feel motivated to respond by reaching out and touching her with our own. The human hand, as well as the close up of a face in agony, is the most touching subject matter that exists in iconography.[44]

And yet, reading it can be ambivalent; maybe the hand is not actually reaching out, but perhaps pushing one away, and thereby indicating: "Please don't take a picture of me." A viewer could ask oneself: "How long will we be voyeurs?" The strong expression of anguish in combination with the outstretched hand could be the reason why this particular photograph was used on several posters, sometimes applied as photomontage with a different background or in combination with other photographs.[45] Ostensibly the poster makers deemed this photograph especially effective to mobilize affective responses that translated not only into empathy but also outrage, and thus suggest support for the anti-apartheid struggle. Butler proposed a close connection between rage and grief: "Open grieving is bound up with outrage, and outrage in the face of injustice or indeed of unbearable loss has enormous political potential."[46] The poster used the affective image of grief strategically and instrumentalized it for political activist purposes and to mobilize by showing black pain and promising to relieve this pain.[47] The exploitation of photographed subjects as mere instruments for a cause almost automatically creates injustice, albeit for a higher goal.

The SUCA poster was printed at the height of forced removals of non-white residents from all urban areas into the townships. In defiance of the state-prescribed destruction of houses and eviction of people, there was protest and mass action. Beginning in 1984 troops had started to enter the townships, and on September 11 of that year the minister of law and order had prohibited all political meetings. In 1985 Nelson Mandela wrote a letter from prison turning down an offer to be released. Following this refusal the offices of the United Democratic Front (UDF)—which was a larger and more outspoken organization than SUCA—throughout the country were raided and more than a hundred activists were detained.[48] Also in 1985 the state announced a "State of Emergency" until March 1986, which meant arrests, detention without trial, the closing off of townships, and other state-sanctioned military actions that resembled a civil war. During this time the documentary photographs used in the anti-apartheid struggle all seemed to be linked with a clear affective message: "Look at this injustice, it needs to stop! Now! Help us change the current situation, which is unbearable." How violence was used by both the government and its opposition during the state of emergency and later photographing extreme violence during the so-called "hostel-war" will be discussed further in the next section to emphasize how pain and suffering of individuals of the African majority were at times visualized strategically and later recognized through the photographic images by a wider community. However, if photographs were created with the aim to have only one interpretation this always also created exploitative images and one-dimensional readings.

Counter-Violence and the State of Emergency—The "Era of the Necklace"

To understand the complexity of violence and its impact in the visual history of shocking photographs from South Africa, one has to also take the counter strategies by the ANC into consideration. On April 13, 1985, Winnie

Mandela made her infamous speech ". . . with our boxes of matches and our necklaces we shall liberate this country" at Munsieville near Johannesburg.[49] "Necklacing" denotes the burning of a suspected traitor, *an impimpi*, with a car tire around the neck.[50] Apparently necklacing first occurred as an act of vigilantism in 1984 at the times of intensified conflict and unrest in the South African townships.[51] The impetus of Winnie Mandela's speech to equate "necklacing" with "liberation" can only be contextualized from the historical context, where one of the aims of the ANC was to make the townships "ungovernable."

As mentioned previously, in May 1985 the "state of emergency" was declared in 36 of the 260 magisterial districts of South Africa by the government of P. W. Botha. This constituted a success for the ANC, but at the same time it was also a major hindrance of its actions. The war-resister and activist David Shandler ironically wrote in a letter *"Greetings from a sunny state of emergency,"* alluding to the ambivalent experience of the apartheid regime failing and at the same time the military and police measures intensifying against its opponents.[52] Also the inner divisions in the townships started a spiral of violence, where the African population started to resist and formed "self-defense units," which became increasingly brutal both against the apartheid state and against "internal" enemies. The state of emergency lasted almost a year until March 1986, during which 575 people were killed in political combat, half of them by the police. The suspension of the state of emergency was short, as it was reinstated as a national state of emergency on June 12, 1986.

In an interview in Soweto with former "freedom fighters," who were part of the Street Committees and Self-Defense Units established in the 1980s, one of the interviewees discussed the practice of "burning traitors." Thabang Motsoeneng said: "Ja, during 1981–1984, we were using molotovs. Petrol bombs, and stones, and tyres. It was the era of the necklace. It was used to burn all informers, police and government agents, which we would find amongst our midst. . . . There were a lot of mistakes because some people were innocent, but it was the struggle, there is nothing we could do."[53] Thus Motsoeneng justifies in hindsight the violent practices as a necessary part of "the struggle," while admitting that not all people punished or killed were actually guilty. The practice of necklacing is discussed in such detail in this section because it reappears in different contexts again during the xenophobic attacks in 2008. Furthermore, it is such a spectacular act of violence that it must be considered to be a "staged" and highly visual act of killing that wants to make a sign for others to see and is therefore entangled with documentation and image production, which will be discussed further by considering a complicity of the cameras and the photographers.

One needs to ask, critically, if there was any kind of *emergence* possible within the state of emergency or only the emergence of more and more violence in a vicious circle and at enormous costs for township residents. What role did visual documentation play in these continual eruptions of violence between apartheid state and ANC? This study argues that photographs of people in pain became icons and could be used strategically, both because of their aesthetic or formal features and due to their strong affective impact when viewed, which makes them memorable.[54]

The Bang-Bang Club

One decade later during the early 1990s the works of a group of four young white photographers, consisting of Ken Oosterbroek, Kevin Carter, Greg Marinovich, and João Silva received international attention. They depicted and portrayed the violence, protest, and unrest in the townships during the negotiation period before South Africa's first democratic elections in 1994. Oosterbroek, Carter, Marinovich, and Silva became quite famously known as the *Bang-Bang* Club, a name that alluded to their daring attitude of *shooting* photographs in difficult and dangerous war-like situations as well as to their images most often showing real shoot-outs with guns and people getting wounded or killed.[55] "Amazing how often these guys were shooting pictures of people committing murder, burning people alive," commented Bill Keller in naïve admiration, who was the executive editor of *The Times* in Johannesburg from 1992 until 1995 and who worked closely with them.[56] At the same time their status as white male citizens of South Africa also offered them protection in general, but specifically when dealing with the South African police force.

Violent incidents in the townships were enacted mostly between ANC and Inkatha supporters, but they were also partly encouraged by white right-wing and police forces to hinder the election process and to "prove" black South African's inability to adhere to "law and order." Often one hostel building complex, which housed hundreds of male African migrant workers from the rural areas, was aligned either with the ANC or the Inkatha party. The people living in the surrounding townships who were urbanized often had an adverse political perspective.[57] The press termed the events the "hostel war" or "black-on-black" violence.[58] As legal scholar Nicholas Haysom has noted in a paper on the rise of right-wing vigilantes in the 1980s: "By referring to all conflict in which both parties were black, as black-on-black conflict, the links and relationships between the conflicting parties and apartheid structures were buried. Furthermore, the label carries with it a racist suggestion of traditional or tribal internecine strife."[59]

In the international press there was a market for these violating images that only showed the surface view of the events. One of the *Bang-Bang* photographers, Greg Marinovich, won the Pulitzer Prize for *Spot News* in 1990 with a series of images that included one of Lindsaye Tshabalala being burnt and knifed by ANC supporters as a suspected traitor (see figure below).[60] Thsabalala, who identified as Zulu, was accused of being a supporter of the Inkatha party by his attackers.[61] The photographs of his torture and death were published and circulated globally. The image shows the unbearable sight of a black man being set on fire by another black man and burning alive. A young man can be seen in the foreground, fleeing the scene. The image may remind one of similar visual icons of humans desperately trying to survive as, for instance, from the Jewish uprising in the Warsaw Ghetto, where the Nazis set all remaining houses on fire.[62] Similarly, the reason why the image from Lindsaye Tshabalala's death became an icon is that it seems to show the existential moment of death, together with the semantically saturated image of flames and fire, thus it draws on the visual archive of religious martyr images.[63] Marinovich's whole series gave prominence to the so-called "hidden war" in the black townships during the preparations for the first democratic elections. But they also strengthened the view of South Africa as a place of "barbarian" violence.

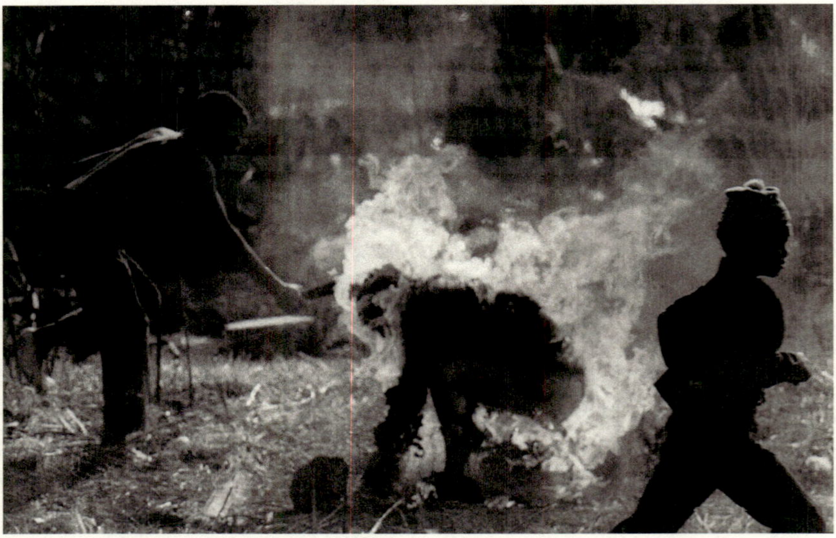

Figure 2.1.5. Greg Marinovich, Inhlazane, Soweto, September 15 1990 (original in color).

The series was condemned by the ANC since it could be interpreted as the black population not able to govern themselves and instead acting out brutal violence. And, yet, the *Bang-Bang* photographers also covered many other aspects of violence, such as the involvement of white policemen in township riots and massacres. They showed white audiences some of the difficulties and struggles of black South Africans. Those photographs, however, were not as widely publicized as the particularly sensationalist ones. The shocking photos, such as the one of the burning of Lindsaye Tshabalala, also seemed to show simple meanings, since it seemed apparent who the perpetrators and who the victims were. Other attempts at explaining the reasons for the violence are summarized by Mahmood Mamdani, from a sociological interpretation he put the blame on the architectural formation of the hostels as prison-like, male-only camps to "cultural" ones, locating a deep divide between township and hostel inhabitants. The hostels were deemed to breed violence as a fight over resources at the margins of society.[64] The Truth and Reconciliation Commissions (TRCs) that were set up in 1995 were able to address some of these proceedings in more complexity and uncover further details of what had happened. This study, however, can only assess the visual depiction of this violence and how these images are remembered and at times restaged.

Ambivalent Witnessing and the Complicity of the Camera

The "era of the necklace" and the state of emergency was publicized through the photographs documenting it. Kevin Carter, another *Bang-Bang* photographer, commented on documenting necklacing: "I was appalled at what they were doing. But then people started talking about those pictures . . . then I felt that maybe my actions hadn't been at all bad. Being a witness to something this horrible wasn't necessarily such a bad thing to do."[65] Hence, while Carter himself grapples with his position of witnessing, he decided, since the photographs started a discussion, to see a value in that, upholding the prime objective of photographers during apartheid as mere acts of "witnessing" and not intervening. These documentary traditions are still very dominant up to this day, but they need to be questioned and further explored from post-colonial and post-apartheid perspectives.[66] And yet Carters whole statement is, of course, highly ambivalent, using the form of double negation and leaving one to wonder if it is "necessarily a good thing" to record such an act. His ambivalent reading and affective state may involve the fact that one cannot watch in the sense of experiencing the other's death, even when being present at the scene. While other events may be witnessed and related to one's own experiences of similar events, death is an exception. There, a true experience of death can only be one's own. To see another person dying underlines the incommensurability of feeling with the other; empathy is impossible and creates at the same time an affective access.

Working conditions and the self-conception of documentary photographers have changed and become the subject of intense critical debates and public scrutiny. Carter himself wondered about an implicit complicity between the perpetrator and the photographer:

> After having seen so many necklacings on the news, it occurs to me that either many others were being performed (off camera as it were) . . . or that the presence of the camera completed the last requirement, and acted as a catalyst in this terrible reaction. The strong message that was being sent was only meaningful if it were carried by the media. It was not more about the warning (others) than about causing one person pain. The question that haunts me is 'would those people have been necklaced, if there was no media coverage?'[67]

In 1994, Carter won the Pulitzer Prize for his infamous image of a little emaciated black girl in Sudan, as a vulture already seems to be waiting in position in the background.[68] The main critique of this photograph is, on the one hand, that it shows African people as passive victims, and, on the other hand, the role of the photographer is questioned as yet another "vulture," preying on people dying without intervening to save their lives.[69] This critique already hints at the complexity of the situation, where African people, like the small girl, were in vulnerable positions, but the action of the photographer was not considered an adequate response. Thus the photograph was condemned in a campaign of indignation. Carter, already troubled before, killed himself shortly after. The photograph, as well as Carter's life and death, has been discussed further through an artistic re-reading by Chilean artist Alfredo Jaar.[70] He re-adapted Carter's famous image and created an installation with the title "The Sound of Silence" to, in turn, challenge what in Rancière's reading of the work is the "duplicity of the system that simultaneously solicits and declines such images."[71] Jaar's work situated the single photograph in the context of Kevin Carter's biography. The question of the complicity of the photographer and the camera with the terror it documents, connects to Judith Butler's analysis of the Abu Ghraib torture photographs, where the act of recording became part of the torture.[72] Of course the setup at Abu Ghraib was different, since the perpetrators were directly involved as soldiers or security personnel. They were taking the photographs and even including themselves in the frame.

Nonetheless, in the South African context there also seemed to be situations of the cameras and, during this era most prominently, the white male photographers becoming complicit in the crimes acted out against people in front of the lens, or to say the least, intensifying the situation. Photography can thus act both as producer of evidence and as catalyst for action. It also seems important to de-mystify the apparent coherence and narrative of progress of violence against apartheid as told through the photographs of the *Bang Bang* photographers, while acknowledging at the same time that the usage of violence and the armed wing of the ANC were instrumental in ending the apartheid regime.

To render the notions of documentary and affective strategies more complex in regard to political protest culture against apartheid in a transnational setting, I want to turn now to a work which, while in the tradition of the dualistic mode of reproach against the apartheid regime, nevertheless offered a new collage technique of working with documentary and against consumerist images. This example, drawn from the realm of popular culture, is the Sun City Protest video that not only experimented with formats but in addition created a particular affective assemblage of wounded images.

Affective Juxtapositions—The Sun City Protest Song Music Video

Protest action spread into mainstream popular culture worldwide; one of the most prominent examples of this is the protest song "I ain't gonna play Sun City". by Artists United Against Apartheid, which was released in 1979. The recording of this protest song was a collective project by an impressive number of star musicians, including Ringo Starr, Peter Gabriel, members of U2, Bob Dylan, Run DMC, Lou Reed, Jackson Browne, Afrika Bambaataa, Gil-Scott Heron, Pat Benatar, Daryl Hannah, George Clinton, and Keith Richards.[73] Steven van Zandt initiated the project and wrote the lyrics. Musically, the song combines elements of hip-hop, hard rock, and R&B.

While the song text addressed the hypocrisy of Western inaction and ignorance with lines like "Relocation to phony homelands | Separation of families | I can't understand | 23 million can't vote | Because they are black | We're stabbing our brothers | And sisters in the back," there was also a music video produced in the United States that mostly documented the production process with the different musicians both in the studio and on location in New York. Paul "Lucky" Goldberg and Paul Allen filmed and produced it, using a Panasonic video camera. In the final edit visual politics incorporated images of black suffering in a collage style that may have maximized their affective impact even further by contrasting them with "pretty," colorful scenes of the luxurious Sun City resort, and staged scenes of the black and white American musicians singing and walking together on the streets of New York City, seemingly promoting racial solidarity and reconciliation.

Besides its overt message of condemning the luxury resort Sun City and attacking musicians who broke the cultural boycott by performing there, the song articulated a tension that was not just in the symbolically political realm. The record cover shows a red sun overlaid with a barbed wire fence, alluding to black and white division. In the music video the images of the entertainment paradise, Sun City, that stood in the West for apartheid injustice and for upper-class, mostly white people living a protected good life, are literally torn open by animated white and black hands and footage of police attacks on demonstrators in the townships appearing in the wounded images (see figures 2.1.6 and 2.1.7 in the color gallery).[74] Thereby, the advertisement images showing the easy, happy life of the elite are accused of being false images that hide the prevalent dire living conditions of the black majority in the townships. Below the glossy surfaces of luxurious hotels, swimming pools, and casinos, a funeral march in the townships with at least four coffins becomes visible, while on the outer margins, still other images remain to be seen.

This aesthetic of cross-fades and layering of moving images, of course, was a technique of video animation and video filters that had only become widely available with new video technology in the 1980s. This experimental way of editing created a heightened intensity and is an example of an "affective assemblage," following Deleuze and Guattari's notion of assemblage: "All this, lines and measurable speeds constitutes an *assemblage* . . . and as such is unattributable. It is a '. . . multiplicity [. . .].' "[75] The video combined footage of people running away from the police or demonstrating with raised fists, which seem to be dancing to the rhythm of the protest song. Here the images of black suffering—including iconic photographs—were integrated into a "united colors" disco beat, which is urging everyone to get up and join the dance (and the protest). The video plays with contradictory affective intensities combining them into a complex affective assemblage, which has the potential of connecting necessary protest and activism to pleasure via the engaging and seductive pop video. Also, it elevates entertainment and youth culture by joining it to a "righteous cause"—political activism against apartheid.

Brian Massumi states that the realm of affect is always part of our somatic and psychic responses to images, but that the affective responses of a viewer may be surprisingly contradictory to our everyday understanding of "happy" as "good/pleasant" and "sad" as "bad/unpleasant."[76] Massumi cites an experiment from 1980 by German media researcher Herta Sturm in which children watched different versions of a short film: "The "sad" scenes were rated the most pleasant; the sadder the better."[77] In addition the "saddest" versions were also the most memorable. In Sturm's interpretation of the results this does not imply an intellectual understanding of what has been seen, but rather a mental overload that she called "the missing half second."[78] Therefore the analysis of affect needs to go beyond notions of rationality and subjectivity. Massumi describes affect similarly to Deleuze as unassimilable intensity, therefore it may have unforeseen effects. Affect always implicates a potential—an aspect of "not yet."[79] In consequence there continues to be a quality of futurity and utopianism of affective forces, since they cannot be captured and stipulated, and yet they cannot be completely separated from politics of representation. To return to the protest video against Sun City: it transported both anger and hope for change and its affective intensity felt pleasurable to viewers beyond the color line and beyond its intended political impact.

In the aesthetic and formal perceptive realm, however, the Sun City video indicated that the luxurious, glossy, color images themselves are under attack and are being accused of hiding or overlaying the images of pain, hidden in their midst or beneath them. Therefore the beautiful, but false, images were wounded themselves and in their wounds the negative *real* images of pain became visible. In the documentary materials, even the iconic photograph of Hector Pieterson's death was included. This collage created a strong argument against the invisibility of black suffering in white, middle-class lives, working visually against what Charles Mills has termed "white ignorance,"[80] both in South Africa as well as in the Western countries that had long cooperated with the apartheid regime. Here, an international production from the United States offers a different framing, while relying on photographs produced in South Africa, which were often censored there. The transnational production settings of the song and the video mirrored the fact that the United States was the prime destination for exiled musicians, photographers, artists, and activists from South Africa. This was partly due to the "common" language, English, and the willingness of the U.S. at the time to grant asylum for black South Africans, as for example the singer

Miriam Makeba or the photographer Ernest Cole. Therefore, there was a lot of cultural and political exchange between these countries.

Besides, even if these images of protest and black suffering were officially prohibited in South Africa, they were still visible through the dialogue with activists in exile and were viewed and distributed by anti-apartheid activists but only in small and semi-private settings like record or bookstores as well as other small leftist venues. The protest song "I ain't gonna play Sun City" was also played at mainstream white clubs and parties in Johannesburg, as white South African journalist Gwen Gill recalled in an interview, "The anti-apartheid song was played in the clubs. I remember that my kids [. . .] went clubbing in Jo'burg at that time [. . .].[81]" However, the music video was not widely watched in South Africa, since television was introduced only comparatively late in South Africa in 1976, and even later in the townships in the 1980s.

Today the protest song and music-video culture have faded away and multiplied on YouTube and alternative media platforms since then without ever ceasing to exist but becoming less present and convincing. Similar affective assemblages constructed from a collage of documentary and advertisement images were pioneered in the art context by artists like the U.S.-American feminist artist Martha Rosler.[82] Rosler's "Bringing the War Home" (1967–1972) series wanted to address the United States' role in the Vietnam War. Rosler cut up magazines and pasted documentary war photographs taken in Vietnam on top of home-decor advertisement photos from American magazines to create unsettling nightmare scenes. The strategy of juxtaposition as it was used in the "I ain't gonna play Sun City" video may in fact have been inspired by Rosler's and similar works.

Putting images loaded with the terror of the Vietnam war into familiar American kitchens and living rooms was Rosler's attempt to make a foreign, faraway fight seem more real, more shocking, and to show the connections between peacetime living in the United States and the battles in Vietnam. Jacques Rancière commented on Rosler's series, "We know how committed artists strove to set the reality of these images of pain and death against advertising images displaying *joie de vivre* in beautiful, well-equipped modern apartments in the country that was sending its soldiers to burn Vietnamese land with napalm."[83] This quandary is at the heart of the debate on how images may or may not be used to induce political change. The first question would be whether images can make one understand or grasp complex sociopolitical relationships. Azoulay would argue that this is beyond the possibility of a single photograph and that the image always needs to be contextualized; this may exactly be the reason why Rosler is making a collage image.

Yet it is complicated further, since even if several images, maybe even accompanied by text, can make one comprehend, this does not necessarily lead to any action, as Rancière comments: "But there is no particular reason why it should make those who see it conscious of the reality of imperialism and desirous of opposing it."[84] The images may even be conceived as fashionable, thrilling or radical chic and simply be consumed and enjoyed by audiences, as partly is the case in the mainstream example of the Sun City protest song and video. Consequently, how images may activate affective responses and in turn political actions is beyond an instrumental relationship and remains highly debatable. Beyond simple calls to actions or equations of images into social reform, however, I argue that there is a politically invested visual discourse that influences society and the political sphere—even if not always in predictable ways. Furthermore, the image producers and artists may add a layer of reflection on the usage of visual media and its particular framings in the work itself, as we have seen in Alfredo Jaar's and Martha Rosler's work that was exhibited in art galleries, of course reaching only a select audience.

Changes and Continuities of Documentary Image Production

After 1994, the mode of working with documentary images has changed in South Africa with regard to both recording technology as well as to who the actors were—in front of and behind the lens. The protagonist of the "Freedom Fighter" from the township during apartheid has retired—but may have been "re-born" as a social movement activist fighting for the landless and migrant people against privatization and slow service delivery by the ANC government. Yet, nowadays black and white photographers, male and female, are documenting events like the xenophobic attacks in 2008 in post-apartheid South Africa. Even though there is no absolute equality, and many whites are still in privileged positions, the situation has changed and more people of formerly and partly still marginalized communities take part in the visual presentation of their own and others' lives. The new political dispensation has—without disregarding its positive impact—multiplied the frontlines and divisions in South African society, and no "easy enemy" (as before the apartheid government) can be located anymore.

Since the 1990s, violating and affective images seem to have lost some of their unequivocal political potency and any one-dimensional connection between image and politics, as was predominant during the struggle against apartheid, has been problematized further. In post-apartheid times images like the one of Hector Pieterson's death or the ones of the *Bang-Bang* photographers have become iconic and are embedded in South Africans' visual memory. This (national) memory is never static though, and images circulate globally and are open to multiple readings, associations, intersections, and updates as can be observed in a later excursion that takes, as an example, the reenactment of a necklacing in a music video clip and thus shows an example of "migrating images" and possibly an attempt to produce "counter-images," to visualize painful history/ies and make claims for justice.[85]

This does not imply that the search for the "just" image in documentary and artistic work is over, but it becomes clear that the image is always "just an image" to borrow Godard's prominent aphorism, and thus not adequately showing "reality" and embedded in complex relations that frame its interpretation.[86] Whether the exploitation of photographs for a fair cause can be vindicated always depends on the circumstances and is not an intrinsic quality of the images themselves. Yet, it is conspicuous that some news images in post-apartheid times look the same as the historical images from apartheid, when one views the media coverage from the xenophobic attacks in 2008. Photographers noticed this aspect themselves, as white, female South African news photographer Nadine Hutton commented:

> There's this weird kind of like almost like bravado machismo of being a photographer as well. Like everybody was like so excited—especially the boys—all the boy photographers were like you know like HARD ON central—for like all the blood and the guts and the guns and all of that all. I'd say 90% of them were like OMG—it's like The Bang-Bang Club.[87]

The above quote establishes an analogy between the violence of the early 1990s in the townships with the 2008 xenophobic attacks, which is a foreshadowing for what will be discussed in chapter 3 "Burning Questions." Besides, Hutton comments on the gendered coding of being a photographer by distinguishing a specifically male excitement in connection to the violence taking place at the xenophobic attacks, which she connects to the occupational (self-)image of the photographer. Nonetheless, she may also be including herself in the feeling of excitement, claiming that "everybody" was sharing in this sentiment. At the same time she stereotypes and thereby denigrates the excitement as sensationalism by hinting that her colleagues already have certain photographs in their heads that only show undifferentiated clichés of violence: "all the blood and the guts and the guns." I propose, however, that today's viewers of documentary media are not satisfied with a single shocking photograph, but that they want to know more about the context. They increasingly question what a photograph seems to obviously show, thereby opening up multiple perspectives on an event. Documentary image producers have also adapted their way of crafting narratives to the new demands and the new technology available and are incorporating and exposing "blind spots" or gaps, as will be discussed further in part 5.1.

Most of the theorization and coming to terms with the history of photography in South Africa still primarily celebrates "struggle photography," when photographed injustice seemed to be smoothly translated into political agendas by using it to codify history as a unified, national narrative.[88] This streamlining and privileging of certain histories and readings of photographs renders others meaningless. As South African photographer's Santu Mofokeng observed, in apartheid South Africa the "everyday was invisible," meaning that only images of extraordinary (and usually violent) events existed.[89] This implies that if there are no visual records, there are also no stories, no words to tell of a historical experience. One may add that even if narratives exist and are recorded by other means than the visual, they are often not as strong as when they are connected with visual evidence. This holds particularly true when proof is sought for previously unknown injustice, systemic disadvantage, or the hardships of marginalized people. African-American writer James Baldwin eloquently named this dialectic relationship of the connection of visibility as proof of events *The Evidence of Things Unseen*, in relation to the Atlanta Child Murder Cases of 1979–81 and systemic violence against African Americans in American society.[90] His title underlined the "commonplace" assumption that there can only be evidence of "things seen," and he instead crafted a memorial to the murdered children by retelling and remembering the events through writing. This can be considered writing a counter-archive into being, a political act against forgetting, and also makes a poignant case for the reconstruction of missing historical documents, a notion which we will return to later when analyzing the works of the South African artists' collective *Center for Historical Reenactments*.

2.2 Affective Images in the "New" South Africa

Visual politics of nation-building and the "new" democratic regime since 1994 are tangible in South African media by what type of affective images are represented and by what can be seen, perceived, and felt. The realm of the political is encoded and mediated by photographic images—people in temporary camps with tents that bear the UNHCR logo queuing for food, outstretched hands with ID cards, men wielding machetes and guns chasing unarmed women and men, a burning shack, a looted spaza shop.[91] Photographic news images and documentary films make things visible for the "public" and show who is included in the nation as citizens and who is visualized as *other*—often as bodies in need of assistance. Of course, in digital times this is no longer limited only to the photographic images on billboards, TV, or newspapers, but includes Twitter, Facebook, YouTube, and similar online social media networks that circulate both moving and still images. The visual realm is one of the prime sites of contestation and negotiation, in what Arjun Appadurai has termed a "diasporic public sphere"—updating Jürgen Habermas's notion of the bourgeois public sphere.[92]

Since there are thousands of photographs circulating between news and social media, the art world and advertisement, often only the particularly sensational and shocking images receive widespread attention. Ariella Azoulay has written sarcastically in this regard about a "hit parade of horrors."[93] "Photographing what exists on the verge of catastrophe thus is an act that suspends the logic of newsworthiness, a logic that is manifested today by what we can call 'the hit parade of *énoncés* of horror. . . . This hit parade is one aspect of the larger conditions of postmodernity. . . .' "[94] Yet it is also important to remind oneself—especially in the South African context, where freedom of the press was severely restricted during apartheid—that not all violent and violating events were visible in the news. During the struggle there were no accurate reports on black deaths during protests, removals, and resistance. I propose that these affective images act as "open wounds" or "affective apertures" that play significant roles in the construction of national and personal history/ies. And yet, Wendy Brown in her re-reading of Nietzsche's *Zarathustra* has cautioned against "identities built on wounded attachments."[95] Since identities built on remembering hurtful events may get caught up in a vicious cycle of revenge and *ressentiment.* Brown suggests: "This past cannot be redeemed *unless* the identity ceases to be invested in it, and it cannot cease to be invested in it without giving up its identity as such, thus giving up its economy of avenging and at the same time perpetuating that hurt—'when he then stills the pain of the wound *he at the same time infects the wound.*' "[96] It is, however, problematic to think of "identity" as a unified unchanging whole, and I rather argue for shifting subjectivities and temporary identifications. In addition, arguing for "forgetting" a history of pain may seem equally cruel. Therefore, this study will attempt to explore the notion of "wounding apertures" of the violating images further, complicating the notion of photographs as wounds by linking them with Spivak's notion of an enabling wound or enabling violation.[97] Spivak developed this concept while considering the construction of the colonial subject and insisted that: "One cannot write off the righting of wrongs. The enablement must be used even as the violation is renegotiated."[98] How can photographs of violent events and black injured bodies not only perpetuate pain and archive suffering, but possibly also act as "enabling wounds" loaded with affects and political effects?

CUT—Tears at the TRCs after 1994

When apartheid officially ended in South Africa, it was not so easy any more to produce images with a single, unequivocal message. The iconography of portraying black suffering and tears changed post-1994: black victims and white perpetrators were expected to reconcile.[99] In 1995 the *Promotion of National Unity and Reconciliation Act* was passed and in order to implement this the Truth and Reconciliation Committees (TRCs) were established. The TRC hearings were set up to uncover crimes committed during apartheid and find out what happened to disappeared people. Many incidents that now came to the public's attention were gross human rights violations. Nevertheless, amnesty was granted to perpetrators if they in turn told the truth. Bishop Desmond Tutu headed the TRCs, as such they existed in a religious as well as a political setting. The process of the victims and perpetrators each telling their side of the story was loaded with affect and painful emotions, as it detailed violence, kidnappings, and killings by the police.

Desmond Tutu cried at a TRC hearing in December 1995, because of the gruesome account of events that was told.[100] The hearing was televised, the viewers saw Tutu clutching his hands and that he laid his head on the table, bowed down in grief, hiding his face. His posture hints at shock or disbelief, creating the impression that he is guarding himself and especially his head against the horrific details. A hand from a woman seated next to him touches his back in an attempt to comfort him. He has completely retreated into his body and looks fragile. One cannot see his tears, yet they were always mentioned in the accompanying title to this photograph. In this court-like context of human rights violations Desmond Tutu's tears were a proof of his empathy, and at the same time his act of crying validated the testimony he had heard.

The public broadcasting of the TRCs hearings exposed, for the first time, many white South Africans to stories of black suffering and tears on their television screens. Often black victims were testifying at the TRCs and white perpetrators were in turn forgiven after telling their side of the story. Yet the lines were not always clearly divided, since there were also black collaborators of the apartheid regime and white resistance fighters. The TRCs managed to form the country's "collective memory" into a shared national history that was judged according to the norms of "universal" human rights. The act of crying together also creates a feeling of a common bond for the audience, a sense of unity and community, and was thus considered important for building a new and united South African nation. This process, of course, also produced certain silences and exclusions as any hegemonic national process of memory construction does.[101]

There were different ways of portraying the crying individual—people in power, holding an office or being attributed with other institutionalized prestige, as in this case Christian-coded stateliness, usually get ennobled and humanized by the act of crying. This can often be seen when a politician becomes more human and credible through the public act of crying a single tear (not actually breaking down crying or sobbing). On the contrary, a female witness, as can be seen in the photo below, is visibly moved and seemingly reduced to the position and hyper-icon of "crying victim." Recently there have been more visual incidents of crying male politicians—Barack Obama, and Vladimir Putin in 2013. In 1995, a male person crying in public was still not seen very often, so the image of Bishop Tutu was very

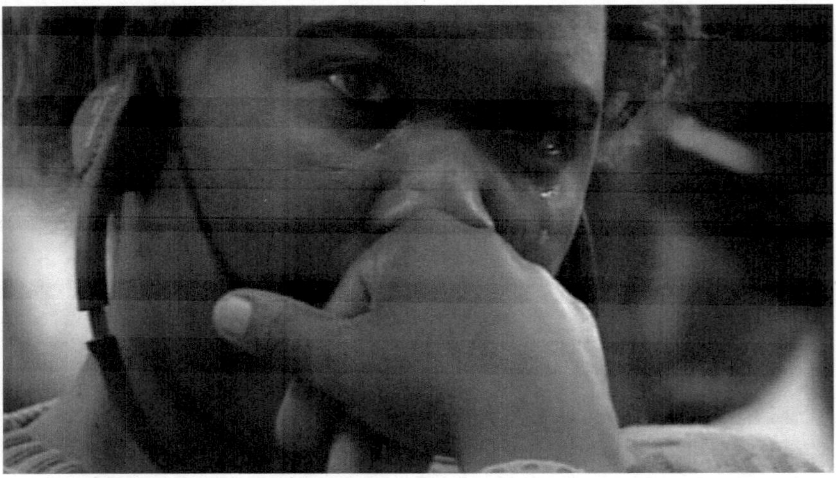

Figure 2.2.1. Still of female witness in tears at TRC hearing, *Facing the Truth*, 1995, by Gail Pellett, gailpellettproductions.com; last accessed 8/9/2014 (original in color).

unusual when it was published, especially in the South African context where masculinity is rigidly connected to demonstrating power and strength, and the disavowal of emotions.[102]

Moreover, tears in a court context like the TRCs beg one to question the links between images of suffering, the status of victimhood and human rights discourses. "More" suffering supposedly leads to more entitlement and compensation, it carries a symbolic and moral weight, yet of course this is not an inevitable reaction. But how can victimhood be proven and how are tears interpreted in the courtroom? Do tears make trauma visible and testimonies trustworthy?

The tales of suffering that were told during the TRC hearings unwillingly or willingly called up the register of certain aspects of melodrama. I want to refer back here to Linda Williams claim that melodrama is a "broadly important cultural mode."[103] Her approach is to analyze this "melodramatic mode" that does not only consider the "tearjerker" or "women's films" but instead takes place in society at large—also in the context of continuing racist stereotypes. She examined several examples and suggested: "To understand racial melodrama is to see why repeated calls for more accurate, or more 'realistic' representations of racially marked characters are powerless to overturn deeply embedded racial stereotypes that seem hopelessly outmoded yet live on in the culture."[104]

The cultural mode of the melodramatic is not only an American phenomenon but is also influential globally, as for example in the increasingly dominant recourse to a discourse of victimization in the global migration debate when the claiming of rights is considered.[105] Furthermore, the court-like setting of the TRCs in South Africa has similarities to some elements that Williams analyzed in the O. J. Simpson case in the United States. As William states: "The study of melodrama has the potential to explain why it is that in a democracy ruled by rights, we do not gain the moral upper hand by saying simply that rights have been infringed. We say, instead, much more powerfully: 'I have been victimized; I have suffered, therefore give me my rights.' "[106] Similarly, as many studies suggested during the TRC hearings, narratives were structured around hegemonic notions of suffering and pain, validated by tears and through gendered coding of the witnesses.[107]

Viewing Tears and Writing about Tears

When confronted with the image of a person in tears one's first affective response may be to look away, or to feel uncomfortable. A defense reaction against tears and sadness often includes anger, defiance, and outrage.

In fact, sadness, shame, embarrassment, and anger are overlapping fields of affect. Questions about the entitlement to watch another person's pain and tears become more virulent when this pain belongs to a body that is already marked as *other* for a Western audience. In addition the scientific or analytical—"cold" gaze may be perceived as betraying the people in tears. The reproach of voyeurism on the one hand and the lack of empathy on the other are important to consider, yet they should not stop one from further analysis. Te ars can, however, be contagious. As affect and film theorist Eugenia Brinkema claims: "In the long history of the philosophy of emotion, the tear has been the supreme metonym for the expressivity of interior states at least as far back as Aristotle's Poetics."[108] At the same time a subject in tears is always perceived as in danger of dissolving into the affect, losing his or her rationality and therefore is not considered to be an equal to an emancipated and composed, i.e., rational subject.

The images in this text are not shown in order to repeat acts of symbolic violence but because they exist in my materials. In effect, there are so many documented scenes of pain and suffering that I cannot neglect this topic. Of course in the process of writing, watching films, and viewing/taking photographs, my own affects are also involved. I cannot maintain my analytical gaze, as tears well up in my own eyes when looking at the painful images again and again, obscuring my field of vision. Naturally, this is one prevailing reproach against "being moved," claiming that affect puts critical distance in jeopardy. I consider my own affective states as part of my analysis and will therefore use them to question and theorize affective responses.

In her seminal book, *Regarding the Pain of Others*, Susan Sontag explores the accusations of exploitation and voyeurism in the context of war photography. She insists that the issues at hand while watching images of suffering are more complicated than what is usually presented by the arguments held against them. A simple refusal to watch may be a defense reaction of persons who are not immediately affected, as Sontag points out with an almost angry undertone. "Citizens of modernity, consumers of violence as spectacle, adepts of proximity without risk, are schooled to be cynical about the possibility of sincerity. Some people will do anything to keep themselves from being moved."[109] I wonder if Sontag in this case takes the term "sincerity" for granted? Sincerity is a moral term, meaning truth-loving, yet there is never one truth.[110] Sontag's statement is additionally highly ambiguous, and I would first ask, if in the moment of refusal to be moved and looking away or turning cynical, one has not been already been touched by an image? In other words, is it even possible to keep oneself from being moved? Is it possible instead that the act of looking away in itself indicates that, in fact, one has already seen too much, and as has become a common saying "one cannot *unsee*."

Sontag herself considers the attempt to reject affect while watching violent images, for instance, by simply not believing that the images are "sincere" and instead believing that they are staged "tearjerkers" attempting to provoke a certain feeling and effect. Instead of repudiating the look, Sontag suggests that one should: "Let the atrocious images haunt us. Even if they are only tokens, and cannot possibly encompass most of the reality to which they refer, they still perform a vital function. The images say: This is what human beings are capable of doing—may volunteer to do, enthusiastically, self-righteously. Don't forget."[111] Thus Sontag encourages the viewers to move beyond cynicism, while reminding them that images can never be taken as complete indices of a situation. The last part—the reminder "don't forget" stands in the documentary tradition of making injustices visible and attributes a pedagogical aspect to the viewing of images urging us to "learn" from history. Especially in the South African civil rights discourse with the still fervent memory of apartheid racism and oppression, again and again the slogan "Don't let History repeat itself!" is reiterated at times of protest.

To conclude, on the one hand tears seem to occupy a privileged space of sincerity and truth, yet, as I have already suggested, on the other hand they are always under suspicion of being a particularly cunning deceit. As such they are close to the documentary film paradigm, which, while being presumed to be a trusted medium delivering the truth, is also always under suspicion of manipulation and showing a false reality. Accordingly scenes of documented tears are a testing ground "under pressure" for documentary films; these are the scenes where the spectator is either completely drawn into or rejects the film. To further analyze the staging of tears and how it raises the stakes and thus the concern of the spectator for the crying subject, the next part considers several audiovisual testimonies in tears from recent South African documentary films.

A "Testimony in Tears"—in Khalo Matababe's *Conversations on a Sunday Afternoon*

Conversations on a Sunday Afternoon directed by the black South African Khalo Matabane is a documentary film which does not hide its fictional elements, making it part of the same hybrid genre as *Come Back, Africa.* However, it will be very pertinent to analyze in detail which scenes were staged and which were not and what their specific function in regard to affective intensity and visual evidence is. The main character in *Conversations*, Keniloe is played by a professional actor (Tony Kgoroge), yet everyone else in the film is not. The quest of the film is to find out more about who lives in Johannesburg's inner city, the residents of which are mostly migrants from other African countries, and to rehabilitate them as people who have a right and a reason to be there. The film was produced in 2005, but even then resentment against foreigners were already palpable, well before waves of violent action against foreigners occurred in all urban centers of South Africa in 2008. The film's structure is built around one documentary scene: the testimony in tears of a Somalian woman, named Fatima Hersi, stranded in Johannesburg.[112] This scene provides the affective urgency and backdrop for all the other people Keniloe encounters who are neither shown in such emotional states nor in such close-up shots of their faces.

The first scene with Fatima introduces the audience to her as a person, and one gets to know her name when Keniloe meets her—seemingly by chance—in a park. Fatima is wearing a long blue dress and a veil that drags behind her over the sandy path in the park. The veil adds an extra marker of otherness. It is noteworthy since it marks her as a Muslim woman and seems to establish a hierarchy in terms of participating in modernity, visibility, voice, vulnerability, religion, and class. This scene was clearly set up—a white sheet is hung behind Fatima, probably to provide more contrast and a clearer background—and we hear her voice as a voiceover. It gives some information on her history, stating that she is a refugee from Somalia, staying in Johannesburg without any of her family members. There is a close-up shot of her hand writing a letter, yet she is not reading what one glimpses of her sentences in the letter—but telling her story in English, adding to the evidence that the scene was restaged later.

The next scene, in which Fatima is present, is her testimony in tears. Keniloe meets her again and she tells him that most of her family members were killed and starts to cry (see figure on opposite page). This scene has a different background than the introductory shots to the scene. The camera is wavering, as if the camera person was undecided about whether to keep filming as Fatima loses control of herself or whether to turn the camera off. Tears are flowing down her cheeks, she cannot continue to talk and wipes away the tears with her hand and her veil as if they are stains. Keniloe whispers: "I am sorry. I am sorry." The scene is deeply saddening when one watches it.

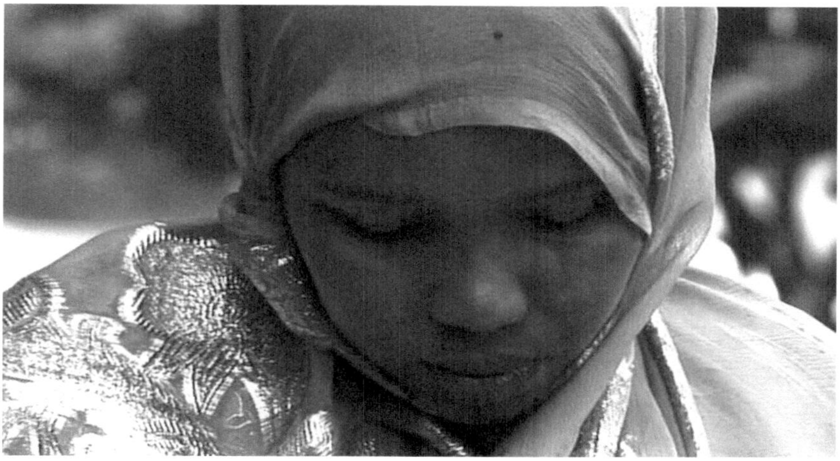

Figure 2.2.2. Fatima's testimony in tears, still from *Conversations* (original in color).

Not only in Western culture is crying an activity connected with shame, and therefore usually done in private, hidden or safe settings and not in public while others are watching. The shame that may be felt by someone who is caught crying by the film camera may also be transferred to the viewers who feel like voyeurs watching it. It was hard for me to watch this scene without looking away. There are cuts in between the filmed material, indicating that either the camera was turned off after all or material was taken out. The sound is unsteady as well, at first it fades out and then later the audio tracks have been cut and reworked, indicating that some sequences were taken out, or possibly some of the talk of the filmmaker or the camera person. The wavering camera and reworked sound make the scene fragile and threatened, it asks me as the viewer to watch closely and hints at the difficulty of filming it. The crying is not subtle, Fatima is sobbing loudly; it addresses the audience directly and asks for immediate and urgent reactions.

In this scene Fatima's image turns into the "crying migrant woman" and is transformed into what I want to call a "hyper-icon." A hyper-icon in my definition is an image that is seemingly overdetermined and thus only seems to have one side and one message. The "crying woman" is a recurring figure in documentary films cast as the ultimate "victim," which is often used to endorse the claims of the films.[113] Connected to this is the notion that female citizens are more vulnerable than male citizens, as the saying "Women and children first . . ."[114] demonstrates. In addition, not only gender but also race adds another layer of possible stereotyping and assumed vulnerability. Within the broader context of visual representation, black women's bodies have often been the subject of voyeuristic consumption, both of their sexuality and also their trauma and pain. This is the common "wholesale" reproach of voyeurism usually held against audiovisual documentary materials, and it is certainly true for the majority of images produced, especially if they are made by Western filmmakers for a Western audience and exoticize the other. Yet it is important in each case to determine which recording and viewing context was used and produced. In the case of *Conversations* the embedding of the documentary testimony into the staged scenes attests to a careful remediation of the situation. One could wonder though if this scene was necessary to include in the final edit of the film?

The answer is that the filmmaker deemed the scene in tears necessary to add an affective impact and to portray "sincerity." The difficulty is that sincerity similar to authenticity is a slippery term, according to Jane Taylor, "[a]nywhere that 'sincerity' names itself, it ceases to exist. It is a value that is vouched for through a circuit of social consensus, in which it cannot itself trade."[115] The quality of "sincerity" is usually directly located within a person and his or her expressions are judged as sincere or not, whereas authenticity is connected to the situation as a whole. In the scene in *Conversations* the documented face is shown in a close-up, revealing all the micro movements of crying. Here the body becomes the prime site for disclosing a deeper truth that seems unequivocal and privileged over words, which can tell lies. The body language is taken as a token for sincerity, since the act of crying renders the documented subject often speechless. Now only the body seemingly conveys the pure and untainted, and thus physical "truth of affect," which will be discussed below. We will leave the crying scene from *Conversation* now, but return to the film again at the very end of this chapter, when it will be someone else's turn to wipe away his tears.

The Truth of Affect—the Documentary "Money Shot"?

The display of affect has become the primary site for the search of a truth. As Marie-Luise Angerer argued the sexual *dispositif* from Michel Foucault is currently shifted to an affective *dispositif*, meaning the truth of sexuality now turns into the truth of affects.[116] Affect holds the promise of being transferrable globally and of being understandable to anyone regardless of citizenship, language, and age. In search for the "true" language of the body, audiovisual recordings of a documentary subject displaying "sincere" affect of pain and despair may thus be considered the most valuable shot in a documentary film. Not only does the affective scene grip the audience and grab their attention, it is also a privileged moment of displaying a "truth," very much sought after in a media age where many displayed images are considered fakes, staged, or reenacted. The moment of crying usually consists of a close-up shot of the face, often with a characteristic slow zooming into the frame. The camera may be shaky, further attesting to the spontaneity of the event of crying happening.

Even if at first it might seem a far-fetched comparison, one could associate the tears in documentaries with the "so-called" *money shot* in porn film, as film theorist Patrick Sjoberg has suggested.[117] The money shot in pornographic films frames the moment of male ejaculation in a privileged manner—full frame, again often with a slow zoom, to center the attention. The money shot means the most indispensable shot. Following Linda Williams's analysis of porn film, the money shot with the prominent scene of the externally ejaculating penis is the visual "proof" that actual sexual pleasure has taken place on screen.[118] What the moment of male ejaculation and presumably orgasm is for the porn film, the shot of tears may be in documentary films.[119] Sjoberg continues: "The uncontrolled secretion of bodily fluids works as a stand-in-index for the faltering photographic one."[120] In the documentary, what tears are meant to affirm is the incontrovertible truth of the suffering depicted on screen. It tells the audience that this was not a fake. A similar view gets repeated in countless sugary pop songs that claim: "Tears never lie." Our media age has been described as taking a turn toward the "confessional" as well as to the natural sciences. Here the body becomes a site of confession, a display of *real* or *true* affect connected to specific physical phenomena that have been scientifically researched and well-described. In both cases the physical events of tears and ejaculation, bodily fluids—lacrymal fluid and sperm—are emitted, proving a "higher truth of the body" than verbal language, which can tell lies. Tears seem to be taken as a token for trauma, thereby giving evidence that the story the person tells is *true*. There is also the dimension of the body here becoming a witness against his or her will, because both actions have a dimension of "overcoming" the subject who temporarily loses control, but of course both actions can be faked as well.

When filming or photographing an event like a person crying, however, this often shows only the aftermath after the real catastrophic event. In addition there is the problem of capturing or translating an embodied affect into the "dry" and distancing (audio-)visual media. Tears are a fleeting liquid, evaporating quickly. A predicament that a recent documentary film commented on in its title: "Tears sent via Skype, arrive dried out." As previously mentioned, crying also immediately arouses the suspicion of an ingenious deceit or fake. Consequently, there is an irresolvable argument staged between the notion of "sincere" portrayal and strategic instrumentalization of tears. This is also an important link to the discussion around the documentary project in crises, due to the possibility of fakes or hoaxes, but also subversion. In this context the term "tearjerker," which is usually a derogatory form for melodramatic films, is of interest, too. "To jerk" means to move something abruptly or joltingly—an insensitive movement. The tearjerker is yanking tears out of an unwilling subject without the subject being able to interrupt this action.[121] Similarly, one could view the subject dissolved in tears as a neutralizing action in which he or she enjoys her tears passively and does not become active in any way. However, in Christian medieval tradition tears were seen as something positive—the *gratia lacrimarum*—tears that were shed as a gift evidencing complete "*Ergriffenheit*" in prayer.[122] Therefore, it is important to remember that tears are not only connected to negative feelings or pain and suffering, but they also were seen as another state, closer to the divine: some of this meaning has been transported into secular times.

And yet to cry seems to be more akin to giving in to a position as victim or passive mourner instead of a position as a fighter or revolutionary, as was discussed by looking at photographs used on protest posters from the anti-apartheid struggle. And while there were already experiments with the projective usage of images by means of collage, there were also examples of photographs and film scenes being used in a way that proposed that they "speak for themselves." Therefore, several different modes to employ images to induce affective responses existed at the same time. While the visualization of tears often points to a larger societal ill, the individual subject shown in tears may also be voyeuristically exposed, especially in connection to the violation of personal physical borders as the next example will demonstrate.

Female Vulnerability Exposed—*Martiné and Thandeka*

An intensification of the hyper-icon of the foreign "crying woman" is the migrant violated (raped) woman, who has a particularly complicated relationship with visual representation. As a result there are few documentary images or films dealing with rape directly, neither of white or black women. The exposed female body is a taboo in documentary media. In addition, the act of rape cannot be recorded by a detached photographer or filmmaker.

This may only be done by the perpetrators themselves, thus becoming part of the crime, which in fact sometimes happens, adding to the shame and injury of the raped person. Some of the difficulties of *showing* and presenting a documentary testimony of sexual violence will be discussed using the film *Martiné and Thandeka* as an example.[123] *Martiné and Thandeka* was produced by the collective Filmmakers Against Racism (FAR) in the aftermath of the xenophobic attacks 2008; here only the scenes with Martiné's daughter will be considered.[124] The FAR Facilitator's Guide states: "This film offers a perspective from women affected by the violence." In the film example a teenage girl and her mother, Martiné, who are African migrants, speak about how the daughter experienced an attempted rape at the temporary shelter at the police station in Johannesburg where they were staying after the xenophobic attacks in 2008.

The scene starts with a text insert that tells the viewer that Martiné's daughter has almost been raped. The daughter, who is never introduced by name, is shown from behind walking through rows of tents at the Rifle Range refugee camp, where hundreds of migrants stayed in the aftermath of the attacks. Her voice starts from off screen to tell her story. She went to the toilet facilities, and noticed: "Someone was following me like he is a security, then I get inside the toilet." The man stepped inside with her into the toilet and held her. Then the man said: "When you scream I will kill you." She did scream, though, and managed to get away. The film cuts to

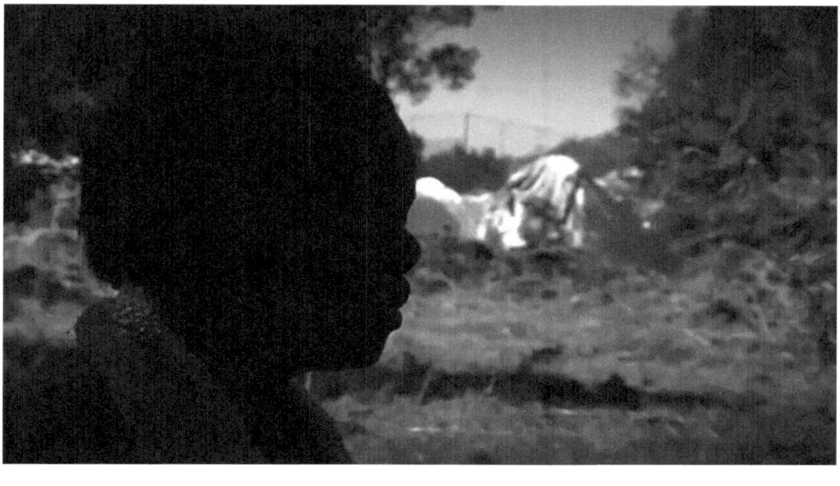

Figure 2.2.3. Martiné's daughter, still from *Martiné and Thandeka.*

the daughter sitting outside in the shade, now talking in real time. Since she is backlit it is hard to see her face at all, it is only a silhouette (see figure below). Obviously this scene has been set up, yet one may wonder if this was just a makeshift background, or if the filmmaker chose it consciously over a more protected space like, for instance, inside of a tent? While recounting the events she starts to cry involuntarily, tears flowing down her face. She tries to suppress them and seems embarrassed. Nobody else is visible in the frame and neither the filmmakers behind the camera nor anyone else outside the frame tries to comfort her.

After the daughter's testimony the film again cuts to her mother, who is always filmed inside a tent where the family is living temporarily. The mother takes her turn to recount the event and also raises the question as to why the offender was not arrested: "They said, they didn't rape her, they tried to rape, but they didn't, so nothing was done to this man. We saw him later out, trying to talk to another woman." The mother is frustrated that nothing happened, she makes a helpless gesture and turns to the camera, simultaneously to the documentary filmmaker and the spectators, in a silent plea to help her achieve justice. She says she had not been allowed to speak to the media by police and security people. The mother seems to harbor some hope in the documentary recording situation that her testimony and account may still in the end change her situation, and thus perhaps believes in the promise concatenated with media attention. At the same time she expresses anger with the police. It is a sad irony that Martiné's daughter was almost raped at the police station—a place that should be the safest of all. In addition, it is unclear whether the police did not allow her any media contact in order to protect her and her family or rather because the police wanted to protect the reputation of their institution.

The discussion of media-ethics and what to show and what not to show thus gets further complicated when considering the vulnerability and exposure of female bodies. Due to their unprotected and often illegalized status, migrant women in general have a higher risk of experiencing physical violence and rape. It is very striking that the main protagonist, Martiné's daughter, remains close to invisible in the film. Was this attempt to "hide" the daughter a conscious strategy of "victim protection"? In addition, her name is also not given, further anonymizing her. But this thought does not seem likely, because even though the audience cannot see her well, one later gets glimpses of her face and might be able to identify her after watching the film. Since the scene starts with a text insert "Martiné's daughter has almost been raped," it seems the filmmaker does not trust the audiovisual testimony by the daughter enough to make the viewer understand what happened and it also does not trust the film images and sounds she was able to record. But the text simply overwrites the images, telling the viewer beforehand what will come, but maybe it is also a gesture similar to a "trigger warning," giving the audience the ability to prepare themselves?

The scene of her in silhouette, re-telling her story in tears, and leaves me wondering if the process of being filmed and having to recount her story in front of the unblinking, neutral stare of the video camera is not re-traumatizing her, and in a way makes her a victim once again, this time exploited by the filmmakers. The daughter seems fully and agonizingly aware of the recording situation the whole time. Documentary filmmaking always has a voyeuristic element but here it is amplified to the maximum. The whole passage left me, as a female viewer of the film, feeling uneasy. It is important to note, though, that the film was directed by female South African filmmaker Xolishwa Sithole. Sithole's work is acclaimed and she has won several awards.[125]

The discussion of the scene in *Martine and Thandeka* has to be connected to larger questions of shame and representation of gendered vulnerabilities, some of which Ariella Azoulay has asked in her text: "Has anyone ever seen a photograph of a rape?"[126] She observes that there is generally an absence of photographic representations of raped women, and asks: "If rape were indeed only an act of violence, as the feminist movement has tried to depict it since the movement's inception, it is difficult to understand why there is such a comprehensive abstention from distribution images of rape or any other iconography connected with it."[127] In addition to the absence of images she observes that the recounting of a rape in the first person still always ". . . remains trapped in the problematic framework of the confessional."[128] The fetishizing of the tears and their privileged inclusion in the film seem to make the incident "worse" since they act as evidence of "suffering." Furthermore, rape victims always have to prove that they did not enjoy the unwanted male attention they received, but on the contrary have been traumatized by it.

A Single Tear on a Mirror

In a different scene later in the film, the daughter is shown doing her hair in the cramped and improvised setting of their tent, while at the same time the mother's voice tells: "My daughter is not the same, because of what happened." On the audio track a small emotional tune is overlaid on this scene as the camera sways to show the daughter's lap where she is holding a mirror—this is due to the fact that they are living in a tent without a proper bathroom and amenities. A single tear can be seen on the mirror, which the daughter must have shed; it seemingly illustrates the mother's statement. The single tear could easily have been missed, since it would have fallen onto the daughter's pants and evaporated, had it not gotten caught by the mirror. Also an extra camera movement was needed to film the daughter's lap, which otherwise would have seemed inappropriate or indecent in this context. Now the tear is framed as the central object, so it is a rather ostentatious view of the single tear, indeed not all that different from a *money shot.* The usage of the music makes one wonder if the documentary is imitating a soap opera, using the melodramatic register as a kind of a last resort, when the makers of the film thought they needed to create strong affective environment to "move" or "touch" the audience in order to gain sympathy for a particularly harsh living situation.

Contrary to her daughter, Martiné is shown at the end of the sequence in a close-up head-shot with sufficient lighting, crying openly. The last scene concentrates on her face and her wiping away tears from her cheeks. Tears of both mother and daughter are thus given a privileged position in the film and frame the account of sexual violation and its aftermath. However, as Azoulay has pointed out in a further footnote on the complexity of photographic witnessing:

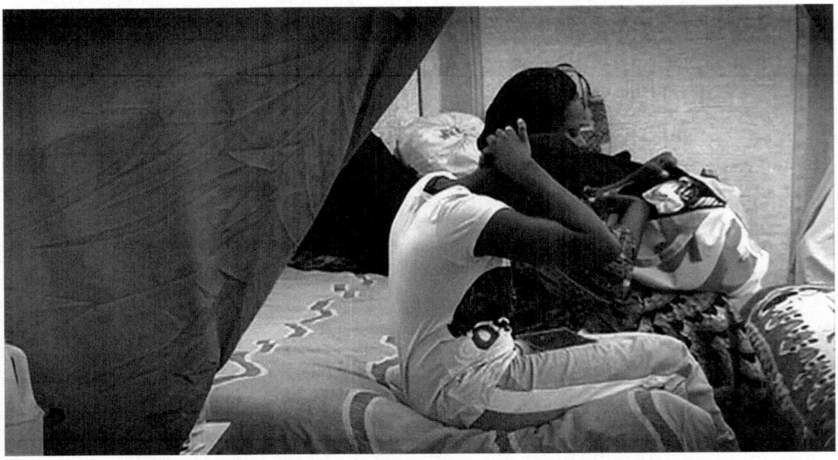

Figure 2.2.4. Martiné's daughter inside the tent, still from *Martiné and Thandeka.*

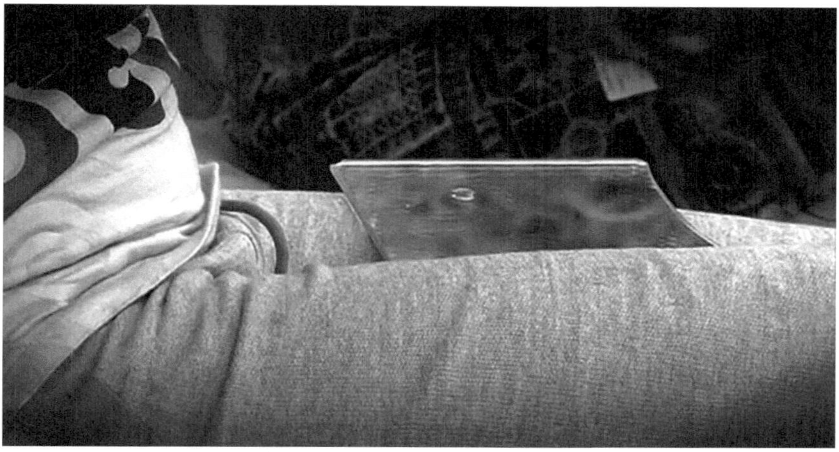

Figure 2.2.5. A single tear from Martiné's daughter, still from *Martiné and Thandeka.*

> . . . exposing women who have survived rape to the gaze is supposed to render rape visible. But an injured person who has survived a traffic accident is not the accident, and when you see a woman who has been raped, you don't see rape. Exposing a rape victim to the gaze doesn't show rape, but merely creates the illusion that rape has become an object of the gaze.[129]

The same, unfortunately, holds true for the portrayal of Martiné's daughter in the film, it re-inscribes her as one of the women that "it" happened to, now suspended in a state of exception, who may become an object of the viewer's sympathy or spite, but who does not emerge as a subject. Azoulay argues that rape cannot have visibility and that it is closer to the notion of an idea. On the contrary, in the sense for a need to show, and to speak about the unspeakable, however, one could argue that it is necessary and important to raise awareness on the issue of rape, especially in the context of vulnerable groups like refugees and migrants. I want to argue that affective images of rape need to be rendered more complex. What can be portrayed more easily perhaps is the reaction of people toward rape victims. A BBC documentary produced by Roger Graef in the 1980s entitled "A Complaint of Rape" only showed the point of view of a woman who came to the police to report a rape, but without exposing her to the gaze of the camera. At the police station three male police officers interrogated her and did not take her seriously. The film, which had adopted a "fly on the wall" approach, was able to capture the menacing behavior of the policemen in such a way that a public outcry followed its screening on public television and the handling of rape victims was reviewed.[130]

Turning the Gaze Around

Women have experimented with different formats of protesting against the silence around rape, trying to include the perpetrator instead of concentrating on the victim position only. A strong silent protest against rape occurred in South Africa in August 2016, when President Jacob Zuma spoke at the Independent Electorial Committee (IEC), briefing the audience on the election results. Four black female activists Simamkele Dlakavu, Tinyiko Shikwambane, Naledi Chirwa, and Amanda Mavuso, stood up, each held up an improvised self-written sign with words in red ink, the first woman holding two, together they read: "I am 1 in 3 #" "10 Yrs later" "Khanga" "Remember Khwezi." Khwezi was the woman who accused Zuma of rape in 2006—ten years ago. She identified as lesbian. In addition she was HIV-positive and the daughter of a late ANC-comrade of Zuma. However, Zuma was acquitted of the charges. "Khanga" was the wraparound garment Khwezi was wearing. "1 in 3" is the alleged proportion of women raped in South Africa. The month of August is officially national women's month. The activists reminded the nation how even in post-apartheid times, the government may fail to support women. Pumla Gqola analyzed the rape trial of Zuma and described it as "a watershed moment" for South Africa's gender inequality. She pointed to the aspect that during the process, Khwezi's sexuality was dismissed and mislabeled as bisexual, while at the same time her previous history of being a lesbian was used to frame her as someone whom it would be "impossible to rape."[131]

Several other documentary photo projects turned the gaze efficaciously around, thereby giving the position of the victim a certain agency.[132] One was called "Project Unbreakable" and was conceived by American Grace Brown, who is a rape survivor herself. In the documentary photographs that she took of rape survivors or that people also took of themselves, they are also holding up signs with handwritten messages quoting what their attackers had said to them. One can upload photographs to the Tumblr website, thereby Brown left all decisions about the way the images look to the participants or negotiated them together when she took the photographs. The only requirements are that the submissions do not give names and that the statements given are in quotation marks. Some of the participants were

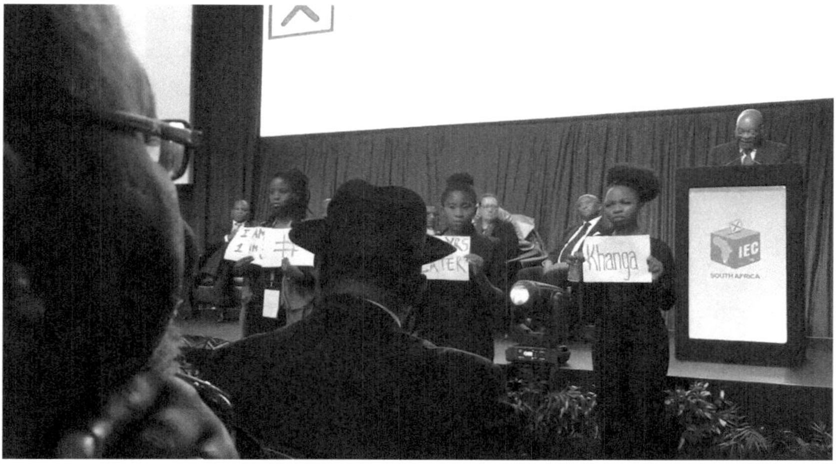

Figure 2.2.6. Silent female protestors during Zuma's speech at the ROC 2016.

hiding behind the signs, some holding the sign up defiantly and looking directly into the camera. This way, the perpetrators were present in the frame as well, and exposed as liars and coërcers, saying things like: "You know, you want it, too."[133] Since the photographs were basically self-portraits and the women chose whether they wanted to expose their faces and look back or remain invisible but expose the assault that happened, they created a very different visibility than the one of "victimhood." At the same time the assault was not hidden, but very present through the words of the perpetrators. The photographs, with their combination of text, a serious and defiant look back, or no face visible, created a complex and moving viewing experience and a unique counter-archive of visible evidence of rape.

Another work that ""shows without showing" is a photograph from black South African photographer Zanele Muholi, simply titled "Aftermath," showing a close-up photograph of a black woman's belly and upper legs, only wearing underwear and protectively cupping her hands over her intimate parts. The photograph had the accompanying text: "Many lesbians bear the scars of their difference, and those scars are often in places where they can't be seen."[134] Muholi's work, while raising awareness on the issue of violence against black lesbians, also always tries to complicate the issue of violence and never portrays the afflicted women simply as victims, either by adding text or abstracting the topic. In addition, Muholi has always emphasized the importance of creating a "positive visibility" beyond shocking images of violence.

The examples of "Remember Khwezi," "Project Unbreakable" and Muholi's "Aftermath" seem to indicate that staged performances in connection with text that are photographed are better able to convey a complex counter-message than simply depicting what Azoulay termed a "woman, it has happened to."[135] Furthermore it becomes evident that the more the people depicted can participate in the construction of their image, the less they come across as "victims." This notion will be taken up again later in part 4.1, in which two participatory photo projects will be discussed in more detail.[136] Yet, also in (documentary) film it is possible to include silences and refusals, counter-narratives and unusual performances of female subjectivities, as will be discussed in the following chapter on a "Refusal" and later in chapter 5, in the discussion of *Conversations*—"Girls Lying Scene."

A Refusal—A Reversal of Tears

As I have hinted before, there are more strategies at work in *Conversations* than simply repeating the "victim tradition" with the hyper-icon of the crying woman. When taking *Conversations* into account as a whole film there are additionally other stories told and other images captured that go beyond stereotypical or hegemonic representations. In the end sequence of the film, after the long search for Fatima is over, Keniloe meets her again. During this reunion it is now Fatima who does not show any emotion and does not want to talk anymore to Keniloe or the filmmakers. She is filmed standing inside a house, behind glass, thus doubly removed and at the same time protected from the intruders. Keniloe expresses his happiness to have found her again and says that he wanted to write about her life. She replies: "But this is my life, and I don't feel to talk no more about it." So the film ends with a refusal or failure instead of a happy reunion and reconciliation. This final scene turns the relationship between Fatima and Keniloe around, now he wants something from her that she refuses to give. Keniloe is at a loss, frustrated and sad for himself that he cannot write about Fatima's life, and he dabs his eyes with his sleeve, wiping away a single tear. This gesture disturbs the seemingly safe subject position that Keniloe as the main character inhabited in the role of the superior male character who interviews others throughout the film.[137]

The externally voyeuristic—but also as an interior state sympathetic—desire of Keniloe and the film's audience to find out more about Fatima, to get to know more details about her life, and maybe even to help her cope is frustrated. But the last scene also shows that Fatima is not a victim, and does not need Keniloe's or anyone else's help, since she is already living her

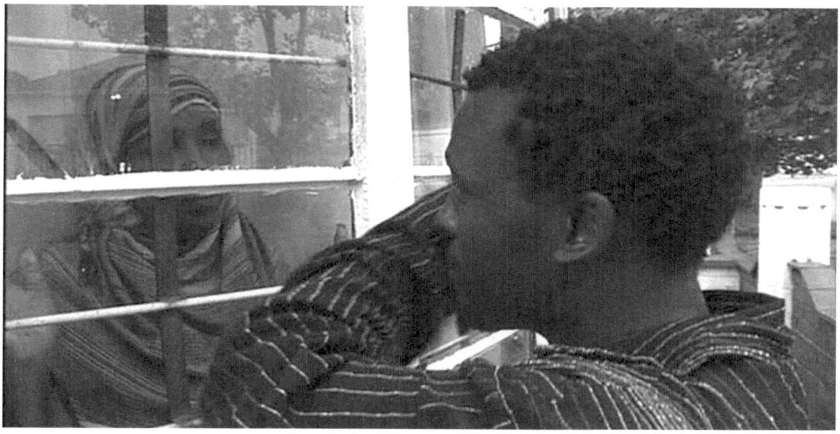

Figure 2.2.7. Fatima refuses the conversation (still from *Conversations*).

own life in Johannesburg in a house in an area where other Somali migrants are living as well. Her hands are painted with henna, as it is a custom for marriage or other festive events, allowing one to imagine that she has a social life. Keniloe's single tear—as one knows that he is an actor and his tear is therefore staged—also reverses the scene of Fatima crying "for real." The act of crying frames the beginning and ending of the film, giving the tears a privileged position. Poignantly, the film *Conversations* offers a different view of Fatima Hersi at the end of the film, in line with a refusal of the victim position that she inhabited earlier in the film.

In this chapter I have discussed the impact of visually presenting pain by showing faces with and without tears. Different strategies exist, each trying to affectively "move" audiences and (maybe) politicize them. Two approaches were predominant in these images—one consists in mourning the invisibility of certain people's tears and the other amounts to a critique of representing tears in the context of marginalized people altogether. These two positions are irreconcilable when taken to their extremes. But one could also argue that the tears shed in front of a camera are not in vain, they are recorded and thus preserved and may be used to evoke outrage and political action or simply to move a spectator to empathy. "Mournability" as Judith Butler states is equal to recognizing other's humanity.[138]

This chapter questioned which agency the presentation of pain and documented tears may still have or not have nowadays. It has shown how far crying can be a de-politicized action as well as be turned into something political. As Judith Butler has analyzed in depth the notion of "mournability" in the context of the Israeli-Palestinian conflict, it is important to pay attention to which losses can be mourned in the public realm and which are neglected or denied. The one that can be mourned is the one that counts as a "human being" or "worthy citizen," adding an ethical dimension to the public display of affect. Butler describes a political project in terms of visualizing the grieving and injured other thus: "Do we apprehend the precariousness of life through the frames available to us, and is it our task to try to install new frames that would enhance the possibility of that recognition?"[139] In this sense the activity of public crying and the possibility of affecting others through the documented presentation of tears may also be a possibility for justice and for making a difference, if this is done in the public arena. This strategy is connected to leftist aims, which have existed since the 1970s, of creating more and just visibility for the disenfranchised other; yet one needs to consider how these strategies may have failed or how the visual remains an ambivalent and complex field where the hope to raise empathy for the other should not be abandoned, yet more visibility is not under every condition preferable in a strategic sense and later chapters will therefore explore possibilities to remain invisible or opaque.[140]

Since the 1980s, images of pain and tears in the South African context have been complicated and become more ambivalent and any illustrative as well as mechanical connection between image and politics, of course always dubious, was now completely blocked. This does not imply that the search for the "just" image in documentary work is futile, but it becomes clear that the image is always inadequate. Nevertheless, documentary scenes of tears and crying bear the possibility of affecting the spectators and may induce the social community to include the formerly excluded. In addition, some of the documentary films and photographs presented offer a level of self-reflection that goes beyond the simple representation of tears and the depicted people as victims. I posit that there exists an interactive, yet indirect, dialogue between the filmmakers, the documented subject and the viewers, which serves to critically examine visual discourse as well as social conflicts, and thus has the potential to directly affect the political sphere. Similarly Hito Steyerl connects the question of documentary images and affect with a utopian project: "For a politics of images, this raises the question of a different politics of documentary affects. On the one hand in the mode of reflection and critique of these affects, but also in the mode of the invention of new documentary affects and connections and the idea of the possibility of a different reality."[141]

In addition, at the end of *Black Skin, White Masks* Frantz Fanon writes about his vision where one is not constantly framed in positive or negative characteristics, and rather one tries to "touch the other, to feel the other, to explain the other to myself."[142] The next chapter takes Fanon's wish as a beginning in the quest to answer urgent "burning questions" in the contextualization of the photograph that became the icon of the xenophobic attacks in 2008.

3

Burning Questions

3.1 The "Burning Man"

After the transition to democracy from 1990 to 1994, following the loss of power of the National Party, the release of Nelson Mandela, and the unbanning of the ANC, South Africa officially overcame apartheid. In comparison, South Africa was one of the last African countries to become a "post-colonial" nation-state.

Three areas of national narratives and images that have become metaphors and national projects in South Africa post-1994 constitute the political framings for the analysis of the visual materials of the xenophobic attacks. First, during the decade after the transition to democracy in 1994, "nation-building" was one of the main goals of the government headed by then-president Nelson Mandela. This included the attempt to reconcile the South African nation by means of the Truth and Reconciliation Commissions (TRCs) as well as the promotion of national unity through the fashioning of new inclusive national narratives, for example in museums and heritage sites such as Robben Island, the District Six Museum, the Constitutional Court, and Freedom Park.[1] These privileged sites of remembrance were attempts to document and display the history of racial oppression and painful memories for both black and white South Africans. As Alison Landsberg has argued on the effect of exposure to such memories by means of visual media, in film, or in exhibition displays, especially for white audiences: "Such prosthetic memories might in turn help them see differently, see . . . with vision that translates into politics."[2] Thereby, the newly developed memory culture was constructed strategically to unify and reconcile the heterogeneous South African population.

Second, with the official end of apartheid it was the image of the "rainbow nation," a term which Desmond Tutu had coined, that became a powerful symbol for imagining the new South African nation. Nelson Mandela used it during his first month in office, when he spoke of South Africa being ". . . a rainbow nation at peace with itself and the world."[3] The metaphoric image stood for the breaking down of racial categories and the constitution of a culturally and ethnically diverse society. It mirrors the new South African flag—post 1994—that includes all primary colors: black, white, blue, green, red, and yellow. The rainbow as a symbol has its own narrative and implies positive progress. In the Christian context it is a symbol of hope—after the great flood and Noah's ark survival—that has been transferred to the secular realm. Since the rainbow is made up of white light that is refracted by the raindrops, acting like a prism, it presents the otherwise invisible fact that white light in fact includes all colors. Metaphorically, the multi-colored rainbow is therefore the perfect symbol for South Africa's national slogan of "unity in diversity."[4]

Third, Thabo Mbeki, Mandela's successor, coined the term *African Renaissance* in the late 1990s to promote scientific, cultural, and economic "renewal" in Africa.[5] In part this updated and re-integrated the Pan-African elements within the ANC's history as well as constituting a strategy to promote cultural integration in the advent of globalization and neoliberalism. Yet the concepts of the "African Renaissance Conference" from 1998 remained vague and varying from the revival of the All-African ideas from the 1970ies to a romanticized Africanized history or philosophy.[6] While the *African Renaissance* lost impact, there are also concrete affirmative-action programs like the Black Economic Empowerment (BEE), but the majority of black South Africans remained disadvantaged regarding access to houses, health care, education, and jobs. In the American context Wendy Brown analyzed that: ". . . a strong commitment to equality, requiring heavy state interventionism and economic redistribution, attenuates the commitment to freedom and breeds *ressentiment* expressed as neoconservative anti-statism, racism, charges of reverse racism, and so forth."[7] These cultural as well as political and socioeconomic factors surrounding nation-building post-1994 may have also led to claims of "authentic Africanness" as the basis for superiority or as Auga has stated, the problem of a "racist anti-racism."[8] As such they have contributed to the emergence of anti-foreigner resentments.

All these overlapping areas—nation-building, the image of the rainbow nation, the African Renaissance, and the question of autochthony, as well as the reemergence and reinvention of difference—were ambivalent movements promising freedom and full citizenship rights for all South Africans, and yet they clearly led to a stronger nationalism and claims of superiority of a certain "native South Africanness." In addition, it led to "sentiments of entitlement," since the ANC had promised an end to black South Africans socioeconomic status of hardship, which was felt to be long overdue. Achille Mbembe astutely scrutinized the political, societal, and economic situation in 2006, after twelve years of limited democracy and before the outbreak of the xenophobic attacks in 2008, as on the verge of catastrophe and

> . . . stirring the darkest brew of South African culture: its addiction to prophecy, consumption and small miracles; its deeply held phallocratic ethos shared by blacks and whites; the corrosive violence that is tearing apart its social fabric; its xenophobia . . . (and) by the increasing viciousness of its rhetoric, forged out of the shards of a conservative urban, migrant, *lumpen*culture whose antics have left countries such as Rwanda, Sierra Leone, Liberia, Congo, Ivory Coast or Sudan bleeding to death.[9]

Mbembe realized the existence of strong xenophobic sentiments in society already in 2006, and located—in line with Marxist theory—the emergence of xenophobia in a "conservative urban, migrant *lumpen*culture," meaning a class of people living a precarious existence at the fringes of society, whose own experiences of migration did not lead them to embrace the plight of others but, on the contrary, to fight them in a hard battle for survival and small advantages. In addition, he mentions the "phallocratic ethos shared by blacks and whites," suggesting gendered hierarchies in society and problematic concepts of black and white masculinity. He is not apologetic, neither toward the black South Africans nor toward the white South Africans in whom he has diagnosed "white melancholia"—mourning for the bygone days of their racial privilege.[10]

Noticeably, the divisions inside the South African society have been amplified even more since 1994, and the metaphorical image of the peaceful "rainbow nation" has lost its meaning in the South African public sphere.[11] The democratic transition in South Africa happened without major economic redistribution, yet service delivery in terms of providing housing, health care, and free education to the disenfranchised majority was promised but not carried out as quickly as had been assured.[12] Consequently, an extreme dissatisfaction has been building up within the majority of the black South African population whose living conditions remained dire—also in the post-1994 South Africa.[13] At the same time the "nation-building" project led to an increased securing of the outside borders of the South African territory against illegal immigrants. Police and government repeatedly talked about "criminal" foreigners.[14] Exclusion already had a *long history* in South Africa, which has been transformed after the official end of apartheid from racial exclusion but has not disappeared, and is now mainly based on class and citizenship.[15] Johannesburg, for example, is still a highly divided and fragmented city even in post-apartheid times.[16] Thereby, the promises of post-apartheid times and the "new" South Africa of the "born-frees" have not all been kept.[17] Yet it is important to expand the critique further than simply blaming the ANC government.

Since the 1980s South Africa had been routinely described in the national and international media as a "violent society." Like many countries that have had civil wars or similar events, South Africa also has a higher rate of "personal" or "private" violent behavior in forms of rape, domestic violence, and homicides even after the conflicts subsided.[18] South African newspapers are rife with nearly daily accounts and images of accidents, murders, rapes, and robberies—despite this fact, the xenophobic attacks and the images they produced, especially the photograph of Ernesto Nhamuave being burnt alive, were generally perceived as notably different, particularly shocking, and affectively moving. The photograph of Ernesto Nhmuave being burnt was immediately recognized as singular, as one of its kind, a photograph that demanded a response, or as Mozambican writer Ungulani Ba Ba Khosa put it "symbolizing all the Nhamuaves that are set alight by the torch of hatred." The image haunted ordinary people, filmmakers, writers, and others. While it is not this study's intention to simply add to the repository of catastrophic images from Africa for the Western audience, the events of the xenophobic attacks and the audiovisual records that they produced, specifically the photograph of the "Burning Man," need to be discussed in detail, since they set a caesura in post-apartheid history.[19]

A Photograph of a Man, Who Was Burnt in 2008

A mob of South Africans had searched for foreigners living in Rhamaposa, an informal settlement in the north of Johannesburg. Two Mozambicans, Ernesto Nhamuave and his younger brother-in-law Francisco Nhamuave, had tried to escape from the area, carrying some of their belongings. Ernesto Nhamuave had grabbed a blanket, some clothes. Both were caught in an open space by their attackers, who beat and kicked them. Francisco Nhamuave was badly beaten but managed to escape. Ernesto Nhamuave was beaten until he was lying on the ground. Then the attackers set his blanket and him on fire and left him to die. A short time later, several photographers and policemen caught up with the event. Some of the policemen tried to dampen the fire. The photographers took pictures. One of the resulting photographs that gained worldwide attention shows Ernesto Nhamuave as he is squatting on the ground and trying to push himself up, maybe to stand up, but he is already too weak. Simphiwe Nkwali photographed it. In the photo Nhamuave's posture shows his desperate struggle. His body is covered with white powder—not ashes but the fire extinguisher's granulate—making him look ghostly. His face seems like a mask. It is unbearable to look at the image, yet, when turning away it has already been burnt onto one's

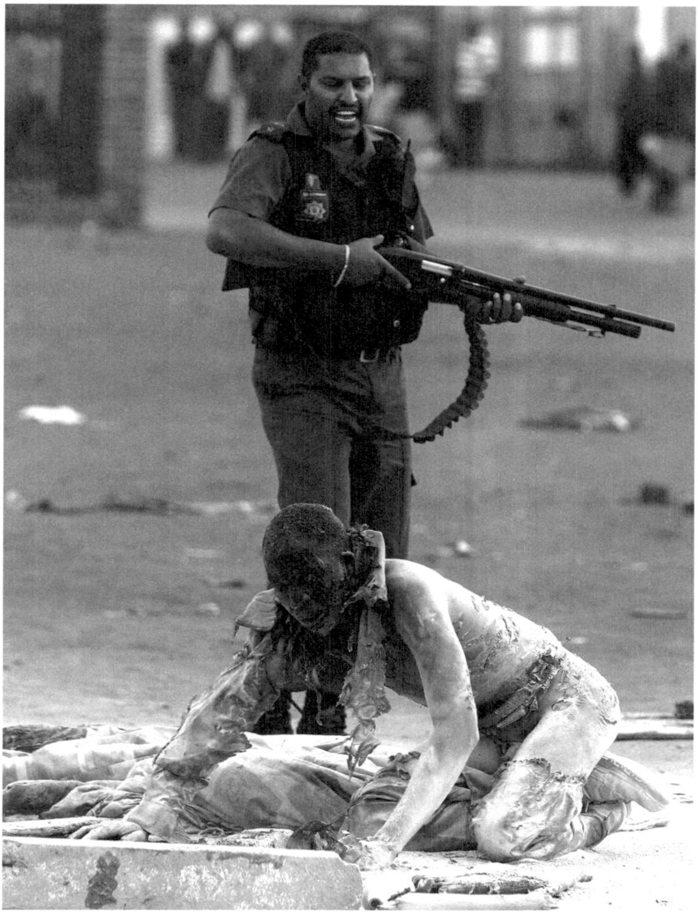

Figure 3.1.1. "The Burning Man," Photographer Simphiwe Nkwali, March 2008.

retina. The photographer, his camera, and the attackers who have set him on fire are all absent from the image, only a policeman is standing behind him. Ernesto Nhamuave is made even more vulnerable by the fact that his male dying body is half naked. His clothes have turned to ashes and shreds, and the man may have also tried to tear off the burning clothes to escape the flames. The photograph shows Ernesto Nhamuave right before he died, marking a specific temporality—as Roland Barthes wrote about a similar image: "He is dead already, and he is going to die."[20] The photographer's camera has caught the man in an eternal death agony. He looks back at the observer without seeing. Ernest Alfabeto Nhamuave was thirty-five-years old.

Photographs are always silent. How can one make them talk? While the photograph does not transmit any sound, both Ernesto Nhamuave and the policeman standing behind him have their mouths open. Black American writer and cultural theorist Fred Moten has pointed out: "The refusal to neutralize the phonic substance of the photograph rewrites the time of the photograph, the time of the photograph of the dead."[21] So how can we hear the non-recorded but visualized screams and make them present again at least in our minds? As I learnt later, Ernesto Nhamuave was not calling for help or in pain and fear. Beauregard, a staff photographer from the *Star*, was present at the scene, and Ernesto Nhamuave did not utter a word. Beauregard explained that when one breathes in fire, one cannot scream or say anything anymore, since it destroys one's lungs.

The policeman, standing behind Nhamuave, was not silent and was shouting at the crowd that is visible at the very top of the photograph as blurry figures, surrounding them, and watching. He may also have been shouting at his colleagues, one of whom—a female police officer—was using a fire extinguisher to try to put out the flames, can be seen in several other photographs that show a wider context to the event. The crowd watching was also shouting; apparently some people called: "Please stop, don't do it!"[22] The policeman could also have called for a doctor, but no medical personnel were visible in any of the photographs of the scene. The policeman looks strangely helpless with his large rifle in his hands. His right arm bears a wrist band; his left arm is framed by the chain of ammunition. The rifle calls up associations of "armed conflict," "state power," and maybe "security," but in this situation it seems completely useless, except possibly to keep the crowd away from the injured Ernesto Nhamuave.[23] The policeman is standing so close to the dying man, yet he is not bending down to touch him, at least not in this frame.

Through the process of writing this text I have debated back and forth whether to include the photograph of Ernesto Nhamuave being burnt—the image of a dying black man—or not, since he is thus exposed once again, to black and white gazes of the reading audience of this text. But I believe it is important to include the images that I discuss, rather than withholding them from the reader. This study analyzes what is problematic in terms of racialized and gendered codings of these images, to get to the bottom of what they show, how they are read, and, last not least, their affective excess. At times it seems that the level of affective intensity is the prime objective against showing them since shocking photographs are often considered "unbearable" or too difficult to view. As Susan Sontag commented in her seminal study *Regarding the Pain of Others*, it is usually the people that are not part of "us" that are shown dead or in precarious and injured positions.[24] This translates into unwritten ethical viewing conventions that mandate, in general, that it is prohibited to show one's "own"—Sontag meaning the American—dead soldiers. To view a body that is on the verge of death is often considered damaging to the honor of the dying person. One could also imagine, though, that it is simply unbearable for the viewers, especially since it often shows the perpetrator's gaze. A common reproach against such a depiction finds it shameless and obscene, calling it documentary "pornography."[25]

Affective Responses, Trauma, and Responsibility

The photograph of the "Burning Man" seems to scream; it is impossible to forget and immediately "wounds" the viewers' eyes, thus creating an affective response. It makes one cry. Following Roland Barthes, the photograph belongs to the group of "shocking" images, or what Ariella Azulay has called "catastrophic" images. The German visual theorist Peter Geimer argues that shocking photographs, on the one hand, are often shown without any thesis, since they are believed to show "everything there is to know." On the other hand, he claims that most image producers/photographers believe that "the shocking image is a counter image."[26] While this conflict is irresolvable, Geimer suggests that it may be more fruitful to discuss the shocking photos as presenting a threshold, a space of negotiating documentary politics.

While I have described so far how photographic images may constitute symbolic wounds overflowing with affect, I now want to consider the "traumatic" dimensions of this particular photograph. This study does not privilege psychoanalytic models to explain affective responses, but violent images and the responses to them cannot be properly discussed without them.[27] The word *trauma* comes from the Greek, meaning both "rupture" and "physical wound," denoting an injury where tissue is sectioned, as well as all other lesions that are caused by outside force. Psychoanalysis has adapted this term to address intense psychic "wounds," represented by a shock or a breach, which has consequences for the entire psychic organization of a subject. Here, trauma is always characterized by a certain "excess" of stimuli that the subject is unable to deal with adequately at the moment of exposure. Within the psychoanalytical model, it is supposed that the traumatic incident is therefore repressed, but keeps haunting the subject repeatedly, seemingly forcing the traumatic situation to be repeated compulsively, albeit in different settings, until the originating incident is consciously uncovered.[28]

Literary theorist Cathy Caruth has conceptualized trauma as a *wound that talks.* She retells the parable of the Italian poet Torquato Tasso whom Freud employed as a poetic illustration of a traumatized person's experience.[29] In this story, the young man Tancred unknowingly kills his beloved, who was disguised. He is devastated when he finds out. Later he is in a forest and strikes a tree with his sword, the wounded tree in fact being again his lover, and it now calls out to him in sorrow and pain.[30] Caruth emphasizes the role of the voice of the injured other. "For what seems to me particularly striking in the example of Tasso is not just the unconscious act of the infliction of the injury and its inadvertent and unwished-for repetition, but the moving and sorrowful voice that cries out, a voice that is paradoxically released *through the wound*."[31]

Caruth reads the parable of Tasso as a larger example of trauma theory. As this study is concerned with the notion of photographs and film as affective apertures and wounding images, reiterating the pain they show, it is worth asking whether or not there might be a positive release through the wound that is revisited in the visual realm. In that case, for example, a photograph silently screaming out like an open wound can also set affective responses in motion and may release the trauma of the event it depicts, possibly leading to further action or a "working through" of painful histories.

Sensual Ensembles

Moten discussed a similar traumatic photograph from a different context, which might add insight in thinking through the questions of affect and responsibility when viewing black pain. Moten wrote about one of the most prominent and widely discussed photographic images of this category—it shows the young dead African-American man Emmett Till, who had been viciously lynched in 1955 in the United States.[32] White American men were the perpetrators of these violent acts by trying to intimidate black men, some of whom had formerly been slaves. This spectacular form of violence was used as a mean of deterrence and warning and to rid a community of "unwanted people." Moten has performed a re-reading of this photograph as a "sensual ensemble" to tease out the ambivalent dialectics of seeing and public showing. He fathomed:

> There is a responsibility to look every time, again, but sometimes it looks as though that looking comes before, holds, replicates, reproduces what is looked at. Nevertheless, looking keeps open the possibility of closing precisely what it is that prompts and makes necessary that opening. But such an opening is only held in looking that is attentive to the sound—and movement, feel, taste, smell (as well as sight): the sensual ensemble—of what is looked at.[33]

Moten argues here for including the sonic level as well as the tactile experience for an embodied viewing of photographs that goes beyond a purely visual and aesthetic experience of seeing. Similarly Brian Massumi has argued that even under scientific experimental setting ". . . 'natural' visual perception is never pure. Vision always cofunctions with other senses, from which it receives a continuous feed and itself feeds into: hearing touch, proprioception, to name only the most prominent."[34]

In a similar vein it was an attempt to connect a first reading of the photograph of Ernesto Nhamuave to include the other senses. This is a task of association and imagination well beyond what can be gleaned through factual knowledge or limited by only that which vision can perceive. The film works that have used the "Burning Man" photo as a starting point further explore these sensual ensembles and will be analyzed later in this chapter.

To return to the question of who looks at these images and why: Moten stresses a "responsibility to look" and "look again" even though there is always something missing, the photograph confronts one head-on with the "problem of the beauty of violence," and thereby the aestheticization and spectacularization of victimhood and murder.[35] Yet it can also lead to identification with the victim and an embodied understanding of racism, Audre Lorde has written in her poem "Afterimages" about Emmet Till's photo:

> However the image enters
> its force remains within
> my eyes
> . . .
> a black boy hacked into a murderous lesson
> recalled in me forever.[36]

Similarly, U.S.-American writer Hilton Als wrote exasperatedly about viewing lynching photographs as both an ongoing experience of understanding racialized violence and feeling pain and fear: "And it's those photographs that have made me understand, finally, what the word *nigger* means, and why people have used it, and the way I use it here, now: as a metaphorical lynching before the real one. *Nigger* is a slow death. And that's the slow death I feel all the time now, as a colored man."[37]

Historical Images of Lynching

In his case study, South African historian Christopher Saunders clarifies that from the 1940s until the end of apartheid there were only a few documented cases of white mobs lynching a non-white person in South Africa comparable to American-style lynching.[38] In the United States one of the most spectacular forms of mob violence was the act of burning the victim at the stake. Yet, Saunders conveys that the newspapers in South Africa did print photographs of American lynching and there were articles and comments on it. In South Africa the historical situation was different as it was a settler and not a slave society. However, in the anti-imperialist novel by Olive Schreiner, *Trooper Peter Halket of Mashonaland*, there was a photograph of a South African lynching published, leading Saunders to the conclusion that "[t]he photograph is evidence that the stringing up of Africans did exist even if not otherwise recorded."[39] Therefore, it is safe to assume that the visual trope of lynching was present in the public imaginary and builds a documentary record in the visual black history archive both globally and locally in South Africa, but it is imbued with different meanings in each context. Further evidence of lynching images resonating in the public sphere is white South African artist William Kentridge's piece "Refusal of Time" from 2012, which includes the scene of a black man hanging from the gallows in its procession of destitute African people. Often Kentridge has modeled his drawings after documentary photographs.[40]

In South Africa, historical sources give evidence that there was no "lynching culture" comparable to that in the American South, but rather a "bureaucratic" tradition that "tolerated private forms of racial violence, which were extensive, but did not condone collective mob violence ending in death, since to do so would have been to risk a racial response."[41] The white minority government wanted to prevent violent protests by the black majority in the case of lynching. Yet Saunders also proves that some incidents of lynching did take place and he assumes that there may have been a larger number of undocumented cases as well. In the 1980s acts of self-vigilant violence in terms of punishment or acts of revenge proliferated in the townships that could not trust the state police system under apartheid as discussed in chapter 2. The images of the *Bang-Bang* photographers captured these events. The photographs of lynching-style killings, however, almost always only showed the victim, and thus the aftermath of the violence, instead of including the perpetrators in the frame. What changed in the 1980s was that both the perpetrators and the victims were black South Africans, and then only the photographers were white men.

All these type of images demand detailed engagement with the question of what constitutes responsible spectatorship. Theorists and writers discuss the questions of the aspects of race and mechanisms of othering in connection to shocking photographs. Here it is possible to see parallels again between the "Burning Man" photograph and the widely known photograph of the lynched Emmet Till in the U.S. Emmet Till's mother had asked for the publication of the photograph of her dead son's face, showing the brutality and violence of the lynching. "The caption of the close-up photograph of Till's face read: 'Mutilated face of victim was left unretouched by the mortician at the mother's request. She said she wanted 'all the world' to witness the atrocity.' "[42] This caption draws a simple connection between showing and viewing injustice and its potential to "move" people and also activate them politically. Here, in this gesture of the mother, we find a returning appeal in connection with documentary photographs that are meant to act as accusations and evidence of injustice to show "all the world."

While this may seem like an inadequate equation, this type of documentary photograph can be considered important "symbolic capital" in terms of making claims for righting wrongs and accusing injustice. It had strong effects on the American civil rights movement. At the same time, since it is the mother of the victim herself asking for publication of the photograph, this repositions questions around sensationalism or voyeurism since it is tacitly understood that a mother has the highest respect for her own child and the right to present him as she chooses. This is a prime example of the intricate blending of seemingly individual private and public matters. The intimate mourning of a mother for her dead child becomes a political issue because it was understood that this death was a symptom of nationwide racism in the United States, producing justified outrage and activating the civil rights movement.

Representations of mothers mourning their dead children are the prime icons of any resistance against violence and they are often likened to scenes of the Christian "Pietà."[43] Global examples of publicly mourning mothers are, for example, "Las Madres de Plaza de Mayo" in Argentina or the "Saturday

Mothers" in Turkey.[44] The Pietà has been reinvented in the repertoire of affective images, since it produces an immediate and intense affective frame with melodramatic overtones and can become political. Moreover, it seems to have been freed of its religious Christian context working trans-culturally since, for example, the "Saturday Mothers" in Turkey are Kurdish.

Victim Tradition?

The depiction of the body, especially in the medium of black-and-white photography also aestheticizes and elevates the fatally injured body into the status of a photographic icon. Thus the photographed dying body of the "Burning Man" may invoke other religious images of suffering, like that of a martyr or even of Jesus. The isolated presentation of Nhamuave without his attackers may visually foster the association that he sacrificed himself as a martyr or a victim, instead of having been killed by people who can be considered to be his peers. This tradition of visualizing black men and women as victims has solidified into a documentary photographic discourse, at least since the 1980s, as Patricia Hayes has yielded: "A very strong theme which emerges in South African photographic icons of the apartheid era is an ostensibly Christian one, involving martyrdom and the suffering of the innocents. The appetite of the west for similar images during the 1980s shows how profoundly and reductively the impact persisted globally."[45] The "Burning Man" photograph is affiliated with this tradition of iconic photographs, which misinterpret violence as an individual rather than a societal "fate," visualizing it as individualized suffering. In this context one has to ask why these images were in such strong demand by the Western press. Is it connected to the reassuring thought for Western audiences that the "real horror" happens elsewhere in the world, as for example in Africa, the place in the West's imagination of catastrophe per se?[46] Hilton Als recognized a "white euphoria" here that asks the racialized other: "Tell me about yourself, meaning, Tell me how you've suffered. Isn't that what you people do? Suffer nobly, even poetically sometimes. Doesn't suffering define you?"[47]

Alternatively, Mbembe has reflected on the relationship of the violated body and asked specifically how it is connected to politics and death: "What place is given to life and death, and the human body (in particular the wounded or slain body)? How are they inscribed in the order of power?"[48] Representations of dead or injured bodies are inscribed by the political and are densely loaded with assumptions, affect, and intersecting interests and strategies of what to render visible and what remains invisible. In addition, for the South African viewers of the photograph of the burning, it may have also reactivated traumatic memories of the trope of lynching and of necklacing in South Africa's public imaginary.[49] According to historian Joanna Ball, ". . . while the distinction between a necklacing and other forms of burning is clear in the physical sense, it becomes blurred in the cultural arena. . . . [I]t is related to its symbolic potency and the graphic horror of burning that it captures. When the victim is actually burnt various forms of burning appear to be interchangeable."[50]

A further question that immediately comes to mind is the title given to the photograph by media: Why was the scene of the killing of Ernesto Nhamuave called "The Burning Man"? The title that was attributed to the photograph curiously shifts the action of burning onto nobody in particular, leaving it open to consider who set him on fire, even including the possibility that Nhamuave could have set himself alight. Should the photograph not have been called: "The Man Who Was Burnt Alive"?

Possible Motivations of the Perpetrators

The photograph of Nhamuave shows the act of burning a man who was perceived as an enemy by the South African perpetrators. One needs to consider whether and how the African migrant man or woman had been coded as a "traitor" in the public imaginary prior to the attacks. The idea that foreigners can be seen as "traitors" makes more sense when one looks at it through an economic lens, as it is intersected by conflicts and stereotypes around class, gender, race, and (national) civic entitlement. Mbembe argues: "After all, more so than class-thinking . . . race has been the ever present shadow in Western political thought and practice, especially when it comes to imagining the inhumanity of, or rule over, foreign peoples."[51] Racist notions about foreigners, especially African foreigners that were considered "darker" than South African citizens, played an important and all too familiar role in the xenophobic attacks. Therefore, European racism and the heritage of apartheid that constructed notions of different capabilities also continue to haunt South African society. South African theorist Pumla Gqola locates here a specific "negrophobic" element in the attacks on African migrants, since "European citizens are not among those foreigners who are safe to violate in a xenophobic manner. This is unthinkable. . . . To repeat, what makes it unthinkable is the clear value *and* whiteness of the safe European versus the disposability *and* Blackness of the brutalized African 'foreigner.' "[52] Gqola thus draws attention to the assumed "nativity" of white South Africans and newly immigrated Europeans that inhabit a more privileged and protected status in South African society than black African migrants.

And yet the perception of migrants as traitors may also have been caused by the strong nation-building rhetoric and project of the African National Congress (ANC), which has become the major political actor since 1994. Since African migrants are living transnational lives, they did not fit into the national project, symbolically or economically. One common reproach is that migrants are not spending and keeping their money within South Africa. Studies have shown, however, that these economic arguments can be easily countered, since a "host" country always benefits from both its highly skilled as well as from the unskilled workers from other countries.[53] There were significant class aspects to the xenophobic attacks, since the African migrants coming to South Africa were often in more destitute positions than the township inhabitants, while at the same time they had a stronger motivation to make a living and earn money to send back to the family in their country of origin. Exploitative working conditions were the result, since the African migrants often took on jobs for lower salaries than South Africa's poor working class. In turn this substantiated the claim that the African migrants were responsible for lower wages and higher competition for jobs. As it is, common civic anger was directed against the weakest in the economic chain, rather than against the South African or international employers who unscrupulously took advantage of hiring African migrants and paying them less, because they knew that they were not organized in the South African trade unions. Often employers also took advantage of knowing that people did not have papers, using their illegal status as a means of intimidating them.

In South Africa, the black South African inhabitants of the former townships are in a position of what Mbembe, following Karl Marx, called—"*lumpen*proletariat," which is not governed, since it lives in a state and place outside of "normal politics."[54] Often police and other state organs do not enter township or squatter camp areas. This implies that since the township inhabitants are more or less on their own, they may be prone to take disciplining and policing into their own hands. Their status is characterized by "subalternity" as Gayatri Spivak analyzed it, because nobody represents them. Yet, they argue for civic entitlement claims on the grounds of nativity and citizenship and for their *de jure* inclusion into South African society to become a *de facto* reality. As Gqola has persuasively argued: "In a context in which South Africans perceive crime as a perpetual problem that the state has failed to curb, 'communities' take it upon themselves to deal with the problem."[55] Burning someone who is called a "traitor" can be related to a long history of vigilante violence and "people's courts" acting in self-justice in South African society and can be seen to be connected to "cleansing" the community of unwanted elements.[56] This history is both connected to apartheid and colonial practices of "native law."[57]

Loren Landau critically commented that one also needs to ask which questions "those attacks raised around the salience of ethnicity within South Africa's black population, the violent basis of local authority and movement of the poor and the potentially dangerous language of 'transformation and positive political values' " and he wonders "whether the very nature of a state-centered social-democratic citizenship might not be as much the cause as the solution to these problems."[58] It is illuminating in this context to consider a quote from an oral-history interview, in which the speaker retraces some of the steps from the overcoming of apartheid in 1994 to the xenophobic attacks in South Africa in 2008.

> The attacks—yes—we were involved—I'll tell that I was involved—not from the negative side of it but from the positive side of it—to say that those who are not born from this country—they need to go back to their own countries. We just came out of the same situation as them and they had their own independence before us so WHY are we supposed to carry the burden—we need to do things for ourselves—FIRST—so that we can be able to do for others.[59]

The speaker, who describes himself as a perpetrator, compares South Africa's political and social situation with the assumed status of the home countries of the African migrants. Thereby, he tries to give reasons why the xenophobic attacks were justified in his view. It alludes to a certain reading of temporalities, of overcoming a state of oppression and entering "independence," yet it hierarchizes different stages of attained freedom, arguing that South Africa due to its late entrance into the post-colonial and post-apartheid state, is not yet "ready" to take on the burden of helping other African states who became "independent" earlier. This indicates a teleological understanding of history as "progress" and of history as a power outside of human actions that, however, people need to observe. In South Africa the notion of overcoming and entering a period of the "post" necessarily refers to both to the "post-colonial" as well as to "post-apartheid" and it does not mean that either colonialism or apartheid has entirely been surmounted. As historian Mark Sanders specified: "In a complication exemplary of postcolonial cultural politics in Africa and elsewhere, the 'past' to be reclaimed is in part a creature of the colonial formation to be superseded."[60]

Gendered Stereotypes: "Foreigners Are Stealing Our Women"

Gender theorist Nira Yuval-Davis has argued convincingly that the role of women in the construction of nation, of who is included in "us" and who is excluded as "them," is to be the "symbolic border guards."[61] As such, women become the "cultural symbols of collectivity, of its boundaries, as carriers of the collectivity's 'honour' and its intergenerational reproducers of culture."[62] This role, however, turns women into goods of economic value that need to be kept pure and secured. One popular myth in South African society prior to the attacks that is also a well-known part of any racism or othering was: "These guys come here and steal our women and jobs." Gqola states this claim in connection with the analysis of black masculinity. "Historically as well as in the contemporary moment, dominant Black masculinities index access to finance as linked to sexual attractiveness and virility. Therefore the loss of both a means of income and the opposite sex is a threat to such patriarchal and heteronormative masculinities."[63]

This statement attests to a perception that non-South African citizens threaten the "ownership" of women as well as of capital and jobs in South African society, and in addition South African women are only supposed to have intimate relationships with South African men. Furthermore, South African women are objectified as bodies to be possessed by South African men; the women can be "stolen" by non-South African men, leaving little agency to women themselves and their ability to make their own decisions. In a twist dominating the perspective of native South Africans, African men from outside South Africa thus become competitors for both economic resources and women as resources. In this case "the obstacles can be eliminated and indeed must be,"[64] as Gqola concludes, thus showing that the violence against African migrants was not "senseless," even if it is based on a mixture of real and phantasmatic claims and identifies the wrong target.

Traumatic Repercussions of the "Burning Man" Photograph

The photographs of Nhamuave being burnt alive are at the same time evidence and accusations of grievance, turning them into "moral memorials." The photographs serve as a document that "this really happened." They preserve an atrocious moment in time. Due to their capacity to fix certain events in documents, visual media as such may counteract on a symbolic level the very acts of annihilation that they witness. The photograph of the "Burning Man," for example, shows a man, injured but still alive, his suffering transformed into an eternal accusation. Yet against this rather positive view of documentary images there is the argument of the camera being a catalyst for more violence, as if the presence of a camera begs people to produce gruesome images, and "act out for it." It is important to consider this double role of the camera, which is far from neutral, as it is also bound to economic interests in certain images from Africa in the Western and international mediascapes.[65]

But to probe deeper, why was the fact that a Mozambican man had been burnt, allegedly for the sole reason of being a "foreigner," so scandalous? Why did his story create such a strong echo in the national and international media? Provokingly, one could argue that many socioeconomic underprivileged African people die every day, and nobody cares, as Mbembe has termed them "throw away or surplus people."[66] Death rates of black South Africans remain high due to HIV/AIDS, violence, and poverty.[67] These structures of epistemic violence are inherited from colonial and apartheid edifices. Yet there must be something that differentiates this photograph from other violent images—perhaps in and of itself or due to the historical moment in which it emerged.

First, the incident of Nhamuave burnt alive became scandalous because it was documented and publicized by well-connected press photographers.[68] It came to resonate with other incidents of (post-)apartheid violence, particularly with images of burning or necklacing incidents.[69] The photograph seemed to belie the "rainbow nation" image of South Africa, complicating the story that promoted a successful overcoming of segregation after a long and intense struggle. It told a very different, more conflictual story of South Africa in 2008, fourteen years after the official end of apartheid, and reminded people of the harsh realities of the aftermath of apartheid.

Furthermore, the photograph hit a nerve in the public imaginary, because it called up photographs from acts of vigilantism and violence during apartheid, and it made a societal conflict visible in all its poignancy that people had refused to see or acknowledge as such before, in post-apartheid times. The reading of it did not fit the familiar narrative of white perpetrators and black victims and created an irritation. The xenophobic attacks were held against South Africa in light of its history of black oppression asking, how can you—who so intimately know the negativity of violence—now repeat it in post-apartheid times? How can you—who successfully fought against white oppression—now not act in solidarity with other black Africans but instead attack them? These are morally charged questions, implying that former victims of similar violence should "know better."[70] As can be seen in similar situations, however, the former victims do not per se act in accordance to their previous experiences of oppression and are not immune to becoming perpetrators themselves.

I argue that certain photographs of the present lead to strong affective responses locally and globally because they also (re)visualize—and thus make memorable—painful moments of the past and racist crimes that are repressed in the dominant historical narratives, exactly because they are too violent and too painful to remember or because the perpetrators want them to be forgotten. The violent photographs of the xenophobic attacks may call up registers of acts of mob violence both during apartheid as well as in pre-apartheid times, for instance certain forms of lynching images that may have also formed part of a global visual repository of documentary images of an imaginary black history archive.

The documentary materials from the xenophobic attacks in post-apartheid South Africa changed and challenged the strategies of documentary image producers and thereby created a gap within the documentary conventions alongside the continued existence of "traditional" documentary strategies. Similarly, as British media-scholar Libby Saxton has argued on photographs that showed the atrocities of the Holocaust, these "haunted images" have served as a catalyst for aesthetic and ethical innovation, for an ongoing search for more responsible forms of witnessing.[71] The photographic image of Ernesto Nhamuave being burnt alive was the trigger for countless actions, from texts, poems, and books, from community outreach programs, soup kitchens, theatre productions, political interventions, and many more expanded image productions in the form of both documentary and fictional films that referenced this image.[72]

The "Burning Man" photograph represents a particular type of "haunted image" as well as an image as wound, emitting affective intensities. These types of wounding and haunted images can be considered sources of ethical as well as historical insight according to Saxton, if one assumes that one can "learn from history" and stop "history repeating itself." However, there are several flaws in this argument, often incidents of seemingly "private" brutality, for example domestic violence and rape, remain invisible. In addition, many crimes against humanity or acts of violence have never been photographed. Abstract and complex regimes of oppression like colonialism or apartheid can never be captured in a single image. As Azoulay postulated: "The situation from which the photograph was taken should always be reconstructed, and the photograph itself attests to the limits of what could be photographed."[73] Photographic images can, however, provide tesserae to form an always fragmented and incomplete "picture" and thus a reconstruction of historical events and a better understanding of the present. To remember the past is at the same time an always incomplete and failing task that can nevertheless not be renounced. Memories are actively reconstructed in the present and often rely on visual and other documents. Those events that are not photographed may be less well-remembered. Photographs and films can and do serve as an affective entry point into the examination of injustice and the construction and negotiation of history/ies.

To summarize some of the findings so far, it becomes evident that several connected arguments need to be discussed when viewing the photograph of the "Burning Man." On the one hand, I argue that one needs to look further than the shocking images from news media to understand the context and history of spectacular acts of post-apartheid violence. Azoulay analyzed the context of photographing someone who lost his citizenship due to catastrophic events: "When presented as an icon, without his own story, he is raped into being only a photograph."[74] Therefore, sometimes it is important to suspend the logics of the iconic image or the "icon making," even though it elevates the victim and may turn her or him into a suffering hero or martyr. One needs to search for more complex, meaning less spectacular, documentary works, and also look at the everyday images of migrant life, for example of socioeconomic inequality, in order to understand the whole scope of the xenophobic attacks in South Africa.

At the same time, however, it needs to be emphasized that an iconic image can also be the starting point for further investigation. In the case of Ernesto Nhamuave's iconic photograph, it was the status of an icon that made the photograph popular and widely known, and this popularity in turn led to the construction of audiovisual memorials attempting to restore his "dignity" and reputation after his death. I argue, therefore, that one still has to look at the shocking images, listen to the burning questions they pose, and should not look away or repress them but let oneself be moved by them. One can only understand the violence of the present through the (lens of the) violence of the past. The photograph of Nhamuave's violent death constitutes a wound, or a wounding aperture, and demanded and spawned further images that will be discussed in the next section.

3.2 The Afterlife of Nhamuave's Photograph

After the xenophobic attacks subsided, several image producers attempted to retrace Nhamuave's life and thus return his personal story to him, making him once again into a person instead of an icon. In that process a second photograph came to prominence; it is a formal portrait of Ernesto Nhamuave, when he was still alive. It is a color photograph, in which he is wearing a black suit, white shirt, and red tie (see below). He looks directly into the camera with a serious expression. This second photograph—the formal portrait—has often been included in the film documents, at times together with a caption giving the date of his birth and death, turning it into an obituary image or a photographic gravestone. This obituary image of Ernesto has also taken on a life of its own after his death; it has traveled through time and space via the Internet. The two photographs—the one of his spectacular death and the formal portrait—were the visual point of departure for several film projects.

The formal portrait returns a representation of dignity, and thus of having been a respectable, strong and uninjured person, to Nhamuave.[75] It is impossible, however, to view the second most widely distributed portrait of Ernesto Nhamuave without remembering the first photograph of his violent death. The two photographs are inevitably linked in one's mind by

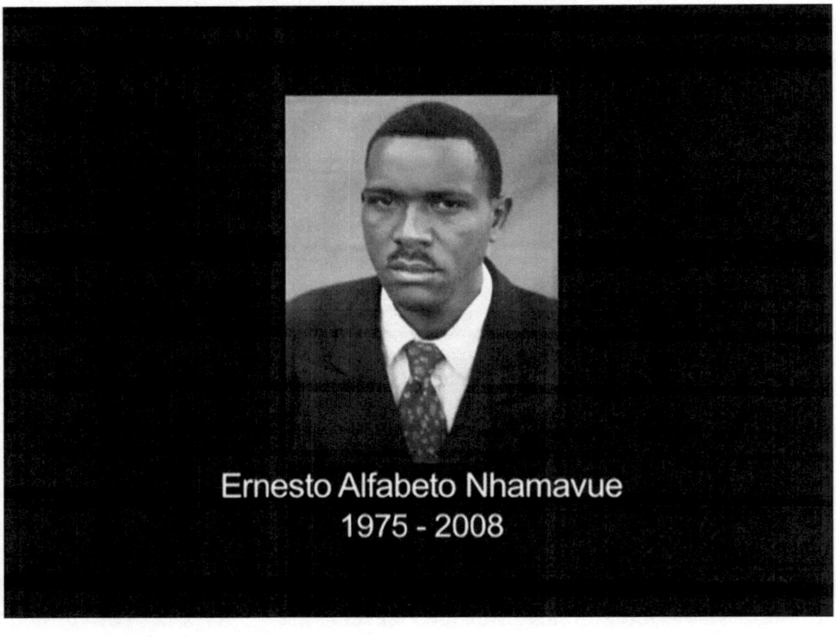

Figure 3.2.1. The portrait photo of Ernesto Nhamuave, which was widely published after his death, still from *The Burning Man.*

their temporal relationship of "before" and "after." They serve as a brutal reminder, saying: "Look what has happened, and how vulnerable a migrant man's life is." While the still photographs solely documented the shocking event, documentary and fiction films can open up a space of reflection to renegotiate the relationships between victims and perpetrators. The next part will consider how the question of guilt, cause-and-effect, and attempted explanations are presented in the aftermath of the attacks by analyzing two films, a short documentary, *The Burning Man*, and a fictional film by Akin Omotoso, *Man on Ground*, wich reenacted the xenophobic attacks.[76]

The Documentary Film *The Burning Man*

The documentary film, *The Burning Man*, chronicles the events that led to Nhamuave's death in the form of a personal investigation by the Nigerian filmmaker Adze Ugah.

Ugah speaks the voiceover himself and is also visible in the film (see figure on the next page). He starts with the assertion that "Thousands of people come to South Africa every year in search of a better life. Ernesto Nhamuave was one of them, husband to Hortencia Nhamuave. Father of three." Thus the film not only recounts some details of Ernesto Nhamuave's life, but also opens up a larger perspective, as Nhamuave's life was exemplary of thousands of migrants' lives who were coming to South Africa.

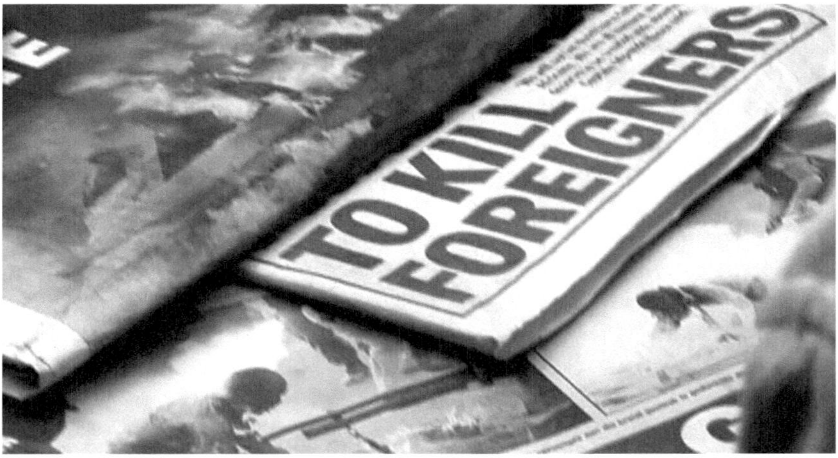

Figure 3.2.2. Newspapers of the event, still from the film *The Burning Man*.

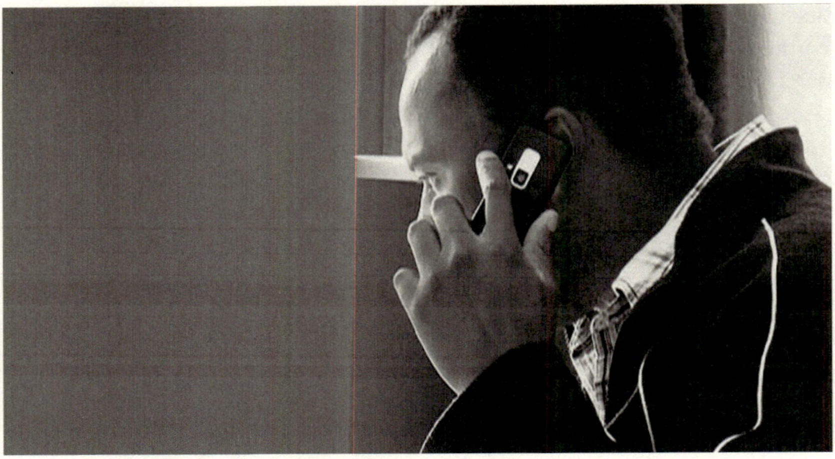

Figure 3.2.3. The filmmaker Adze Ugah, still from the film *The Burning Man.*

Thereby, the film is also a documentary perspective on the by-now already common story of migration to Johannesburg and thus the "Jim Comes to Joburg" theme. Furthermore the filmmaker's own perspective, as a Nigerian national living and working in South Africa, is included in the film, immediately drawing parallels between himself and Nhamuave. Ugah's perspective is therefore not congruent with the one commonly found in documentary films of an "outsider" looking into another world, but instead he shares some of his own experiences of being a foreigner in Johannesburg.

Following this, several photographs are shown of the xenophobic attacks that are intercut with the sound of a camera shutter and a police siren's wailing, creating an intense affective assemblage. The images show people being attacked and three dead bodies lying face down on the ground. Next it cuts to a pile of newspapers that all show a similar photograph: the one of Ernesto Nhamuave set on fire (see figure 3.2.1). At the location in Ramaphosa where the mob had set Nhamuave on fire, the filmmaker tries to imagine what it must have felt like, but of course he fails, and is outraged, saying repeatedly "Nobody deserves this." A neighbor of Nhamuave recounts the incident, while the camera shows the crime scene, now simply an empty sandy open place, intercut with the still photographs of the event, always reminding one that this is a film, constructed in the aftermath. Ugah also admits to being scared for his own life and not getting out of the car the first time he went to Ramaphosa.

In addition to the affective personal engagement, the film tries to make a claim for justice, in order to restore Nhamuave's reputation, who was called a "criminal" after his death, apparently in an attempt to justify his murder. A few sequences will be analyzed in more detail to emphasize how the film reasserts Nhamuave's "normality" and therefore tries to take a stand against the common reproaches against migrant men as deviant. To reiterate an earlier point, foreign men who were choosing South African women were not only crossing national but also intimate sexual borders. Nhamuave, however, did not have a South African wife, but had left his Mozambican wife and children back home. He came to South Africa with his brother-in-law Francisco Nhamuave.

"A Normal Family in Mozambique"

Idyllic shots of Ernesto Nhamuave's home village of Vuca in Mozambique are shown, where his wife and children live and which is said to be the opposite of Johannesburg.[77] The images have a warm color and are carefully crafted. They could just as easily have been used in an advertisement for a holiday in Vuca. The filmmaker shares subjective memories about his own home village in Nigeria and stresses the point that people have difficult lives in the rural areas all over the African continent, trying to survive from subsistence farming.

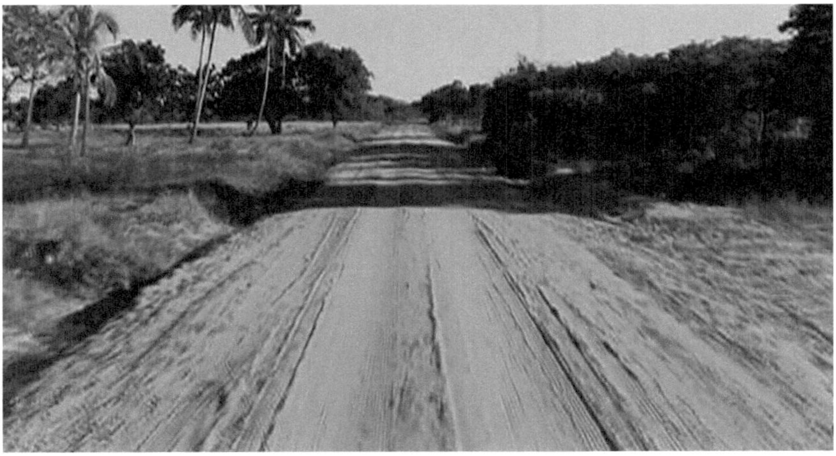

Figure 3.2.4. Road and landscape in Vuca, still from *The Burning Man.*

Living conditions are sparse, there is no electricity and running water. The film then portrays all of Ernesto's three children individually. The most attention is given to Ernesto's eldest son, Alfabeto, who is twelve years old and attends high school. The children are not shown talking. The camera seems to be an intrusive presence, yet keeps some distance, while showing the children in their daily activities of playing house under a tree. The filmmaker's voiceover tells us, "When asked about his father, Alfabeto went silent and began to weep." The camera shows him crying for a few seconds at the right edge of the frame, somewhat sheltered by a few branches of a bush, ashamed, wiping the tears away with his T-shirt, then cuts to a shot of him walking away (see figure 3.2.5).

This filming from behind seems to be a conscious strategy and is mirrored in sequences with other family members while they are walking. This decision can be read as an attempt to protect them from the camera's gaze. Later, though, there are also interviews with Nhamuave's sister and brother-in-law and finally with his wife, showing them in frontal view. Yet, even the interviews do not ask every detail and maintain a dialogue with the filmmaker's inner monologue or experience, as, for example, when the brother-in-law Francisco is interviewed. Francisco still suffers from injuries that he obtained when he was beaten during the xenophobic attacks. In the scene Ugah shows him photographs of the attacks on a laptop but then stops, commenting in the voiceover: "His anxiety started to rise, so I decided

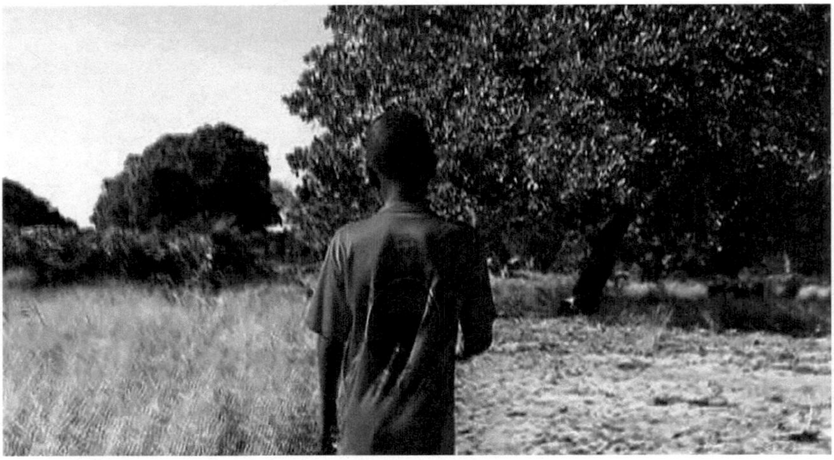

Figure 3.2.5 Ernesto's son seen from behind, still from *The Burning Man.*

to spare him the painful memories." Here the logics of total visibility and voyeuristic consumption of another man's pain, as is commonly seen in conventional televisual documentaries, are suspended and halted through the empathetic and authoritative voice of the filmmaker himself.

Witnessing—*The Funeral Scene Told by a White Photographer*

The funeral scene of Nhamuave is put together in retrospect, again from photographs, since Ugah and his film team were not present. The South African newspaper, the *Star*, had sent their white photographer Shayne Robinson to document the funeral. Ugah uses Robinson's photographic images, and he interviews Shayne Robinson about his experience of what he witnessed. At the same time, on the sound track what sounds like the singing of women at a funeral is audible and the interview is intercut with more photographs. Robinson tells his story a little uncomfortably as if he is shy and unused to talking about his experiences since usually he only shows the photographs. He appears to be still affected by the horrific event, maybe feeling guilt and pain. Even though he does not verbalize his feelings, they are present through his body language, for example his clenched hands and hesitant speech, as if he were trying to keep his emotions inside. He answers in short sentences like, "Then there was a lot of singing." Thereby, Robinson brings the auricular dimension back into the silent photographs. In his photographs of the funeral, one can see Hortencia Nhamuave, Ernesto Nhamuave's widow, who is wearing a white dress. The color white, rather than black, symbolizes mourning in Mozambique. Ugah commented on this in the voiceover, that the color white is meant to show "a life lived fully" instead of only reminding one of the death. By documenting Nhamuave's funeral and showing his coffin the act of mourning can be realized and shared even with the larger community of the spectators of the film.

The usage of the white South African man to retell the funeral, one of the most intimate and moving scenes of the film, is a particular choice. It symbolically reconciles white and black men, recognizing the humanity of the *other*. It puts a white man into an affective situation that de-centers his authority and instead exposes him in the context of emotional states, in which he seems to feel for the dead black man. At the same time the black filmmaker gives a white male voice a special importance here. This scene may make it easier for white audiences to sympathize with Nhamuave's family and makes a visual argument for "transracial" unity in mourning in a country where until 1994 apartheid was the law, which meant that affective ties—between white and black—had been rare, one seeing the other group as the "enemy." At the same time the "color line" became less and less important in certain groups of society as in the anti-apartheid protest movement, and it is important not to essentialize black and white divisions.[78]

"Real Men" and Martyrs?

The final sequence of the film starts with more still photographic images of the attacks while Adze Ugah's voice is heard reciting a poem written by the white South African woman Margie Orford: "If being a South African means, hanging over my garden fence and watch the smooth skin of a man blister as he is being burnt alive, then I am a foreigner. . . ."[79] After the poem, music starts again, we see a panoramic shot of Johannesburg's inner city. The next frame reveals the filmmaker himself, sitting in a car; the voiceover continues—now in Ugah's own words—while still images of Ernesto's children are being shown and music dramatically underlines the statement: "A man's life is not judged by how long he lives, but by how well. . . . He was prepared to make every sacrifice to give his family a better life." Now the second most famous photograph is shown—the formal portrait picture of Ernesto Nhamuave, which is intercut with the date of his birth and death like an obituary notice in a newspaper, while the filmmaker's voice issues a final statement: "That's what real men do."

The whole film had focused the attention on a portrait of Nhamuave's family in Mozambique to re-assert that he was just a "normal" family man, a caring father and good husband. Hence it resorts to heteronormative, conservative values to prove his "humanness." At the same time it creates or simply affirms a code of "correct behavior" for migrant men in the meantime, in the sense of: "Don't fall in love in the new place you live and work, and always support your family back home." The last assertion that Ernesto Nhamuave was a "good father" who worked hard and sacrificed himself for his family, as well as the statement "this is what real men do" creates a very positive—almost saintly—picture of him. It could lead one to think that Ernesto Nhamuave was a "martyr."[80] At the same time the usage of terminology like "real men" stays inside a certain *macho* and often stereotypical heterosexual discourse. The common male ideals of the South African context—regardless of black or white masculinity—are often powerful, aggressive, violent, and adventurous, thereby demonstrating the wish to reaffirm a gender regime that endorses men being in a dominant position in public space as it represents access to both symbolic and economic resources. While it has often been stated that both black and white "masculinities" are in crisis in South Africa, the insistence on "real men" as responsible and caring fathers could also be read as an attempt to create another, more positive concept of manhood. The Sonke Gender Justice Network, for example, is attempting to change the behavior of men in the context of domestic and sexual violence and opts for taking on responsibility in the light of the HIV/AIDS crisis.[81]

Visible Mourning and Icon-Making

When a death remains invisible and the sight of the corpse is withheld, the usual affective transactions of mourning are blocked for the family and community, but the film successfully counteracts the invisibility of many migrants' death. The film powerfully stages a memorial to Ernesto Nhamuave and the other victims of the xenophobic attacks. This is accomplished in a first-person narrative, offering the viewer an entry into a "foreigner's" experience through Adze Ugah's personal, gently spoken voiceover. By first learning about Ugah's travel to South Africa and his current work and life here, the viewers are able to relate to a person who is still alive, but who shared some important biographical details with Nhamuave.

Moreover the film starts a metareflection on the visual media as such and the difference between photograph images and film images in particular by comparing the two and repeatedly interspersing the film with still photographs. The single photograph that shows iconic moments—"larger than life"—is at times also used as stills in sequence, halting and delaying the flow of the film, making one aware of the "artificial" action of the camera, framing and recording certain images. Importantly, the film does not remain in the individualized story of suffering, since Ugah says in his voiceover: "The men who burnt him believe that there is a direct link between the presence of foreigners and the problems in their community." This statement is rather presented as an open question without any answer, leaving the audience to reflect on their own explanations of the events. Ugah challenges his own and our complicity by asking directly, even if rather abstractly: "Is there a darker side to all of us?" Yet, this statement is in danger of diffusing the responsibility of the perpetrators and therefore should be refrained.

After his death, Ernesto Nhamuave was turned into an icon—as either a hero or a saint—this portrayal even extended to his family, who show no signs of anger or desire for revenge. At the same time, we learn that Ernesto's wife is unable to provide for herself and the children without the income of her husband. Adze Ugah has noted in a conversation that the film was also made as an attempt to raise funds for Ernesto's family, so this plea for support may already form the strategic mise-en-scène of the Nhamuave family in the film.[82] All told, the film, *The Burning Man*, manages to give a more complex and complete account of Ernesto's life than the single shocking photograph, which nevertheless was the departure point of the cinematic endeavor. In the medium of documentary film it is also easier to include a layer of reflection both on the production of the film itself and the role of the filmmaker told by the filmmaker's voice in the finished product.

The Fictional Film *Man on Ground*

The second film that was dedicated to Ernesto Nhamuave's memory was *Man on Ground*, a fiction film directed by Nigerian actor and director Akin Omotoso.[83] The film's script is based on the events during the xenophobic attacks and dedicated to Ernesto Nhamuave, but events are fictionalized. To start with a short synopsis, *Man on Ground* tells the story of the Nigerian man Femi, who leaves his country, escaping from personal as well as political prosecution. In very short flashbacks in the beginning, he is shown crossing a river with other refugees. Femi ends up in Johannesburg, South Africa. There is a short but telling scene at the IOM (International Organization of Migration) office in Johannesburg, shot in documentary style. A disinterested IOM employee tells Femi that he cannot receive any government assistance. He then tries to make a living for himself by setting up a small shop. In the xenophobic attacks he gets injured and loses his shop. A South African woman helps Femi nurse his wounds and find a new job at her husband's construction site as a security guard in a township area. In the film the fictitious name "Extension 6" is given to the area. But the community at Extension 6 is convinced that foreigners are getting the government houses meant for them. They hold anti-migrant rallies and stir up hate. Later a group of men takes Femi and burns him in a car as a revenge on the foreigners. Femi's brother is a businessman from Nigeria and comes to visit South Africa with his girlfriend. The tragedy of Femi's life and death is slowly uncovered in the film by his more successful brother and Femi's girlfriend, as the two are searching for him together.

Man On Ground again tells a "Jim Comes to Joburg" story, showing both a victim of the attacks—Femi—and black South African men as perpetrators. In contrast, the black South African woman is the only person who shows empathy with Femi, a desperate and wounded foreigner, and acts as his temporary savior. However, the film ambiguously implies that the only reason Femi had to die may have been because the other men wanted to discipline the wife whose act of caring created jealousy. Thereby, the film raises sympathy, if hesitantly, for the perpetrators and de-legitimatizes transnational solidarity. Femi does not emerge as an individual, but rather comes across at the ultimate victim, haunted by his experiences of being bullied by his brother as a child and later by political enemies in Nigeria.

Fetishized Flames

Images of flames and fire get fetishized in *Man on Ground*. A close-up shot of the striking of a match is repeated many times throughout different sequences. This shot leads up to the sequence where Femi is burnt inside a car. The car acts like an eye protection. While the scene is well-composed, it is agonizing to watch, even though it spares the viewer the direct graphic view of a human being burnt alive. The film thereby strategically positions what can be seen on-screen against what happens off-screen and is only imagined. According to film theorist Christian Metz, "cinema literally plays with the terror and the pleasure of fetishism, with its combination of desire and fear."[84]

The image of the striking match (see figures 3.2.6 and 3.2.7 in the color gallery) seemed like a heavy-handed metaphor, pointing the viewer excessively to the conclusion of "Look, violence starts here," and also: "Now, don't play with the fire."[85] In some ways it seemed to infantilize the perpetrators, who had "played with the fire" and then could not stop it anymore, as if violence were a force of nature. The film's perspective thus seems to be interested in raising understanding for the perpetrators as it asks whether the South African perpetrators are not also "victims" in the bigger picture, as they are seemingly the "losers" or "underdogs" in South African post-apartheid society?

This section explores the ambivalent connotations of the motif of fire, flames, and burning both as cultural myths and narration, and recurring real and symbolic images in the South African public imaginary in order to understand how the perpetrators may partly be excused for their violent deeds through their strategic representation in *Man on Ground*. Burning as an extreme form of punishment is an existing theme in South African literature, art, and film. The South African writer J. M. Coetzee explores burning as a form of violent revenge in his novel *Disgrace*, in which a group of black men raid a white farmhouse, trying to set the white male protagonist on fire. This act seems to be interpreted by Coetzee as one of justified anger and revenge for colonial and apartheid oppression.[86] To understand these acts of post-apartheid violence in South African society, they need to be related to forms of apartheid and colonial violence.[87] As Kylie Thomas has argued: "Thinking the relation between violence during apartheid and post-apartheid violence, necessitates first thinking against the powerful narratives that read the violence of late apartheid as signaling apartheid's end."[88] Burning and fire may refer both to acts of resistance as well as of destruction and to acts of revenge and punishment as was captured by the *Bang-Bang* photographers.[89] And yet, *Man on Ground* does not contextualize these practices of violence historically.

The reason why the photograph of the "Burning Man" received such special attention is also connected to the history of the representation of fire and flames themselves. Fire, flames, and the scene of burning are a highly charged cultural trope with a long history of depiction in painting and documentary photography. Universally the presentation of fire envelops archaic and modern means of both annihilation and force, which also holds true in South Africa's visual tradition. "If something is to stay in the memory, it must be burned in: only that which never ceases to *hurt* stays in the memory."[90] This quote by Friedrich Nietzsche attests to the connection of affect, pain, morality, and memory.[91] It also speaks of the dimension of unbearable pain when a living being is burnt. The act of burning thus always leaves visible and invisible scars. Wendy Brown uses Nietzsche's quote in her analysis of how metaphorical scars are created—as already explored in the previous chapter.[92] Hilton Als defines the memory of lynchings for African Americans: "That is their rite of colored male passage: having to drag all those lynchings around with them, around their neck: those are their ancestors. Too bad when violent deaths define who you are."[93]

Burning occurs both in the material sense as cases of arson, setting something on fire and thereby destroying it, as well as in the symbolic meaning of flames spreading, for example, as a small fire igniting a big change. *Man on Ground* visually creates exactly this strong narrative of a small flame that cannot be extinguished, but instead grows into a large fire. This cultural trope of starting a fire is not only imbued with negative associations in the South African national memory. During the struggle against apartheid in the late 1970s, the resistance movement was metaphorically likened to the image of a small fire that would soon ignite the whole nation and could not be put out again and in the end would overpower the white minority. This trope was, for example, memorialized in the lyrics of Peter Gabriel's song on the murder of ANC activist Steve Biko.[94]

> You can blow out a candle
> But you can't blow out a fire.
> Once the flames begin to catch
> The wind will blow it higher.

Oh Biko, Biko, because Biko
Yihla Moja, Yihla Moja
—The man is dead.

And the eyes of the world are
watching now.[95]

The lyrics also attest to the virtue of attracting attention by the motif of fire combined with death, as is reflected in the line, "and the eyes of the world are watching now." This metaphorically positive view of the anti-apartheid struggle could subconsciously put the perpetrators of the xenophobic attacks in line with the anti-apartheid fighters even though they were historically separated by several decades. While the imagery of flames and fire can thus be imbued with positive values such as in this song or in the mythical image of "Phoenix rising from the ashes," of course the xenophobic attacks and especially the photograph of the "Burning Man" showed the horrific effects of fire in violence and killings. Thereby, it is impossible to understand why, aesthetically, *Man on Ground* is fascinated with spectacular images of fire and burning, visually bathing in the flames. These shots are highly aesthetic, staged and more interested in the gorgeous spectacularity of the flames than in the destruction and horror they bring, for instance when Femi is burnt inside the car (see figures 3.2.8 and 3.2.9 in the color gallery). While they seem to be invested in a "Nollywood" style of dramatic and stylized cinemtatography, this "beauty of violence" is highly problematic in the context of a film on the xenophobic attacks.[96]

Civic Entitlement and Class Issues

The film *Man on Ground* does not offer a happy ending, in fact in the final scene the perpetrators and others who were also at the anti-foreigner rally are seen talking to a Pakistani tuck shop owner in a township area, telling him that he has to leave, because only South Africans should be able to have shops and do business there. The film, likely irrespective of good intentions to humanize the victim, thereby creates a narrative of people "on the ground" being dissatisfied with government and thus taking action into their own hands. The film shows the conflict around civic entitlement only as a conflict between South African blacks and people of color, all the characters in the film are non-white. In some ways this represents the post-colonial and post-apartheid society but it also erases all historical traces of the former regimes of oppression. And yet, *Man on Ground* does show how this conflict of civic entitlement breaks out along new and old divisions of class—Femi's brother is a very rich and successful businessman from Nigeria. His status protects him from the mob. Also, the property owner who shelters the brother belongs to a different class and has a higher education than his striking and murdering workers.

It is almost a little surprising to see the dedication to the "Burning Man" Ernesto Nhamuave in the final credits, since the film gives quite a different account of the events and does not use any of the actual biographical elements of his life, like his nationality or the circumstances of his death. The film *Man on Ground* attempts to create a sympathetic understanding for the mob violence on the verge of a lynching. Thus it is reactionary in its political aim. The perpetrators are shown as dissatisfied and illiterate working-class people who almost had to take their fate into their own hands. The audience, however, does not gain much insight or information into their living conditions, and can feel "safe" and relieved from any shared responsibility for the attacks.

The Expanded Image Space of the Xenophobic Attacks[97]

In the events of the xenophobic attacks 2008 one cannot so much recognize "classical" racism, but rather a new form of "hegemonic citizenship" with national entitlement claims that seek to repeal the de-privileging of the African majority of South Africa's population at the cost of African migrants who are not South African citizens. The films *Burning Man* and *Man on Ground* follow different paths to comment on this new form of racist nationalism. Yet there are also some obvious similarities—both films are by genre "bio-pics" and tend to heroize the main character, who is doomed to die. While *Man on Ground* is apologetic and seems to imply that the perpetrators were justified, it is nevertheless an attempt to look at both the victim and the perpetrator's side. However, it shows them only in collective action with no single person being responsible, as compared to the individualized "heart-wrenching story" of Femi, who remains a singular victim, disconnected from larger themes like capitalism, neoliberalism, and migrant labor streams.

The perpetrators acted as a collective affective assemblage, as a violent mob, in a desperate act of self-legitimating, leading a war not only against their non-South African neighbors, but also against the moral capital of South Africa "shattering the image of the peaceful rainbow nation," not willing to remain silent, unseen, and destitute any longer. Often in this context it has been stated that: "Burning is a 'call' when no one listens."[98] Thereby, the act of burning is acknowledged as a strategically used "language" or medium of communication that already has a long history in violent protests and self-vigilance in South Africa. In addition, this interpretation of arson means that it is not irrational violence, but rather a strategically used act, and therefore rational. What happens discursively if a certain expression of violence is called "senseless" is, since the perpetrators are not taken seriously or that they may act with impunity, that "they get away with it" if their violent acts are deemed culturally legitimate. These are important political questions.

One also needs to ask, in relation to *Man on Ground*, who was being constituted as perpetrators and what type of subject formation was initiated by the discussion and negotiations of "xenophobia." It becomes obvious that "xenophobia" is a discursive formation and not a monolithic concept operating outside parameters of cultural and historical context. Instead, while it has universal and global dimensions it is also always imbued with local readings of who is included and who is excluded and why.

The conflicts in post-apartheid South African society can no longer (if they ever could) be translated directly into photographs that "do not need any explanation," as was the case with the documentary photographs showing the injustice of the apartheid regime.[99] Yet the new struggles try—consciously or otherwise—to build on this visual heritage and still seek to produce iconic documentary images. The images successfully construct an affective framing that can serve as an entry point into politics. Here one can also return to the question of traumatic recurring images in the documentary realm. My observation is that these images have to be looked at, uncovered, discussed, and worked through, together with the affective responses they instigate, over and over again. One cannot and should not stop the flow and production of documentary images to then start with a "clean slate" and politics proper without the distraction of claims and accusations made through and with images. Both spheres belong together and are in constant dialogue, yet they can never be entirely congruent. Documentary and fictional affective images provoke rethinking of the history, present and future, and challenge normative readings of the present, but they can also perpetuate stereotypes.

Aesthetically this leads to a further hybridization of the documentary form as can be seen in *The Burning Man*, which uses essayistic and poetic elements, as well as the personal reflection of the filmmaker, and still photographs to make an experimental documentary film as an open format. However, it is especially the unfinished state, the openness and indecisiveness of the film, that manages to defend a space of reflection and catharsis of moral questioning beyond the shocking image and the logics of the actuality and fast pace of documentary news media. *Man on Ground* fails to offer much aesthetically and politically, it heavy-handedly basks in the metaphor of fire and flames, sparing no cost to stage beautiful shots of shacks, cars, and warehouses burning down to the ground. They are filmed in central perspective, as back-lit tableaus at dusk or dawn, apparently trying to make the audience shudder and enjoy the fascination of evil and destruction.

The xenophobic attacks in 2008 that occurred in South Africa were termed "Flames of Hate," alluding both to the metaphorical and to the material realm of this outbreak of violence against alleged foreigners. But only few cultural practitioners linked the attacks to global *ressentiments* against migrants, as Ba Ba Khosa, who wrote about the xenophobic attacks indicates:

> When caught by the whirlwind of hate, all they saw was Zimbabweans, Malawians, Ethiopians, only foreigners. To all of those they directed the hatred they felt for their own miserable lives. It was tough. And even tougher was when we saw the images of Ernest Nhamuave burning alive. They wrote "Burning Man," "Burning Nation." But what was burning away wasn't only South Africa, but also the world; the world that burns with misery and hate. The world that killed Jorge Gomondai in Dresden up there in the white north, also burns. And now in the black south, Nhamuave burnt away, [. . .] symbolizing all the Nhamuaves that are set alight by the torch of hatred.[100]

Ba Ba Khosa links the "flames of hate" in South Africa to racist hate crimes against African migrants in former East Germany since both its targets were migrants from Mozambique. In his metaphoric text the attacks that produced the photograph of a man being burnt to death are themselves likened to the image of a flame that starts a fire and gets out of control, spreading all over South Africa's townships and the whole nation, while at the same time there are already similar racist "fires" burning in other countries all over the world. Khosa reminds one that acts of spectacular mob violence, as well as structural violence, in the form of racism also take place in Germany and elsewhere in the northern countries, thus pointing to a global dimension of racism and so-called xenophobia.[101]

However, this link was neglected in most visual documents, while a great demand to show this specific image-space of the xenophobic attacks persisted and attests to the acuity of the conflict around migration and civic entitlement, national inclusion and exclusion in South African society. One more example is given in the following short excursion on the restaging of a necklacing in a hip-hop video. Afterward, in chapter 4, this study will analyze everyday, ordinary images of African migrants, which shows them beyond the shocking images of the xenophobic attacks.

Excursion: Reenactment of a Visual Icon—*Violent Images Now*

The South African music video "Powa" from 2011 is a current example of restaging necklacing in popular culture in which it becomes obvious how visual discourses between documentary and fiction are always interdisciplinary and cross-platform—and how violent images once connected to political protest like punishing a suspected traitor also get staged and reenacted in popular culture. While this video constitutes a problematic example, nevertheless it is important to contextualize it, as it attempts to be a counter-document to violent masculinity, and to help provide understanding of why certain types of violence seem to get repeated, as in the xenophobic attacks.

"Powa," of course indicating "power," was produced by black South African hip-hop artist Tumi Molekane in 2011, who quoted the instrumentals of Kanye West with a new self-written text.[102] Molekane was born in exile in Tanzania in 1981 and returned to South Africa. He said he had been provoked to write the song by the high rates of violence against women in South Africa. In the music video the practice of necklacing is performed here under different auspices—of a (possibly emancipatory) fantasy of women fighting back—but it could also be read as a revisionist male fantasy. Thereby, the video forms part of the discussion about gender-based violence in South Africa.

A sample of the disturbing, violent, and very explicit text of Tumi's song "Powa" is given below:

> To every girl I cheated on
> Disrespected, beat on, called a whore,
> Peed on, had sex with illegal, put hands on
> Raped, slapped, love you, didn't say it back,
> Ladies I disappointed lied to and misinformed,
> No one man should have all that power.
> We put our seeds into school they get deflowered
> From sweet sixteen to 20 something sour
> When Mandela dies, who gone really care about us?[103]

The opening lines of the text detail the abuse of women, clearly criticizing the performance of male violence in post-apartheid times. The song has several verses, each starts with a specific address to women, specified as "every girl," "every sister." In the final verse it says: "To every sister annoyed / pissed with these ignorant boys / That took what you built / destroyed" showing a critical reflection of the erasure or forgetting of women's accomplishments in South Africa, whose role was crucial in the fight against apartheid. The verse above, however, ends with a certain pessimistic line: "If Mandela dies, who is going to really care about us?" apparently internalizing the perception of the rest of the world, that Africa is a place of problems, and only outstanding, famous individuals—"heroes" like Nelson Mandela—can make a difference, because we do not know any other Africans who can.

South African artist Thenjiwe Nkosi cautiously remarked after Mandela's death: "I fear that when we invest our hope in some figure, some savior, alive or dead, we risk absolving of contributing, of acting, or making change."[104] Tumi Molekane is not the only South African man grappling with the questions of personal responsibility and violence against women—the topic, while under-discussed, is starting to surface in literature and visual media. Another example is South African writer Kgebetli Moele's novel "Untitled," which details the life of a young black woman from the townships until her rape at age seventeen.[105] The novel is written completely from a female perspective, including diary-like texts and poetry, such as:

My Pleasure
My pleasure is not being naked
My orgasm is not sex
To enjoy I don't have to be sexed
To rejoice I don't have to be drunk.[106]

Thereby, Moele creates a very different perspective on female desire, opposing it to male desire and multiplying the perspectives. Importantly, even though Moele is writing as a black male author, he takes an unflinching look at South African macho culture that forces black women and girls into sexual submission. Although this study is not the place to pursue a detailed analysis of Moele's novel, it needed to be mentioned to show that there is an ongoing discussion around violence, sexuality, and gender roles in South Africa in different public arenas.

To return to the Molekane's "Powa," it was released with a carefully produced black-and-white music video. In the video the text of the song is not illustrated by showing examples of violence against women, instead a group of white and black school girls are taking revenge on a black man. Thus the video seems like a reply and at the same time a replay with reversed roles of a "hate crime" and gang violence and rape, usually perpetrated by a group of young men, who see "women . . . as objects that the different gangs compete for."[107] In the "Powa" video, a group of teenage girls is seen, performing acts of assault and causing trouble that is usually attributed to male teenagers. They are noisy, bump into people, steal a piece of fruit, and intimidate pedestrians. They come across a large black man by himself and start harassing and chasing him. In the final scene of the video the girls are burning the strong looking man with a tire around his neck (see figure below). This is a reversal of the usual setup and thereby clearly a transgressive fantasy; at the same time it questions the *status quo* of women and men in contemporary South African society.

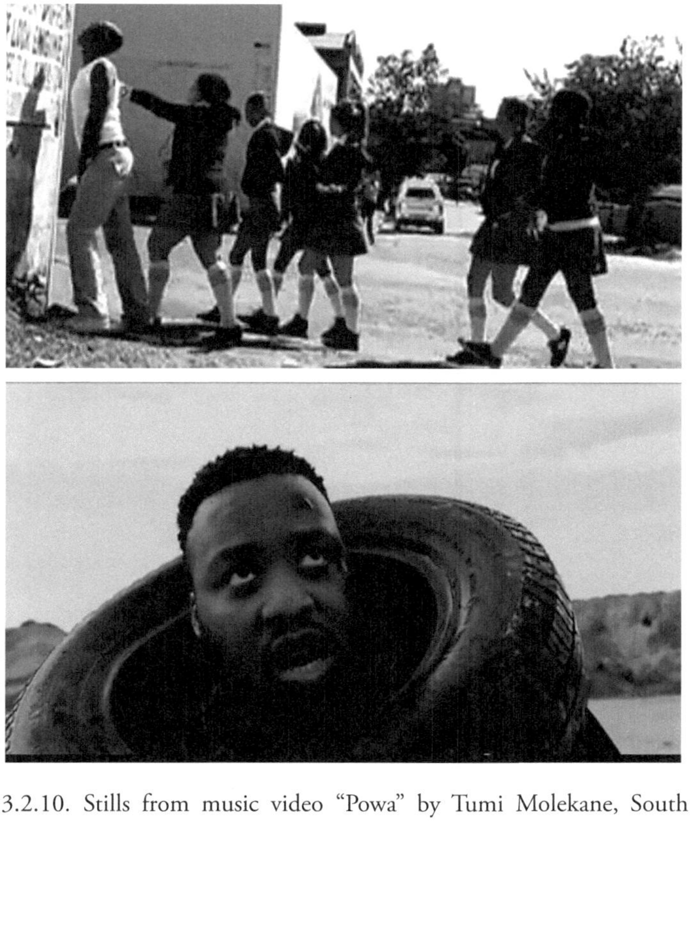

Figure 3.2.10. Stills from music video "Powa" by Tumi Molekane, South Africa 2011.

The final shot shows how a match is lit and thrown after which the focus goes soft, sparing us from the images of the man being burnt alive. This scene quotes numerous photographs of necklacings by the *Bang-Bang* photographers that were discussed in chapter 2. These historical necklacings were usually performed by impromptu people's courts that were judging and punishing traitors, criminals, or spies—or, in 2008, African migrants. Therefore, I want to argue that certain images get repeatedly restaged in settings of violent masculinity in reality, as news media do not tire to point out, calling these incidents "Justice Breakdown."[108] On the contrary, in the video a fictional staging takes place under changed auspices in a collage setting. These scenes are carefully crafted in order to call up well-known "historical images."[109] They are used with a different meaning—here as a seemingly justified act of revenge of suppressed women against misbehaving men. The women in the video are not victims but instead act as perpetrators. Henriette Gunkel has rightfully cautioned against the production of stereotypes if the label "violence against women" is invoked: "The gender-based violence discourse, in particular, sustains the gender regime as women are continuously reduced to the role of the passive victim in need of protection—without any actual effects on the statistics."[110]

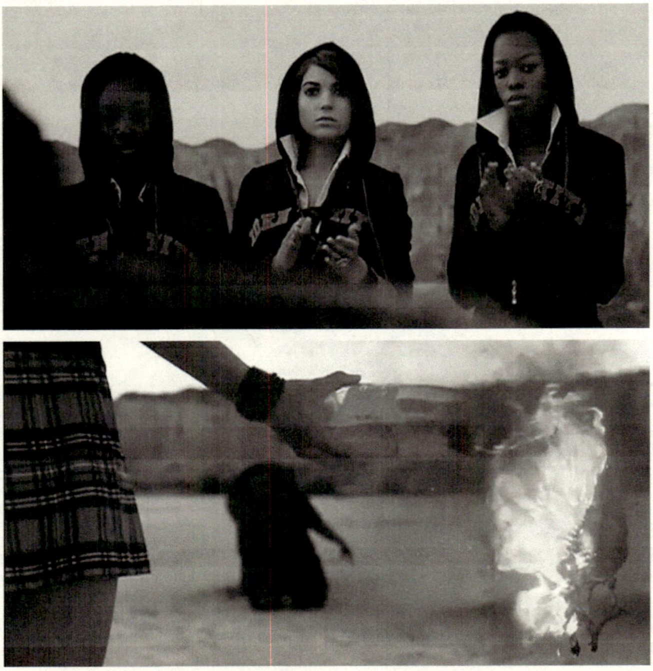

Figure 3.2.11. Stills from music video "Powa."

The video is an expression of visual politics by showing "counter-images" to the ones that prevail in the public sphere. Violent masculinity in post-apartheid times needs to be connected to the militarized male citizenship of white and black South Africans that was created during apartheid, as has been discussed earlier. "On the one side, this shows that the men involved are policing and disciplining not only femininity but also female sexuality through the act of violence. On the other side, the collective nature of the crime shows that in undertaking the attack together the men not only discipline the woman's sexuality, they also discipline one another's (militarized) gender identity."[111] Therefore the men also police themselves into heterosexual norms. Recently, organizations have started to work on issues of masculinity in South Africa, instead of focusing on "violence against women." Their aim is to work with men who may become perpetrators and try to prevent them from retreating to violence. These organizations have the same aim of "protecting women," but have understood that this cannot be achieved without actively influencing the behavior of men, as well as societal roles and symbolic ideals of violent masculinity. South Africa has the reputation of being "the rape capital of the world," which is a problematic and shocking label.[112] Hence, a critique of the violent performance of masculinity is justified.

Viewed in this light rapists in the video could be seen as traitors to society who are punished by their own means. It is questionable, though, if the glorification of violence is an appropriate method, even if an oppressed group of society is exercising it. The video seems like a staging of a scandal but avoids the direct attribution, this strategy is often found in popular culture and is an empty gesture without concrete results. At the same time this piece does create a strong and different counter-image of women as capable of defense and who stand together and on their own, which is a highly unusual visibility contrary to the one of women as passive victims. Moreover, black and white female teenagers are cooperating against a black man. This seems to be a utopian vision that is a far cry from the reality of South African society, which is still highly divided along race and class lines. It is problematic to assume a united or universalized feminism as Spivak and other post-colonial theorist have criticized. To change Spivak's famous dictum "white women usually want to save black women from black men"[113]—all the while forgetting their own involvement in black subordination and their benefitting from white privileges.

Furthermore, the video spells out one of the contradictions of post-apartheid South African society: the obvious aims of "gender-equality" as expressed in the post-1994 constitution are in stark contrast to the everyday lived experiences and practices. While South Africa has one of the most progressive constitutions promoting gender equality and women's rights, it also has one of the highest rates of violence against women—both black and white, even though there exist differences in the status of vulnerability on different axes of sexual preference. "Normative femininity is, above all, defined through sexuality—and, more precisely through (presumed) heterosexuality and its appearance."[114] Black lesbian women are therefore at the highest risk of being subjected to violence, including the crime of "corrective rape."[115] The need for security and visibility of the female body thus leaves many questions open. Masculinity needs to be recognized as a determining factor that structures society and culture and social reality of institutions and the identities of women and men. Molekane's "Powa" video is the reversal of a typical performance of violent "masculinity" that is historically specific and should not be equated with "males" or "men" per se. It shows an attack as it is usually performed on "foreigners" or deviant women, for example lesbians. However, as Gunkel reminds us: "At the same time these power relations cannot be regarded as linear or fixed, instead they need to be recognized as being ambivalent since several power relations overlap concurrently."[116]

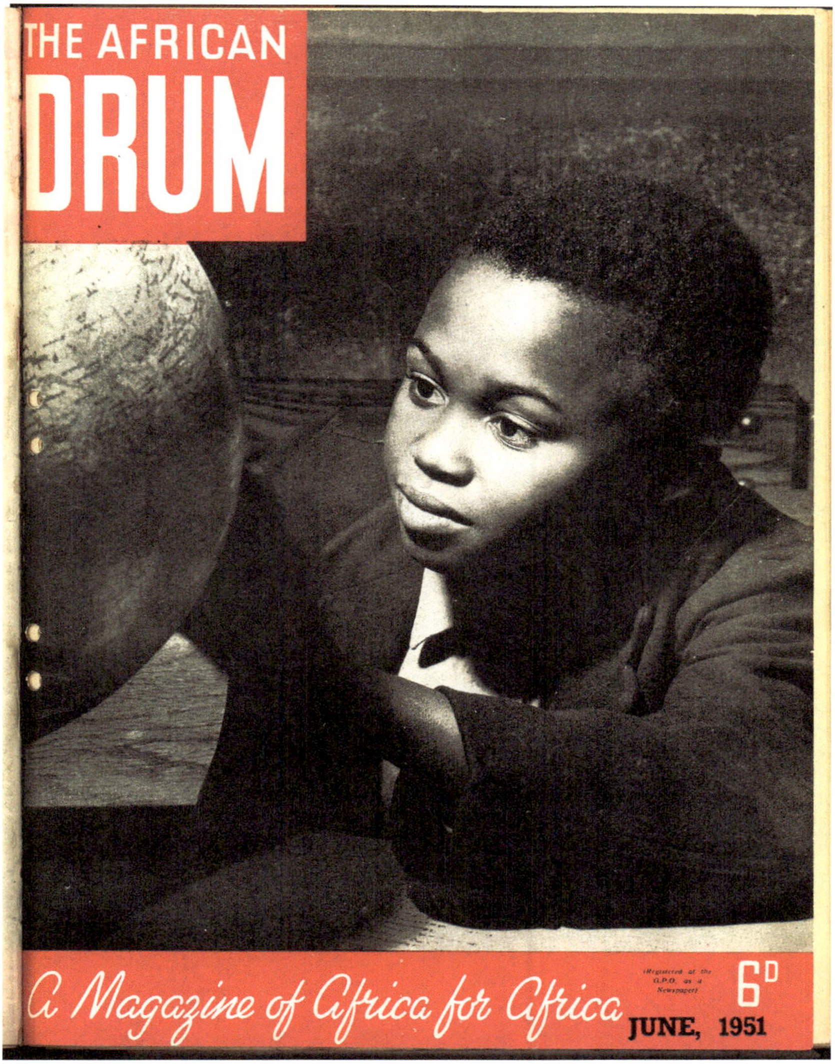

Figure 1.3. *Drum* Cover from June 1951, Bailey History Archive.

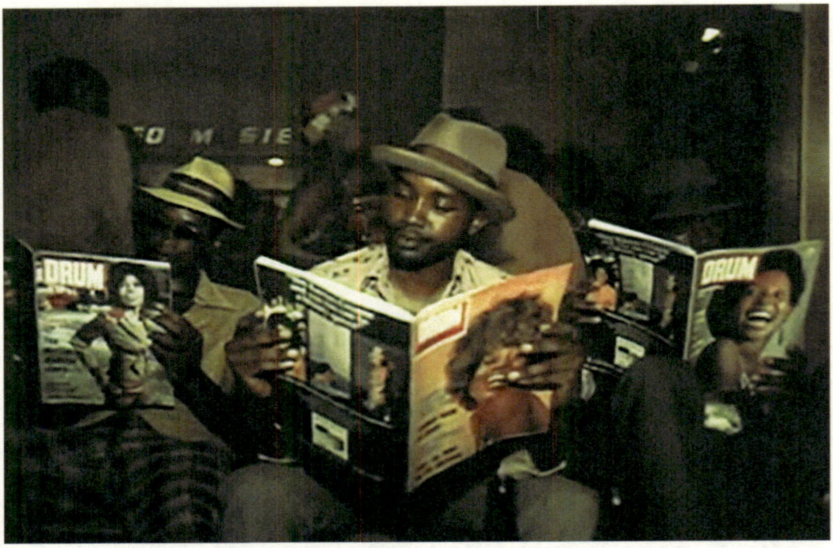

Figure 1.4. Still from the music video "Got Till It's Gone."

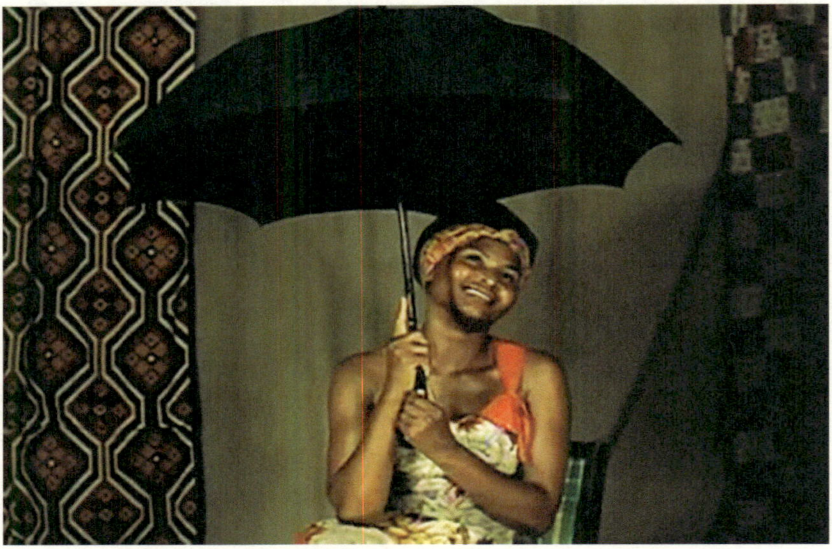

Figure 1.5. Still from the music video "Got Till It's Gone."

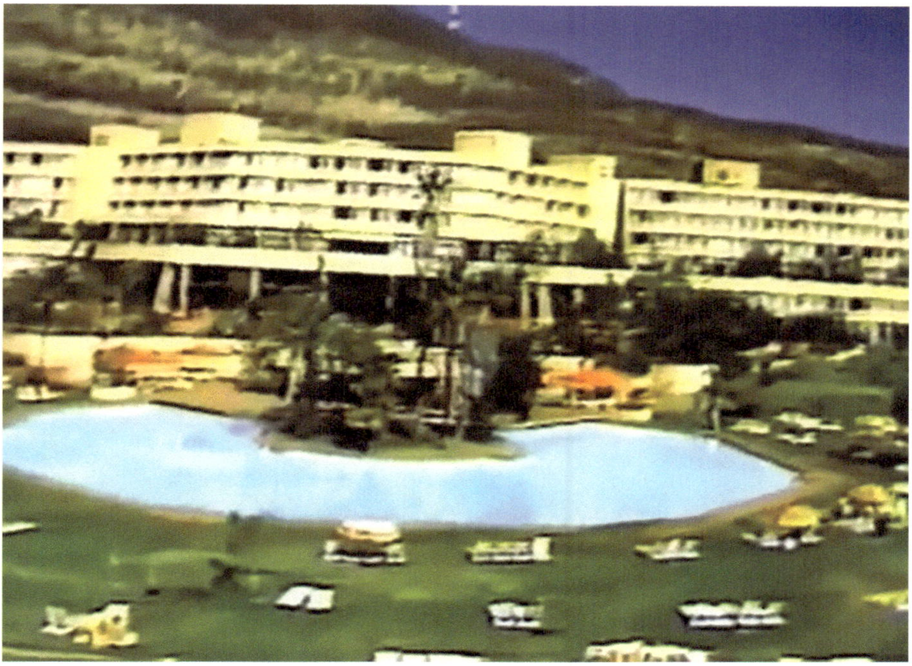

Figure 2.1.6. Still from the music video “I ain’t gonna play Sun City.”

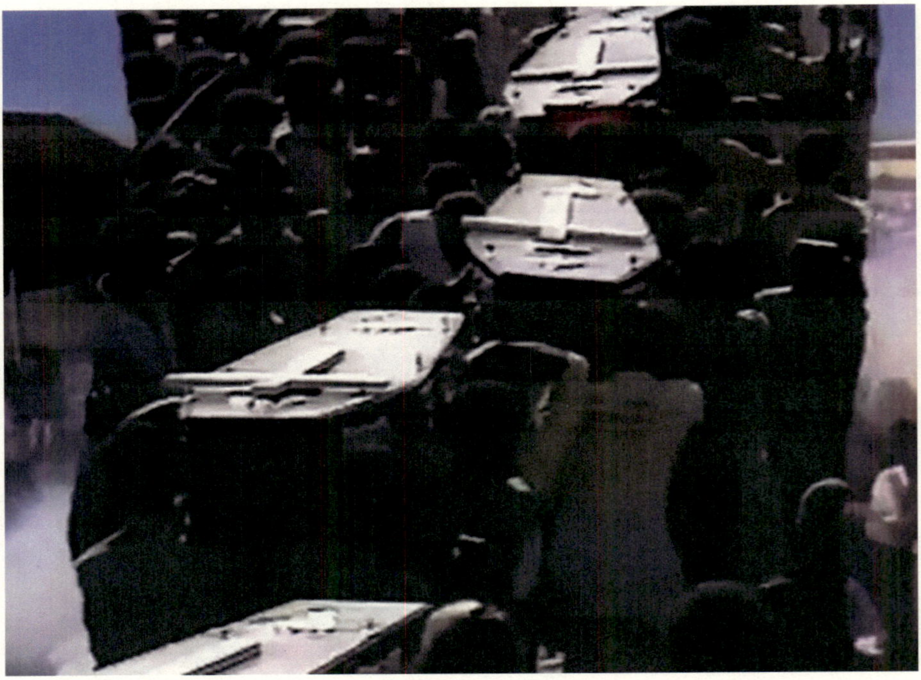

Figure 2.1.7. Still from the music video "I ain't gonna play Sun City."

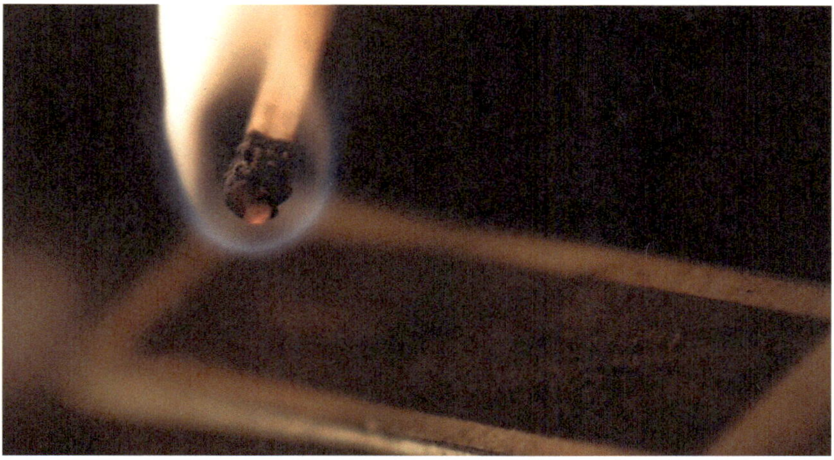

Figure 3.2.6. Striking a match, still from *Man on Ground.*

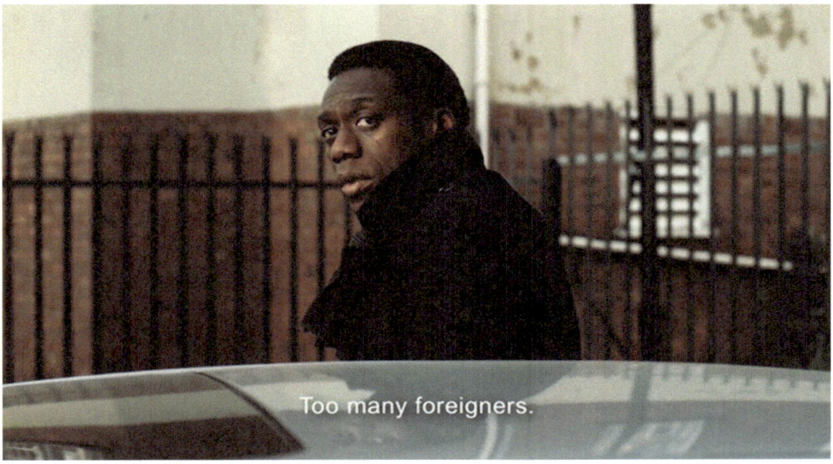

Figure 3.2.7. The statement "Too many foreigners," still from *Man on Ground.*

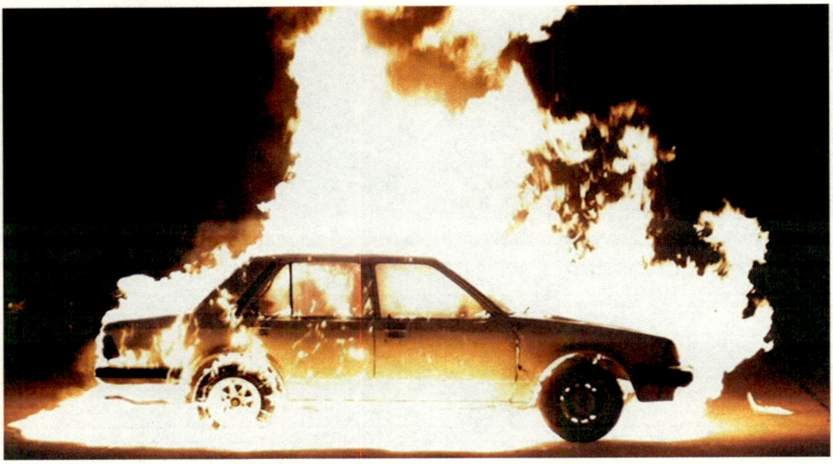

Figure 3.2.8. Car burning with Femi inside, still from *Man on Ground.*

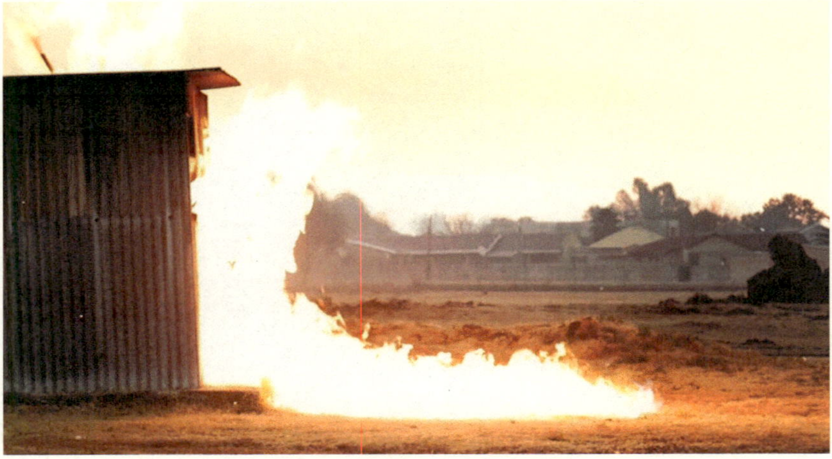

Figure 3.2.9. Shack burning, still from *Man on Ground.*

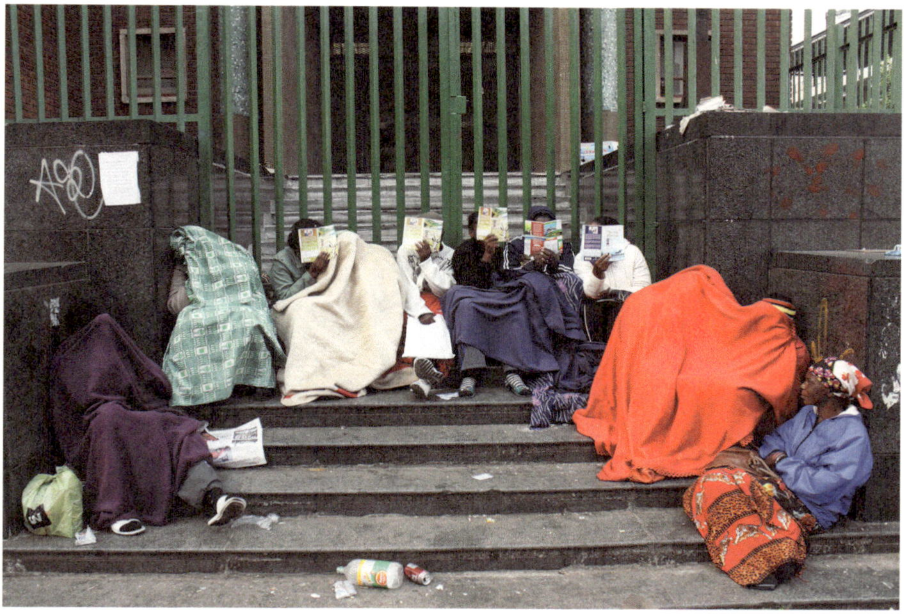

Figure 4.1.4. Zimbabwean Nationals waiting at Home Affairs in Johannesburg, photographer Believe Nyakadjara 2011.

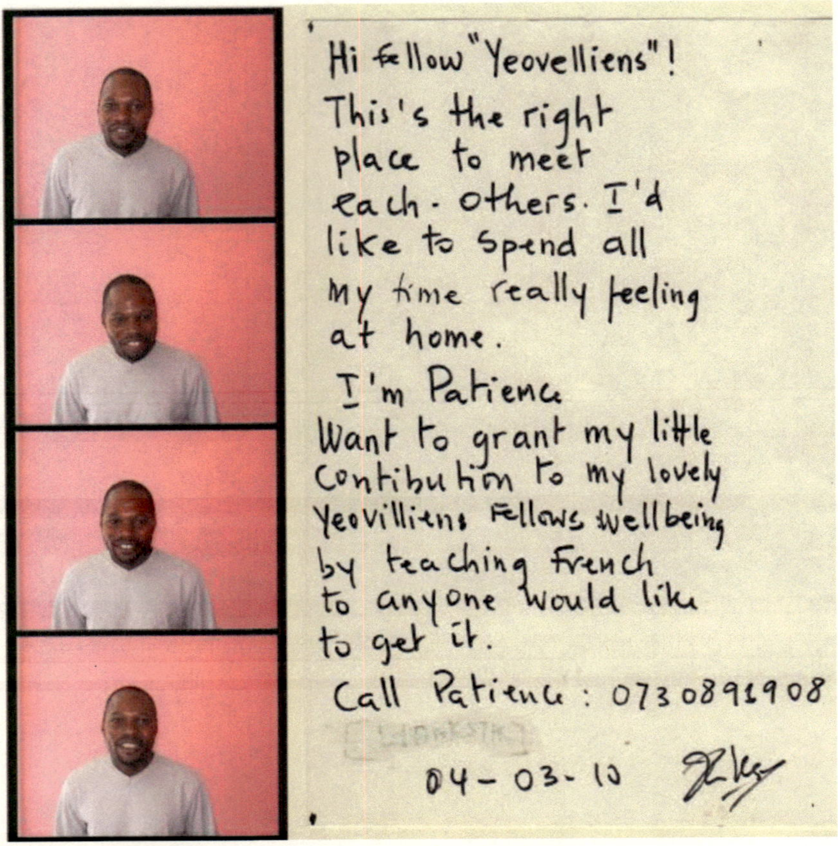

Figure 4.2.1. Self-portrait and text of Patience produced at *Hotel Yeoville* © Terry Kurgan & Hotel Yeoville.

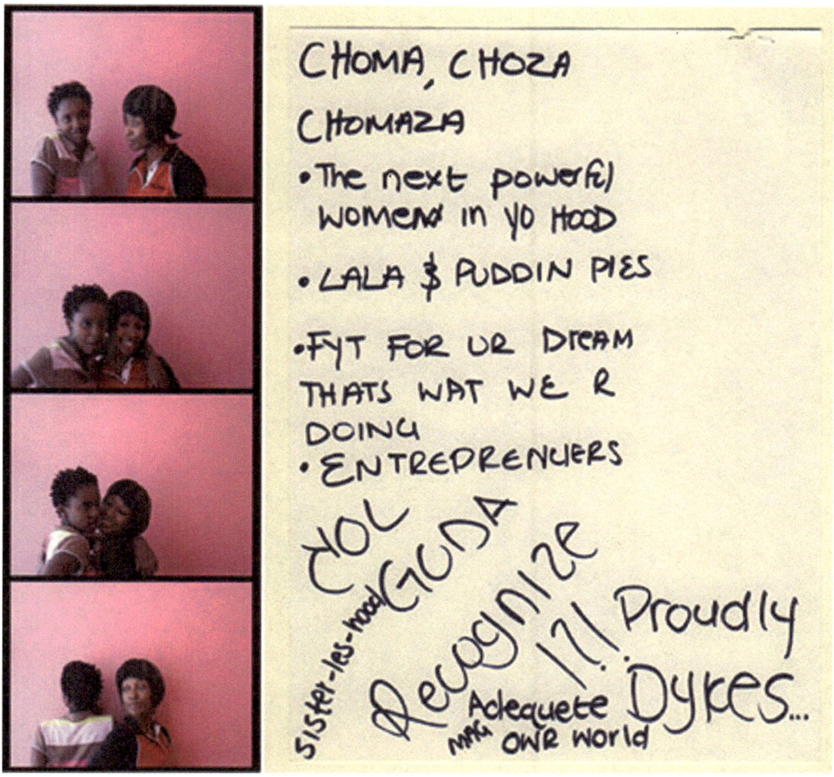

Figure 4.2.2. Self-portrait and text taken in the photo booth at *Hotel Yeoville* © Terry Kurgan & Hotel Yeoville.

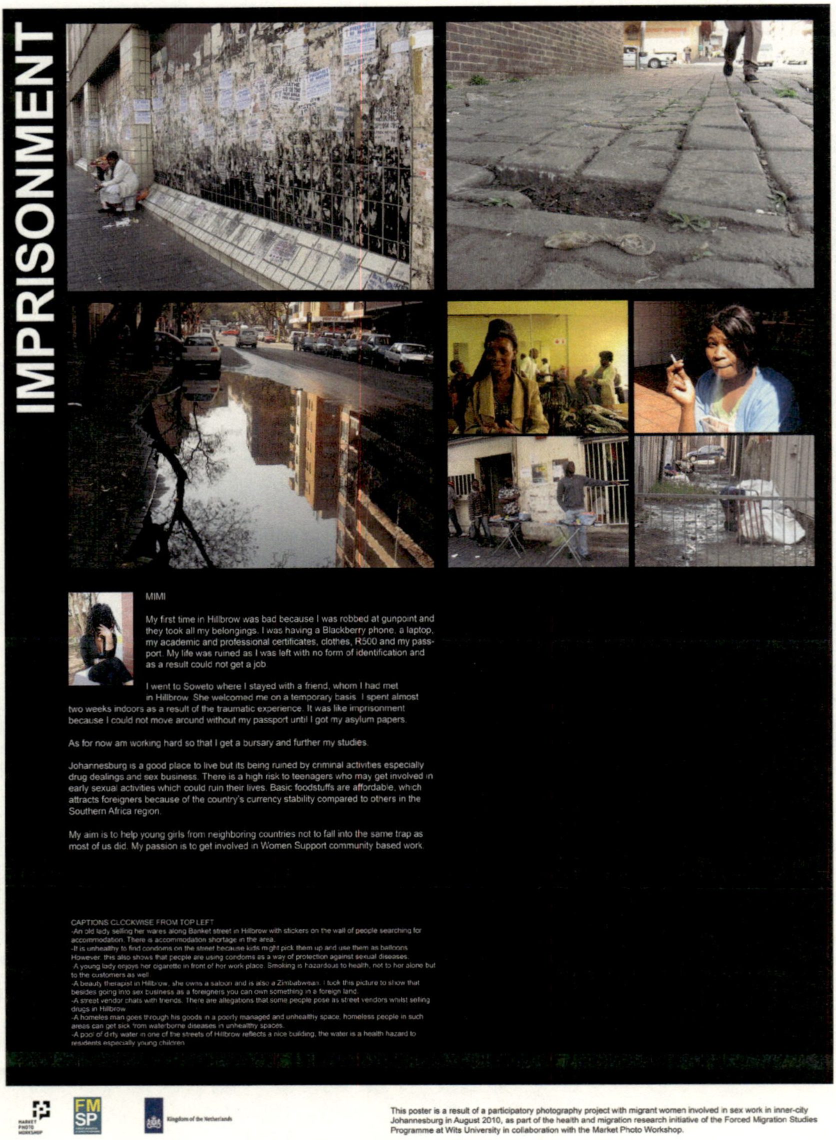

Figure 4.2.3. *Working the City,* poster presentation of Mimi. African Centre for Migration & Society (ACMS), the Market Photo Workshop (MPW) and, the Sisonke Sex Worker Movement.

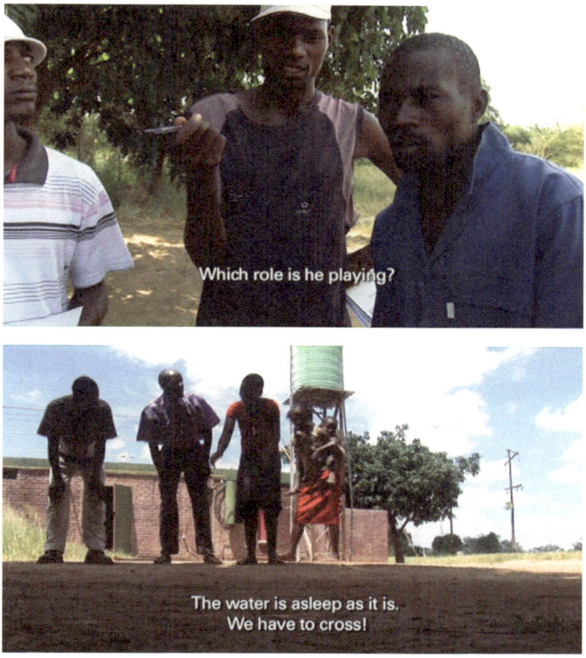

Figure 5.1.5. Stills from *Border Farm*.

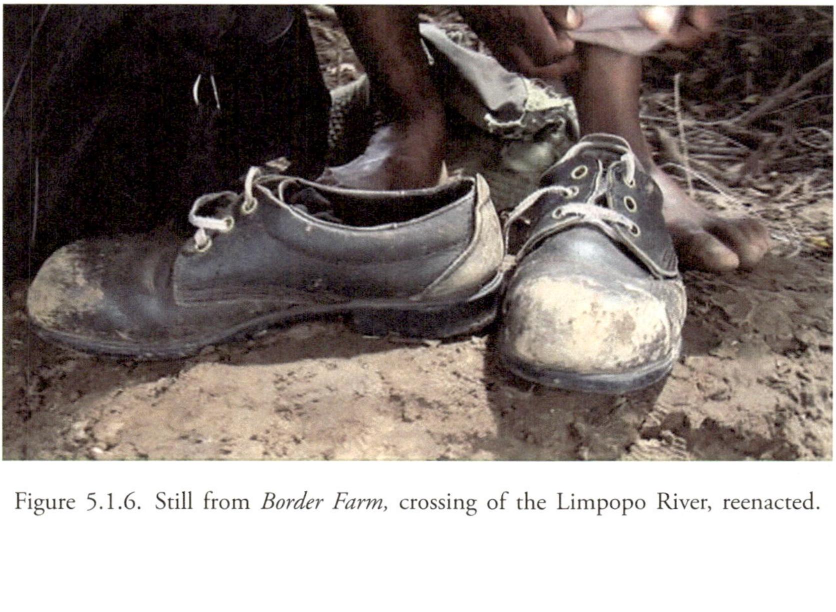

Figure 5.1.6. Still from *Border Farm*, crossing of the Limpopo River, reenacted.

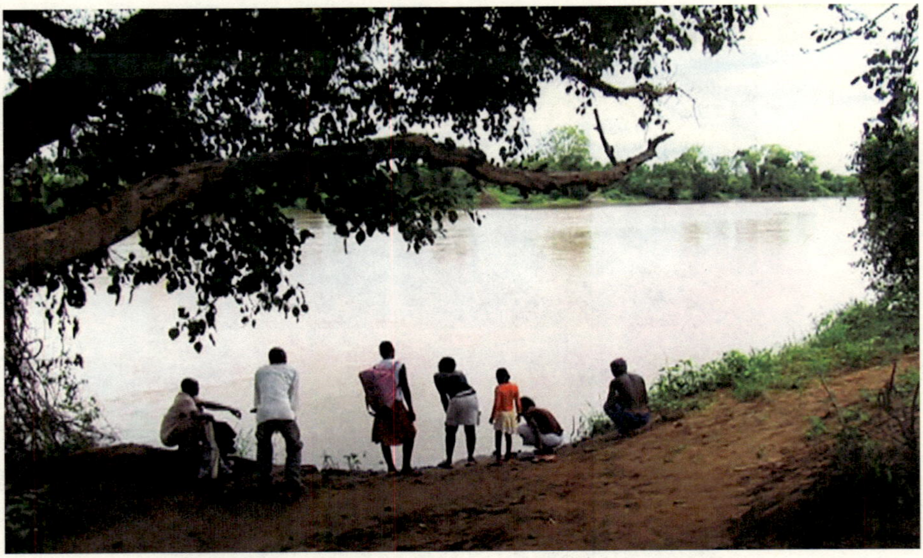

Figure 5.1.7. Still from *Border Farm,* crossing of the Limpopo River, reenacted.

4

Photographic Speech Acts

4.1 Migrant Life and the Image[1]

As an entry to the subject, I want to look at a photograph that I took in the inner-city suburb of Hillbrow in Johannesburg, which is home to many African migrants.[2] Often, when speaking about Hillbrow, the term "migrant community" is invoked. This is nonetheless, to borrow a phrase from Jacques Derrida, "a community without community" of those who don't belong to any community, and thus a precarious community, without any common essence.[3] At the same time, I want to point out that migrant inhabitants of Johannesburg, South Africa, often do share some common experiences

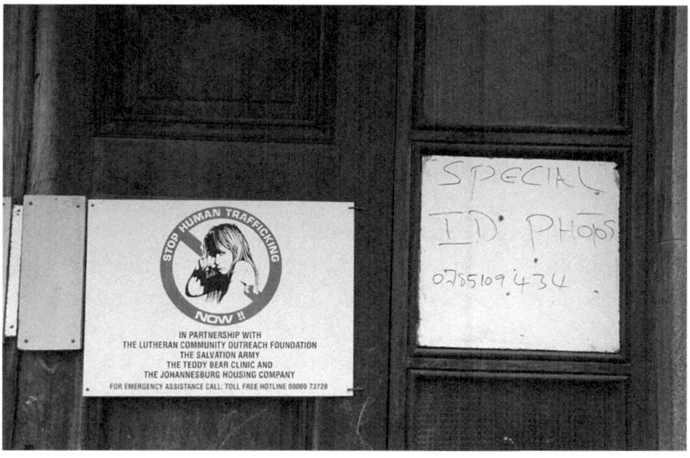

Figure 4.1.1. Boarded-up door with signs in Hillbrow, 2011, Marietta Kesting.

of repeatedly having to renew their legal permits, of being harassed by the police, and of facing difficulties in finding jobs and accommodation and other obstacles.

The photograph shows the boarded-up doorway of an apartment building on King George Street in Hillbrow. This photograph has several layers of meaning—both on its surface that includes another image and text, and as a metaphor. Visible on the left-hand side of the photo is a sign for an anti-trafficking campaign, supported by various local aid organizations. Also, one notices, the door has no handle and small pieces of wood have been nailed over to cover that area, to keep the door shut at all times; it has become an extension of the wall of the house. As the house was likely unoccupied at the time the photograph was taken, locking the door permanently was probably a measure against squatters. According to Médecins Sans Frontières (MSF), "the inner-city slums of Johannesburg are the destination point for many survival migrants seeking opportunity, transit, or simply to hide among Jo'burg's millions of inhabitants. But finding safe shelter here is extremely challenging."[4] Recent arrivals to the city often need to share accommodation, which is frequently rented out at very high prices, shrewd landlords capitalizing on the knowledge that many migrants do not have any other place to go and may not have legal papers.

To return to the photograph and one of its possible readings, certainly this door no longer serves its original function of letting people pass through. The closed door can be seen as not only hindering people in Hillbrow from entering this house, but may also be analogous to the national politics of closing the borders and trying to control the influx of people. The semi-transparent glass bricks, visible on the right, are dusty and dark—one cannot actually see what is inside. The sign on the left reads "STOP HUMAN TRAFFICKING NOW!!" and includes a drawing of a stylized weeping white woman or girl, highlighting the common conflation of migrant women and children in the public imaginary.[5] The image has a pedophiliac tinge, leaving the viewer potentially uncomfortable. Her raised right hand may be seen either as the girl/woman wiping the tears from her eyes, or even as a raised fist in counter-attack. She looks at the viewer from beneath her long bangs, her raised left shoulder a possible sign of her trying to protect herself, or as a display of fear and discomfort. Someone has used the white space to the right of the sign to pin up a hand-written advertisement, offering "Special ID Photos" and giving his or her phone number. I still wonder what the "special" stands for. Maybe especially cheap or well-made? It is certainly not a coincidence that the advert for identity photographs is written next to the "Stop Human Trafficking Now" sign. Indeed, the person offering the photo service might have assumed that its placement would give it extra attention, and maybe even that a person who might consider calling the number on the left could also be in need of some ID photos, as offered on the right.

There are hardly any public photo booths in Johannesburg's inner city.[6] Because of this, the informal ad for ID photos may actually be more "useful" to a migrant person in Hillbrow in trying to get papers than the well-intentioned sign on the left, since the NGOs working "against trafficking" usually assists the government in deporting migrants back to their countries of origin. The campaign illustration of a supposed victim on the left—even though it is fictional and soliciting for effects and affects—and the informal advert for ID photos on the right may reveal the ways in which migrant life is visually framed by NGOs and the national laws imposing identification procedures. Both types of images—the assumed victimized migrant woman and the identity photograph as such—will be discussed in detail in the following sections.

Identity Photos and Passport Photos

The passport photo needed for identification, as well as for travel and legal documents, deserves further consideration, since it shows how one is made visible by and to the nation-state. As indicated by the first image, photo services are in demand within the everyday life of the migrant community, since identification photos are necessary to register and obtain the legal permits that are often required in order to secure employment or legal status to remain in the country. With a cell phone or other camera that people may have access to, it is very difficult to take photographs that are acceptable as official identity photos. Often national institutions only accept photographs produced on their premises or by a specifically validated service, since these photos have to adhere to certain standards and rules: "The photograph should consist of a close up of your head and top of your shoulders so that your face takes up three quarters of the photo."[7] Moreover, the face needs to be frontal with even lighting, sharply in focus, with enough contrast, and a uniform, neutral background. These standards are becoming ever more sophisticated in the age of terrorism and biometrical passports. The photos are supposed to provide unequivocal recognizability of the person depicted, even though this is never entirely accomplished. Today the identity documents often include a recorded electronic fingerprint.

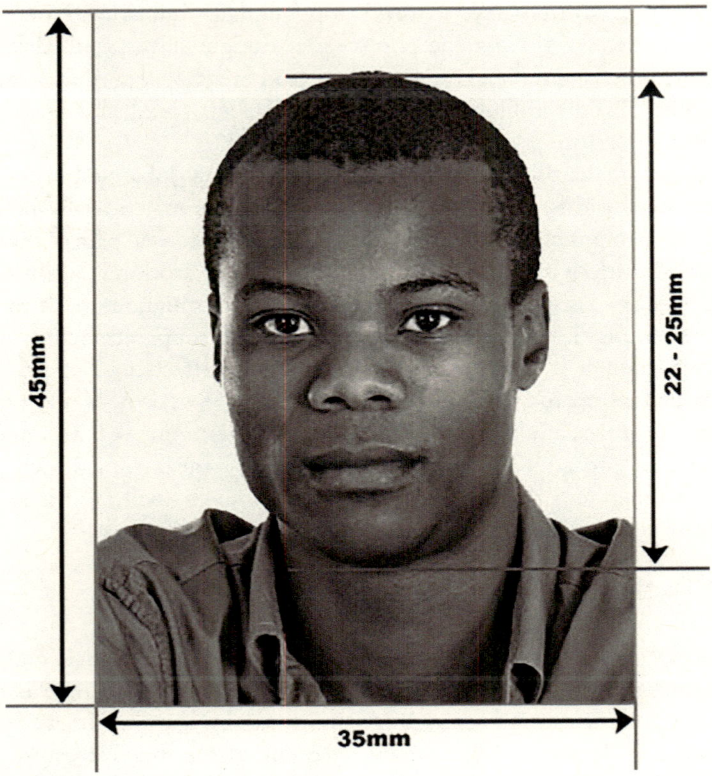

Figure 4.1.2. Example of a correct South African passport photo, source: Passport Agency Website.

The identity photograph is particularly relevant and can serve as a poignant example of the ambivalent qualities of the photographic self-portrait: on the one hand documenting and codifying, and on the other hand as a means of empowerment, self-expression, and pleasure. The passport photo reduces the subject and presses him or her into a certain category, thereby limiting individuals' aptitude to produce their own images according to their own ideas, desires, and standards. Another dimension to consider is the affective response to passport photos—the subject almost always de-identifies with his or her documentary portrait. Most passport photos are shown with the remark: "Don't look at the picture, it makes me look bad. In reality I don't look like that, it makes me look like a criminal." This is especially true nowadays with the new passport photo regulations where smiling is forbidden. Therefore, on a formal level the mandatory identification photos may turn every citizen into a criminal look-alike as on a "wanted" poster.

In addition, the legal papers with a valid identity photo that tie a person's place of birth, country of citizenship, and other information together through a passport with a name and nationality are often an integral part of preparing to deport him or her back to his or her country of origin. Therefore, another strategy used to defy the nation-state system may include remaining invisible to state and legislative control altogether. This would mean staying illegally in a country without papers and under the state's radar. Or becoming "someone else" by taking on a new identity, the legal option being to get married and take on your spouse's nationality and thus, usually for women, altering your surname; but there are also illegal options, for example destroying your papers or forging an identity document. These tactics of invisibility will be discussed in more detail in part 5.1.

When considering this, one should never forget that identification photos are always already framed by historical discourses of borders, immigration policies, and national security, all of which resonate with control and surveillance, especially in the South African post-apartheid and post-colonial context.[8] During apartheid and colonialism the registering and dominating of Africans by Europeans relied heavily on bureaucratic means of identifying, counting, and granting or denying passports and entry permits. Some aspects in regard to in/visibility of black South Africans during apartheid may be comparable to the precarious visibility of African migrants in South Africa today.

To return to some of the points already raised in the discussion of the migrant labor system: during apartheid all South Africans who were classified as "black" were foreigners in their own land. They had only limited citizenship rights in the ethnicized "homelands."[9] Under various acts of the South African apartheid government following the doctrine of "separate development" of the different "races," the homelands or "Bantustans" were created in order to control and exclude black South Africans in pseudo-independent territories. The Bantu Homelands Citizenship Act of 1970 completed this process. Black South Africans residing outside of their nominal "homeland" had to carry pass books that soon included identity photographs, and work permits that at times included fingerprints, therefore, their freedom of movement was largely restricted, as noted in the following text:

> B had to register and be given a pass-book—the tool by which the government effected laws that kept blacks out of the cities

> unless they were gainfully employed. 'The old pass was just a piece of paper. It had no photo, so we could borrow someone else's,' B remembered, but the pass laws became more sophisticated and more difficult to evade. . . .[10]

Especially in the South African cities—which were imagined as "white" areas by the apartheid government—the status of black South Africans was precarious. As is known, black South Africans thus did not have the same rights as white South Africans, who had the status of "citizens." Instead, their position might be described as what Ariella Azoulay has called "flawed citizens."[11] She has explained "flawed citizenship" as a situation in which: "The state may be interested in the specific goods this population can provide or obtain, but is definitely not interested in their permanent assimilation into the rolls of the citizenry, and thus their status remains transient. . . . What the state wants is something that is in their possession—labor, power, bodies, sex, knowledge, and skill in certain areas—but this interest is not enough to alter their transient status."[12]

Black South Africans were subjected to a long history of exclusion in what would have been their own country. At the same time, during apartheid in "white" South Africa any black African, almost regardless of his or her nationality was perceived as a foreigner or a trespasser. In addition, as Mbembe has argued, the colonial epistemology denied colonized people self-representation and self-expression. They had "no freedom, no history, no individuality in any real sense," rather "he/she simply 'represented' a sort of eternal presence."[13] The racist ideology of apartheid has often repeated and thus doubled the weight of the colonial heritage in South Africa. Yet there was a lot of resistance by the population classified as "African" as we have already seen in the very first photograph of the pass-burning protest in Soweto.

Here one should be reminded of the famous photograph by Eli Weinberg of Nelson Mandela burning his pass book in 1960.[14] The black-and-white photograph shows Mandela crouched down in the yard of a township home. He is burning the pass in a tin pot. His gaze is fixed on his task, at the same time his eyes are half-closed from laughing. He seems at ease and very content with his action. All that remains visible of the pass are the pieces of the dark rectangular cover inside the pot, already engulfed in flames. There is no smoke, but the flames are visible, Mandela seems to be touching them with his left hand, as if he were urging them on. The burning of his pass book took place publicly during the ANC's defiance campaigns in 1960. The abolition of the pass laws and the freedom of movement for all was one prime objective of the African National Congress. President Hendrick Verwoerd extended the pass laws in 1959 to include women, leading to nationwide protest. In the same year, at the annual conference of the ANC, its president Albert Luthuli had declared, "1960 will be the year of the pass."[15] One of these anti-pass campaigns, organized in March 1960 and supported by the Pan African Congress (PAC), led to the Sharpeville Massacre 1960.[16] Black people not only burnt their passes, they also approached the police station and offered themselves for arrest for not carrying their pass books.

The burning of passes as acts of defiance against an unjust government is echoed today by the act of some migrants globally to burn their papers before crossing a national border. The migrants know that they are breaking laws, but they also insist on their mobility. Therefore, they burn

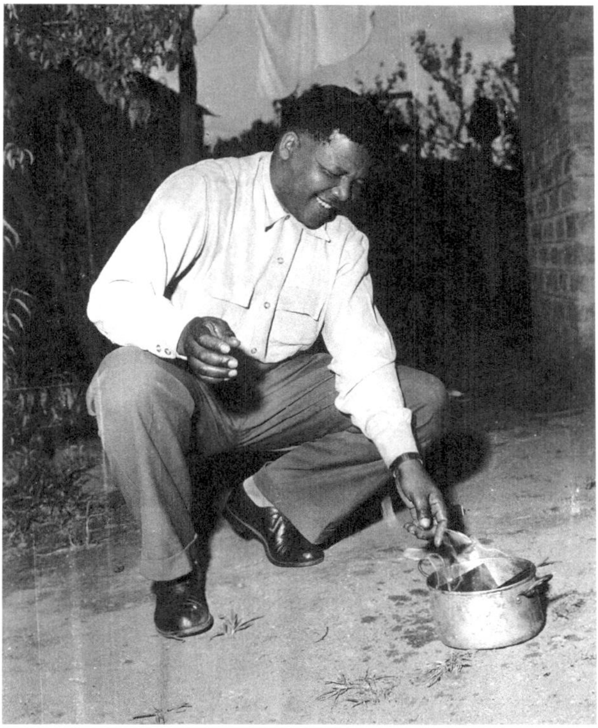

Figure 4.1.3. Nelson Mandela burning his pass, photo by Eli Weinberg 1960. University of the Western Cape, Robben Island Mayibuye Archives.

their passports in order to be unidentifiable and thus not to be deported. This practice occurs globally, as Papadopoulus and Tsianos have observed. Migrants waiting in Tangier to cross the Strait of Gibraltar are called ". . . 'Herraguas,' the burners, people prepared to burn their documents when they reach the Schengen border in Spain order to avoid being resent to their country of origin."[17] This tactic might rather lead to an argument for a right to remain outside of visualization, a "right to opacity," not to be read, documented, included, or excluded that Martinican writer Édouard Glissant once proposed: "Why must we evaluate people on the scale of the transparency of ideas proposed by the West? . . . As far as I'm concerned, a person has the right to be opaque."[18] While an imagined "right for opacity" is an important notion, it does not, of course, translate directly into any change of legal border policies at this point. African migrants who try to enter South African territory or the Schengen area cannot claim this "right to opacity," as there is no larger national or international political organization supporting such a right.

Becoming Visible

Nonetheless, there is also the opposite movement, fueled by an equally strong desire among migrants to become visible and documented and thereby to obtain legal status in South Africa. Only legal status affords assured access to certain jobs or education, housing, and other services. The next photograph I would like to discuss shows Zimbabwean nationals waiting at the Home Affairs Office in Johannesburg in order to register to get legal papers. Since at the exact moment the photograph was taken they are without papers, they are not legal, yet. Therefore, they did not want to be recognized in the image taken by a Zimbabwean photographer who was studying at the Market Photo Workshop in Johannesburg. It seems ironic that these people hiding from the photographer are waiting in line to have their official passport photo taken. Which modes of photographic imprint are legitimate and which delegitimize the subject become a matter of huge importance in these liminal moments (see figure 4.1.4 in the color gallery).

The photograph was taken using a wide-angle lens, producing distortion, most visibly in the warped lines of the stairs that the waiting people are seated upon. It looks almost like a stage set. The vanishing point shows a locked gate integrated into a green fence, leaving no room to escape, nowhere to go, adding a slightly Kafkaesque dimension to the scene. In the foreground there is trash—a juice bottle, a soft drink can, and some plastic wrapping are visible on the first and second steps, maybe attesting to the long time period people have had to wait having to sustain themselves, however meagerly. The steps have stains and crumbs on them, looking sticky and dirty. Anyone who chooses to sit down here and rest could only be someone with no other choice. The people waiting here, melding with the rubbish surrounding them, are a kind of human detritus, superfluous people, unseen and unnoticed by South African passersby who are rooted in their jobs, lives, and everyday routines. The standout of the scene, the "punctum" for the spectator in the Barthesian sense, is the woman on the far right of the picture who chooses not to hide her face and instead seems to look on stoically.[19] In this way the photograph resists an all-too-easy reading or explanation, showing with her defiance that there are alternative actions available.

The nation-state is the "author" or the power that requires every citizen and non-citizen to be identifiable and thereby controllable. The passport or identity document is usually the material object where photography and citizenship interface and assist the nation-state to symbolically produce or construct the male or female citizen with a fixed nationality. A legal document requires identity images that one could argue are the most "documentary" images there are in the genre of documentary portraits, supposedly "true" and "factual," where subjects are turned into objects in order to then be subjected to national and international laws. The passport photo, together with a valid passport, is literally the essential document allowing one to "pass," to move, to enter, to make one's way or not, and it can also mean access to services and protection, usually reserved for citizens.

Documentary Masks

After having discussed the passport photo in detail, I now want to look at an image that may at first look somewhat similar to a passport photo, but explicitly anonymizes the person depicted in it. Figure 4.5.1 was used in the South African Anti-Trafficking Campaign and shows a young black woman who cannot speak.[20] The smaller text next to the image states: "Human Trafficking is Slavery," establishing a parallel between colonial practices and current times. Another image from the series shows the same woman unable to see, because her eyes have been blotted out with red. This creates a powerful image with violent connotations, which is also associated with illegalization, as the hidden eyes, covered by a bar or pixelated, are often used when people are charged with a crime, but not yet convicted, to make it impossible to identify them.[21]

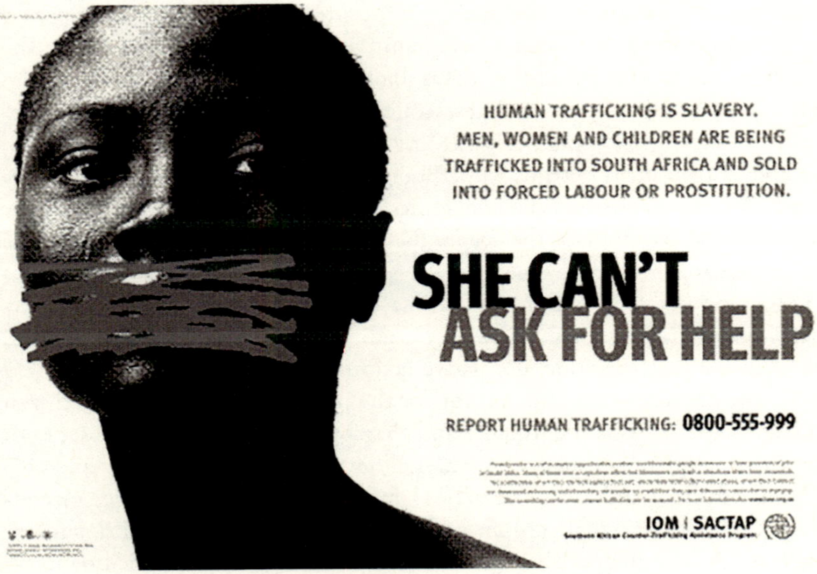

Figure 4.1.5. Flyer of the IOM and SACTAP Campaign Against Trafficking.

The woman in the image above looks at the viewer while looking away at the same time, it seems. Her gaze looks serious, and she has a scar on her right cheek. Her mouth is crossed out with red paint. The color red signifies "blood," "attention," "life and death," "danger," but at the same time it indicates "lust," "emotion," and "anger" amongst others, and in this context sensationalizes the woman further. Yet the woman may also come across as very seductive. No trace of clothing can be seen, leaving the viewer to conclude that the woman seems to be naked, further pushing the idea of her as ready to be (sexually) consumed. This image and the way it is presented are rather more reminiscent of a slick ad campaign than of the typical documentary photograph. Yet their monochromatic quality—except for the color red—calls up black-and-white documentary photography. The images are highly stylized and were probably shot with a model only for the purpose of the campaign.

The intergovernmental organization IOM (International Organization for Migration) and the regional public work SACTAP (Southern Africa Counter-Trafficking Program) feature prominently on the poster. The IOM prides itself in advancing "humane and orderly" migration.[22] This image of an assumed migrant black woman that imitates a documentary look but is part of a stylized campaign is a typical representation of the hegemonic idea of women as "silenced, blindfolded victims" in the context of sex work and—thus labeled illicit—sexuality.[23] Furthermore, it scandalizes and criminalizes black migrant women. Cross-border mobility is delegitimized.

A similar image could be found promoting an exhibit of Médecins Sans Frontières (MSF) held at Constitution Court, Johannesburg, albeit without the sexual overtones. This was also an exhibition dealing specifically with migration, entitled "Solidarity for Survival."[24] The text banner of the exhibit silences the female face (figure 4.1.6), which is—again—printed on a red background; only her left eye looks straight at the viewer. The woman depicted is wearing a headscarf. Although it is uncertain if this has a reli-

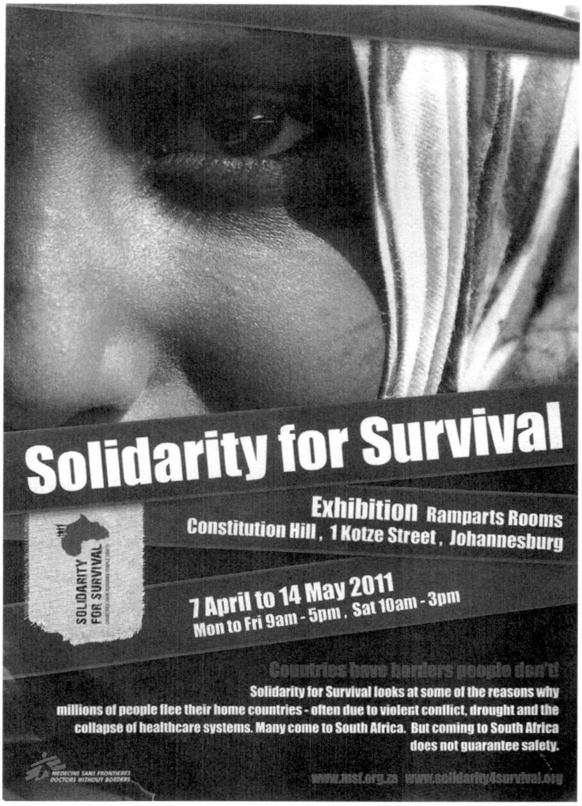

Figure 4.1.6. Poster for exhibit by Médecins Sans Frontières, 2011.

gious connotation, it seemingly marks her as a non-Western other. There are slanted red banners overlaid on the photograph, one over the woman's forehead, the other covers her mouth. As if she is peeking through a fence, only a small rectangular frame of her face remains visible. It may remind one of the red cordons, marking sites of danger or construction on the street.

This silencing of the woman seems unintended, since the exhibit has the opposite aim of raising "solidarity for survival."[25] It begs the question as to what kind of solidarity one can have with a character that has no voice? This can only mean that others—in this case MSF, or myself as the viewer of the poster—are empowered to speak for this silenced victim who cannot speak for herself. This creates an unequal partnership, where one partner has to care for the other and no real dialogue is possible.[26] The last two images are common examples of the highly selective ways in which migrant women are visualized by counter-trafficking and awareness-raising campaigns. They demonstrate why it is important to "draw on critiques about the focus on the sexuality of people from marginalized groups and the consequences thereof, but equally show how contested claims to represent 'vulnerable' groups have significant implications for how resources are distributed, how one makes claim to be or is labeled a victim or perpetrator, and the kind of migrant one can claim to be."[27] This means that migrants have only limited choices of how to portray and present themselves in the public sphere. Of course presenting oneself as a "victim" is also a label that may be used strategically. And yet, it is meaningful to emphasize that historically other depictions of "women as victims" have also existed in South Africa that included more militant and self-assertive connotations.

A struggle poster from the 1980s may serve as a visual example of the powerful iconography of that time (see figure on oppopsite page). This poster was printed in 1982. BSS stands for Black Students Society at the University of the Witwatersrand. The text reads: "Detention won't stop us." The image of a female figure, with a shaved head, standing defiantly with a clenched fist behind a wall and bars, as if in a prison cell, makes a strong aggressive impression. She looks like a fighter and not like a victim. She is holding a small child in her arms; the child looks directly at the viewer, as if asking how one can let this injustice happen. While this image clearly calls up Christian religious registers of motherhood and alludes to images of Mary with Jesus, it also moves beyond them.

In 1954, the Women Charter of the African National Congress was established, which called for the right for women to vote as well as other matters of removing discrimination.[28] The ideology of motherhood was as efficacious in African as in the white Afrikaans nationalism, yet in African nationalism it had a different connotation—it was considered a social

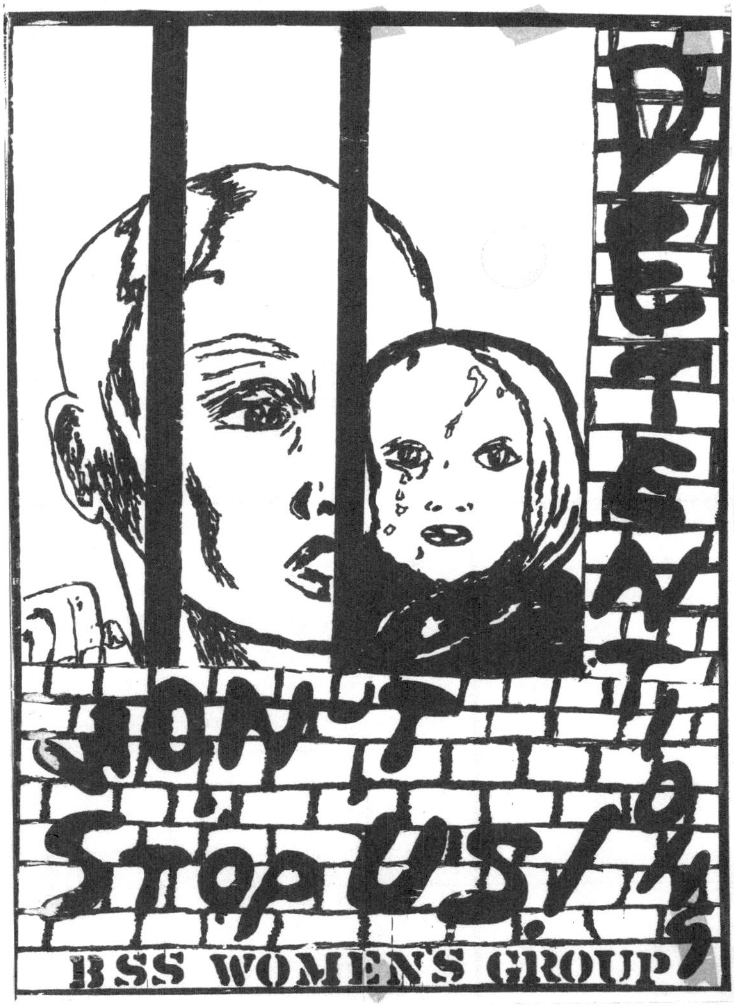

Figure 4.1.7. Poster by the Black Women Studies Group, 1982, SAHA.

category instead of a universal and biological one. African women have debated and expanded its meaning and developed a perception of themselves as "mothers of the revolution" since the 1970s, a self-naming which had significant militant undertones. Slogans of the times were "A Nation will Never be Free Unless its Women are Free," and "A Woman's Place is in the Struggle, not Behind Bars," but also the utopian "Speak Up, Make your

Dream Come True," possibly quoting Martin Luther King's famous speech from 1963.[29] In addition, in the aftermath of armed conflict and civil war women often have a higher number of survivors and are the ones who start building up society again, which also applied to South Africa.

The continued effect of apartheid structures also in post-apartheid times has led to the demise of traditional family structures, yet the extended family remains an important support system. Often children are raised in women-led households or, due to the HIV/AIDS crisis, even in child-led households, but this fact has not had much effect on the societal status of women and children.[30] Especially in Hillbrow, most families consist of migrant mothers and their children, sometimes the father has stayed behind in one of the neighboring African countries or left altogether. However, the "family" and structures of kin remains the central matrix for how to organize and imagine social relations, even if these are not thought of as biological concepts and consanguine relationships. Close friends are often described as "brothers" or "sisters," or depending on age as "uncles" and "aunts." So while there may be fewer and fewer "functioning" families, the symbol of the family as a unit of solidarity between individuals as well as a symbol for national unity remains important. Many visual documentary works are structured around the concept of a "family portrait" or a "family history," constructing arguments of, for instance, the loss of a family member against an idealized normal and functional family.[31] It is often argued by gender studies scholars that the symbol of the family needs to be updated and expanded in order to create a more just and equitable position for women. New images and alternative imaginary spaces are looming, but have not found consensus. One could even wonder whether the role of women after the consolidation of the "new" democracy is not even more regressive than her active militant position during the anti-apartheid struggle.[32]

Self-Portraits as "Kwerekwere"

To return to the Médecins Sans Frontière exhibit, one curious fact was that it included the possibility for "selfies:" the spectators could get involved and take their own digital self-portrait as a "Kwerekwere"—a derogatory term for foreigner in South Africa.[33] This action tried to promote the idea that "We are all foreigners, in most places." I myself had my photograph taken, wearing the "Kwerekwere" campaign T-shirt (see figure on opposite page).[34] The images were later uploaded to an online photo gallery, where one could see hundreds of smiling people wearing a "foreigner" T-shirt; many of the persons posing were white. Viewing the images had the effect of creating a slight

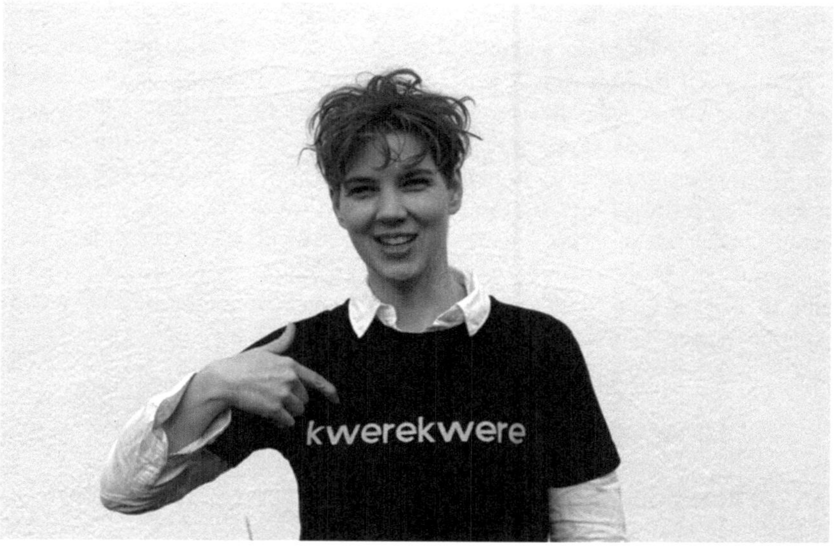

Figure 4.1.8. Example of the self-labeling as a foreigner. The author is wearing the "Kwerekwere" campaign T-shirt, Marietta Kesting.

disturbance between the self-assured look of people, representing themselves, feeling "normal" and part of society, and the derogatory label "Kwerekwere," which is usually only used for black foreigners in South Africa. The label did not seem to match, seemingly provoking the viewer to say, "What—these people are foreigners? They don't look like them at all. Could I be a foreigner then, too?" It was designed to lead one to the recognition that the norm is usually invisible and that if one feels that one belongs to the norm, one can go about one's life unlabeled. Then it is not so subversive to "out" oneself as a foreigner. Whereas a black foreigner could wear the T-shirt as an act of reappropriation, of "talking back"—"You call me a bad name? Well, look I am already calling myself that"—dampening the impact of the derogatory term. The "Kwerekwere" portraits were of course completely removed from the actual experience of navigating Johannesburg as a black foreigner from an African country. Yet, they created a fruitful disturbance and also showed how different (self-)portraits look when people have volunteered to have them taken in an active and assertive performance.

While the passport photo and identity document are part of the measures to control national borders, populations, and individuals, people taking their own photographic self-portraits can also experience this positively, even when wearing a certain label, as the "Kwerekwere" T-shirts attested. Photographic self-portraits are at times empowering if the subjects can actively craft their own images freely and creatively according to their own wishes. Therefore, the next chapter will consider two participatory photo projects in Johannesburg that promote self-representation. One is artist and photographer Terry Kurgan's *Hotel Yeoville* and the other the Market Photo Workshop's collaboration with migrant women sex workers. These projects may be important tools in counteracting the representations of the colonial and apartheid past and creating photographic images of migration and gender beyond narratives of victimhood.

4.2 Documentary Participatory Photography and Politics

Self-portraits I: The *Hotel Yeoville* Photo Project

Yeoville is an inner-city suburb of Johannesburg, bordering onto Berea, Hillbrow, and Bellevue. Historically it was a white area, built for the newly arrived European immigrants in South Africa. In the 1970s mostly Jewish immigrants lived there, but the area also attracted students, artists, musicians, and left-wing political activists. After the influx control laws were lifted in 1986, however, Yeoville went through a process similar to that of Hillbrow and Berea. Black people moved in, white people moved away, and with them the capital relocated to Sandton in the north of Johannesburg.[35] Many of the buildings were built as "hotels," but for a long-term stay for the new arrivals, that is, single men or women. At the same time "hotel" also serves as a good description for Yeoville's post-apartheid role in being a first home or maybe one of multiple homes for Johannesburg's transient black population. My first example of participatory self-documentation creating a different type of affective image is Terry Kurgan's participatory photography project, *Hotel Yeoville*, from 2010.[36] Terry Kurgan is an American artist and photographer based in Johannesburg. During 2010 *Hotel Yeoville* resided and took place inside the newly renovated Yeoville public library that had an allocated exhibition space.

Terry Kurgan's project mapped the inhabitants and visitors of Yeoville (audio-) visually—similar to a visual census, but participation in this public art piece was voluntary, of course. The questions that participants were asked started with: "What's your name? Who are you? Where do you come from? Where have you traveled? And what has been your experience, living in Yeoville?" People could choose if and how they wanted to answer. "The exhibition installation was comprised of a series of private booths in which visitors were invited to document themselves through a range of interactive digital interfaces and online social media applications, thereby bringing various forms of personal expression and intimate experience into public circulation."[37]

The project thus had a physical presence in the library, where content was produced, and a virtual presence provided online. Mostly, photographs were created, but people could also record short videos, write text, and record oral accounts. In addition Terry Kurgan archived all the images and included them in her own artistic body of work.[38] The self-description claims that "the exhibition's carefully considered surfaces and spaces not only functioned as invitations and prompts, for the users of the exhibition, but in fact relied on the traces and gestures—the engagement and participation of visitors—to produce both the website and the exhibition's content."[39] All the images, texts, and oral accounts created in the documentation and storytelling booths were uploaded to the website and mixed together with other resource content: migrant and refugee guides and advice, online discussion forums, classifieds, and a business-listing directory.[40] *Hotel Yeoville*'s webpage alluded at first sight to a geographically circumscribed social media platform not too dissimilar from Facebook. The photo booth was by far the most popular space and used by many different people each day. The photo booth's setup simulated a passport photo booth, even though the technology used was different—a digital camera and the images were printed out on the computer and not in a completely automatic mode. Thousands of self-portraits were produced here in sets of two copies, accompanied by short self-written texts. Participants were allowed to keep one copy of the photographs for themselves; the project team kept the other copy and the written text. Kurgan described the resulting images as existing "at the very threshold between private and public space, and these personal, utterly commonplace images have the power to resonate in much broader public and political spheres."[41]

One example would be the self-portrait of a francophone African man by the name of Patience (see figures 4.2.1 and 4.2.2 in the color gallery). He is looking straight at the camera, with little variation between the four frames, aside from the slight movement of him turning his head. He describes himself and advertises his ability to teach French to his "lovely Yeovilliens fellows," even giving his phone number, attesting both to the sincerity of his offer as well as maybe to his urgent need to generate some income. Patience claims Yeoville to be his *home*—where he would "like to spend all my time really feeling at home." This short message is paradigmatic for many other messages. They expressed an ownership and identification with "Yeoville," many said "Yeoville is my home." This showed that Yeoville indeed had become a new home where a community was established and where life was livable.

But what could be the political and social role and lasting impact of very ordinary, everyday domestic snapshots? And how would they gain relevance in the larger arena of the public sphere? These are worthwhile questions to pinpoint—it is uncertain if these images had any political agency besides saying "I am here, and I am beautiful" and "I love you all," which of course is an important gesture, but also quickly forgotten unless it is accompanied by further research into the everyday discrimination faced by African migrants in Johannesburg.

At the same time the project was a successful intervention against *othering* processes, since it emphasized the common desires of all inhabitants of Yeoville regardless of their nationality or citizenship status. Yet, while the project was consciously set up as a space removed from everyday reality and day-to-day politics, the political was reintroduced in some of the images, remarkably, via the decisions people made about how to present themselves and what to share with the public. In one image (see figure 4.2.2 in the color gallery), for example, two black women, explain that they are "proudly dykes" and describe themselves as "the next powerful women in yo' hood," claiming a positive visibility for black lesbians who are often *othered*, excluded, and marginalized similar to African migrants.[42] As Gqola has argued, black lesbian bodies were in South Africa "highly visible manifestations of the undesirable."[43]

The self-written text of the two women oscillates between claiming a female space in the city, self-assertion "sister-les-hood," and an invocation of a future: "FYI [For your information] for ur dream / that's wat we r doing / entrepreneurs," but not specifying if the dream (yours or ours?) has materialized and what their business is, further stating "You guda recognize!?! Proudly Dykes. . . ." This message opens up a desire for futurity, making an affective statement that includes, however, a question mark after "you have gotta recognize," playing with ambivalent meanings.

Kurgan states: "In an attempt to create a poetic distance from politics, and also to free the work from a referential dependence upon the harshness of xenophobic violence, we very consciously made 'Hotel Yeoville' a utopian or idealized space. The frame we produced was warm, pink and happy."[44] From my personal experience of visiting the *Hotel Yeoville* space in the public library of Yeoville I can agree that the design of the photo booth, which was pink and called "love booth," definitely made one smile. The whole space was modeled in the retro-design of an old cinema and the walls were painted by a former movie-poster painter. The color pink foremost associated with "kitsch," Barbies, and little girls was a bold choice that added another layer of campy staginess to the space. The setup acted as a prompt for people to "perform" themselves, often striking several different poses in each of the four frames. It also seemed to equate the act of photographing with spreading love and friendship, and in fact many people took images together with their friends and family. This probably also significantly mitigated the reluctance to participate. While photographing in Johannesburg on the sidewalks in the inner city is not a welcome activity, here—at *Hotel Yeoville*—photographing oneself seemed safe and inviting. One question to be mused upon is whether the "feel-good" framing of the project also only produced mostly "feel-good" responses, leaving little space for criticism and contestation.

Looking back at the project, Kurgan elaborates further on her evaluation: "If we accept the claim that all photographs bear the trace of the encounter between the photographer and the photographed, then some of the traces that these images carry is that utopian desire—a world in which power (us) and citizens (our participants) existed on a plane of co-dependence and equal exchange."[45] I would argue instead that it remains an open question as to whether the participants in the *Hotel Yeoville* project—largely consisting of the African migrant population of Johannesburg—actually had equal citizenship status (both in reality and\or symbolically) as the conveners of the project. If they were treated as citizens in the project, this does not necessarily extend to their daily life experiences in South Africa, in which they may often be treated as non-citizens or "flawed" citizens. Mbembe has used the term "disjunctive inclusion" to describe these mechanisms of post-apartheid society.[46] Nevertheless the project, of course, cannot and never set out to document the *reality* of discrimination, and in itself it was generally a positive and an affirmative experience for its participants.

The colonial epistemology denied colonized people self-representation and self-expression. They had "no freedom, no history, no individuality in any real sense," rather "he/she simply 'represented' a sort of eternal presence."[47] The racist ideology of apartheid has often repeated and thus doubled the weight of the colonial heritage in visual representations in South Africa. Therefore, participatory photography projects may be important tools in counteracting the representations of the colonial and apartheid past. However, it is important to note that even if colonized people "had no freedom for self-expression" in the eyes of the colonial state and were subjected to mechanisms of dehumanization, there were always elements of representation that escaped control. As is evident from countless sources of life under apartheid and colonialism, people have always aspired to be "more" and "other" than what the state defined them to be.

Hotel Yeoville succeeded in building a counter-archive of photographic portraits of the everyday life of African migrants living in Johannesburg and thereby worked against the assumed invisibility of their lives, producing photographic images that were both meaningful for the participants and to some extent resonated in the public sphere. The second example of a participatory photo project, *Working the City*, which will be discussed after a brief excursion and that also produced self-portraits, was started from a political context, rather than an artistic one.

Working the City—A Project with Migrant Women Sex Workers

Before looking at my final example of self-portraits of African migrant women, it is important to briefly position the Market Photo Workshop, which initiated the project. South African white photographer David Goldblatt founded the workshop in the late 1980s in order to provide training and education to African photographers, who were excluded from other tertiary institutions by apartheid policies. Therefore, it was never *only* a school of photography but also a space of political protest and defiance: a social, political, as well as educational and aesthetic project. While during apartheid there was a clear mission for the school and clear "enemies," the post-apartheid situation is complex and confusing—full of hope, but also facing corruption—having to negotiate post-Fordist neoliberal work settings, as well as other problems.[48] The Market Photo Workshop educators and students are at the forefront of the discussions on the shortcomings of post-apartheid society, about representing marginalized people, and trying to integrate this critical awareness into their own practice. Among other remarkable projects, the Market Photo Workshop succeeded in doing a collaborative project with migrant women sex workers, a social group that usually either remains invisible or receives negative visibility, framed as victims, as we have seen in some of the previous examples.

Working the City was collaboratively conducted by the Market Photo Workshop, the African Centre for Migration and Society (ACMS) at the University of the Witwatersrand, and the Sisonke Sex Worker Movement.[49] "*Working the City* sought to bring to light the experiences of migrant women involved in sex work within inner-city Johannesburg through a visual medium."[50] The project joined students of the Market Photo Workshop and migrant women both from within South Africa as well as from neighboring African countries. A part-time workshop was conducted, during which the students first recorded the stories of how the eleven participating women had arrived in Johannesburg. For example, a woman named Sbu explains: "I moved from Kabuli Natal to Johannesburg in 1995 to look for a job. I could not get employment, so I started selling fruits and vegetables on the streets."[51] The next step involved the students sharing some rudimentary parts of their photographic knowledge and thereby assisting the women in taking photographs. Then the women were asked to take images to illustrate their own lives in the inner city of Johannesburg. Afterward, the participants worked with students to edit their images and write captions and texts. The oral account of each woman was printed in white letters in the lower middle part of the posters. The photographs were printed in different sizes and arranged in sequences on a black background to produce one poster for every participant.

A portrait photograph of each woman was included—usually in the lower-left corner of a poster. These (self-)portraits are highly significant for my specific focus, since here again one can see different strategies of becoming visible or staying invisible. In the poster below, the personal story of Mimi is told, which starts with her being robbed, losing all her belongings, including her passport, on first arriving in Hillbrow. In her words: "My life was ruined as I was left with no form of identification and as a result could not get a job." Here the loss of an identity document is immediately linked with the loss of employment opportunities, forcing this woman, as she tells the story, to take up sex work. In addition she explains that she could not move around without her passport and it was like "imprisonment . . . until I got my asylum papers." While the portraits of friends and acquaintances in the upper-right corner of the poster show one woman smiling and another looking serious, as well as some men who work as street vendors, the woman called Mimi herself did not want to show her face and is hiding behind her hair and her hand. This may be because she did not consider her current living situation as "good" and therefore presentable, or maybe she was ashamed of being a sex worker or feared retribution, since sex work is still criminalized in South Africa under the Sexual Offences Act 23 of 1957.[52] Yet her gesture is also one of defiance, refusing to be fully interpolated into the exposure implied by portrait photography

While handing over the camera can to a certain extent be an empowering—or as in the previous example of *Hotel Yeoville* simply just amusing—experience for the participants, there are obviously still power relations involved; and the project supervisor in fact has the final control of the editing of the materials. The project initiator is also usually the person with a higher social status and education, as was also the case with the students and the migrant sex workers. Therefore, it is tremendously insightful to include photographs that show a participant defying the act of being portrayed and thereby adding a meta-reflective layer to the final poster (see figure 4.2.3 in the color gallery).

The *Working the City* posters were presented as a traveling exhibit and shown in different locations—including art galleries in Johannesburg. The first aim of the exhibition was to raise awareness, since the criminalization of sex work leads to difficult and often violent and unhealthy working conditions. Many migrant women have had experiences with sex work; this raises the question of whether sex work ("prostitution") can be considered an active and self-determined strategy of survival or if it usually means oppression of and violence against women, and how the women identify or dis-identify themselves in relation to their work. Moreover, this leads to the question if in the age of capitalism this differentiation can still be made? The *Working the City* project included the women's aspiration for their future without condemning their present situation. For example Mimi said: "As for now I am working hard so that I get a bursary to further my studies." It is important to remember in this context that migration policies of the state always favor well-educated migrants over the ones who work in the informal sector, for example, as sex workers, nannies, or touting goods on the informal market.[53]

Second, this project attempted to humanize the migrant women involved in sex work, who are often perceived as people involved in "dirty work" by the mainstream media and in the public's imaginary. Instead, it wanted to show who these women are, why they do the work that they do, and what their fears, hopes, and everyday lives are. African migrant women were long neglected in mainstream migration studies, but have now become the center of attention of some initiatives in South Africa and especially in Johannesburg, ranging from Caroline Kihato and Terry Kurgan's Visual Diary Project of Migrant Women to supportive measures by Sisonke and special classes offered at the Methodist Church by social workers in order to educate women about rape and its aftermath.[54] Certain other themes besides their working conditions, however, also surfaced repeatedly in the personal narratives:

> Additionally, tales are told of very difficult lives, and harrowing experiences. It is important to note that a high level of xenophobia is expressed in many of the stories, a fact that reflects

> some of the difficulties and harsh realities of these women's lives but also an issue that is extremely problematic particularly in a country of unacceptable levels of xenophobia and tendency toward xenophobic violence.[55]

Here intersections of race, class, immigration status, and occupation all influence individuals' life situations and may aggravate each other. Moreover, the organizers of the project connected the subjective experiences of these migrant women to the larger picture of South African post-apartheid society and which problems are present here. Participatory projects thus can act as seismographs of societal constellations or as a means of social mapping that can be a starting point for political interventions. As art theorist Grant Kester has remarked: "While each practitioner comes to collaborative work with a unique perspective, these individual creative choices, taken in the aggregate, reveal much about both the current political moment. . . ."[56] Even as it is problematic to assume that the site of political transformation is always in the discriminated other—to refer to Hal Foster's critique—nevertheless non-stereotypical images can render the perception of minority groups in the public sphere more complex and less schematic.[57] Photographic (self-) portraits are consequently reconfiguring the sphere of representation and are ways of "world-making" and affective engagement.[58] While *Working the City* acknowledged the difficult life settings of the migrant women sex workers, it did not portray them as victims in need of saving, but rather as active individuals in different modes of subjectivization.

In conclusion, while the normative passport photograph as we have seen in part 4.1 only frames the African migrant in an attempt to identify and control him or her, I want to argue for the need to complicate the frames and framings of African migrant subjectivities in photography. The intentional hybridization of the documentary photographic genre including reenactments and fictionalizations can accomplish this and thus give the former "objects" of the camera's gaze an active part in photographic image production. There also needs to be the choice, however, to remain invisible, since migrant subjects are often already framed as normative discourses of victimhood or deviance that they cannot directly influence. Butler states: "Bound to seek recognition of its own existence in categories, terms, and names that are not of its own making, the subject seeks the sign of its own existence outside itself in a discourse that is at once dominant and indifferent."[59] The act of taking self-portraits can intervene in this outside discourse and may initiate an introspective meta-reflection on one's own situation, thus the photographic self-portraits of migrants frame subjectivities in different states of becoming and oscillate between self-expression within normative frames or the choice to stay invisible. The question of invisibility will be taken up further in the next chapter. Photographic interventions of participatory projects are meaningful tools in current mediascapes to add complexity and multiply the frames already available, since photographic portraits circulate in private and public arenas.

5

In/Visibilities and Reenactments

5.1 De-Identification and Multiplication?

Investigating notions of invisibilities and affective images of others connects to questions of post-representation and blackness. Post-representation would imply abandoning the photographic discourse of indexicality, visibility, and evidence.[1] Conflicts around the images of others, national borders, immigration policies, and inclusion and exclusion exist worldwide. In Europe there are recurrent waves of racist, anti-immigrant sentiments, in the United States racism persists and has led to the new movement "Black Lives Matter."[2] Violence is often not only connected to the actual presence of people deemed "foreigners" but to the imaginary beliefs and fear constructed around "them." Pogroms against Sinti and Roma, for example took place in spring 2008 in Naples, Italy, as well as against African refugees in internment camps farther south in Lampedusa, as well as in Germany.[3]

The list of violence against "foreigners" is endless, proving that this form of violence is not a specifically South African problem. Film and photographic documentary images play a crucial role in all of these conflicts. An understanding of how images become political and also how they are consequently used in politics is necessary to define how we will continue to treat these visual media in the future. At the same time, in the documentary genre the goal of making the invisible and suffering migrant visible has already turned into a much criticized cliché that is counterbalanced by an approach of considering the "autonomy of migration" and the agency (even if it may be precarious) by migrant subjectivities as exemplified by the works of migration theorists Vassilis Tsianos, Dimitris Papadopoulus, and others.[4]

Beyond the globally occurring dimensions of resentment against alleged foreigners, what is specific in South Africa, however, is that after 1994 a new visibility of blackness—and specifically as a by-product of nation-building and Mbeki's project of an "African Renaissance"—"South Africanness" emerged. Some theorists like Gqola have spoken in this context of a "Black-against-Black" racism or of "negrophobia."[5] There are other discourses on migration happening in South Africa that do not only construct *visible minorities* as they occur predominantly in Western Europe.[6] And yet, the questions of skin "color" and shades of "blackness" are still a powerful momentum to discourse formation in South Africa, too. Racist judgments about Zimbabweans having "darker" skin than South African blacks resonate with historical European racist discourses, which continue to operate even in post-apartheid times. The reinvention of difference in South Africa therefore points back to inheritances from apartheid history and the failed processes of reconciliation and compensation within the impoverished township areas. Non-South African, yet African foreigners, were specifically singled out by pseudo ethnic and lingual markers in the buildup to the xenophobic attacks.

Visibility can be an empowering act of a Deleuzian "becoming" in the sense of a hybridization of the subject which implies becoming "minoritarian,"[7] and it could even mean to temporarily inhabit the space of a "political subject" instead of a victim. Yet, visibility can also codify stereotypes, normative frames, and clichés about others. Often these stereotypes are sexualized in such a way as to delegitimize peoples' status as "good citizens." As has been noted before, the documentary landscape of visual image production in South Africa is often over-determined by the traumatic visual documents of the past, exemplifying black suffering under apartheid. All current images are read and held up against those iconic images from the past.

Until the last decade in contemporary migration theory in South Africa, a dual mode of thinking reigned, which on the one hand usually featured the economic thinking of African migrants as a useful and exploitable workforce in the unacknowledged tradition of the colonial and apartheid migrant labor system, and on the other hand addressed the humanitarianism of refugee studies alike. In the theorizing of migration it is therefore important to step out at least temporarily of the individualized anti-trafficking discourse in the framework of the nation-state of migrants as victims or criminals from the smuggler mafia and instead consider the "autonomy of migration" and the desire for mobility. In South Africa, as has been exemplified, there exists a long history of forced and at times voluntary African labor migration that needs to be accessed, remembered, and indeed consciously owned.

Current migration scholars have used Deleuze and Guattari's unsettling concepts for challenging fixed notions of what migration entails: "For example the Deleuzian concept of *becoming* can help us to overcome the liberal discourse of the new migrant as a useful and adaptable workforce as well as the logic of victimization prevalent in NGO paternalistic interventionism."[8] The tension between representation, hegemonic representations of public visibility, and blackness in connection with the political and modes of becoming will be discussed and applied to the analysis of more visual materials in this chapter.

Invisibilities—*We Are Nowhere* (To Be Seen)

The documentary film *We Are Nowhere* by white female South African filmmaker Andy Spitz was shot in the aftermath of the xenophobic attacks on the outskirts of Johannesburg and offers poignant scenes that hint at a meta-reflection on visibility and images. One Zimbabwean migrant is accompanied by the filmmaker as he re-visits the site in the informal settlement, where his home, a modest shack, used to stand. Everything has been torn down, ransacked, and mostly burnt. He asks a neighbor if they have seen his official college documents which were packed in a padded courier envelope with the logo 'RAN.' Nobody has seen them, but a woman gives him a black-and-white passport photograph of his wife that was found lying not far away in the unpaved, muddy street. The photograph is bent and dirty, the white background covered with dust and scratches. The camera frames his hand, holding the image upright on a lower corner, in the middle of the frame, drawing all attention to it (see figure 5.1.1 on next page). Even though the passport photo is curved, one can recognize the face of a serious woman; her eyes look directly at the viewer. Her forehead reflects the flash.

The man is shocked and exclaims: "She found it in the street, which means the thief was dropping things in the street without thinking." It also denotes that the "thief" was likely a neighbor, going through the booty on his way home. In addition he finds a partially burnt photograph of his wife's sister. These two images are all he can recover from his belongings. Why is he taking the images? They are worthless in monetary terms, yet they have an affective and symbolic value.

This man has lost evidence of his professional qualifications due to the xenophobic attacks and the looting of his possessions, thus he is now relegated to the sphere of unskilled worker. He now inhabits a less acknowledged and less visible position in society. At the same time he regains some—if precarious—visibility as a subject in Spitz's documentary film,

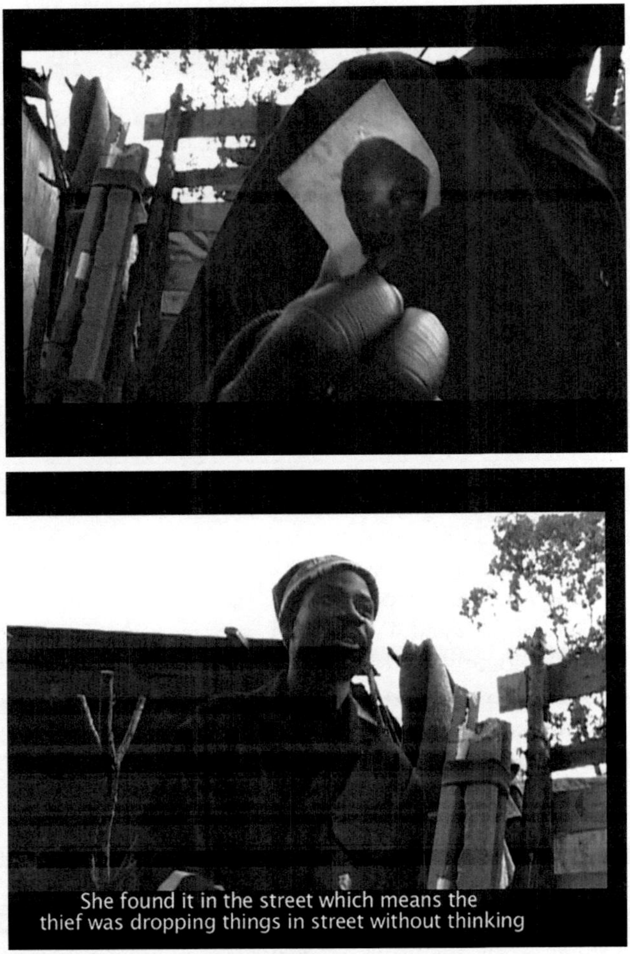

Figure 5.1.1. Stills from *We Are Nowhere.*

which captures his image and his search for his documents. He is depicted as a married man, attached to his wife, who is present in the scene through the retrieval of the degraded photograph, humanizing him and showing the audience that even though he is portrayed in the film alone, he is part of an affective relation. W. J. T. Mitchell has extensively written on the idea of images being "alive" for us, as becomes blatantly obvious in this case, where the dirtied photograph of the woman makes one feel as if she herself had been treated badly, illustrating our fetishistic belief in images.[9]

The title of the film *We Are Nowhere* is actually a quote from some of the perpetrators of the attacks who live a life on the margins of post-apartheid society. One could complete the sentence as "We are nowhere to be seen in South African society," a reproach against a post-apartheid situation that has not upheld its promises of freedom and "good" life for all. And yet, it could equally be transferred to the situation the man from Zimbabwe and the other African migrants find themselves in, stranded in a hostile environment in South Africa without proper identification and documents. The film manages to draw attention to the problematic living situation of both the perpetrators as well as the people targeted in the attacks on the margins of visibility in mainstream media. While not excusing the perpetrators, this film is one of the few documentaries that dares to include the perpetrator's view with all its problematic connotations, complicating the picture, instead of only showing the "poor victims."[10]

I want to read the scenes from *We Are Nowhere* against other documentary film scenes to tease out the ambiguous potential of becoming invisible and imperceptible and in order to show that it can also have aspects of resistance and choice. The following examples will complicate the notion of visibility and voice by showing possibilities of defying identification and remaining silent or respectively telling lies.

De-Identification and Multiplication

As I am writing this chapter, I am also in the process of editing a short documentary film about photography and migration in Johannesburg with the title *Howzit? Migrant Life in Joburg*.[11] The film uses both interviews and documentary footage as well as reenacted events. Filmmaking functions differently than critical writing and analysis, and yet both could be mutually informative. Questions surface from the materials: What audiovisual documents may exist of a state of becoming invisible or imperceptible? Is it even possible to visually represent how African migrants oppose the control and identification procedures by the nation state in their everyday lives? Some scenes from the raw footage have become stuck in my mind and are replaying there again and again. One of them is from an interview in which a migrant from Tanzania explains:

> "I am against the government, you see, and I have to be, life pushed me to be against the government, but I don't want to

> be against the government each and every day for the rest of my life." He continues: "You know me by my name 'Simon' but if you go to the streets now, there is nobody there who knows this name. I go by different names, you see? I have maybe five names, and each person I meet, I see which name I will give to them to call me with. Even these cops now that are looking for me they don't know my name and they don't know my face, either. So even if they find me, I can tell them, that is not me, that is somebody else."[12]

This testimony is a provocation of the documentary recording setting that is "still" trying to capture authenticity. Instead, this statement attests to the self-reflection of a minority position "against the government" and on also the conscious negation and refusal of a relatively banal knowledge like the *real* name of the interviewee.

In addition, "Simon" deliberately de-identifies himself as a small act of resistance and as part of his acquired survival skills in inner city Johannesburg and making a living in the informal sector. The act of resistance and staying imperceptible is, however, not targeted against global consumer

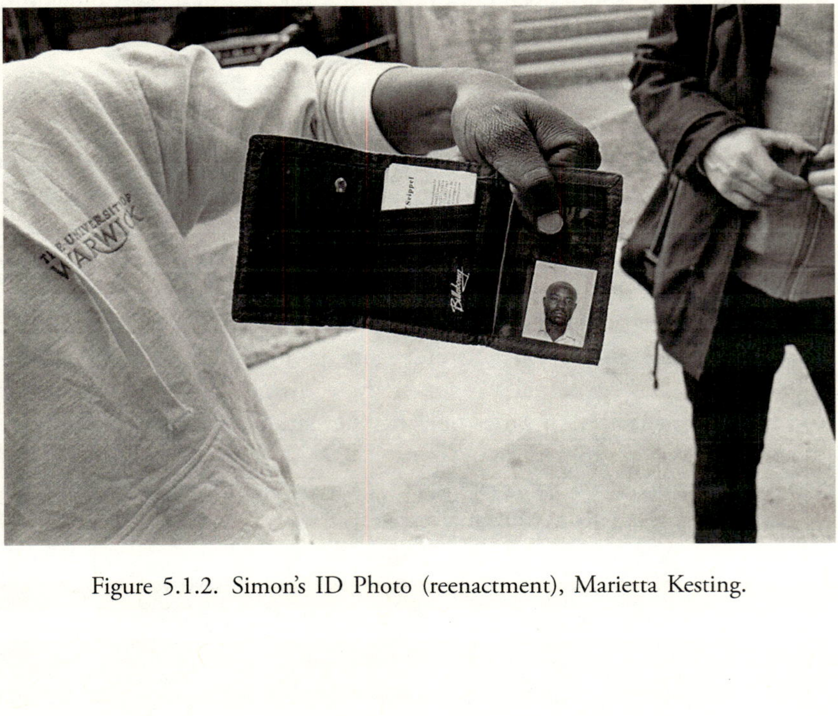

Figure 5.1.2. Simon's ID Photo (reenactment), Marietta Kesting.

culture, instead it is outside of it and at the same time submerged in it—Simon is wearing a sweater with the logo of the "University of Warwick." He has never been to the United Kingdom, and yet, of course, he takes part in a global realm of images of desire, fashion, hopes for education, and careers and international travel.

This act of de-identification is not an act of disappearance; instead it is to become imperceptible by multiplication, thus becoming "more than one." It is therefore an insistence on a presence in the here-and-now by becoming not one person, but many—"I have maybe five names"—including the possibility of making up new ones as needed. Tsianos and Papadopoulous have theorized this practice critically, suggesting that:

> . . . de-identification is not primarily a question of shifting identitarian ascriptions; it is a material and an embodied way of being. The strategy of de-identification is a voluntary de-humanization in the sense that it breaks the relation between your name and your body. A body without a name is a non-human human being, an animal, which runs. It is non-human because it deliberately abandons the humanist regime of rights.[13]

This strategy signifies a never finished state of becoming, which Tsianos and Papadopoulos have theorized by building upon Deleuze and Guattari's concept of becoming that can impregnate and change an entire social field.[14] As it has been clearly spelled out in the quote by Tsianos and Papadopoulous, it is important to stress that this process of de-identification should not be taken lightly or romanticized since it is a very precarious position. Whoever inhabits it can no longer claim any of the formal rights from the UNCHR refugee convention or the like. In most countries, including South Africa, non-nationals who lie on their applications when applying for legal status and a right to stay are—if found out—immediately expelled.

Is it possible to connect the notion of imperceptible politics and de-identification to José Esteban Muñoz's concept of disidentification to theorize modes of subjectification that do not quite belong in the national framings and are located in-between? Muñoz proposed: "These identities-in-difference emerge from a failed interpellation within the dominant public sphere."[15] But instead of insisting on being "normal," usually alluding to the normative ideal of white or black masculinity, and being human like the hegemonic parts of society, the practice of disidentification instead involves actively becoming and inhabiting the *other*, the animalized or de-humanized and "raced" body, but with a critical turn.[16]

Yet, even in the situation of "disidentification" and possibly illegalization, there are still sometimes ways for individuals to negotiate, be it through connections to people working for the department of home affairs or crossing a national border and re-entering. Many African migrants challenge national laws and actively promote their presumed right to move freely. This strand of thought on de-identification can contribute to opening the visual discourse on migration beyond the simple equations of migrants as the eternal victims or the eternal criminal and instead thinking in terms of a politics of imperceptibility that include positions of ambivalence. This positioning in-between may at times include a strategic identification and self-labeling, yet without fixing one's identity, a process akin to what South African writer and artist Sinethemba Twalo has called "othering myself."[17] This is multiplying Spivak's notion of "strategic essentialism."[18] All these strategies to escape identitarian positions will be explored further in the next part that discusses the "telling of lies" and "hiding" in documentary recording settings.

Telling Lies and Staying Invisible in *Conversations*

Now we return to the film *Conversations on a Sunday Afternoon* that was introduced in chapter 2. Keniloe, the main character, visits Lindela, the detention and repatriation center of Johannesburg toward the end of his reenacted search for the Somalian woman Fatima. Lindela is where the illegalized migrants are held before they are sent back to their countries of origin—so this is an almost inevitable place to search for a refugee woman. When Keniloe enters the Lindela detention camp, nobody wants to speak with him.[19] He tries to befriend some young women and asks them about Fatima, but they do not answer.[20] They remain silent, are looking away and giggling. When he insists, they hide in a shed. Keniloe points his finger to the inside and makes a begging pose toward another woman, who also withdraws. Keniloe, and with him the camera, hesitantly follows them into the room. Inside the room the girls are lying on the floor in a sad play-room with Superman paintings on the wall, hiding very inadequately, because there is nothing to hide behind except a game board that is too small but that one of them has put over her back. The others turn their faces away and put their bodies toward the floor and their backs to the camera, defying the act of being recorded. Keniloe enters the room, tries to talk to them again. and demands: "I am not going to talk to you, when you cover your faces like that." Reminding us that after all there are proper ways to talk, which means face-to-face, and that is also what *Conversations* has been delivering so far: all straight "into" or "for" the camera statements.

At the detention camp, where no one stays out of his or her own accord, this changes. The scene is very unusual and also to an extent violent, even though the girls are not touched physically. But their strong defensive action suggests that there may be reasons for their mistrust and the gaze of the camera is also violating their personal space, of course. And yet, the scene manages to expose the power relations of the asymmetry of being "illegal" as well as being "safe" behind the camera or exposed in front of the lens.

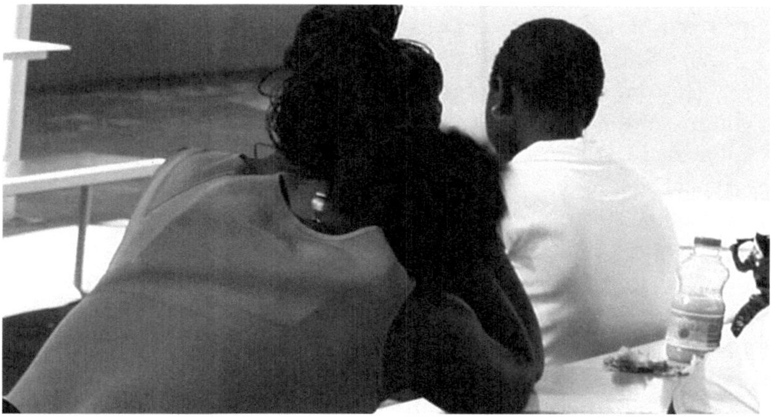

Figure 5.1.3. At Lindela Detention Center, women hiding—a still from *Conversations.*

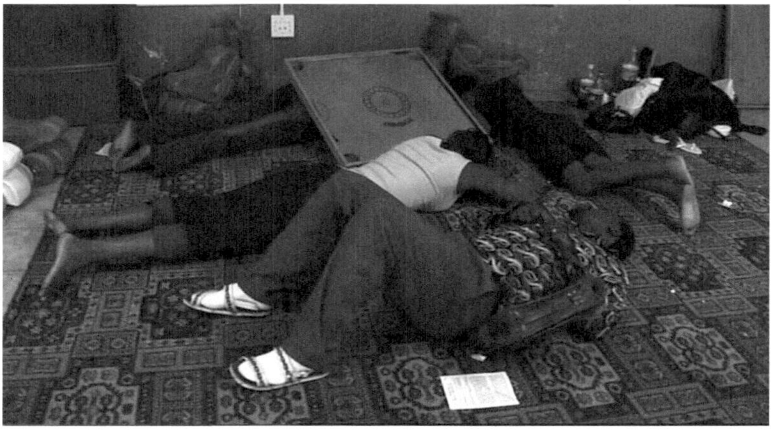

Figure 5.1.4. At Lindela Detention Center, women lying on the floor and hiding—a still from *Conversations.*

Keniloe adopts the same pose on the floor, except that he is lying on his back and looking at the ceiling. He waits patiently for the girls to open up and he asks them questions, but they won't answer. He asks them where they come from: "Are you from Zimbabwe? From Mozambique?" This is the most basic question that a policeman stopping them on the street or anyone trying to identify them would ask. The reply is always: "No." They won't tell him anything. He tells them that they must be lying. Their answer from underneath their covered faces is brisk and clear: "Then don't talk to liars." After some more time goes by—as can be deduced from the cut in the material filmed—Keniloe gives up and leaves again. This kind of scene of a "failed" interview would normally not be included in the final edit of a film. The scene also unsettles Keniloe's safe male subject position, since his authority to question others is undermined here. There is some double meaning in the scene as the girls are "lying on the floor" and "lying"—in the sense of "telling lies." This reminds one of the proverb: "Lies have short legs," meaning they cannot run far before they are outrun and apprehended. The scene offers a visualization of this saying, since the girls are grounded on the floor, not using their legs. Additionally "telling lies" could also be read as "lies" that are "telling" meaning, that they carry great weight and produce a marked effect.

The dialogue in this scene is a poignant reminder that for illegalized migrants there may not only be nothing to be gained by participating in a documentary film project, but additionally any act of clear identification could be considered a danger. One survival strategy is to avoid being recorded and to remain invisible and unidentifiable. This also begs the question of whether it is ethical to include footage of people who obviously did not want to be filmed. On the contrary, the migrant inhabitants of Johannesburg that have some kind of legal status and who were interviewed on the streets seemed to have no concerns about talking in front of the camera. By leaving this scene in the finished edit of the film, however, it opens up a space to think about the whole documentary project: what is constructed as truth and what as lies, the notion of staging and authenticity besides the information it offers on the living situation of some of Johannesburg's inhabitants. The film also makes visible the concept of a national hierarchy of "good" migrants (legal) and "bad" migrants (illegal) that are held in a prison-like camp like criminals.

In addition, as Michel Foucault reminds us, the interview in the court context is always already suspicious, since its technique is historically derived from the religious confession or judgment of God.[21] Hito Steyerl has followed Foucault's line of thought and then re-phrased Gayatri

Spivak's famous question "Can the subaltern speak?" into "Can witnesses speak?" Steyerl concludes that the witness may not be able to talk depending on which group or context she or he belongs to.[22] Similarly, pioneer of intersectional analysis Kimberlé Crenshaw observed that victimized women are usually presented by documentary media in "the classic view of the pathological 'other': the viewer peers through the dimly lit window into her life; they see the violence she experiences, but they cannot and do not understand why she stays."[23] These questions of voice, agency, visibility, and the political have already been negotiated in films like Godard and Gorin's *La politique et le Bonheur*, 1972, where an interview with workers on strike is shown, but you cannot hear the words of the interviewed person, only the mute thoughts of the woman standing next to her.[24] Films are thus clearly part of the discourse production and advance the reflective process on questions of representation and having "a voice."[25] The strike scene in Godard and Gorin's film conveys that it also depends on the tonality and the context of what is being said and not just the content, or as Rancière commented on the societal framings and power relations:

> There is politics because speaking is not the same as speaking, because there is not even an agreement on what a sense means. Political dissensus is not a discussion between speaking people who would confront their interests and values. It is a conflict about who speaks and who does not speak, about what has to be heard as the voice of pain and what has to be heard as an argument on justice.[26]

Often only a stereotypical speech act, that is pure kitsch—the "voice of pain"—what everyone already expects to hear comes across in the mainstream media when "the worker," or "the victim," or "the crying woman" speak. *Conversations* works against the stereotypical speech acts. It does so by showing the silences and the gaps, which are usually omitted in the final edit of the film.

Documentary film can accordingly be a testing ground for modes of subjectivization, as well as a stage for the political and a mirror for society at large. Simultaneously, it records events and shows modes of thought and of subjectivization. In this context the Brechtian question of "who's to blame for a certain injustice" is evoked, as most documentaries are committed in one way or other to make society's ills visible and enlighten the audience on what the underlying cause is.[27] Therefore, a connection between documentary studies and political science exists, which wants to analyze structures of power.[28]

In the case of *Conversations* the South African public got the message—after the screening the audience asked the director—"Is this how we are? Are we really this ignorant and bad?"[29] In spite of not being able to provide any quick answers, images—moving or still—have the potential to express and pose complex questions. In *Conversations*, for example, there is an allegorical image of protest that may speak for the state of the political today and that will be discussed in the last part of this chapter. First, however, after the analysis of a refusal to speak in a documentary interview situation, let's take a look what happens when the migrants become "actors of themselves" in a process of restaging their border crossing into South Africa.

Reenacting Migration: *Border Farm*

A film that complicates the visibility of African migrants in South Africa, allowing for agency and desires to be expressed is *Border Farm*, 2011. It is a collaboration between the South African artist Thenjiwe Niki Nkosi and the Dublibadzimu Theatre Group of Musina. *Border Farm* presents documentary footage of Zimbabwean migrants who reenact and fictionalize their own acts of border crossing, and interviews with individual members as well as a meta-perspective on the whole project.[30] This semi-documentary film—again advocating for a hybrid genre—portrays the lives, hopes, and dreams of black migrants that are working on a farm by the South African town of Musina, which is located right next to Zimbabwe. The Limpopo River acts as a natural border between the two countries.

As an introduction the film shows documentary shots of the work being done on the farm—the harvesting of watermelons and working in the fields. As such it visually and thematically links the current work situation of illegalized Zimbabwean immigrants to African migrant labor during apartheid times but without spelling it out verbally. And yet, the question of work and sustaining oneself resurfaces in the interviews. An older Zimbabwean man by the name of Ephraihm Nhema, indicates, as most interviewees do, that he never intended or dreamt about coming to South Africa, that also he did not have a passport, but that in the end he came for "greener pastures" and because the situation in Zimbabwe was impossible without money or jobs. In the final sequence of the film Nhema expresses his disappointment that now in South Africa he is working a job that requires no skill whatsoever, when in fact he has an education. He muses, "pastures are the same everywhere."

The images of black men and women working in the fields are followed by a reflection of how they secretly passed into South Africa. The legal situation when the film project was realized stated that Zimbabweans might cross the border into South Africa, as far as the South African immigration officials were concerned, but the Zimabwean authorities wanted to keep the borders closed. Therefore, people who wanted to cross the river needed guides who knew the secret paths and holes in the border fence. These guides were often organized into gangs—the "guma-guma" (hustlers). They not only asked for high fees, but often they also stole all money and papers from the migrants, who were completely at their mercy.[31]

The initiator of the theatre group Meza Weza wrote a script, together with the participants, in which they incorporated their own experiences of how they had crossed the Limpopo to reach South African soil. But the actual experiences were fictionalized in the process: "We each experienced this, but we now acted as if it had happened to all of us together."[32] After completing the script, they began rehearsing, which is also documented in the film (see figure 5.1.5 in the color gallery). First the theater group practices the crossing of river and border fence on the grounds of the farm without getting their feet wet. Weza gives instructions: "Now, when you pass, just do it as you did, don't look into the camera." Precisely the inclusion of the instruction "not to look into the camera" emphasizes the artificiality of the recording situation and directs the attention to the strategic reenactment of an already past, yet actually experienced, incident. Subsequently, in the film, the actual restaged crossing of the Limpopo is shown. The scenes of the passing through the river are accompanied by dramatic music and added close-ups of the muddy banks of the river, in which the naked feet of those anxious to make the crossing sink in deeply. This makes the situation look more dangerous than it probably actually is. As the viewer I am anxious as well as affected in spite of knowing full well that I am watching a fake. On the contrary, knowing about the fake and at the same time experiencing that the dramaturgy of the film "works" to create an affective state increases the pleasure of watching, since I, as the viewer, am in on the secret and do not feel duped.

For *Border Farm* Rancière's analysis is valid: "Documentary cinema is not bound to the 'real' sought after by the classical norms of affinities and verisimilitudes that exert so much force on so-called fiction cinema. This gives the documentary much greater leverage to play around with the consonance and dissonance between narrative voices, or with the series of period images with different provenances and signifying power."[33]A documentary that is partly reenacted by the people concerned has the freedom to construct memories and experiences and to structure and reassemble them in new ways. In Nkosi's film the people involved are allowed to keep their secrets. In the personal interviews the conversation is cut right after the statement: "I just had to go." The reasons for leaving Zimbabwe and crossing the border do not have to be told or are only vaguely alluded to. The flow of the film is interrupted and instead shows the process of the playful and theatrical staging of the act of becoming different persons—a farmworker, a theatre director, a border crosser, an actor or actress (see figures 5.1.6 and 5.1.7 in the color gallery). "Becoming is essential to mobility. The trope of becoming animal is only one of the options migrants employ in order to claim their freedom of movement. Becoming woman, becoming child, becoming elder, becoming soil, becoming fluid, becoming animal is the migrants' answer to the control of their desire."[34]

Importantly the film complicates the story and does not make a simple case for the migrants as victims, but includes their everyday conversations, perceptions, and aspirations. As Norman Masawi, a younger man, relates in an interview, he was scared to cross the big river that has a strong current and crocodiles and hippos, yet at the same time he proudly emphasizes: "I liked the adventure. And now I am one of the few people who can say I crossed the Limpopo on high tide."[35] This statement bears witness to the power of affect and a trace of imperceptible politics that is an insistence on the present and the body's experience, and particularly the force of desire. Tsianos summarized this type of embodied politics as:

> Situated in the present historical regime of control, imperceptible politics involves *remaking the present* by *remaking our bodies*: the way we perceive, feel, act. Imperceptible politics transform our bodies. Loving the present, existing in the present, imperceptible politics is practiced in the present. It works with social reality in the most intimate and immanent ways, recalling the whole history and practice of escape, [. . .] and rethinking it anew.[36]

The remaking of bodies in the present can lead to the creation or performance of counter-images and counter-memories challenging the hegemonic views of the mainstream discourse in media and society and thusly helps envisaging, for example, another immigration politics or concretely another concept of who has a right to stay where.

Let us now consider an image of "staged protest" from *Conversations* that pushes the analysis of blackness, (post-)representation and the political even further.

Staging of Protest

How can politics that take place in the realm of imperceptibility even be shown at all in documentary films? In contrast, one could also wonder if a film may automatically become "political" by filming a demonstration? A fundamental lack in political documentaries is the difficulty of representing "community" and "society," since it is much easier (and more manageable) to concentrate on the fate of an individual.[37] However, there is an extraordinary scene of a small united crowd in Khalo Matabane's film *Conversations on a Sunday Afternoon*.[38] This scene shows a small protest. I want to argue that this scene is a "dialectical image," an image as a "reflection-space" in the sense of Walter Benjamin's "Bildraum"—image-space—as "Denkraum" and as "Leibraum," where image-space may become body-space, meaning the body enters into a space for reason and reflection.[39]

The scene starts with the camera following the main character Keniloe, who is walking the streets of Hillbrow, an inner-city quarter of Johannesburg, surveying the migrant urban geography and social landscape on his staged search for a Somali refugee. Suddenly and unexpectedly he passes through a small group of protesters who are carrying black signs and wearing black masks. The signs are empty and have no demands. They do not even talk but walk in silence, like a funeral procession. Keniloe and other bystanders watch them in confusion but no explanation is given as to who they are and what they are protesting against.

In discussions of the film, director Khalo Matabane himself has purposefully left the question unanswered as to whether this scene was staged or not. Of course, one could also argue with Habermas that nowadays, in modern times, everything is always staged—all the time.[40] But it is such

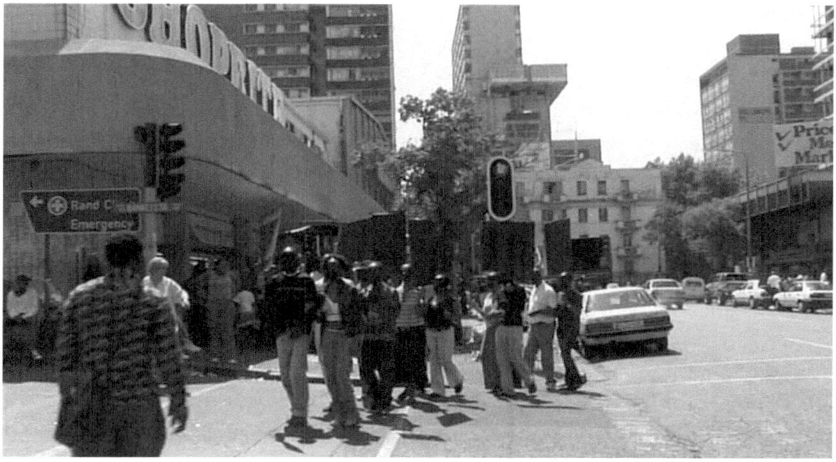

Figure 5.1.8. A staged demonstration, still from Conversations.

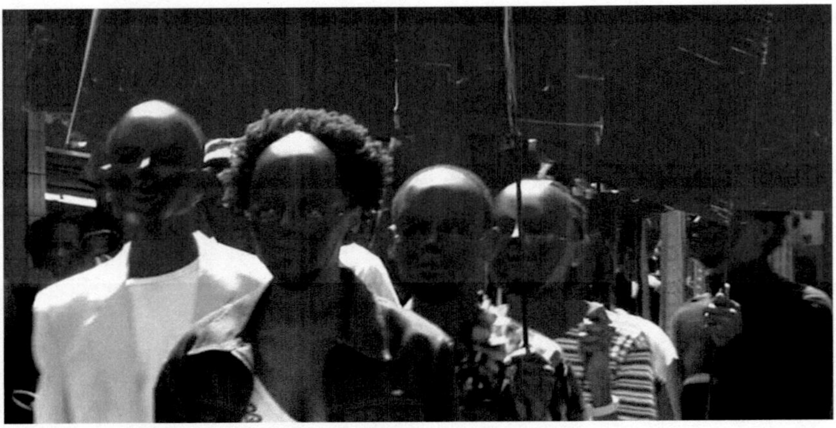

Figure 5.1.9. A staged demonstration, still from Conversations.

an evocative scene! Why are there no demands on the signs? Presumably because it is no longer possible to formulate simple demands? Or because "the people" do not believe anymore that protest changes anything? Or possibly because "the voice of the people" will not be heard anyway, as Godard has exemplified in some of his films? Or is it a critique of the film representation of the usual concept of "voice of the people" and easily readable political messages? As Hito Steyerl commonly has stated in documentary film: "The voice of the people is conceived as the unity of differences, of different political groups, and it reverberates within the resonator of a filmic space-time, the homogeneity of which is never called into question."[41] Here, however, the "voice of the people" remains silent and unreadable.

In addition, African people are wearing black masks—"black skin, black masks"—which of course references Frantz Fanon's *"Black Skin, White Masks."* Could this be an inversion and thus maybe a truly post-colonial gesture?[42] As gender researcher Emily Ngubia Kuria commented during a presentation, in her opinion only "white skin and black masks" would be a complete reversal of Fanon's seminal statement.[43] Fanon himself clearly stated: ". . . the Negro suffers in his body quite differently from the white man."[44] Therefore he argued that whiteness is not the reverse of blackness, since "the black man offers no ontological resistance to the white man."[45] And yet, the film playfully experiments with the Fanonian heritage.

The film image could also be read as the black masks double-signifying the "fact of blackness"[46] and thereby as a comment on the failure of the dissolution of identity politics that are often limiting and essentializing; yet the only one who can afford to step out of them is someone whose body and position is not constantly framed, reinscribed and coded by his or her race, nationality, gender, class, age, and ability. Fanon further asserts blackness as an ontological quality beyond a category, and beyond an opposition to anything else: "My Negro consciousness does not hold itself out as a lack. It *is*. It is its own follower."[47] Therefore blackness or black consciousness cannot be equated or exchanged in Fanon's perspective. Sinethemba Twalo recently updated Fanon's notion by speaking of "multiple blacknesses," complicating any simple readings or assumptions about what "blackness" might further mean.[48] Wearing a black mask may be one attempt to show these present multiplicities. However, putting on a mask also makes it possible to make oneself anonymous: being visible but at the same time hiding one's identity. It can thus be an act of self-assertion against the pressure of the different prescribed framings or stereotypes around blackness, "South Africanness," nationalism, and gender. Thereby, it opens up a scope for possible actions outside or in-between measures of control or expectation. As filmmaker and artist Clemens von Wedemeyer stated: "The camera and the mask are related devices which generate 'culture' through concealment and division."[49] One could ask, in addition, if the scene also provides a memory image connected to historical practices of blackness in connection with masks, questioning old and new communal rituals—in post-colonial times the "ritual" of protests and demonstrations "to change the world." In addition, the donning of masks at demonstrations—not only to stay unidentifiable—, ut also to refer to historic struggles—has had a surge of popularity in the rise of new social and protest movements worldwide.[50]

These performative acts cry out to be photographed and filmed, thereby visualizing protest and crafting affective images, however, Jodi Dean has argued on the performative and visible practice of democracy in the United States:

> As drive democracy organizes enjoyment via a multiplicity of stagings, of making oneself visible in one's lack. Contemporary protests in the United States, whether as marches, vigils, Facebook pages or internet petitions aim at visibility, awareness, being seen. They don't aim at taking power. Our politics is one of endless attempts to make ourselves seen. It's as if instead of looking at our opponents and working out ways to defeat them, we get off on imagining them looking at us.[51]

This re-reading of visual politics as proposed by Rancière would imply that visibility is today an end in itself, a "reason without a cause," or an endless act of repetition. Maybe the staged protest in *Conversations* with its empty signs is mocking this desire to be seen. But is Dean's interpretation really doing justice to the emerging political movements coming into existence all over the world? She implies that there should be something more important happening or a "deeper" engagement than the superficial "making ourselves seen." While this may be a common reproach in disguise—the endless repetition of the argument against the visual realm as "just on the surface," misleading, dazzling, and duping people—the political project of protest and of visibility, of course, has been questioned since the 1970s by filmmakers and more recently by theorists and artists. We have already discussed that "visibility" should not supply a goal in itself, and the whole post-colonial project of the "decolonization of the mind" has often been connected to changing and criticizing racist or colonial image conventions and thereby expand and empower visibilities of formerly disenfranchised people.

Let us further consider the idea of the citizen as a person who takes part in protests a little, in a small digression. The scene of the silent demonstration in *Conversations* shall be read against another scene, a literary image, still set during apartheid, which the author Ivan Vladislavić described in his novel *Double Negative*. It is a similar tableau of a graffiti mural, in front of which a crowd of *white* citizens has gathered due to a bomb alarm:

> Everyone flapped about, outraged and delighted, full of righteous alarm. Model citizens. Along the façade of the building was a mural, a line of black figures on a white background, and this separate-but-equal crowd drew my attention. They looked on solemnly, although their eyes were popping. The masses, I thought, silent majority, observing this self-important European anxiety with Assyrian calm.[52]

Which allusions and interpretations of South African society and history get transported in this quote? What has happened to the "silent majority" of the African population in South Africa, who watch the self-righteous Europeans without talking, now in post-apartheid times? I am interested in the way in which this account manages to compare different ways of acting like "citizens" and performing community. I want to borrow the term "model citizen" since it is useful in thinking through an idea of who is believed to be a "good citizen" versus who is considered "deviant." Vladislavić comments on and implicitly criticizes the belief that the "model citizens" of

South African society are the self-assured white Europeans. He points out that the majority of the population who do not speak and who exhibit a different behavior than the "model citizens" are "black figures." Yet the term "masses" with "Assyrian calm" is also problematic—to see the African part of the population only as a mass and not as individuals. However, in the silent demonstration scene in *Conversations* there are not "masses." Instead it is a rather small group of people, but they are radiating a calmness that is palpable. The improvised jazz tune adds a slightly haunting note to the encounter, which the viewer experiences from Keniloe's point of view, who is startled but not alarmed, passing through the protest group and moving on.

An imaginary right to opacity was discussed when analyzing the identity photograph in the previous chapter. There should be a possibility to stay invisible, out of sight, silent, unwritten, as a possibility for different states of becoming beyond any prescribed notion of citizenship and society. This entails not just a possibility of escape for people on the margins like illegalized migrants who live in a field dominated by (mostly negative) hyper-visibility on the one hand and invisibility on the other, but also the possibility for hegemonic subjects to see themselves differently.

Staying outside of the realm of (documentary) images, is often also a strategy not to be deported. Yet there is an imperceptible politics acted out in these everyday practices against the control of the nation-state.[53] The term "imperceptible politics" together with the "autonomy of migration" provides concepts beyond simple activism and new dogmas. The remaking of our bodies in the present, the way we perceive, feel, act"[54] provides a powerful insistence on the state of continuous becomings. What kind of artworks, photographs, and films can be made with this in mind (sometimes defying the visual scope altogether)? The fight for just representation and inclusion of migrants may be an outdated activist approach, and I quote Tsianos, Stephenson, and Papadopoulus again: "Despite all these variations in the treatment of migration the main question was the assignment of rights and representational visibility to migrants."[55] Yet this does not mean that so-called outdated formats of visual politics like the activist film or the practice of counter memory, which often consist of putting a name and a face to the forgotten, have ceased to exist. They remain meaningful and effective for example in the context of Spivak's "strategic essentialism." However, in the visual domain more and more image producers and artists are already using complex reenactments and stagings, and follow the direction of fiction and abstraction to make a statement about the various reality/ies of migrant life. Migrants as well as other subjectivities on the margins of South African society are thus leaving the position of victims and instead are reenacting their experiences, like in Thenjiwe Nkosi's film *Border Farm*.

The next chapter will move from documentary to fiction and back by looking at *real* aliens, complicating the notion of the other in South African society and a look at migrating images and recurring historical images in the double mirror provided by the South African feature film *District 9*.

5.2 From Documentary to Fiction—and Back: *District 9*

District 9 showcases a dystopian depiction charged with affective images of South African post-apartheid society, directed by white South African Neill Blomkamp.[56] The film narrates the arrival and long-term stay of extraterrestrial aliens, whose situation mirrors both the injustices of the apartheid past and the recent events of xenophobic violence against African migrants in South Africa in 2008. *District 9* moves between genres; it has been called a "science fiction film," yet it works and looks very different from the typical Hollywood sci-fi flick. I argue that the film uses certain Afrofuturist themes.

Moreover, the film presents images of "alien migrants" who are stuck on Earth as well as W. J. T. Mitchell's "migrating images," in this case the restaging of historical images, which have moved from other contexts.[57] Mitchell's notion of "migrating images" indicates images that have left their original context and reappear in a different one, sometimes still bearing traces from their former location. "Migrating images" is a meta-picture, a term that denotes a reflective image and starts a second order discourse on visualizations. However, Mitchell develops his argument further by equating the control of the visual sphere with other forms of control like forced removals or ethnic cleansing, claiming that "[t]he removal of images, of sacred sites, and of persons is all one process."[58] This adds another denotation to his "migrating images" theory, where images are considered to have agency and are treated as quasi-organisms.[59]

It seems theoretically seductive to connect this with the idea of controlling the look of a city, and constructing a white "European" city, by forcibly removing the African people, as was done in apartheid South Africa, and as is done with "informal settlements and squats" in post-apartheid South Africa. The visual regime structured around the topics of sanitation and overcrowding, "decent" living situations, and "civilization" has arguably changed since apartheid and colonial times, however there are certain continuities now under the changed auspices of neoliberal capitalism in post-apartheid.[60]

District 9 can be seen as a paradigm of a film that is staged and fictional, yet deeply invested with documenting current situations and commenting on *real* society and history. It locates the extraterrestrial species right in the middle of Johannesburg and thus centers around the question of who is "us" and who are "the foreigners" using hybrid visual and narrative strategies. As American post-colonial film scholar Marguerite Waller has claimed: "Science-fiction films . . . often take a certain decolonization of the imagination as one of their aims, projecting futures that magnify the dark areas of the present and past."[61]

Flashbacks of the repeated images of colonial, apartheid and post-apartheid and global history in *District 9* are deciphered and analyzed in terms of how they are used to construct evidence through imitating documentary film strategies and by creating affective images. In a second thread the construction of the aliens as the *other* in South African society is examined, as this references the living situation and stereotypes surrounding the real African migrants and specifically also the "Nigerians," as well as the possibility of an Afrofuturistic dimension of these fictional aliens.

Aliens in Johannesburg

District 9 is included in my selection since it is a prime example of the proliferation of the strategies of a mixed-media collage and combination of several image-spaces. The film is a hybrid, narratively split into several parts, starting as a "mockumentary," showing staged television news footage. A very large spaceship has broken down and is hovering over Johannesburg. The aliens, who are only males and considered to be some kind of workers, are rescued from their unusable ship and start living in a shantytown.[62] They are here to stay indefinitely in South Africa, much to the distress of the local population, who are scared of the foreign species, looking akin to armored insects; and they fear crime and insecurity. Only the Nigerians, who are equally marginalized, interact with the aliens. Over a period of twenty years, the fronts harden and the local communities begin organizing protests against the alien camp. When the tensions between the stranded aliens and the locals turn violent, the politicians assign the private security company MNU to evict and resettle the aliens in a camp farther away from the city.

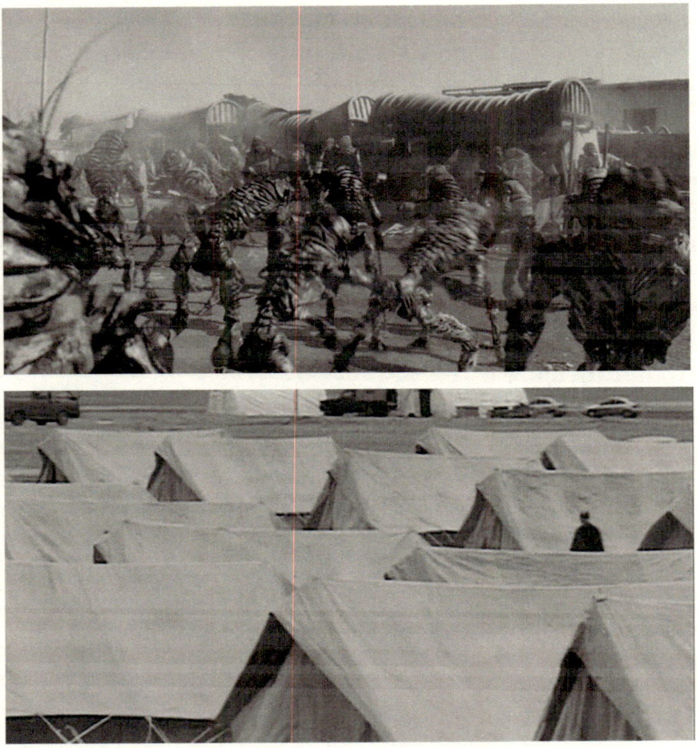

Figure 5.2.1. The aliens on Earth, and the camps that they have to stay in, stills from *District 9*.

The main character is the white South African Wikus van der Merve, who is to implement and oversee the MNU operation. In this part *District 9* turns into a typical action film. In the process of the evacuation Wikus becomes infected by an alien substance.[63] As a consequence his body slowly turns into an alien form over a period of several days. Wikus subsequently changes sides and now fights together with an individualized alien by the name of "Christopher" against the humans to restart one of their spaceships. In the end, through the cooperation of Wikus and the aliens against the aggressive MNU fighters, Christopher and his son manage to fly away in a small spaceship. Wikus survives and lives in his changed body among the aliens, waiting for Christopher's return.

The actuality, multiple points of reference, and poignancy of *District 9* immediately stirred up heated discussions in film magazines, newspapers, and blogs in South Africa, as well as in the United States, England, and Nigeria. Some criticized *District 9* as yet another tale of the white male hero's redemption, others appraised it as an example of "New African Cinema."[64] In my reading of the film, however, I will demonstrate that both of these judgments are over-simplified by moving beyond simple equations of representation and also looking at the self-reflective elements inherent in this film.

Staged Documents and Affective Intensity

District 9 uses confessional speech acts and testimonies to create a high level of intensity and intimacy with the viewers. Interviews in a reportage television style and as a so-called "home story" are used in the beginning and ending to create a live feeling and an affective assemblage of excitement and danger. These speech-acts are playfully staged like common documentary television formats, such as the docu-soap. The first seconds show no image; the screen is black, while only the main character Wikus's voice is heard as he is self-consciously testing the clip-on microphone and chattering with the television crew as in a making-of-scene, conveying that the viewer is being shown something private, or exclusive.

Then—as if the camera has accidentally just been turned on—the image appears. Here the audience first encounters Wikus in his office where a "home story" is shot prior to the start of the evacuations; the logo of the company MNU, which stands for Multi-National United is visible in the lower right corner of the frame. A few moments later, the recording situation itself is commented on for a second time with a self-reflective irony; when Wikus has now settled for his "official" statement, a text insert has been superimposed on the image in the lower-left corner, giving both his and his company's name. He then asks the camera operator, "Must I look here?" In reply, he is told to "look right at the lens" for his statement.

The command "to look someone right into the eye"—here through the camera at the audience—is associated both with the delivery of confessions and with testimonies in a court context. It is commonly believed that people will tell the truth if they have to exchange direct gazes with another, and that they are unable to lie in this situation, or if they do in fact lie, the other person will be able to detect it in their face. Usually, in fiction films the presence of the camera is unacknowledged by the actors, who never look directly into it, except by mistake, since it destroys the suspension of disbelief between the fiction and the audience, in theatrical terms the so-called "fourth wall."[65] Thus the acknowledgment of the recording situation and the direct addressing of the camera and by extension of the audience is normally one important distinction between documentary and fiction film. *District 9* purposefully blurs the line between the two genres and manages to portray "sincerity" and "live-ness" by including this staged scene of "making-of," using the concept of a film inside the film.

The second unexpected performance by Wikus is that he shows the TV crew a photograph of his wife—calling her "his angel": this affectively charges and personalizes his statement.[66] It also characterizes him as a loving partner and not just a professional doing his job. The scene, in combination with his acted camera-shyness in front of the television crew, makes Wikus a lot more likable and humanizes him, since every person likes to look at and show photos of a loved one; it is a universal gesture. At the same time the film oscillates here toward the fictional again, as it already foreshadows that this happy relationship is in danger and his wife will lose him, thus calling on normative storytelling conventions. The scene with the private snapshot is repeated at end of the film, acting as a narrative bracketing, when the wife now longs for Wikus who has disappeared, and whom she has not seen since he transformed into an alien. She looks at an old photograph of him as a human, thus the two personal photographic snapshots frame the whole plot of *District 9* and strategically use the affective power of the personal documentary portrait.[67]

Replaying CNN

All sequences that introduce the arrival of the aliens are edited in a breathless stream of live images pretending to be *real* documentary footage from official television newscasts, surveillance footage, eye-witness accounts, filming from a helicopter—,all MNU's footage as embedded journalism documenting their own operation, as well as a reportage on Wikus's family. Typescript and text inserts on top of the documentary images signify liveness. The frequent cuts and layered accounts create an affective intensity of excitement and foreboding. The story of what has happened since the aliens' arrival twenty years ago to the point of the now-time of the film is seemingly naturally spliced together from these different sources, cutting back and force between news reports and the voices of experts, a sociologist, a police officer, a technical scientist and a female aid worker, who insists that "at first a lot of attention was given to giving the aliens proper status and protection," as there was a lot of pressure on South Africa with "the whole world watching." The whole section is a sophisticated CNN persiflage, a matrix of the media age of our times.

The film cuts to the interview with a "concerned citizen," portraying different voices from "the man or woman from the street," as for example a black woman who complains about the governments' action: "They are spending so much money to keep them here, when they could be spending it on other things. But at least they are keeping them separate from us." Interestingly enough these short statements often do not name the aliens as such, but just talk about "them" or "they." As another woman explains: "They can take the sneakers off your feet, or your cell phone and they kill you." This leaves it open for the audience to fill in the information about whom they exactly mean by "they." Here no images of the aliens are shown, and they are just stand-ins for people's fears. In fact, director Blomkamp had asked people on the street what they were thinking about the human African migrants, and these were the answers he received.[68] "The aliens must just go, I do not know where, but they must go," relates a black family father, while a white man speaking in Afrikaans proposes releasing a "virus, a selective virus, near the aliens," basically calling for their complete extinction.

Then the film returns to the main character Wikus, who explains that the removal of the aliens into a fenced of camp—euphemistically called "Sanctuary Park, Alien Relocation Camp"—200 km away from Johannesburg is the better solution for both the humans and the aliens, who he also calls "prawns." This separation of humans and aliens in South Africa immediately reminds one of the apartheid doctrine of separate development, the re-zoning of inhabited settlements, and the practice of forced removals and eviction of non-white people from urban areas into the townships and "homelands."

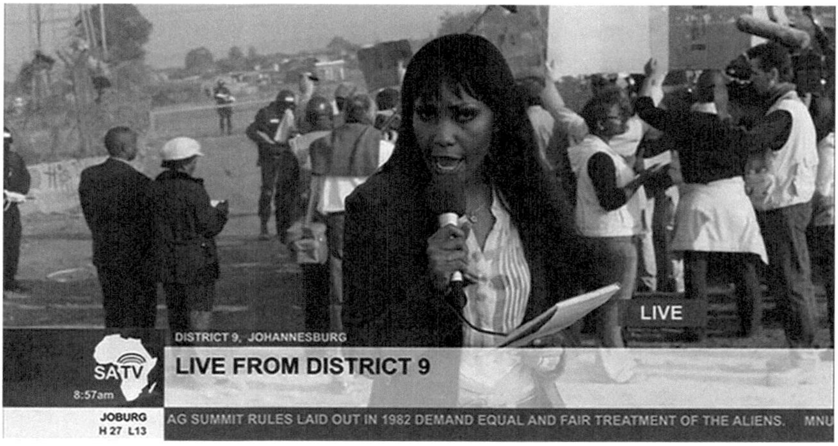

Figure 5.2.2. Staged news cast, still from *D9.*

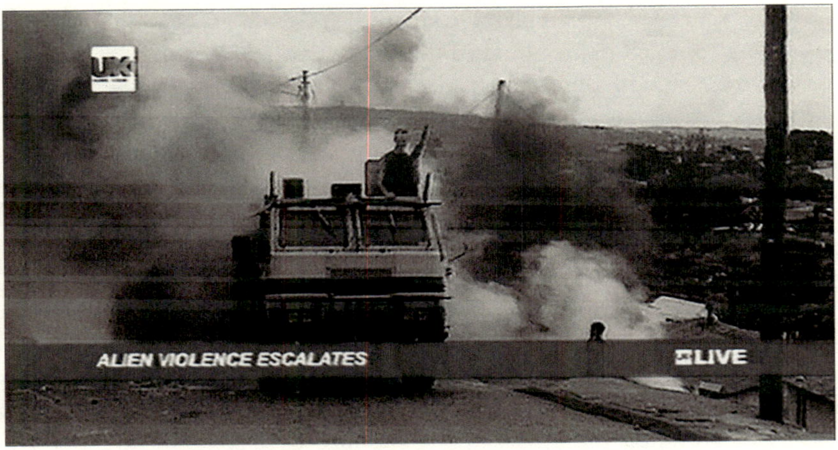

Figure 5.2.3. Staged news cast, still from *D9*.

The text "Alien Violence Escalates" is highlighted with the color red and the words LIVE in the right corner (see figure 5.2.3 above). One can see an armored vehicle, the Casspir that was also used by the South African apartheid police, with a white policeman standing on lookout presumably shouldering a rifle. The vehicle is driving through fire and flames, and large parts of the frame are filled with varying shades of heavy smoke. On the lower-right side a black person is visible and some roofs of small buildings, a typical location of a former township. Many of the documentary images presented were taken from the 2008 reporting on the xenophobic attacks and protests. Only the voiceover and small details, for example the signs, add the narration of the spaceship and the aliens. The real audio-visual documents are restaged here under fictional auspices. On the day when the eviction of the aliens is about to start, a female black reporter speaks live from the location of conflict in an unidentified township setting (see figure 5.2.2). In the background some black and a few white people are protesting, holding self-made cardboard signs; one can glimpse the handwritten text "We love Prawns" with a heart on one. Reporters and policemen surround them. "Alien Rights Will be Monitored," the commentary says; this is a pro-alien demonstration by a human rights group.

Simultaneously, the preparation of the MNU operation itself is intercut with interviews with members of Wikus's family and employees, who already comment on the proceedings in hindsight, so here we again encounter different time levels folded on top of each other to heighten the affective intensity and give the audience the hint that the operation will not go as planned. One of the high-ranking MNU's armed employees, called "cowboy," seemingly strikes the camera person. The camera sways and only shows shaky images of the ground, while on the audio track one can hear the captain snarl "get the camera out of my face!" It is thus implicated to the audience that they are getting to watch something exclusive that some people are trying to keep invisible. Furthermore, a young black man, who is specified as "Fundiswa Mhlanga, Former MNU Trainee" says: "I just want everyone to watch this right now to learn from what has happened," while another MNU employee, a white man, says: "I don't think he can be forgiven, because what he [Wikus] did was like a betrayal."

As the detailed analysis of the beginning sequence has shown, *District 9* has crossed formal borders and already changed the way of addressing the spectator several times in its very first minutes, thus it is "hyper-reflective on its own status as a medium."[69] Later the film image repeatedly switches to a black-and-white control monitor image, as if the footage of a second security camera is spliced into the film, suggesting both the *liveness* of the situation, as well as the panoptic vision of always yet another camera watching, even if just on automatic mode, thus also commenting on the prevalence of CCTV for security.

Moreover, the film presents not just a meta-discourse on seeing and documenting or on aliens arriving, claiming space, staying on against the will of the locals. In a nutshell all of the prevalent conflicts of post-apartheid society are already drafted in this beginning sequence: the question of documenting and learning from history, pressure from the international community, the negotiation of human rights, the question of who is a foreigner in South Africa, as well as the impossible act of forgiveness and the reproach of betrayal. These conflicts and how they interleave the conventional storyline will be further unraveled by looking at the historical quotations and the material presented on exclusion and othering.

Overlapping and Folded Time Layers in *District 9*

When the archival footage of the arrival of the aliens is shown, the year 1982 is visible in the lower corner, indicating that the spaceship arrived when apartheid was still in place, and thereby linking it to the past. For a

South African audience *District 9's* very title is already a historical quotation, as it refers to the location of "District 6"—a "mixed" living area in central Cape Town, a lively social hub of colored and black culture. Due to the implementation of the Natives Resettlement Act of 1954, "District 6" was declared a whites-only area in 1966 and in 1968 removals of non-white residents and the demolition of their homes started. In 1982 over 60,000 people had been evicted and were moved to the Cape Flats township, which was 25 km outside the city and lacking in services and transportation. In comparison the aliens in *District 9* are moved to a euphemistically named "Alien Sanctuary Park" that is 200 km outside of Johannesburg.

The real historic location of "District 6" became a privileged site of remembrance with its own museum after 1994.[70] Yet besides the nominal reference and the looming prospect of its destruction and the evacuation of its inhabitants, there are not many other parallels between the historic "District 6," which had a vibrant life, and the informal settlements in the film location of *District 9*, mostly consisting of shacks and no real houses, where the lives of both humans and aliens seem to be only about precarious survival. The ghetto-like space of the aliens that look like a refugee camp that has become permanent, are presented as an unreadable place of danger and despair, sin and filth, where sensational events like inter-species prostitution, fights, illegal gambling, and other informal economic activities are happening.

The now-time of the film, however, when the riots between aliens and humans started, is given as 2002, meaning that the aliens have already stayed for twenty years in their informal camp outside of Johannesburg and are now living in post-apartheid times that do not treat them any better. In the final sequence one is informed that 2.5 million aliens continue to live in *District 10,* the new camp after *District 9*, and that it is growing. Another haunting parallel is that during the shooting of the film in Chiawelo, a section of Soweto, the black people living there were in fact also removed, not due to the film set, but because the whole area was marked for evacuation. Apparently, some people received RDP-houses, whereas others had nowhere to go.[71]

"It's Real!"—Maps, Zones, Posters, and Signs

The film's release was accompanied by a whole cross-platform viral media campaign. Similarly to the film, the carefully designed *District 9* website repeated images from the South African national documentary memory archive, making it look "all too familiar" for the South African audience as well as for an international audience aware of rudimentary parts of apartheid history. The still images here acted as authentication strategies to create evidence to make the audience feel that "this is real" and to construct an affective involvement that seemed uncannily familiar.[72] The *District 9* website presented the viewer with a bird's-eye view of many shack settlements, the repletion of the colonial or imperial gaze of an area with informal settlements. It also included a compass. Maps have the function of presenting places for (visual) consumption and thus constructing relationships among space, identity, and representation.[73] They are a special kind of operational images. The film's website imitates similar sites like *GoogleMaps*, offering the viewer the possibility to zoom into the zone where the aliens reside, which is cast as dangerous through the accompanying text that spells out "Local Alert System," and "Community Watch." All of these key words allude to the heavy securitization and restrictions of movement in post-apartheid society, where surveillance cameras, private security firms, motion detectors, and community watch groups are the rule.[74] Moreover, the aerial view also recalls iconic historical footage of violence in the townships, most prominently from the Soweto Uprising 1976, which was often filmed from the air, as well as in more recent times of the helicopter shots of police raids in news footage.

The signs that were used on the website and in the advertising campaign made the viewers familiar with the idea of alien/human segregation. When entering the website one had to click on a button, choosing whether one wanted to enter the site as a "human" or as an "alien." Similar signs were included in short scenes in the film itself, where it says "No Non-Human Loitering" or "No, not Welcome." Below the image a fictitious law sentence is given, "Mandate 114-118 Enforcement Area," thus constructing a whole official-looking system of pseudo-laws concerning the aliens. Yet these signs and texts also look very similar to post-apartheid anti-hawking signs in the inner city of Johannesburg, only that these in reality do not target extraterrestrial visitors but rather poor African migrants trying to eke out a living in the informal sector.

Iconographically they stand in the tradition of pictograms signifying who is not allowed in a certain location with the silhouette of an alien in black crossed out with red. The text asks the viewer to report non-humans. In the small print it also says, "This restaurant reserves the right to refuse service to all non-humans," reminding one immediately of the separate restaurants and hotels during apartheid. Further signs also warned about the risk of "infection," communicating the idea that the aliens are carriers of diseases that can harm humans. All of these images allude to apartheid signs of "For Whites only,"[75] or repeat struggle poster terminology and iconography both from the anti-apartheid protest as well as from the more recent protests against "xenophobia" after 2008.

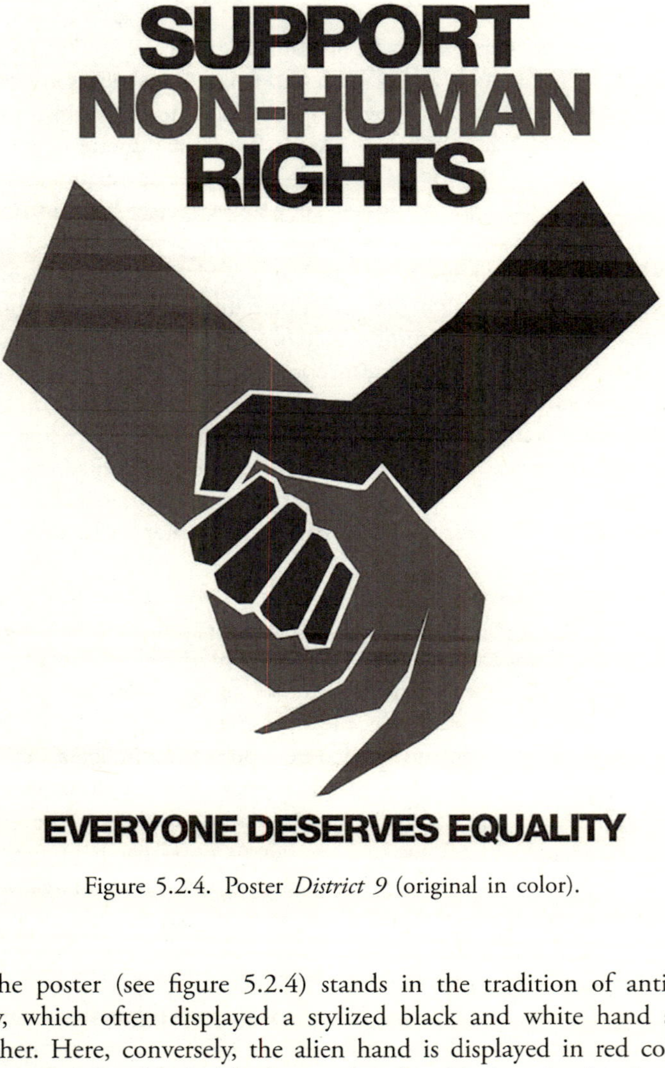

Figure 5.2.4. Poster *District 9* (original in color).

The poster (see figure 5.2.4) stands in the tradition of anti-racism imagery, which often displayed a stylized black and white hand shaking each other. Here, conversely, the alien hand is displayed in red color and the human hand in black. The human hand in black grabs the alien's wrist quite firmly, almost looking like a "black power" symbol of the raised black fist.[76] The hand is the foremost body part that people who do not know each other may touch. The handshake is a human gesture with many functions, from greeting to an act of forgiveness or to close a business deal. Accordingly, it is the privileged motif when trying to opt for sympathy with strangers and trying to establish a connection or asking for reconciliation.

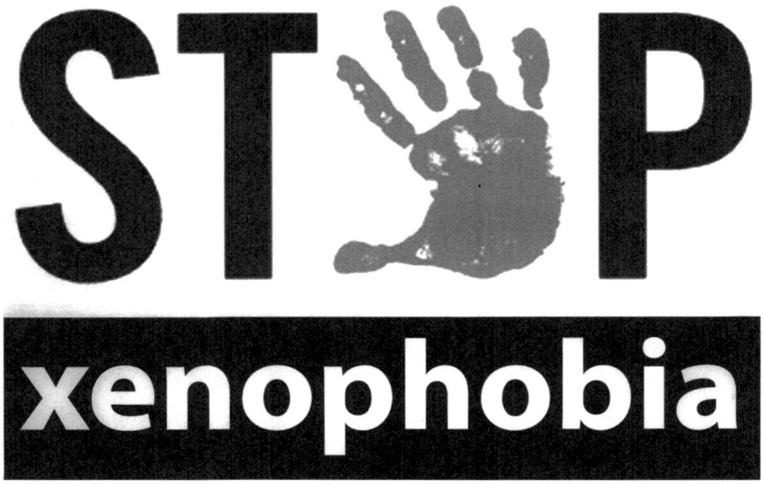

Figure 5.2.5. Poster by the APF "Stop Xenophobia," 2008, SAHA (original in color).

Not surprisingly, current posters that were created after the xenophobic attacks in 2008 used similar motives of a handshake or a hand as part of their emblem, such as on a poster by the Anti-Privatization Forum (APF).[77] Here the yellow imprint of a hand substitutes the letter "o" in the word "Stop." It looks as if it had been plunged in finger paint, and as if the hand wanted to block the violence, making itself as large as possible. The hand-print that is never perfect but instead always shows some areas with less paint, or where the hand failed to press hard enough against the surface, reminds one that this is only the trace of a real hand and alludes to the fragility of the human body. The other letters of the word "Stop" are purple—the complementary color of yellow, making both colors stand out and intensifying their luminance. The word "xenophobia" employs a similar color contrast of white lettering on a black background.

The "helping hand" or the reconciliatory "handshake" are thus a well-known icon moving through history and different contexts—an example of a Mitchellian migrating image. The film playfully combines all of these images, visual quotations, symbols, and signs as an energetic affective assemblage to create an intensity and recombination of codes that start a reflection beyond simple analogies to the use of motifs in art history.[78]

Afrofuturist Themes

The first outstanding image of *District 9*—the stranded spaceship over Johannesburg—is visually a hijacked metaphor of the Afrofuturist mothership. In the mid-nineties Mark Dery coined the term "Afrofuturism" to describe science fiction by African-American writers:

> African-American signification that appropriates images of technology and a prosthetically enhanced future—might, for want of a better term, be called Afrofuturism. The notion of Afrofuturism gives rise to a troubling antinomy: Can a community whose past has been deliberately rubbed out, and whose energies have subsequently been consumed by the search for legible traces of its history, imagine possible futures?[79]

The African-American musician and artist Sun Ra became one of the prominent figures of Afrofuturism, claiming that he was from outer space and creating a mystical alter ego that merged science fiction, space travel, and Egyptian mysticism.[80] Sun Ra stated: "I never wanted to be a part of planet Earth, but I am compelled to be here, so anything I do for this planet is because the Master-Creator of the Universe is making me do it. I am of another dimension."[81] The "mothership" from outer space is the reverse of the slave ship, and creates an imaginary history of African Americans, living on the margins of American society, as being from another planet and waiting for the return to their motherland; but it also became a powerful tool to imagine new fantastic black futures. Afrofuturist themes of space travel, use of new technology, life on other planets, and the creation of a new hybrid race were further developed in music and literature.[82]

District 9 alludes to the possibility of hybridization beyond the color line and of becoming the other. It is made from a white perspective with the anti-hero Wikus, being a white male South African, and yet is a view from the post-colonial periphery.[83] In the end, Wikus merges not only with the alien, but also with their technology, as he becomes a cyborg, a fighting robot to help the start of the spaceship. In this portrayal of the aliens, and Wikus as becoming alien, the film drafts life beyond the anthroprocentric frame.

Double-Seeing the Aliens

The aliens in *District 9* need to be seen in two contexts: first they are subject to similar laws as were people classified as "Black" or as "Colored" during the

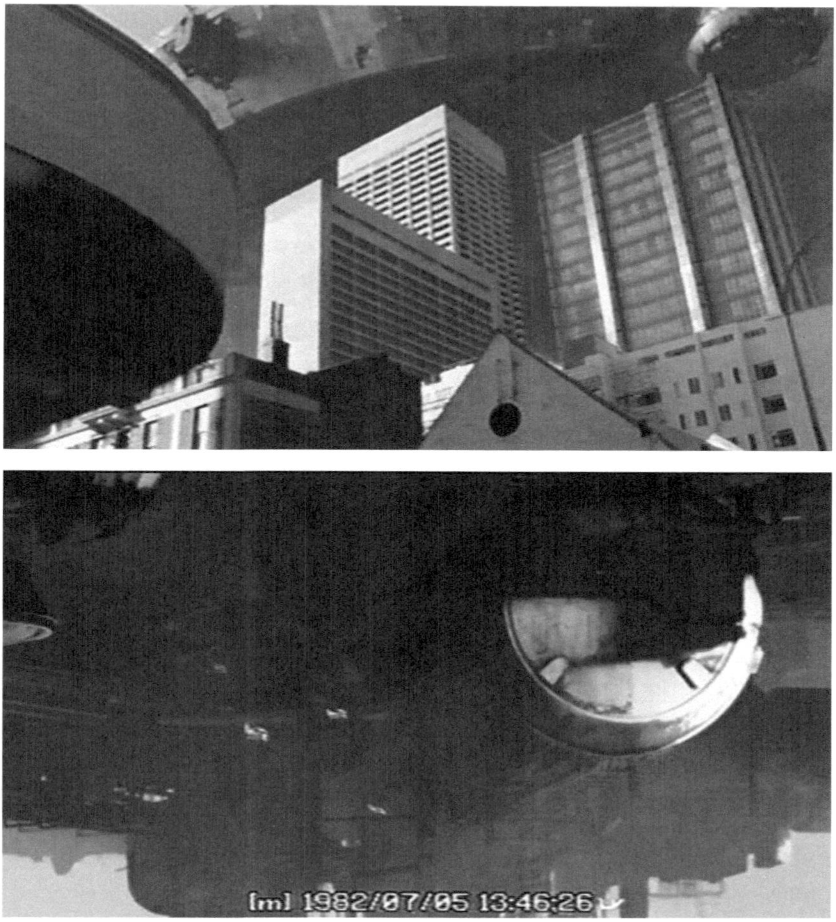

Figure 5.2.6. Spaceship over Johannesburg, stills from *D9.*

apartheid regime, and second they face discrimination similar to that against the African migrants in post-apartheid South Africa. In a telling scene the aliens are delivered eviction notices twenty-four hours before their removal is scheduled. Naturally the aliens cannot read or understand the notices, yet they are asked to "sign here." Seemingly adhering to "democratic norms" and laws, this scene spells out the injustice of the bureaucratic measures and again relates back to zoning practices and forced removals. All of the aliens are conceptualized as males only, as a working population that was sent out into the galaxy, parallel to the migrant labor system under apartheid.

The majority of the aliens are presented as inhabiting an area similar to the space of colonized people and are derogatorily called "prawns" by the human population. "Prawns" are one of the lowest types of animal, not even being mammals, and therefor far removed from humans, often considered to be without much intelligence or agency. However, the behavior of the aliens resists any too easy comparisons. The South African human experts ambivalently describe them as "helpless and malnourished," but also as "seeing violence as a recreational activity," for example, de-railing human trains, stealing electricity, and taking human lives. Yet in another scene an alien's statement is subtitled as saying "We just want to go home," which is the prime statement of any homesick migrant always wanting to return home, which is nostalgically cast as the better place.

A sociologist describes them as "bottom feeders, scavengers," another scientist adds "aimless." The characterization as "aimless" echoes with descriptions of the colonized Africans by the European colonizers, who deemed human intervention necessary on behalf of others who seemed unable to take care of themselves.[84] As Fanon analyzed, the imperial powers saw only "torpid creatures, wasted with fevers, obsessed by ancestral customs, form an almost inorganic background for the innovating dynamism of colonial mercantilism."[85] The aliens are thus unreadable, animal-like creatures to the human population. The "normal" South African people cannot understand them. This not-understanding is an experience similar to what Fanon described as "colonial neurosis." Colonial neurosis has several symptoms—one being that the colonizer is incapable of identifying with the colonized.

Yet one of the aliens is presented as the caring father of a young and bright son. This individualized father is also given the human name "Christopher." Again this is an analogy to the apartheid government, which gave anglicized names to the African population in their pass books.[86] The alien, called Christopher, is the only one that the audience may be able to identify with and he becomes the best friend of the main human character, Wikus. The film cleverly produces an inversion: while one may at first have feared the aliens, by the second half of the film, I as the viewer have changed sides together with Wikus and now fear the humans, especially after witnessing their cruel medical experiments on the aliens and Wikus.

In addition, the aliens' living situation references the recent fate of thousands of African immigrants who sought asylum from poverty and war-torn regions. Film director Blomkamp had interviewed black South Africans about what they thought of black Nigerians and Zimbabweans.[87] The aliens have to stay in makeshift camps outside the city, similar to those of the African migrants after the attacks, but also structurally analogous to the former townships during apartheid and informal settlements in post-apartheid times. There are not only allusions to specific South African history, though, but also to global history, as the Holocaust is cited through the cruel and deadly lab experiments that the white scientists perform on captured aliens. The humans presented in *District 9* thusly regard the aliens as "unworthy to live" life. Yet the aliens are not simply victims or docile creatures, but in fact are cunning, non-integrating, and resisting, as well as violating codes of the human society. They are not "model citizens" and have no interest in dialogue with the humans beyond rudimentary trade transactions, and thus they could be described with the figure of "preferred silence" as an intentional strategy, not wanting to share their intelligence and knowledge about their source of energy as well as the technology of their space vessel with the humans.[88]

The film is very ambivalent in its portrayals, unnerving the viewers and compelling them to make up their own minds about the aliens, who are only introduced through the ways the humans perceive them. While they are shown as wild and dangerous creatures in the television footage, eating raw bloody meat and scavenging through garbage, the individualized alien Christopher is later shown acting completely differently in his shack-turned-science-laboratory. In this private realm, sheltered from the outside, Christopher seems to live a human-like existence and works meticulously on restarting the broken-down spaceship.

Wikus, however, is tracked as becoming more and more "barbaric," at least on the "outside," as he turns into an alien. This seems to be a conscious restaging of white stereotypes about blacks, now projected onto the white man who transforms into an alien, thereby revealing that it was always already inside of him, too, and that it is only the white's abject self that is now becoming visible.[89] Moreover, this could also be read as a coming dimension of the future, of developing a new hybrid race that goes beyond the humans. It is Wikus and the aliens who achieve success together in the end by cooperating on the now-repaired and flying space vessel. Christopher and his son inside the ship is a sign of hope—the aliens persevering over the evil humans from MNU.

"Look and Don't Look!"—The Presentation of Nigerians

As the eviction notices are delivered by Wikus and his crew, who are all afraid of the aliens and protected by gunmen, more information about the aliens and their living situation is revealed. The aliens are addicted to cat food. "Nigerian drug dealers" are making business out of the alien's obsession, as the white female sociologist explains: "The Nigerians were involved in various scams, one was the cat food scam, where they sold cat food to the aliens for exorbitant prices." The "Nigerian drug dealer" is a stereotypical trope in South African public discourse, in the public imagination every person from Nigeria is seen as a drug dealer: "Nigerians appear frequently as stereotyped caricatures in the South African media."[90] However, one cannot escape the clichés, and therefore this film stages them provokingly. The stereotyping is part of *District 9*'s aesthetic strategy, which is applied equally to all presented groups.

In the beginning of the film a walkie-talkie sound byte informs us that we are "Entering the Nigerian compound." Here, for the first time we see African people—"Nigerians"—who are interacting with the aliens normally and without fear. A scene of a fight between two giant scorpion-like beasts, similar to illegal cockfights, is shown. Nigerians and aliens are betting with money bills, the winner is quickly determined and the crowd cheers happy and excitedly. The female expert's voice continues: "Not to mention inter-species prostitution, and they [the Nigerians] also dealt in the alien weaponry." An image of a beautiful, black woman in a dress is shown, and then some black men and aliens with fantastical weapons. A white male expert explains: "The Nigerians in District 9 are headed by a man called 'Abi Sanja' "—a black man sitting in a wheelchair, looking menacingly and majestically is shown—"a very powerful underground figure in Johannesburg." The image cuts back to Wikus saying to his colleague: "You don't want to be playing with these boys, they'll cut you in four pieces." He laughs, but at the same time is also seriously scared of the Nigerians, telling his crew: "Now don't look at him." meaning it is too dangerous to disturb or provoke the Nigerian boss by looking him openly in the face. They all lower their gazes and tiptoe away. The reverse shot shows the Nigerian boss staring menacingly back at them. This also calls to mind, though, how one would behave with a dangerous wild animal, for instance a savage dog, and thus puts the Nigerians on the same level as animals. But in this scene the film restages the visual regime of who has "the right to look," reversing the colonial power dynamic of the white male gaze and the black male gaze, where in this case the white male has to cast down his eyes, while at the same time denigrating the Nigerian men as hyper-violent and animalistic.

Yet to complicate the stereotypical presentation of the Nigerians and their status as "aliens" in South African society further, it is important to note that the clichés about foreigners gave the director the idea for the film narrative on "aliens in Johannesburg." Therefore, the film follows its own logic that the Nigerians who are stand-ins in the film for all other groups of African migrants in South Africa get along well, at least in terms of cooperating economically with the extraterrestrial aliens with whom they share experiences of discrimination. Later in the film, however, one learns that the Nigerians are also eating parts of the aliens' bodies in order to be able to use their weapons. In this context the African "muti"—a "traditional" medicine or object with healing power—is explained and ridiculed.[91] The Nigerians are portrayed as believing in African traditional healing and are thusly considered backward and not "modern."

In addition, that scene conveys that there is no "friendship" between aliens and humans, since all humans, even including the Nigerians, only use the aliens for their own interest in making money or trying to acquire the knowledge of their advanced weapons and technology. The Nigerians could be read as the most powerful group of humans, and the least fearful and most business-savvy, even though this portrayal remains firmly rooted in racist and colonial prejudices, alluding to "blood-thirst," physical violence, and hyper-masculinity. Yet the film makes clear that it never shows the viewer what the Nigerians or the extraterrestrial aliens are "really like," since one only sees them through the eyes of a normative cross-section of South African society.

Intense Reactions

District 9 was developed right in the buildup to the xenophobic attacks, and Blomkamp had made a short precursor film, *Alive in Joburg*.[92] This short piece was shot quickly and with almost no budget in 2005, but it already explored all the themes that were then used and expanded in *District 9* in a "rough cut version." This short film may indeed have acted like a seismograph, as Siegfrid Kracauer once posited, which shows social and societal phenomena—in this case racism and violence—before they are registered elsewhere in the mainstream or academic discourse.[93]

Moreover, *District 9* had reality effects even though it was fictional, because of its strong affective impact, the allusion to real historical events and the construction of "truth claims" about post-apartheid society, which were partly achieved through the usage of pseudo-documentary strategies. While the reference to the situation of African migrants living in South Africa was usually viewed as positive in the discussions and reviews of *District 9*, the stereotypical representations of Nigerians has met sharp criticism and even led to diplomatic tensions between Nigeria and South Africa.[94]

The film seems to develop sympathy for the ultimate "other"—the alien, at least in the individualized "Christopher"—while repeating stereotypes about real Nigerians. Yet, as Homi Bhabha observed, the stereotype is not problematic because it is a false representation but because it is a "fixity."[95] The film satirically spells out the stereotypes that are already prevalent all over the South African media, including academic discourse, and that influence police and immigration practices.[96] Thereby, it exposes these stereotypes toward African migrants that are held by both black and white South Africans and starts a discussion about this. In addition, it is important to keep in mind that no group in society is portrayed sympathetically in *District 9*, and one must question the wish to belong to this dysfunctional society.

The humans also betray Wikus and try to hunt him down. His public image is destroyed by a smear campaign on television that shows him having sex with an alien. It is made clear that this is homosexual sex, since all the aliens are male, which is considered scandalous and disgusting. Typical othering strategies are employed in terms of sexualization and pathologization outside prevailing normative categories, thus *District 9* cannot be heralded as innovating new ways of seeing the other and never offers the other's point of view. It manages, however, to complicate the framings and perspectives where the others become visible and by whom they are seen. Furthermore, it exposes typically white male (and at times female) speech acts, which describe the other and at the same time perform the ongoing effects of white privilege in post-apartheid society.

District 9 is foremost a critique of the present state of South African society in post-apartheid times; it shows modes of exclusion and the precarious clinging to the power of white masculinity, even though many key positions are also staffed by blacks. Furthermore, South Africans do not love the aliens.[97] Thereby, the anxiety of what counts as human and a radical rethinking of the boundaries of species becomes possible.[98] The film is pointing at the old wounds of "inherited" racism and segregation and in addition highlighting newly developing xenophobia in post-apartheid times. *District 9* deals with history/ies in a post-modern, mash-up collage style—in its strategy to create visual evidence by restaging documentary footage it alludes to history without caring about detailed historical accuracy and rejecting conventional aesthetics of the narrative-driven history drama.[99]

In my analysis I have concentrated on the documentary strategies used, the double mirror provided by the aliens, and the play with stereotypes and clichés. One can thus see the past and present juxtaposed, colliding, seeing both the details of everyday post-apartheid society—the proliferation of new securitization, and inner-city borders, and the abstraction of the extraterrestrial aliens—provoking one to think about who is included and excluded in post-apartheid society. Director Blomkamp explicitly stated: "In my opinion the film does not exist without Jo'burg. . . . I think Johannesburg represents the future. What I think the world is going to become looks like Johannesburg."[100] It critically examines the South African metropolis in the present and picks up topics of bio-politics and migration, and privatization of police and military. The film does not offer any solutions but inevitably raises questions about whether one can learn from history, or if historical injustices may be repeated over and over in new guises, while at the same time offering glimpses of a futurity beyond the human.

With its meta-dialogue on the image-space of apartheid documentary images *District 9* starts a reflection on the continued effect of historical visualization techniques and visual memory-making in the here-and-now. While these images seem uncannily familiar and to have "migrated" from apartheid into post-apartheid times, at the same time *District 9*'s ambivalent timeframe of taking place both in the past and in the present conveys an impossibility to overcome the past and conceive of a future. The viewer may become a "tourist in the past," which provides her with the opportunity of retrograde ordering and constructing a master narrative about apartheid.[101] And yet, this safe subject position of "overseeing and understanding" the past gets interrupted again through the links to the present societal situation, and through the quotations of the xenophobic attacks in 2008.

6

Conclusion

Affective Images of Belonging Re-Visited

In South Africa an asynchrony has crystallized in the two decades after the official end of apartheid. On the one hand an ambitiously ethical vocabulary has been inherited from Nelson Mandela's discourse on reconciliation and nation-building, on the other hand nefariousness and self-vigilant acts persist even after the end of the armed struggle against the apartheid government. In terms of image production, however, South Africa's situation is special since it has a group of national and international artists, photographers, filmmakers, and activists, who actively comment on these developments, combining aesthetics with the political and affective realm, and additionally construct a meta-discourse and add a layer of reflection. Despite their different approaches, the documentary images in photography and film encourage the viewer to think about historical and cultural representations of (South) Africa, particularly in relation to the question of community, belonging, and migration—"us" and "them"—always entangled with and complicated by questions of gender and race.

This study started by looking at a black-and-white documentary photograph of a pass-burning protest in Soweto outside of Johannesburg in 1961; it ends in a different time with an advertisement clip from Nando's, filmed in 2012 in color in the inner-city of Johannesburg, and a video installation by the Center for Historical Reenactments.[1] At first glance these two sources may have little in common. Yet when considering what is at stake in both of them, the affective contestations over citizenship, land, and belonging grounded in history/ies, they may act like a prism, offering us a last example of a visual dialogue and tying together all the topics explored in this study. Nando's is an international fast-food chain that started a "Diversity" campaign after the xenophobic attacks in South Africa. Nando's is notorious for their provocative advertising campaigns—especially their short film clips that often address societal or political problems—but the company is also actively involved in social work and funds cultural events.[2] The Center for Historical Reenactments is a collective of artists and writers based in Johannesburg with a keen interest in history that is not, however, narrowed down to a concern over historical facts or "truth."[3]

Nando's "Diversity" video shows a reenacted scene of African foreigners crossing the border somewhere—in a typical no-man's land. At the same time a voiceover states: "You know, what's wrong with South Africa? All you foreigners! You must all go back to where you came from." As to mark the point, a dry explosive sound is heard, and one of the persons that just went through the fence is dissolved in a cloud of smoke.

The film cuts to Johannesburg. The next scene is on a sidewalk in Hillbrow, where a tent is marked with a sign "Immigrations," in front of which a queue of black men and only two women has formed. The voiceover pipes in: "You Cameroonians, Congolese, Pakistanis, Somalis, Ghanaians and Kenyans." Every time a group is mentioned, some of the persons waiting in line are turned into a smoke cloud, speeding up in a staccato rhythm. "And of course you, Nigerians." Cutting to a scene that shows the stereotypical image of a Nigerian as a drug dealer on a street corner, making a

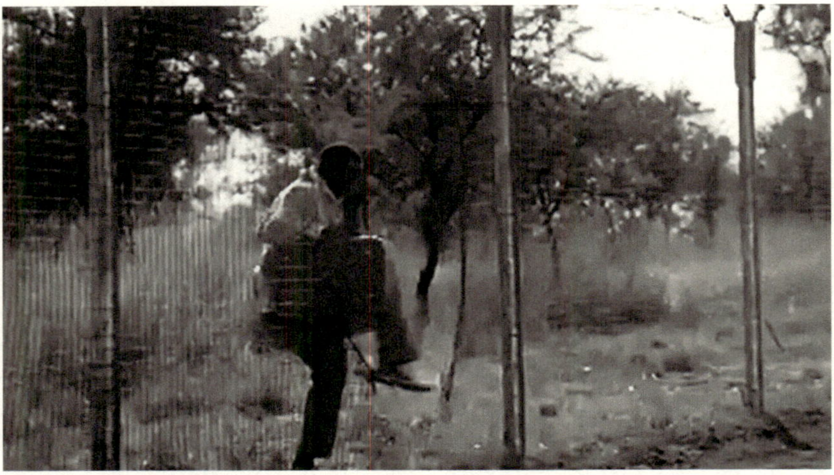

Figure 6.1. Still from Nando's "Diversity Clip."

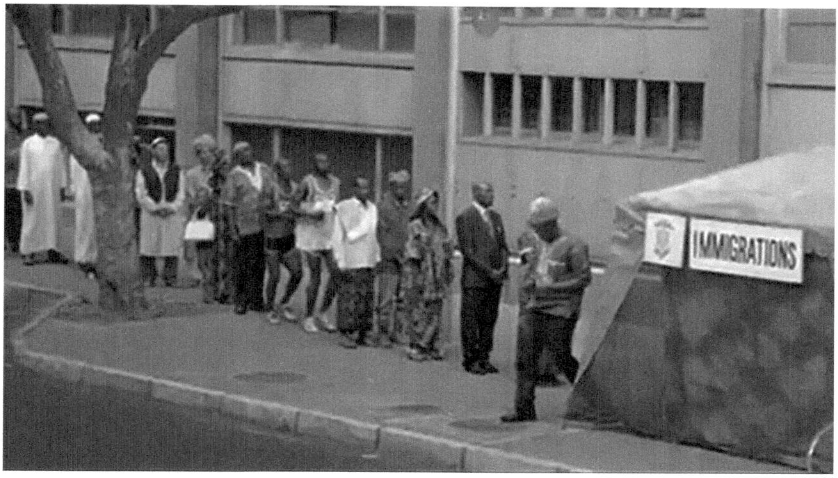

Figure 6.2. Still from Nando's "Diversity Clip."

transaction with a white couple in a posh car.[4] As if something has just come to his mind the speaker continues: "And of course, you Europeans," adding "Let's not forget all you Indians and Chinese." Next it cuts to a rural landscape with an older white Afrikaans farmer in a truck: "Even you, Afrikaaners." A view of the black African workers riding in the back is shown and hastily it adds: "Back to Swaziland for you Swatis, Lesotho for you Sothos, Tswana, Venda, Zulu—EVERYBODY."[5] Now one sees a cultivated field where a man looking like a Khoi-San stands in traditional attire half-naked, holding a bow and arrows.[6] He seems upset and is presumably talking in his native language, which is subtitled in English: "I'm not going anywhere. You found us here." The subtext of the clip "We are all foreigners here"—except the Khoi-San—reverses the idea of racist exclusion that was acted out during the xenophobic attacks in 2008.[7] While the clip has its strength as it playfully defines that everybody belongs to the new South Africa, and constructs a universal history of migration as the underlying common denominator of this diasporic nation, it does so through the reiteration of stereotypes. A variety of responses were elicited from public, and the broadcasting committee even banned the clip.[8] While journalist Maria Hengeveld observed: "South African advertising is known for its eagerness for political commentary; very little ends up being off-limits,"[9] one has to take into consideration that all advertisement tries to provoke and takes its prohibition into consideration for more publicity.

Artist Kemang Wa Lehulere, who was part of the Center for Historical Reenactments, was highly critical of the Nando's advertisement for a different reason, claiming that its subtext can also be read in such a way that the formerly disenfranchised black South Africans have "no right to the land now since everybody is a foreigner," and therefore "all have equal rights to the land."[10] This reading unveils the inherited injustices between the economically disadvantaged majority of the population of black South Africans and the predominantly white landowning people, dating back to the "Native Land Act" in 1913, as has been historically unraveled in the first chapter. South Africa still remains, in post-apartheid times, one of the countries with the highest social and economic inequality.[11] There has been no large-scale redistribution of land after 1994.

When read in this manner of everyone being "equal," the clip erases colonial and apartheid oppression by making everybody a non-native, a new arrival with the same rights as anyone else and in addition being "color-blind" to the continuing effects of racism. It adopts an epic temporality, as if zooming out of the historical context and pointing back to the pre-colonial times in Africa by citing the Khoi-San. On the positive side the diversity clip also renders the idea of "nativity" or a "real South African" obsolete and thus shines a critical light on the limitations of the post-1994 nation-building efforts. The final remark "Real South Africans love diversity" is a tongue-in-cheek comment on the national slogan "United in Diversity," and yet in the clip the diversity is ironically iterated as being about consumer choices between different fast-food meals.

Let's read another documentary and artistic video piece against the erasure of the specific histories of forced removals as presented in the subtext of the "Diversity Clip." South African emerging artist Michelle Monareng's video installation with the title *Removal to Radium* starts a different dialogue with the past as a concrete examination of black South African's dispossession of land by white missionaries, linking colonial with apartheid and post-apartheid history.[12] Monareng's installation was presented by the Center for Historical Reenactments at the Berlin Biennale 2014 and elsewhere. The piece consists of three separate video loops and mixed media—photographs and texts from Monareng's grandfather Sonnyboy Abram Shikwane's personal archive.[13] Removal to Radium portrays Shikwane's community's history of a loss, as well as the sustained inequities in the present.

In 1875 the white Reverend Herman Düring arrived in Rietspruit from the Berlin Lutheran Church. He consequently convinced the "native" community members that their documents and land title deeds would be safer in his care in the iron-corrugated church rather than in their thatch-roofed houses.[14] The 1913 Land Act further empowered Düring to dispossess the black community of Rietspruit, which was eventually relocated to Radium, a barren area in the Kalahari desert in 1965 under apartheid laws.[15] Monareng used photographs, documents, and video footage from her grandfather and also revisited the place herself and recorded her own video footage there. She has also visited archives in Berlin while on an artist residency trying to uncover more details of this contested history; her project is still continuing, adding different materials to the project at each stage.[16]

She wanted to "emphasize narratives that are excluded from official historical narratives," since she believes that what has been omitted "reveals more about the past."[17] Her installation contextualizes who once lived there and how this land was extracted from the community of Rietspruit.[18] In Monareng's video an old black man clad in light clothes is kneeling down on one leg, bowing, and touching the ground with his right hand (see figures below and on the next two pages) as if he were blessing it. It adds a tactile, dedicated presence to the abstract notion of land ownership, as an embodied affective gesture. In a second video one sees a person on a meadow covered in mist, a bull coincidentally enters the frame. Both the bull and the human figure almost merge with the background, stepping in and out of visibility, giving off a ghostly presence. The video loops showcase both

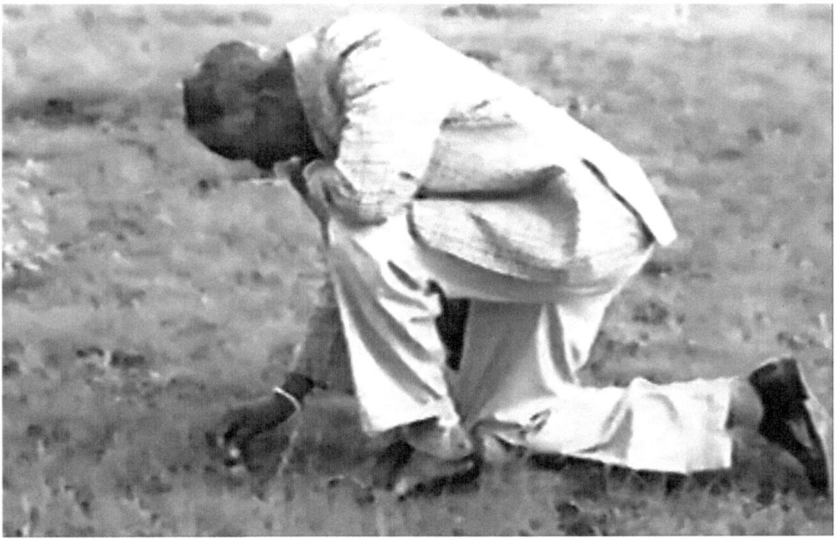

Figure 6.3. Still from Michelle Monareng's *Removal to Radium.*

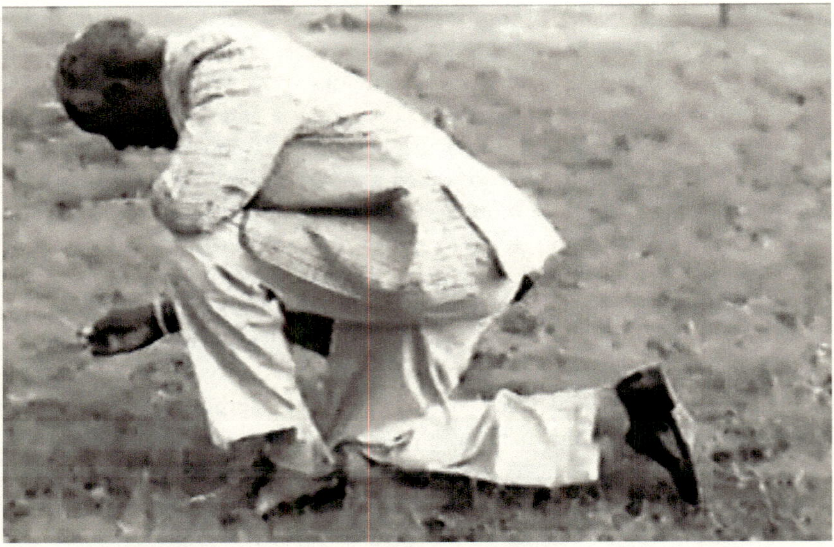

Figure 6.4. Still from Michelle Monareng's *Removal to Radium.*

the documentary as well as the manipulative aspects of video technology by using juxtapositions, repetitions and different play-back speeds of the visual footage of an empty landscape. M. Blackmann, reviewing Monareng's work, stated:

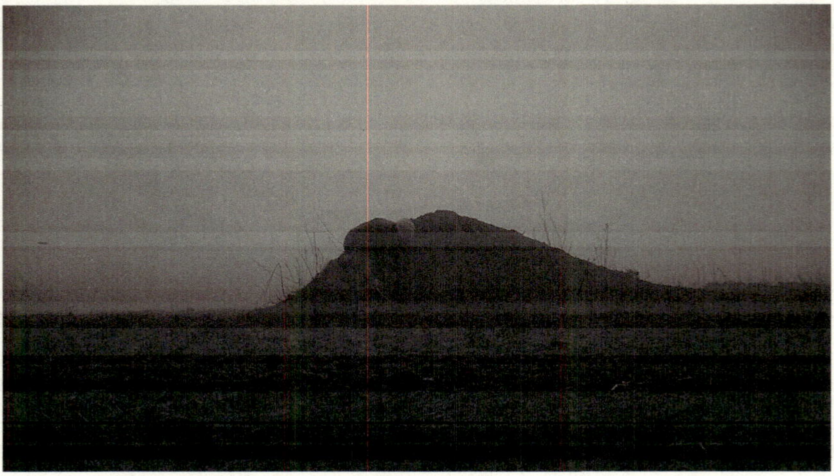

Figure 6.5. Still from Michelle Monareng's *Removal to Radium.*

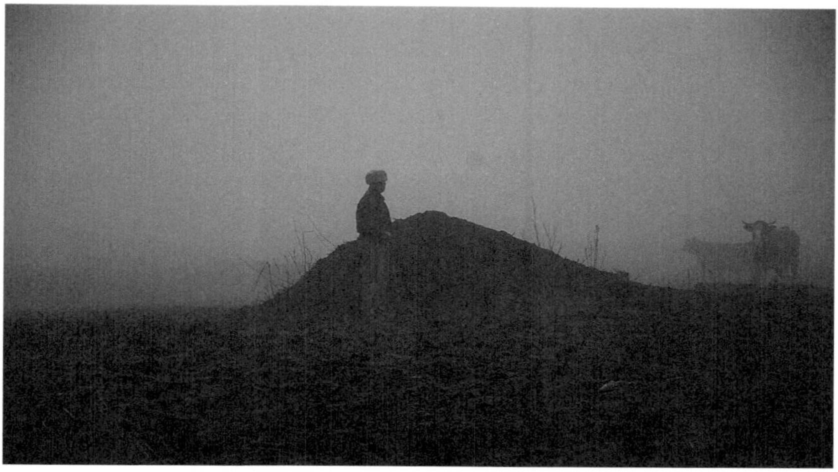

Figure 6.6. Still from Michelle Monareng's *Removal to Radium.*

> The video of a man digging and placing sods of earth onto a mound while cattle, half seen, pass by in the mist, captures something both emotive and politically significant without the need to explain with essentialising sentences. The chance happening that the one bull decides to take more of an interest in the man's work adds to the drama of the scene, again managing to convey many of the issues that surround land in South Africa: fear, ownership, labour, exclusion, utopian ideas of the pastoral, a helpless lack of clarity.[19]

Furthermore, *Removal to Radium* memorializes an eviction, thousands of which happened—undocumented—during apartheid, thus building a black visual archive. It conveys that while black South Africans fought against the pass laws during apartheid for their "right to move," at the same time they fought for a "right to stay" on their own land—or as has been discussed in chapter 1—for a right to live in the cities. Mobility and presence always need to be thought of as inherently connected, as is evident in the last two examples. For a critical production of historical and present visibility, there is neither truth nor essence, but an emphasis on multiple perspectives and minoritarian or marginalized points of view. It can take the format of an audio-visual dialogue with existing stereotypes, as in Nando's clip, or a "digging up" of painful pasts, beyond a narrative of linear progress of overcoming, as has been discussed with the piece of Monareng, but which also hold true for the Center for Historical Reenactments general engagements with history in all of their projects. The last two examples first reconnect with the contestations over land ownership, memory politics, and representation that have been an underlying thread in this study. Second, they expose the wide-ranging changes that have taken place in South Africa with the downfall of apartheid, and that have changed in/visibilities and who is included in the "rainbow" nation. Third, the advertisement clip and the video installation incited affective responses. Furthermore, they both attest to the power of documentary image strategies in the face of South Africa's unresolved history/ies.[20]

In this study different documentary perspectives and materials have been examined that sometimes exposed their construction as "staged documents" and sometimes tried to appear "realistic." The concept of staged documents connects with the production of Landsberg's "prosthetic memories" since they authenticate the second-hand memories and provide them with relevance.[21] This notion of staged documents and prosthetic memories helps to conceptualize an expanded sense of archive that includes documents lost and forgotten due to colonialism and apartheid. These missing records may in part be recreated, reactivated, and restaged through artistic practices, interventions, and re-readings. Reenactment, replaying the archive and fictionalization, and thus rendering history multidimensional and polysemous, is something positive and progressive in the South African context, which for a long time was predetermined by one-dimensional propagandistic truths and counter-truths and binary thinking. I have argued for a right to look, to show, to record, and a need to feel, to be empathic and affectively moved, while at the same time always questioning what is visible in the frame and what may have been left out.

This study has compiled and analyzed new images of post-apartheid affect from documentary materials and produced alternative ways of reading staged documentary materials. And yet, it has been revealed that each current image has a visual history of its own and resonates with intervisual connections, quotations, and transferals. The study has argued that all documentary materials are always staged to a certain extent, and yet it underlines that it is important to reflect the variations and degrees of "staged-ness" and construction in each work and to locate it in its historical and social context. Reading documentary artifacts through the lens of "affective images" enables us to see that they were always—and still are—bound up with the political in different ways. Fictional images presented as staged documents turned history-telling into propaganda or ideology. Documentary images were used as affective and at times effective "weapons" in the struggle against apartheid.

Sometimes the explicit staging of documents and their fictionalization was a useful strategy to start a meta-discussion of the documentary "truth claim," as we have seen in *Border Farm, Conversations,* and *District 9.*

A Right to Look and to Take Your Own Image

It is important to note that as in any unjust and oppressive regime, the apartheid government tried to control the public sphere of visibility and to ban shocking images to curb protest both within the nation as well as internationally. The shocking images were withheld from the public and were not screened on national television. As is testified to, for instance, by a short documentary film with the telling title "Don't Shoot" by white South African director Lucilla Blankenberg.[22] As one interviewed black South African woman explains: "What you saw during the day on the street, and what they screened at night on the SABC news, it was two completely different worlds. Of course, we could not believe anything we saw on the news."[23] This history of the attempt to ban certain photographs and films forms the heritage and justification of South Africa's critical documentary practice in post-apartheid times, implying both a "need to document" and a "right to look."[24]

Not only were the shocking documentary images of suffering suppressed, but also the positive ones, which were a symbol of hope for the black South African majority, as for example any photographs of Nelson Mandela. The ANC leader was imprisoned on Robben Island for twenty-seven years and thereby doubly hidden away from the public's view. As black South African director Khalo Matabane muses in his latest film Mandela, the Myth and Me, the lack of images led to the creation of fantasies about Mandela and to the making up of new images.[25] Mandela, the Myth and Me restages the traumatic images of the past but at the same time manages to convey that new myths are still being constructed in post-apartheid times as well, even if they appeal to diverse "truth claims." This is why documentary work in South Africa is so important and so highly charged with ethical, affective, and political questions. There is always the impetus "to learn from history," which is tied to the claim that "ethical thinking could be enhanced by memory practices."[26] Furthermore, it emphasizes the post-colonial project of recapturing one's own history in the face of so many losses and ruptures caused by imperial and colonial conquest. This commemoration of the past is by no means purely factual or objective. Instead it is charged with affect, trying to recover what people may have felt like and trying to feel with them but not like them.[27] In addition there is a message of hope implied in it, which links understanding history to changing the present and future in order, for example, not to repeat the crimes committed during colonialism and apartheid.[28]

It was argued that documentary photos and films were used as "weapons" in the struggle against apartheid, especially at the end of the 1960s. After apartheid, their role and significance changed, and they seemed to lose their apparently unequivocal, dogmatic "message" in the political realm, yet they are restaged and recycled again and again.[29] The representation of injured or suffering black bodies, which often became iconic, has been paradigmatically sketched out and critically questioned from the past to the present. In addition the gendered coding of the witness in audio-visual documentary productions has been interrogated, particularly the hyper-icon of the "crying woman" with its long history in Western art history from the Pietà to its contemporary reincarnations.

In the Mirror of the Other—Changing Perspectives of the African Migrant Worker

The figure of the migrant has been the focal point of this study since it is predestined to offer reflection about the self and the other making movements of (national) inclusion and exclusion, border conflicts, and issues of community and "tolerance" visible. Photographic images of the other, the foreigner, the traveler, the migrant, and the alien are in addition always deeply intertwined with the ethnographic heritage of documentary film and photography. Othering techniques and the concept of race are historically connected to the invention of photography and film, marking bodies and constructing certain in/visibilities.[30] Moreover, visual media have been considered objective or true image producers, and therefore they were used in the natural sciences as well as in ethnography, anthropology, medicine, and many other disciplines. Even though today, in the age of digital media, photographic images have lost some of their credibility due to the endless possibilities of digital manipulation, the very same images still play a fundamental role in the construction of social categories like race, class, and gender.

The "African migrant worker" has emerged as a central figure in documentary images across history in South Africa and has appeared throughout this study since the first chapter. Post-1994 South African migrant workers have become equal citizens with equal rights, at least in theory, whereas migrant workers from other African countries have been constructed as "illegal aliens." After an extended period of neglecting the topic migration in South African media—due to the national project of nation-building and "reconciliation" post-1994—there has been a renewed interest in portraying migrants in photography, art projects, and film. This attention to surveying the population of South Africa in post-apartheid times occurred even before the xenophobic attacks, which produced images of crisis and violence that were begging for action.

The shocking documentary materials from 2008 were the starting point for a nationwide discussion of citizenship, nationalism, modes of inclusion and exclusion, identity, and migration in South African society. Accusations and demands were expressed toward the South African government, as well as in the academic field and within NGOs and activist groups.[31] The visual material also triggered a critical analysis of the constructions of gender, of how masculinity was visibly performed during the attacks, and about the production and re-invention of "violent differences."[32]

The status of citizenship in South Africa is precarious and contested due to its colonial and apartheid heritage.[33] Therefore, while the legal status of South African citizens promises equality, the social reality of South African citizens is highly unequal and is divided by class, race, and other fault lines. Migration and, on the other hand citizenship and nation, were paradigmatically explored along several lines of different subjectivities residing in South Africa today. The question "Who is a foreigner in South Africa?" has been answered very differently by the different groups claiming to belong. It has provided insightful answers by looking at South Africa through the "lens of migration," thereby complicating the notions of community, mobility, nativity, nationhood, and inclusion and exclusion—both historically and in post-apartheid times. Historically, the "Great Trek" of white migration was heroically remembered and reenacted, whereas migration of Africans was at the same time often forced and prohibited.

Now the black South Africans, who only gained full citizenship rights in 1994 and who had been treated as "foreign natives" in a South Africa imagined as white before, comprise the majority. Similarly, there are African migrant workers from Zambia, Mozambique, and other neighboring countries had a similar status to black South Africans during apartheid, but did not receive citizenship rights after 1994 and often faced deportation and a restriction of their status as workers in South Africa.[34] Yet many of these migrant workers had already established themselves in South Africa and were not willing to leave. Thus they stayed on "illegally" or in a position that maybe could be called "late modern nomads"—traveling back and forth as informal traders between South Africa and their countries of origin, staying nowhere permanently.

During the xenophobic attacks in 2008 an African migrant worker from Mozambique, Ernesto Nhamuave, became an icon in a shocking photograph as was discussed in chapter 3 with the analysis of the image of the "Burning Man." The photograph of Nhamuave's violent death constituted an open wound, or a wounding aperture, and asked "Burning Questions." Thereby, it spawned further image productions, which were partly memorials to him and partly renegotiations of post-apartheid citizenship. This part focused on the tension of shocking photographs as evidence and accusation and argued that one can only understand the violence of the present through the (lens of the) violence of the past, and that affective witnessing is a necessary part of this. The problem of the sexualization of the victims and at times of the perpetrators has surfaced repeatedly, and especially when discussing the photograph of the "Burning Man" but also in visualizations of migrant women, even though sexualization at times was used to humanize the victims and to re-integrate them again into the "national body." In addition, images of both victims and perpetrators may take on "lives of their own" and in turn influence the political sphere.[35]

In the years following 2008, at least in terms of public visibility, the African migrant worker—so far usually denoted as male—has changed gender. In present-day Johannesburg the female African migrant worker has become part of participatory photo projects like *Working the City*.[36] The work situation has changed—while farm work in the rural areas has remained relatively stable if underpaid—as was visible in Nkosi's *Border Farm*; the jobs in the mining industry, however, have decreased (even though mining continues and persists to be on the forefront of images).[37] Especially in urban areas, informal businesses are often the only choices available. The "aliens" in *District 9*, who are also migrant workers—albeit from another galaxy—also do not work for humans in the formal job market at all, and simply persist through informal and illegalized activities. Thereby, they deconstruct the popular equation of migrants having to equal "good workers" in order to have a right to stay. District 9 visualized a thorough critique of post-apartheid society, while also including glimpses of futurity and the unfinished processes of becoming.

I argue for the importance of "re-writing your own history" and "re-taking your own photographs," as has been exemplified by looking at participatory photo-projects in chapter 4 that have changed discourses around authorship and production. The actors in front and behind the lens have been replaced, when comparing it to the white male *Bang-Bang* photographers. The role of the camera as technical apparatus has also evolved. American writer Susie Lienfield recently observed a changing approach to war photography and documentation, in which the camera "would become a tool with which to proclaim and affirm, rather than fight against, the most hideous aspects of war."[38] However, while the complicity of cameras in documenting atrocities certainly has intensified, the notion of images as "trophies" has existed since the invention of photography.[39] What has changed significantly is the position of the photojournalist, who is nowadays often displaced by a certain "embedded" person present at the sites of violence, who takes pictures in accordance with a military unit and its overseeing army commander, thereby only representing an officially sanctioned perspective that was given imprimatur.

A different development derived from the prevalence and availability of mobile phone cameras, turning any citizen into a potential documentary photographer.[40] In fact, many newspapers and media networks seek out amateur photos of newsworthy events, euphemistically calling on "citizen reporters" to email their photographs, thus also cutting production costs. At the same time the perception of which action is conceived as political action and what is described as "senseless violence," and thus deserving or undeserving of being photographed, has undergone transformations in post-apartheid society. While social media, Internet components, and availability of cell phone cameras have changed the visual regime, trained photographers are still in demand and larger media productions like films still need special skills and funding. Mediascapes, modes of production, and display have diversified, however, and have become more representative of the diverse South African society.[41]

"It All Looks Too Familiar"

> It marks a re-turn rather than a "clean" beginning—it points towards things we do not know have passed, yet still haunt the present, like stumbling on an un-marked grave "a location without coordinates"—or an inability to stand firmly on the ground, for fear it may cave in beneath ones feet.[42]

As has become painfully clear throughout the study, history never ends. Instead the present is pierced through with historical flashbacks, look-alikes, zombies, and phantoms. And yet the revenants of historical images are distributed unevenly. Therefore, this study has shown which images are privileged, remembered, and restaged over others, which remain unseen. Attention is divided unequally—black African migrants received the least of it, until they became the protagonists of the shocking photographs of the xenophobic attacks.

Some of the historical and current photographs constituted both "wounding apertures" and open wounds as has been developed in part 2.1. "Photographs of Black Suffering and Violence."[43] "Aperture" refers to the opening or hole in the optic lens of the camera through which the light travels to form an image. The meta-picture of a "wounding aperture" alludes both to the photographic process to create these images and to the affective responses they may incite. This study has argued that these painful images also open up something up, creating an aperture through their affective content. Thereby, a certain setting-free can happen through the wound that is revisited in the visual realm. In that case, the photograph silently screaming out can also set affective responses in motion, and may release the trauma of the event it depicts, possibly leading to further action or a "working through" of painful histories. Thus, the affective entanglement of past and present, and apartheid and post-apartheid, in the visual materials has become palpable.

The current South African constitution is one of the most progressive in the world in terms of offering rights to minorities, including LGBTQ people, and to the formerly marginalized black majority.[44] But despite having a strong human rights discourse, the country is stricken by gross violations of these very rights again and again, as evidenced by the massacre of protesting miners at Marikana in 2012 or the ongoing clashes between police, security staff, and students during the student protests since 2015.[45] One recent example of disregard was the violent incident at a varsity protest at the University of KwaZulu-Natal, where security personnel shot a law student—Bokenga Mntaka—at close range with rubber bullets.[46] The photograph of the incident shows a fellow student carrying Mntaka to safety. This event recalled memories of the brutal apartheid police practices. Its images that looked all too similar to historical events, like the aftermath of the Sharpeville massacre, prompting the question of what has and what has not changed over twenty years into democracy.[47] And yet, there were also differences to be seen: all the police in the photograph were black South Africans, as were the victims. However, as has been proposed by several studies, apartheid police practices have often continued, even in post-apartheid times.[48]

Certain images, as we have seen with the one from "Hector Pietersen" and the "Burning Man," create intense affective assemblages that are remembered and lend themselves to the transferal of particular meanings, which may not be able to be fully verbalized and which become visual icons. Their iconic status is based both on their affective excess, seemingly screaming at us, and on their allusions to already known images. While these images are uncannily familiar and have "migrated" from apartheid into post-apartheid times, it is not enough to recognize the structural analogies; one needs to probe further: "If it looks the same, does it also mean it is the same?" To conclude, the fact that exclusionary practices still exist in post-apartheid society is a starting point for an analysis of the present situation where the categories of difference have diversified but not disappeared. South Africa is not a post-racist society, even though that is what it aspires to be.

In May 2014, South Africa had general elections and as "always" the African Nation Congress (ANC) has gained the absolute majority of 62 percent in parliament. This result is almost analogous to the first free elections in 1994 after Nelson Mandela's release from Robben Island. The repeated success in 2014 can only be explained by the ANC's historical role in the fight against apartheid and its still radiating image as the party of Nelson Mandela who is the imaginary "father" of the new South Africa and thus its symbolic capital.[49] This is another example of how the history/ies and the affective images connected to them have ongoing effects on South African society. In 2016, in the municipal elections, however, the ANC only earned 53 percent of all votes, indicating that the sustained criticism of the ANC and Jacob Zuma finally shows changes in the political landscape and opposition parties have gained more influence, especially in three key metropolitan regions—Johannesburg, the city of Tswane, and Nelson Mandela Bay in the Eastern Cape.[50]

Wounding Apertures Reexamined

This study has examined the painful affective images and referred to Wendy Brown, who cautions against identities built on historical pain, stating that: "Revenge as a 'reaction,' a substitute for the capacity to act, produces identity as both bound to the history that produced it and as a reproach to the present which embodies that history. . . . that reiterates the existence of an identity whose present past is one of insistently unredeemable injury."[51] Being aware of this danger of "wounded attachments," not remembering the past and the suffering of the formerly oppressed black South Africans, is not viable either, and yet Brown's work makes one aware of the delicate questions that surround the politics of visual memory.

In post-apartheid South Africa there has been an understandable attempt to retrieve and in part institutionalize the black perspective and history, as it was in large parts missing due to apartheid's distorted way of overlooking, neglecting, and depreciating black life and culture. Thereby, the historical images of black South African suffering have in some areas become iconic in a Mitchellian sense; as has become evident in my analysis, this is connected to new (national) myth-making and, in part, to deadly nationalism. While remembering the past and actively engaging with the visual documents of apartheid and pre-apartheid history, I have extended the concept of wounding apertures with Spivak's notion of "enabling wound" to imagine how the painful images of the past may get incorporated and not silenced in spite of their affective intensity. Documentary and artistic strategies can widen perspectives and add multiple new axes of vision and points of views. These photographs, films, and installations argue against and complicate, as well as subvert, any notions of fixed identities and citizenship as close-minded, exclusive, and violent nationalisms, as well as masculinity (both black and white).

South African photographer Zanele Muholi, filmmakers like Khalo Matabane, Andy Spitz, and artists such as Thenjiwe Nkosi, Michelle Monareng, and the Center for Historical Reenactments strive to not always repeat the same painful images, and thereby do not re-inflict the same wounds again and again, which may lead to staying in a subjective mode of "victim;" but rather they imagine otherwise, and use documentary strategies to open up a realm of futurity. This study has made the case for a representation beyond victimhood, particularly in part 2.2. "Affective Images in the 'New' South Africa."

The link between photography and surveillance and control of the othered parts of the population was unraveled, which specifically meant the black people in the past and the African migrants in the present, by analyzing the passport and identity photograph. Furthermore, racist images that were made by Europeans in South Africa were deconstructed. While racism and xenophobia can be based on visual distinctions, there is always an affective and medial excess, and there is more to see than the filmmakers and photographers may have intended. In/visibility was problematized as a discourse formation, Deleuze's concept of visibility is helpful here, about which he stated: "Visibilities are not defined by sight but are complexes of actions and passions, actions and reactions, multisensorial complexes, which emerge into the light of day."[52] This expanded understanding of visibility can help envision "postcolonial visibilities" that neither negate colonial subject formation nor stay limited to these conceptions.[53]

In this connection the study has asked if photography can "overcome" its troubled history. This indeed may be possible. Photography can also be used to produce and stage subjectivities in a non-normative fashion; it can open up a perspective on desires and futurity, as has been analyzed throughout and specifically detailed when discussing the participatory projects *Hotel Yeoville* and *Working the City*. Even passport or identity photos, arguably the most normative portraits that exist, have not only been burnt, but were challenged and creatively reworked.

During apartheid, when separation, forced removals, and migrant work became prevalent experiences of the black South African population, studio photography and snapshots entered the lives of families. They show black life framed differently than the apartheid system of negation, negativity, and segregation, even though sometimes the very same photographs from the identity document were used. At times they were the only photographs available. For example, a black couple wanted to have an idealized wedding picture of a "white wedding." For this purpose an image from the passbook may have been used together with a snapshot; they were retouched and recombined and finally hand-colored with a white wedding dress, a fashionable suit, and blue skies. These images became treasured family possessions, attesting to people's dreams and aspirations, creating the type of life and self-image that they wanted to have, at least in the visual realm.[54] The irony of black South Africans aspiring to have an image of a "white wedding" should not be lost, but at the same time it is exactly here that I want to locate, with all insistence, a resistant potential, an unexpected appropriation of the visual realm to incorporate desire and self-representation. It is the creation of a cliché image, which is askew.[55] According to Butler it is this "refusal of the law in the form of the parodic inhabiting of conformity that subtly calls into question the legitimacy of the command."[56] This could also be called a "queering" of the image space of portraiture, similar to the members of the LGBTQ community in New York who reenacted model shows, beauty and dance contests on their own terms with the prominent practice of vogueing, as has become famous through the film *Paris is Burning*.[57]

The practice of idealized images within black South African portraiture is upheld today and, of course, expanded through the endless possibilities of digital retouching with Photoshop and other tools. These self-fashioned portraits are imbued with completely different connotations of love, dignity, and personal memory-making than the "wounding images" of black pain that the international press featured of South African black life.[58] This practice presents the local visual politics of the everyday within South Africa versus the visual politics of the catastrophic, pursued by the shocking photographs that were circulating internationally.[59] The re-usage of passport photographs is an example of a resistant appropriation that does not condemn the visual.[60] Historically, as well as currently, photography has always been used in creative ways, breaking out of the normative, prescribed usage, showing other images even in the midst of the colonial and apartheid archive. Nevertheless, it is also important to argue for a space of "opaqueness" of othered people who are not (white) male and normative, and who thereby inhabit a space in society that is both invisible and hyper-visible, as was explored throughout.

Documentary Strategies and Affective Politics *Now-Now*[61]

With my selected examples and their approaches toward history, I want to argue for a radical practice of documentary—including fictionalization and reenacting that goes beyond post-representation but rather multiplies perspectives of whiteness and blackness. However, as has become obvious, the affective visual realm is always the battleground of representations and the political, where societal conflicts become palpable. Stereotypical representations produce affect and create effects and can perpetuate racism and violence. One always needs to ask, who is looking at what images, who produces and archives them and why? As Christina von Braun has proposed: "Clichés always become dominant, when the self does not have access to its own language."[62] While visual representations always have voyeuristic elements and bear the danger of reproducing stereotypes and clichés, one needs to inquire further: How can multiple stories be told in several languages? And how can one theorize and imagine a post-identitarian visual representation in order to move beyond a too one-dimensional and seemingly clear representations?[63] Black South African artist and writer Rangoato Hlasane cautioned: "Everywhere I turn, I see images of the black body, and these images are not necessarily flattering, despite their well-versed relevance."[64] The documentary artistic media production beyond the news media images in South Africa often includes a utopian dimension—the hope for a different future, the promise of reconciling race and gender conflicts and moving beyond identity politics, and thus also a dialectic element—the wish to understand the past and present in order to be able to create other prospects for all.[65]

In a world where the political sphere often relies on documentary materials, images of pain and tears can and should not be renounced without further ado, because the intricate relationships of affect, agency, and address need to be acknowledged. While it is never possible to feel the other's pain like one's own, affective intensities transmitted and created through images and films are one of the few realms of how we may develop empathy for the other and let ourselves be moved. Accordingly, affective images have a potential for re-imagining the political. Jasbir Puar has asked what new strategic alliances could be formed between the affective and the political: "If we transfer our energy, our turbulence, our momentum from the defense of the integrity of identity and submit instead to this affective ideation of identity, what kind of political strategies, of 'politics of the open end,' might we unabashedly stumble upon? Rather than rehashing the pros and cons of identity politics, can we think instead of affective politics?"[66] This rethinking of the political combined with the affective realm is necessarily connected to material and immaterial images that also need to become open to restaging, re-reading, and re-combination.

Similarly, on the final pages of his seminal study of cinema and affect, The Movement Image, Deleuze pointedly asked: "An image must emerge from the set of clichés. . . . With what politics and what consequences? What is an image, which would not be a cliché? Where does the cliché end and the image begin? . . . The new image would therefore not be a bringing to completion of cinema but a mutation of it."[67] South Africa is a vibrant site of (documentary) image productions, re-workings, new interpretations, and contestations, and thus certainly a site of "cinematic mutation" in a positive sense. It is a ground of experimentation of a visual culture bound up with high moral stakes and ethical questions and in constant dialogue with image productions of other African countries, as well as with Europe and the United States. These works of visual culture, which orient themselves toward a documentary aesthetics, offer impulses for reflection and a meta-discourse of the genre as a whole and thus consist of a thinking through and with images in affective relations with the political. They spell out the visceral connections between looking and feeling, empathy, affect and action, self and others, framed by normative categories of black and white bodies, male and female, and yet always also trying to disturb these very categories through unexpected images and sounds and thus multiplying perspectives of belonging.

Notes

Introduction

1. Soweto, the South-Western Township was a large township close to Johannesburg, where black South Africans were forced to live under the apartheid urban planning system that conceived the cities as white spaces, where only Europeans were allowed to reside. Cf. chapter 1: "Mapping Context and Place."

2. The terms "race," and accordingly "black" and "white," as well as "gender," are understood in this study as social constructions and not in an essentialist way. It is important to acknowledge, though, that these social constructions have "real-life" implications. Therefore I want to underline that these terms are ideological terms while being central and relational for the analysis of power and hegemony in this study. The same holds true for the terms black, white, and colored that may both be quoting apartheid terminology as well as current self-labeling and strategic political usages. Particularly, the term "race" has a very destructive and overtly problematic history. In this study, however, the concept of race is being applied in the tradition of anti-racist disciplines like post-colonial studies and critical race studies, which employs the term both as a reminder of its historical dimension in the process of racialization, but also in its anti-essentialist and strategic sense for anti-racist analysis and counter-positioning. For further discussion on "race," see, e.g., Ina Kerner, *Differenzen der Macht. Zur Anatomie von Rassismus und Sexismus.* (Frankfurt a. M.: Campus Verlag, 2009), 113–40.

3. The president of the African National Congress (ANC) Albert Luthuli had declared 1960 as the "Year of the Pass," a series of mass-actions of protest were planned. Cf. South African History Archive (SAHA) www.sahistory.org.za/topic/sharpeville-massacre-21-march-1960; last accessed 8/11/2014. In South Africa the "pass-port" was also called "pass-book" or abbreviated as "pass."

4. Ian Berry moved to South Africa in 1952 and photographed for *Drum* magazine. In 1962 he was invited to become part of Magnum Photos. Cf. www.magnumphotos.com/; last accessed 8/1/2014.

5. The history of the pass-system and the identity photograph in South Africa and what effects and affects it produced for the people subjected to it will be analyzed further in chapter 4.1 on "Migrant Life and Image."

6. I saw this photograph by Ian Berry for the first time when I was working as an editorial assistant at Magnum Photos New York in 2002.

7. W. J. T. Mitchell, "Offending Images," in: *What do Pictures Want? The Lives and Loves of Images.* (Chicago, London: University of Chicago Press, 2005), 127.

8. For the analysis of the white skin as the norm by unmarking and a surface of projection, cf. Jana Husmann, *Schwarz-Weiß-Symbolik. Dualistische Denktraditionen und die Imagination von "Rasse."* (Bielefeld: Transcript, 2010).

9. Similarly, there were women of all different groups of the population involved in front of and even behind the lens, since there was also a white female photographer, Gille de Vlieg, who was part of the Afrapix collective, but who did not become as well-known as her male colleagues. Cf. Kylie Thomas, "Wounding Apertures: Violence, Affect and Photography during and after Apartheid," in *Kronos*, 38(1) (2012), 204–18. Also see Claudia Marion. Stemberger, "Spot On South Africa: Women Photographers," an interview with Pam Warne, Curator of Photography and New Media at Iziko Museums (South African National Gallery) in Cape Town, in: *EIKON—International Magazine for Photography and Media Art*, No. 70, 2010.

10. Patricia Hayes, "Santu Mofokeng, Photographs: 'The Violence is in the Knowing,'" in *History and Theory*, 48, 2009, 36.

11. Roland Barthes, *Camera Lucida.* (London: Vintage Random House, 2000 (Seuill, 1980)), 93–94.

12. Cf. especially the works of photographer Santu Mafokeng and the works of the Market Photo Workshop and the Afra Pix Collective.

13. Jacques Rancière, *The Politics of Aesthetics: The Distribution of the Sensible.* Trans. G. Rockhill, (London, New York: Continuum, 2004).

14. Trinh T. Minh-ha, "The Totalizing Quest of Meaning," in Michael Renov, ed., *Theorizing Documentary.* (London, New York: Routledge, 1993), 90. Trinh T. Minh-ha follows the Vietnamese system of listing last name first.

15. Abigail Solomon-Godeau, "Who is Speaking Thus," in id. *Photography at the Dock: Essays on Photographic History, Institutions, and Practices.* (Minneapolis: University of Minnesota Press 1991), 169–83, here 169.

16. Abigail Solomon-Godeau, "Who is Speaking Thus," 169.

17. Trinh T. Minh-ha, "The Totalizing Quest of Meaning," 99.

18. Irit Rogoff, "Studying Visual Culture," in Nicolas Mirzoeff, ed., *Visual Culture Reader.* (London: Routledge 1999), 14–26; and Roland Barthes, *Mythologies* (New York: Farrar, Strauss and Giroux, 1972), Martin Warnke, ed., *Aby Warburg, Der Bilderatlas Mnemosyne. Gesammelte Schriften,* Band II.1 (Oldenbourg: Akademie Verlag, 2008), Elisabeth Bronfen, *Crossmapping.* (Zurich: Scheidegger & Spiess, 2009), Christina von Braun, *Die schamlose Schönheit des Vergangenen: Zum Verhältnis von Geschlecht und Geschichte* (Frankfurt a. M.: Verlag Neue Kritik, 1989).

19. Linda Williams, *Playing the Racecard: Melodramas of Black and White from Uncle Tom to O. J. Simpson* (Princeton, NJ: Princeton University Press, 2001).

20. Trinh T. Minh-ha, "Speaking Nearby," Interview with Nancy Chen, in *Visual Anthropology Review*, Vol. 8, No. 1, Spring 1992, 87.

21. The theoretical term "xenophobia" does not fully describe the situation and has some problematic connotations. One could also call the attacks "racist" or as Pumla Gqola suggested "negrophobic." Cf. "Brutal Inheritances: Echoes, Negrophobia and Masculinist Violence," in Shireen Hassim et al., eds., *Go Home or Die Here. Violence, Xenophobia and the Reinvention of Difference in South Africa.* (Johannesburg: Wits University Press 2008), 209–22. However, I have decided to utilize the term "xenophobia" since it is most commonly used in the South African academic context. Cf. e.g., Tara Polzer, " 'Xenophobia,' Violence Against Foreign Nationals and other 'Outsiders' in Contemporary South Africa," Migration Issue Brief 3, June 2010, Forced Migration Studies Program, University of the Witwatersrand, Johannesburg, South Africa, www.migration.org.za/uploads/docs/brief-3.pdf; last accessed 8/9/2014. "Perceived" foreigners because in fact some of the people injured and killed were also South African citizens, but belonging to a minority group. These "ethnic" categories were constructed and implemented during colonialism and apartheid. Cf. e.g., Mahmood Mamdani, *Citizen and Subject: Contemporary Africa and the Legacy of Late Colonialism* (Princeton, NJ: University of Princeton Press 1996).

22. Cf. Worby et al., "Introduction: Facing the Other at the Gates of Democracy," in Hassim et al., *Go Home or Die Here*, 2.

23. "Nigerians" are the group of African migrants that are seen stereotypically as "bad drug dealers" in South African society. This campaign sought to turn this stereotype around.

24. *Chimurenga* is a pan-African magazine and radio station, based in Cape Town. The Chimurenga team also sometimes edits books, curates art exhibitions, and manages concerts. Their radio is called pan-African space station (PASS), alluding to Afrofuturist themes, cf. www.chimurenga.co.za/; last accessed 9/9/2014. "Chimurenga" is a word from the Shona language, roughly translating as "revolutionary struggle" or "liberation." It also refers to a contemporary Zimbabwean music genre that was popularized by Thomas Mapfumo.

25. Loren Landau, "Mobility and Metanarrative: Revisiting South African Social Science Through Migration and Displacement," inaugural lecture, 6/18/2014. University of the Witwatersrand, African Center for Migration and Society (ACMS). Johannesburg, South Africa. Cf. www.migration.org.za/uploads/docs/landau-lecture.pdf; last accessed 6/20/2014. There were three important historical exhibitions of photography in this context: First, *The Short Century* 2001–2002, curated by Okwui Enwezor, first shown at the Villa Stuck, Munich that looked at liberation movements in Africa. Second, *Kwere-Kwere. Journey into Strangeness* 2000 curated by Rory Bester, first shown in Johannesburg, that focused on the construction of foreigners in South Africa. Third, *Rise and Fall of Apartheid. Photography and the Bureaucracy of Everyday Life.* 2012, curated be Okwui Enwezor and Rory Bester, first shown at the International Center for Photography, New York.

26. Rory Bester, "City and Citzenship," in Okwui Enwezor, ed., *The Short Century: Independence and Liberation Movements in Africa 1945–1994.* (Prestel), 219–24, here 223.

27. W. J. T. Mitchell, "Migrating Images—otemism, Fetishism, Idolatry," in Petra Stegmann and Peter C. Seel, eds., *Migrating Images: Producing . . . Reading . . . Translating* (HDKW: Berlin, 2004).

28. I have spent extended research stays in South Africa, mostly in Johannesburg, since 2005 consecutively as a researcher and documentary filmmaker and photographer, which were funded by the DAAD, the Goethe Institute, and DFG travel grants.

29. Cf. Worby et al., "Introduction: Facing the Other at the Gates of Democracy." Desmond Tutu coined the description of South Africa as the "rainbow nation."

30. Cf. The role of private security personnel in the student protests since 2015. Chris Webb, "Impatient for Justice: South Africa's Youth Are Leading an Uncompromising Movement to Right the Wrongs of the Post-Apartheid Era." In *Jacobin*, 12/18/15, https://www.jacobinmag.com/2015/12/south-africa-fees-must-fall-jacob-zuma-apartheid/, last accessed 9/8/2016.

31. Cf. e.g., Hilton Judin, *Blank. Architecture, Apartheid and After.* (Rotterdam: NAi Publishers 1999); Marietta Kesting, *Politik und Sichtbarkeit in Johannesburg* (Berlin, Vienna: LIT, 2009).

32. Cf. Patricia Hayes, "Santu Mofokeng Photographs. The Violence is in the Knowing," in *History and Theory 48* (2009), 43. Nicole Wolf, *Make it Real. Documentary and other cinematic experiments by Women Filmmakers in India* (Dissertation, Frankfurt O., 2007).

Rancière has written on the relation of "poetics and politics," quoting that "Godard said ironically, the epic was for Israelis and the documentary for Palestinians." In Jacques Rancière, Fulvia Carnevale, and John Kelsey, "The Art of the Possible" in *Artforum*, 2007. Similarly, black South Africans were also ascribed to the documentary image, at least in the hegemonic construction of the history of the struggle against apartheid.

33. Santu Mofokeng, *Black Photo Album/Look at Me 1890–1950.* This was a commissioned research project by the University of Witswatersrand, Johannesburg.

34. Sigmund Freud, "Five Lectures on Psychoanalysis" (1910), in *Standard Edition of the Works of Sigmund Freud*, 11, 31.

35. I will not reproduce these images here, but only later in the chapter that specifically deals with them. By doing so I do not want to simply recount, re-illustrate and thereby re-traumatize or re-practice structural violence. Yet it is important to include the discussion of these images in my project and at times also show them, since they are the images of crisis and suffering that involuntarily will always be brought up when one hears "migrants, violence, xenophobic attacks." The image will be discussed in more detail in chapter 3 on "Burning Questions" and the analysis of the film *The Burning Man.*

36. Cf. Arne Perras, "Ernestos tödlicher Irrtum," photograph by Simphiwe Nkwali, *Sueddeutsche Zeitung,* June 3, 2008.

37. The scene was recorded by several photographers and exists in slightly different versions.

38. Jacques Rancière, "The Intolerable Image," in *The Emancipated Spectator* (London, New York: Verso, 2011), 83.

39. Rancière, ibid.

40. Luc Boltanski, *Distant Suffering: Morality, Media and Politics* (Cambridge, UK: Cambridge University Press, 2005), 57.

41. Rancière, "The Intolerable Image," 83. Cf. also Susan Sontag, *Regarding the Pain of Others.* (New York: Picador/Farrar, Straus and Giroux, 2003), Judith Butler, *Frames of War: When is Life Grievable* (New York: Verso, 2009).

42. Nadine Hutton, South African photographer, interview quote from: Gina Shmuckler, *The Line,* original play, (Johannesburg 2012) written and directed by Gina Shmukler, premiered on July 18, 2012, at the Market Theatre in Johannesburg. Emphasis on witness mk.

43. Ariella Azoulay, *The Civil Contract of Photography* (Cambridge, MA: MIT Press, 2012), 355. While it is certainly not a coincidence that Azoulay speaks of the photographer as "him" and many photographers taking images in such contexts are men, I want to note that the quote given on this page belongs to a female South African photographer.

44. Cf. for the notion of "vulnerability" Judith Butler, *Precarious Life: The Power of Mourning and Violence* (New York: Verso, 2006).

45. In this context discourses of critical whiteness studies are important but also need to be approached critically. Cf. Gabriele Dietze, "Okzidentalismuskritik. Möglichkeiten und Grenzen einer Forschungs-perspektivierung," Gabriele Dietze et al., eds., *Kritik des Okzidentalismus, Transdisziplinäre Beiträge zu (Neo-)Orientalismus und Geschlecht* (Bielefeld: Transcript, 2009). Susan Arndt, ed., *Mythen, Masken und Subjekte. Kritische Weißseinsforschung in Deutschland* (Münster: Unrast, 2005).

46. Christina von Braun, "Die unterschiedlichen Geschlechtercodierungen bei NS-Tätern und Täterinnen unter medienhistorischer Perspektive," in Ulrich Weckel and Edgar Wolfrum, eds., *"Bestien" und "Befehlsempfänger." Frauen und Männer in NS-Prozessen nach 1945,* (Göttingen: Vandenhoeck & Ruprecht, 2003), 257.

47. Cf. Definition of "affect" in Oxford Latin Dictionary, (Oxford: Oxford University Press, 1982).

48. The analysis of "affective images" will be pursued in more detail in chapter 2.

49. See for this also Brian Massumi, who builds on Deleuze and Guattari's work on affect: Massumi, *Parables for the Virtual: Movement, Affect, Sensation* (Durham: Duke University Press, 2002), 35.

50. Yet as some recent theories argue, affect is also always already structured by culture and does not exist outside of it. Cf. Anu Koivunen. "An affective turn? Reimagining the subject of feminist theory," in Marianne Liljeström and Susanna Paasonen, eds., *Working with Affect in Feminist Readings: Disturbing Differences* (London, New York: Routledge 2010), 8–28.

51. Christina von Braun et al., eds., *Das Unbewusste. Krisis und Kapital in den Wissenschaften.* (Bielefeld: Transcript, 2009).

52. Carolyn Pedwell, and Anne Whitehead. "Affecting Feminism: Questions of Feeling in Feminist Theory." In *Feminist Theory* 13.2: Special Issue: Affecting Feminism (2012), 115–29.

53. It is important to differentiate between reactivated traumatic memories and the notion of "secondary" or transferred trauma that is disconnected from a subject's own experiences. Connected to this is Alison Landsberg's notion of "prosthetic memory," which is not directly experienced but instead transmitted through media like film or exhibitions in museums. Cf. Alison Landsberg, *Prosthetic Memory: The Transformation of American Remembrance in the Age of Mass Culture* (New York: Columbia University Press, 2004).

54. For the analysis of contagious affects transmitted through visual images, see Katrin Köppert. "Contagious! The Affective Politics of AIDS Scrapbooks!" in Theresa Wilkie et al., eds., *Photography and the Album.* (Boston, Edingburgh: Museums etc., 2013), 142–75.

55. For the notion that "an image seems to demand something from us," cf. W. J. T. Mitchell, "Migrating Images—Totemism, Fetishism, Idolatry," 16.

56. Hito Steyerl, "Documentary Practice Is Always Already an Action," Interview with Hito Steyerl by Reinhard Braun, *Camera Austria*, # 14, 27.

57. Brian Massumi, "Navigating Movements: An Interview with Brian Massumi," interview by Mary Zournazi, *21 C Magazine,* www.21cmagazine.com/issue2/massumi.html; last accessed 6/2/2014.

58. Judith Butler, *Frames of War.*

59. Gilles Deleuze, and Felix Guattari, "Percept, Affect, and Concept," in *What is Philosophy?*, 163–99.

60. Ibid., 164.

61. Baruch (Benedictus) de Spinoza, *Die Ethik nach geometrischer Methode dargestellt.* Dt. Otto Baensch, (Hamburg: F. Meiner, 1955). Relatedness refers to the German "*Bezogenheit.*"

62. Judith Butler, *Precarious Life: The Powers of Mourning and Violence* (London, Brooklyn: Verso 2004); Emanuel Levinas. "Ethics and the Face," in *Totality and Infinity.* Trans. A. Lingis, (Pittsburgh, PA: Duquesne University Press, 1969), 197–201.

63. Serhat Karakayalı, "Regime der Alterität. Affekt und Politik," in Angelika Baier et al., eds., *Affekt und Geschlecht. Eine einführende Anthologie* (Wien: Zaglossus, 2014), 288. Translation mk. Cf. Gilles Deleuze, *Spinoza und das Problem des Ausdrucks in der Philosophie.* Trans. U. J. Schneider (Munich: Fink, 1993) and Étienne Balibar, *Spinoza and Politics.* Trans. P. Snowdon (London, New York: Verso, 1998), 109.

64. Deleuze and Guattari, *A Thousand Plateaus: Capitalism and Schizophrenia,* 265.

65. Ingrid Palmary et al., eds., *Gender and Migration: Feminist Interventions* (London: Zed Books, 2010), 6.

66. Cf. e.g., Pumla Gqola, *What is Slavery to Me: Postcolonial/Slave Memory in Post-Apartheid South Africa* (Johannesburg: Wits University Press, 2010); Christina

von Braun and Bettina Mathes, *Die verschleierte Wirklichkeit. Die Frau, der Islam und der Westen* (Berlin: Aufbau, 2007); Christina von Braun, *Versuch über den Schwindel* (Zurich, Munich: Pendo, 2001); and Dietze et al. eds., *Kritik des Okzidentalismus, Transdisziplinäre Beiträge zu (Neo-) Orientalismus und Geschlecht.*

67. Judith Butler, *Bodies that Matter: On the Discursive Limits of "Sex"* (New York: Routledge, 1993), 48–49.

68. FAR, Filmmakers Against Racism: *Reflecting on Xenophobia. Documentary Filmmakers Respond to the Violent Attacks that Hit South Africa in 2008.* Film Facilitator Guide, South Africa, 2009.

69. Maurice Halbwachs, *Les Cadres Sociaux de la mémoire* (1925). German translation: *Das Gedächtnis und seine sozialen Bedingungen* (Frankfurt a. M.: Suhrkamp, 1985). At the same time the role of "forgetting" also needs to be considered: Elena Esposito, *Soziales Vergessen.* Formen und Medien des Gedächtnisses der Gesellschaft (Frankfurt a. M.: Suhrkamp, 2002).

70. Halbwachs, *Das Gedächtnis und seine sozialen Bedingungen.*

71. Butler, *Frames of War: When is Life Grievable.*

72. Christina von Braun, "Das kollektive Imaginäre," in *Versuch über den Schwindel. Religion, Schrift, Bild, Geschlecht* (Zurich: Pendo, 2001), 260.

73. Alison Landsberg, *Prosthetic Memory: The Transformation of American Remembrance in the Age of Mass Culture* (New York: Columbia University Press, 2004).

74. Landsberg, *Prosthetic Memory*, 3.

Chapter 1

1. Nadine Hutton, South African Photographer, quoted from Gina Shmuckler, *The Line*, original play, Johannesburg, South Africa July 2012, 3.

2. Cf. www.freiburg-postkolonial.de/Seiten/Bley-Kongokonferenz.htm; last accessed 6/17/2014; and Andreas Eckert: "125 Jahre Berliner Afrika-Konferenz: Bedeutung für Geschichte und Gegenwart" (Hamburg, 2009). GIGA German Institute of Global and Area Studies—Leibniz-Institut für Globale und Regionale Studien, Institut für Afrika-Studien ed., (GIGAFocus Afrika Nr. 12), nbn-resolving.de/urn:nbn:de:0168-ssoar-274593; last accessed 6/17/2014.

3. Walter Benjamin, "Excavation and Memory," in *Walter Benjamin: Selected Writings*, Vol. 2, 1927–1934 (Cambridge, MA: Belknap Press of Harvard University Press, 1999), 576.

4. Benjamin, "Excavation and Memory," 576.

5. Leslie Witz, *Apartheid's Festival: Contesting South Africa's National Past* (Bloomington, IN: Indiana University Press 2003). April 6 was a public holiday in South Africa, called "Jan van Riebeeck Day" until 1974.

6. Mirzoeff, *The Right to Look*, 17.

7. Witz, *Apartheid's Festival*, 180.

8. Mahmood Mamdani, *Citizen and Subject* (Princeton, NJ: Princeton University Press, 1996).

9. *Voortrekker* is Afrikaans and literally means "the forerunners" or "pioneers."

10. Anne McClintock, *Imperial Leather: Race, Gender and Sexuality in the Colonial Contest* (London: Routledge, 1995), 369.

11. Ibid., 369.

12. Solomon Thsekisho Plaatje, *Native Life in South Africa.* (London: PS King and Son, 1916), 302.

13. The Natives' Land Act, 1913, cf. www.polity.org.za/polity/govdocs/legislation/misc/nla1913.html; last accessed, 5/10/2014.

14. T. R. H. Davenport, *South Africa: A Modern History* (London: Macmillan, 1991) and C. F. J. Muller, ed., *Five Hundred Years: A History of South Africa* (Pretoria: Academica 1981), 393–96.

15. There were different films produced for white and black audiences. Cf. Gutberlet's and Els's project on the "B-Schemes," cf. www.arsenal-berlin.de/en/living-archive/projects/visionary-archive/b-schemes.html; last accessed 6/13/2014. The censorship boards decided who was considered "mature" enough to watch certain films.

16. Tomaselli, *The Cinema of Apartheid*, 14.

17. Cf. Hannah E. Britton, *Women in the South African Parliament: From Resistance to Governance* (Chicago, IL: University of Illinois Press, 2005).

18. Cf. Robert Young, "Women, Gender and Anti-Colonialism," in idem, *Postcolonialism: An Historical Introduction* (Oxford, UK: Blackwell, 2001), 366–67.

19. Jan Smuts, "Native Policy in Africa," from *Towards a better World* (World Book Company, 1944), 322–27; quoted in John Clare, ed., *Captured in Time: Five Centuries of South African Writing* (Johannesburg and Cape Town: Jonathan Ball Publishers, 2010), 30. Smuts is an ambivalent figure, born in South African on an Afrikaans farm, educated in Cambridge, later entering the Afrikanerbond and starting the war against the British ("Anglo-Boer" or "2nd Boer" War that started in 1899) and promoting racial segregation and white minority rule. Cf. *Encyclopaedia Britannica*, britannica.com/EBchecked/topic/550198/Jan-Smuts; last accessed 8/10/2014. In Johannesburg, however, a prominent street in Johannesburg is still named "Jan Smuts Laan" (in Afrikaans "Laan" translates into "Street"), indicating that there has not been a thorough coming to terms with the past and renaming of streets.

20. Mamdani, *Citizen and Subject*, 218.

21. McClintock. *Imperial Leather*, 324.

22. South African artist Mary Sibande has created a memorial to female domestic work, producing sculptures and murals of black women in Sibande's newly designed extravagant domestic workers' uniform that were inspired by a Victorian queen's dress. By doing so, she is also commenting on her own family history, some of her female relatives had been domestic servants. Cf. Mary Sibande, "The work of South African Artist Mary Sibande," (8/26/2012); *The Guardian*, www.theguardian.com/artanddesign/gallery/2012/aug/26/south-african-artist-mary-sibande; last accessed 8/12/2013.

23. In addition, this was also Rogosin's preferred way of making films as documentary-fiction hybrids. Compare, e.g., his film *On the Bowery* (USA 1956, 56 min.), which was produced in New York City, with a similar setup, however not having to fear prosecution by the American government the same way as in South Africa. He was, however, accused of being a communist, which hindered his career. Cf. www.onthebowery film.com/ and www.imdb.com/title/tt0050800/; both last accessed 8/1/2014.

24. The genre of the "Jim comes to Jo'burg" narrative was established in film with *African Jim*, by Donald Swanson, (50 min., B&W, South Africa 1949).

25. White South African author's Alan Paton's novel *Cry, the Beloved Country* was first published in New York in 1948, before apartheid was institutionalized. The novel discussed the injustice of racial segregation and drafts a promise of reconciliation between black and white from a Christian perspective. The novel was also adapted to a screen version and made into a fiction film in 1951 directed by Zoltan Korda. Cf. www.imdb.com/title/tt0043436/; last accessed 9/17/2014, and Jacqueline Maingard, *South African National Cinema* (New York: Routledge, 2007), 106–24.

26. Cf. Lindiwe Dovey, *African Film and Literature: Adapting Violence to the Screen* (New York: Columbia University Press, 2009), 150.

27. Lewis Nkosi, *Come Back, Africa: Fighting Talk.* February 1960, no pagination; quoted from: Ntongela Masilela "*Come Back, Africa* and South African film history."

28. Darryl Els, "Shifting Grounds: Reflections on National Identity in the Archive," in Arsenal, ed., *Living Archive: Archive Work as a Contemporary Artistic and Curatorial Practice* (Berlin: b_books, 2013), 69–75.

29. Els, "Shifting Grounds. Reflections on National Identity in the Archive," 73.

30. Frank Wilderson III, "Biko and Problematic of Presence," in Amanda Alexander et al., eds., *Biko Lives: Contesting the Legacies of Steve Biko* (New York: Palgrave Macmillan, 2008).

31. Incidentally, *Come Back, Africa* was the first film that started the collection of the Arsenal Film Archive in Berlin, as the director gave a 16-mm print to the founders of the archive, Erika and Ulrich Gregor. This is more than just an anecdote, instead it points to the postcolonial entanglements of spaces and spheres in the realm of cinema and image-making as well.

32. Masilela, "*Come Back, Africa* and South African film history."

33. Cf. *Visionary Archive* series, www.arsenal-berlin.de/en/living-archive/projects/visionary-archive/it-all-depends/it-all-depends-1.html; last accessed 7/7/2014.

34. Tomaselli, *The Cinema of Apartheid*, 222.

35. Cf. Tony Sutton, *Drum 1976–1980: An Exhibition from the Pages of Drum Magazine*, 2006, www.coldtype.net/Assets.06/Essays.06/0606.DrumBook.pdf; last accessed 8/7/2014.

36. It hast often been said that within *Drum* magazine office apartheid did not exist. There is, however, a remarkable absence of female photographers or

writers, either black or white, like in most other editorial departments during that time.

37. Newbury, *Defiant Images*, 6.

38. Cf. Enwezor, "A Critical Presence: Drum Magazine in Context."

39. Janet Jackson, *Got 'Till It's Gone*, together with Q-Tip. Album The Velvet Rope. Virgin Records 1997. The music video was shot by Mark Romanek in Los Angeles and won 1998 the Grammy Award for the Best Short Music Video.

40. For Malick Sidibé's work see, Michelle Lamuniere, *You Look Beautiful Like That: The Portrait Photographs of Seydou Keita and Malick Sidibé* (Harvard Art Museum, 2001).

41. Jacob Dlamini, *Native Nostalgia* (Sunnyside, SA, 2009), 108.

42. African Media Online, Drum Cover Collection, cf. www.africamediaonline.com/; last accessed 8/24/2014. Cf. for example in this context also the story of Sandra Laing, a black child born to white parents, she was classified "white;" at eleven years old this was changed into "black" and two years later changed again to "white." This was a scandal in the Afrikaans-dominated white society, since it also alluded to the unspeakable idea of "interracial" sex. Sandra Laing—A Spiritual Journey. Documentary Film by Karien van der Merve, (26 min., 2001), www.journeyman.tv; last accessed 9/2/2014.

43. Hilton Judin, and Ivan Vladislavić, eds., *Blank—Architecture, Apartheid, and After* (Rotterdam: NAi Publishers, 1999).

44. W. E. B. Du Bois, *The Souls of Black Folk*, (1903). (New York: Signet, 1995), 45. For a thorough discussion of the veil in the African-American context, cf. Therese Steffen, " 'Leben unter dem Schleier': Afroamerikanische Texte und Kontexte," in: Bettina Dennerlein et al. eds., *Verschleierter Orient—Entschleierter Okzident. (Un-) Sichtbarkeit in Politik, Recht, Kunst und Kultur seit dem 19. Jahrhundert* (Munich: Wilhelm Fink, 2012), 181–202.

45. Ivan Vladislavić, *Double Negative.* (Cape Town: Umuzi, 2011), 13.

46. For the American context on Adrian Piper's writing and artistic work on "passing," cf. Adrian Piper, "Passing for White, Passing for Black," first published 1992, reprinted in: *Out of Order, Out of Sight, Volume I: Selected Essays in Meta-Art 1968–1992* (Cambridge, MA: MIT Press 1996).

Chapter 2

1. Deleuze, *Cinema I: The Movement-Image*, 103.

2. David Smith, " 'Racism' of early Colour Photography explored in art exhibition," in *Guardian*, Jan. 25, 2013, www.theguardian.com/artanddesign/2013/jan/25/racism-colour-photography-exhibition/print; last accessed 7/20/2014. Kodak introduced a new film stock in the 1980s that was better able to render the details of dark skin.

3. Compare e.g. Christina von Braun, "Ceci n'est pas une femme. Betrachten, Begehren, Berühren—von der Macht des Blicks," *Lettre International* 25,

1994, 80–4; and, e.g., Tobias Nagl, *Die unheimliche Maschine. Rasse und Repräsentation im Weimarer Kino* (Munich: Edition Text + Kritik, 2009).

4. Cf. Christina von Braun, "Die schamlose Schönheit des Vergangenen," in *Die schamlose Schönheit des Vergangenen: zum Verhältnis von Geschlecht und Geschichte* (Frankfurt a. M.: Verlag Neue Kritik, 1989), 116.

5. Hannah Arendt, *On Violence.* (New York: Harcourt, 1970, 1969), and Judith Butler, *Precarious Life: The Power of Mourning and Violence* (London, New York: Verso, 2004).

6. Hannah Arendt, *On Violence.*

7. Cf. e.g., Roland Barthes's discussion on "Schockphotos" (shocking photographs) in *Mythen des Alltags* (Original title in French: *Mythologies*) (Frankfurt a. M.: Suhrkamp, 1964), 55–58.

8. Ernest Cole, *House of Bondage* (New York: Random House, 1967).

9. "Bondage," however, also has inadvertently sexual overtones of S&M practices.

10. The pass laws and resistance against them were already briefly introduced with the first photograph in the introduction, explained in more detail in chapter 1 and will be picked up again in chapter 4 when discussing identity and passport photos.

11. Marie Wentzel, "Historical Origins of Hostels in South Africa: Migrant Labor and Compounds," in Anthony Minaar, ed., *Communities in Isolation: Perspectives on Hostels in South Africa* (Pretoria: Human Sciences Research Council, 1993), 3.

12. In fact, the pass-photos have been used in one exhibit to tell the story of African migrant labor in the Lwandle Township Museum. Cf. Witz and Murray, *Hostels, Homes, Museums*, 62–66.

13. John Cook, One-Man Truth Squad. *Mother Jones.* Issue May/June 1997, www.motherjones.com/politics/1997/05/one-man-truth-squad; last accessed 12/23/2012.

14. Okwui Enwezor, "A Critical Presence: *Drum* Magazine in Context," in O. Enwezor, O. Obuibe, and O. Zaya, eds., *In/Sight: African Photographers 1940 to the Present,* (New York: Guggenheim Museum, 1996), 16.

15. Cf. John Fels and Denis Wood, *The Power of Maps* (New York: Guilford Press, 1992).

16. Deleuze and Guattari, *A Thousand Plateaus*, 3–4.

17. Patrick Laurence, "Twenty-one hanged in seventy-two hours." The article originally appeared in the *Weekly Mail* 11/12/1987, mg.co.za; last accessed 6/6/2014.

18. Thandeka Gqubule, "Soweto Ungoverned." The article originally appeared in the *Weekly Mail*, 08/26/1988, mg.co.za; last accessed 6/6/2014.

19. "Umkonte we Sizwe" in *isi*Zulu for "Spear of the Nation."

20. Patrick Laurence, "Twenty-one hanged in seventy-two hours." Capital punishment in SA was abolished in 1995 after a five-year moratorium. During the 1980s South Africa had one of the highest rates of executions in the world. Cf. Howard W. French, "South Africa's Supreme Court Abolishes Death Penalty," in

New York Times, 6/7/1995, www.nytimes.com; last accessed 6/16/2014. The UDF was formed in 1983 and was a coalition of about 400 organizations from all different sectors of society. It had a close relationship with the then-banned ANC.

21. Namibia had formerly been the German colony "South West Africa" from 1884 until after WWI, then it was part of the South African Union that treated it as a colony and only gained full independence from South Africa in 1990.

22. Cf. e.g., Jacklyn Clock. "Gun Violence and Masculinity in Contemporary South Africa," in Robert Morrel, ed., *Changing Men in Southern Africa.* (London: Zed Books, 2001), 43–55. Nonetheless black South African men (77,000) had been enlisted to fight in the South African Army in the 2nd World War on the side of the British without being allowed to carry arms, acting as "logistical support" for the white soldiers. Cf. South African History Archive, saha.org; last accessed 7/6/2014.

23. The Verwoerd apartheid government prosecuted the ANC and its leaders as a "terrorist" organization whose aim it was to overthrow the state. Cf. South African History Archive. www.sahistory.org.za/topic/rivonia-trial-1963-1964; last accessed 8/15/2014.

24. Gunkel, *The Cultural Politics of Female Sexuality in South Africa*, 90.

25. South Africa has a wide diversity of African languages, after apartheid eleven languages are officially recognized: Zulu, Venda, Sotho, Northern Sotho, Tswana, Xhosa, Tsonga, Swazi, Ndebele, English, and Afrikaans. Of these eleven official languages, nine are African languages.

26. The photograph was taken by Sam Nzima with the caption: Hector Pieterson, a school child, shot dead by police, Soweto Uprising 1976, www.sahistory.org.za/people/hector-pieterson; last accessed 6/20/2013. As a bitter footnote of history, Mbuyisa Makhubo and his family were not left in peace due to the famous photograph, later the very same year Mbuyisa disappeared as his mother Nombulelo Elizabeth Makhubu testified at the Truth and Reconciliation Commission hearings on April 30, 1996, cf. www.justice.gov.za/trc/hrvtrans/methodis/makhubu.htm; last accessed 06/24/2013.

27. As Azoulay has described in relation to similar images from the Israeli-Palestinan conflict, the Palestinians seem not to be able to declare a *real* case of emergency, since they are not considered citizens by the sovereign power. An observation that holds similarly true for the South African context. Cf. Azoulay, *Civil Contract,* 292–95.

28. Ibid., 302–03.

29. Smaill, *The Documentary: Politics, Emotion, Culture*, 139.

30. Rancière, "The Intolerable Image," 83. Cf. the definition of "intolerable image" in the *Introduction.*

31. Judith Butler, *Frames of War*, 38–39.

32. Ibid., 140.

33. As can also be observed in visual politics of the Israel-Palestine conflict time and again with the images of injured or dead children from Gaza. Cf. Richard C. Schneider, "Über Gaza berichten. Gegen die Bilder ist unser Text machtlos." In: *FAZ*, August 4, 2014.

34. The Hector Pieterson Museum, cf. www.southafrica.net/za/en/articles/entry/article-southafrica.net-the-hector-peterson-museum; last accessed 9/11/2014. In addition, June 16th has been turned into the national "Youth Day" in South Africa.

35. Cf. South African History Archive (SAHA), www.sahistory.org.za/topic/british-anti-apartheid-movement?page=5; last accessed 6/22/2013.

36. Kylie Thomas, "Wounding Apertures: Violence, Affect and Photography during and after Apartheid." *Kronos*, 38 (1) (2012), 204–18.

37. Thomas, "Wounding Apertures," 204.

38. Ibid., 207.

39. Williams, *Playing the Racecard: Melodramas of Black and White from Uncle Tom to O. J. Simpson*, 148.

40. Cf. "The Abolition Project," abolition.e2bn.org/campaign_14.html; last accessed 9/7/2014. Cf. for a discussion of the iconography of the anti-slavery movement, e.g., Gabriele Dietze. *Weiße Frauen in Bewegung* (Bielefeld: Transcript 2013), 60–61, Simon Strick, *American Dolorologies: Pain, Sentimen-talism and Biopolitics* (Albany, NY: New York University Press, 2014).

41. Paul Gilroy, *Darker than Blue: On the Moral Economies of Black Atlantic Culture* (Cambridge, MA, London: The Belknap Press of Harvard University Press, 2010), 64.

42. Paul Gilroy, ibid., and Luc Boltanksi, *Distant Suffering: Morality, Media, and Politics*. Trans. G. Burchell. (Cambridge, UK: Cambridge University Press, 1999).

43. On the issue of images in combination with text, see W. J. T: Mitchell. *Iconology: Image, Text, Ideology* (Chicago: University of Chicago Press, 1986).

44. The hand, or two hands together are a recurring motif in the visual materials of this study.

45. See some of these other posters in the South African History Poster Collection. www.saha.org, last accessed 8/7/2014. The representation of tears, of course, has a long history in Christian iconography, especially in depicting martyrs. Cf. e.g., Emile M. Cioran, *Tears and Saints*. Trans. I. Zarifopol-Johnston.(Chicago: University of Chicago Press, 1995). Further contemporary visualizations of tears will be discussed in the next chapter.

46. Butler, *Frames of Wars*, 38–39.

47. Again, this aesthetic and affective strategy has parallels to the usage of images in the U.S.-American abolition movement.

48. The UDF was one of the most important anti-apartheid organizations with about 3 million members.

49. Cf. www.sahistory.org.za/topic/nelson-mandela-timeline-1980-1989; last accessed 12/12/2012.

50. *"Impimpi"*—"traitor" in *isi*Zulu. Cf. for a discussion of photographs of necklacing: Thomas, "Wounding Apertures."

51. The Truth and Reconciliation Commission covered this case: "Truth Commission Looks at First 'Necklace' Murder": SAPA. February 4, 1997, www.doj.

gov.za/trc/media/1997/9702/s970204c.htm; last accessed 9/17/2012. Cf. Wilfried Scharf and Baba Kgcokoto, "Images of Punishment in the People's Courts of Cape Town: 1985–87: From Prefigurative Justice to Populist Violence," in N. Chabani Manganyi and Andre du Toit, eds., *Political Violence and the Struggle in South Africa* (London: Macmillan, 1990), 371. This does not imply, however, that necklacing only occurs in South Africa. There are other reported cases globally.

52. Letter from David Shandler to Matt Meyer, War Resisters League, September 18, 1986. Historical Papers, University of the Witwatersrand, AG1977—End Conscription Campaign, A4.2.2; www.historicalpapers.wits.ac.za/; last accessed 6/7/2014.

53. "Battle: Excerpts from a conversation," Interview with Mpho Mathebula, Lindelani Mathebula, Thabang Motsoeneng, Jabulani Ngcobo, and Jerry, September 29, 2012, in Dorothee Kreutzfeld & Bettina Malcomes, eds., *Not No Place, Johannesburg, Spaces and Fragments of Time* (Johannesburg: Jacana Media, 2013),103.

54. As Massumi established, strong affect is connected to memory. Cf. "And it was the emotional version that was most remembered." Cf. Massumi, *Parables for the Virtual*, 23.

55. Greg Marinovich and João Silva, *The Bang-Bang Club: Snapshots from a Hidden War* (London: Arrow Books 2001). Also a fiction film was made with the same title, directed by Steven Silver in 2009. It includes some reenacted documentary interview footage of Kevin Carter. Cf. www.imdb.de/title/tt1173687/; last accessed 9/2/2012. The *Bang-Bang* Club was not a self-chosen name, but taken from the headline of an article that was supposed to be called "Bang Bang Papparazzi." "Bang-Bang" has inadvertently male heterosexual connotations, it also means informally "to have sex with."

56. Cf. lens.blogs.nytimes.com/2009/08/20/showcase-38/; last accessed 9/2/2012. Photographer Ken Ooster-broek died from a stray bullet in 1994.

57. For a detailed study of the violence in the hostels, cf. Mahmood Mamdani, *Citizen and Subject*, 218–84.

58. Lauren Segal, "The Human Face of Violence: Hostel dwellers speak," in *The Journal of Southern African Studies*, Vol. 18, No. 1, March 1991, 190–231.

59. Nicholas Haysom, "Mabangalala: The Rise of Right-wing Vigilantes in South Africa." Occasional Paper No. 10, Centre for Applied Legal Studies, University of the Witwatersrand, Johannesburg 1986, 1.

60. These images also seem to have been the blueprint for the flashback sequence in Khalo Matabane's film, looking acutely similar, showing their ongoing status as visual icons in post-apartheid times that get repeated in films such as: *State of Violence*. 79 min., 2010. Cf. www.imdb.com/title/tt1722517/; last accessed 9/25/2012.

61. Cf. Mamood Mamdani study of violence on the Reef: "The Rural in the Urban: Migrant Workers in South Africa," in *Citizen and Subject*, 218–84.

62. Cf. Tobias Ebbrecht, "Migrating Images: Iconic Images of the Holocaust and the Representation of War in Popular Film," in *Shofar*, An Interdisciplinary

Journal of Jewish Studies, 2010, Vol. 28 (4), 98. Holocaust images are also referenced in the film *District 9,* which will be discussed in chapter 5.

63. A more detailed analysis of the motif of "burning people," fire, and its multiple connotations will be given in *Burning Questions*, chapter 3.

64. Mahmood Mamdani, *Citizen and Subject*, 223–25.

65. Tim Porter, "Covering War in a Free Society," February 18, 2003. Cf. www.timporter.com/firstdraft/archives/000071.html; last accessed 9/17/2012.

66. Cf. e.g., Newbury, *Defiant Images*.

67. Tim Porter, "Covering War in a Free Society," and Scott Macleod, "The Life and Death of Kevin Carter," *Time Magazine*, Johannesburg, Sept. 12, 1994.

68. E.g., Caroline Wanjiku Kihato criticized Kevin Carter's image during her presentation at the African Studies conference in Leipzig 2010, similarly Okwui Enwezor in *Snap Judgments: New Positions in Contemporary African Photography* (New York: International Center for Photography, 2006), 16–18.

69. Carter committed suicide shortly after receiving the Pulitzer Prize in 1994.

70. Cf. Alfredo Jaar, *The Sound of Silence,* alfredojaar.net, Roberta Smith, "One Image of Agony Resonates in Two Lives," in *New York Times*, 4/15/2009, www.nytimes.com; both last accessed 7/18/2014.

71. Rancière, "The Intolerable Image," 99.

72. Butler, *Frames of War*.

73. Cf. Dan Solomon, "Steven van Zandt tells the story of 'Sun City' and fighting apartheid," www.fastcocreate.com/3023454/steven-van-zandt-tells-the-story-of-sun-city-and-fighting-apartheid-in-south-africa; last accessed 8/10/2014.

74. Video available on YouTube "I ain't gonna play Sun City" Music Video; www.youtube.com/watch?v=TlMdYpnVOGQlast accessed 6/2/2013. Compare for the ambivalent role of Sun City during apartheid: Aljoscha Weskott and Marietta Kesting, eds., *Sun Tropes: Sun City and (Post-)Apartheid Culture in South Africa*.

75. Deleuze and Guattari, *A Thousand Plateaus*, 3–4.

76. Cf. Brian Massumi, *Parables for the Virtual*, 23. Brian Massumi cites a study by Herta Sturm of children watching different versions of a sad short film and tracking their reactions measured by galvanic skin response on a pleasant to unpleasant scale as well as a sad to happy scale. Galvanic skin response according to Massumi implies an unconscious, physical reaction that the children were not able to consciously influence. For a thorough critique of Massumi see Ruth Leys, "The Turn to Affect: A Critique," in *Critical Inquiry,* Vol. 37, No. 3 (Spring), 434–72.

77. Massumi, *Parables for the Virtual*, 23.

78. Herta Sturm, "Wahrnehmung und Fernsehen: die fehlende Halbsekunde," in *Media Perspektiven*, No. 1, 1984, 58–65.

79. Marie-Luise Angerer, *Vom Begehren nach dem Affekt* (Zurich, Berlin: diaphanes 2007), 14.

80. Charles W. Mills, "White Ignorance," in: Shannon Sullivan and Nancy Tuana, eds., *Race and Epistemologies of Ignorance* (Albany, NY: State University of New York Press, 2007).

81. Gwen Gill in: Aljoscha Weskott and Marietta Kesting, eds., *Sun Tropes. Sun City and (Post-)Apartheid Culture in South Africa* (August: Berlin, 2009), 123.

82. Martha Rosler, "Bringing the War Home." Cf. theexposureproject.blogspot.de/2008/11/martha-roslers-bringing-war-home-1967.html; last accessed 8/2/2012.

83. Rancière, "The Intolerable Image," 84.

84. Ibid., 85.

85. Cf. e.g., Kerstin Brandes, "Visuelle Migrationen—Bild-Bewegungen zwischen Zeiten, Medien und Kulturen," in *FKW, Zeitschrift für Geschlechterforschung und visuelle Kultur*, No 5, June (Jonas: Marburg, 2011), 5.

86. Cf. Marcia Landy, "Just an image. Godard, cinema, and philosophy," in *Critical Quarterly*, 43, 2001, 9–31.

87. Nadine Hutton, quoted from Gina Shmuckler, *The Line*, 10.

88. Cf. Newbury, *Defiant Images.*

89. Hayes, "Santu Mofokeng: 'The Violence is in the Knowing.'"

90. James Baldwin, *The Evidence of Things not Seen.* (New York: Owl Books 1995). While the comparability of the African-American and the black South African context is not always constituted, and without romanticizing a pan-African connection there exists a mutual influence and appreciation that is evident both in popular culture as well as in other intellectual productions.

91. I saw these photographs in the book Hassim et al., eds., *Go Home or Die Here*, and on the blog from FAR. A *spaza shop*, also called tuck shop, is an informal small shop providing household items and that is usually run from home. These shops exist in South Africa typically in the former townships that are far away from formal shopping areas. Many of these shops are run by non-South Africans—often Somali or Pakistani immigrants. These shops are regularly the target of anti-immigrant violence and are robbed and looted.

92. Jürgen Habermas, *The Structural Transformation of the Public Sphere* (Cambridge, MA: MIT Press, 1991) and Arjun Appadurai, *Modernity at Large* (Minneapolis: University of Minnesota Press, 1996).

93. Azoulay, *The Civil Contract of Photography*, 291–92.

94. Ibid., 291–92.

95. Wendy Brown, "Wounded Attachments," in *States of Injury: Power and Freedom in Late Modernity.* (Princeton, NJ: Princeton University Press, 1995), 52–76.

96. Wendy Brown, "Wounded Attachments," 73.

97. Spivak on "enabling violation" in: "Righting Wrongs," *The South Atlantic Quarterly* 103 2/3, Spring/Summer 2004, 524.

98. Spivak, "Righting Wrongs," 524.

99. Of course there were also black collaborators with the apartheid regime, and white victims of it, yet the majority of victims were black South Africans.

100. From: "The Times Heritage and Memorial," cf. heritage.thetimes.co.za/memorials/ec/DesmondTutu/article.aspx?id=640927; last accessed 6/15/2013.

101. Kistner, *Commissioning and Contesting Post-Apartheid's Human Rights.*

102. As was already discussed also in chapter 1 on "militarized citizenship" in South Africa.

103. Williams, *Playing the Racecard*, 17.

104. Ibid., 9.

105. For example, in the context of the decision-making process of accepting asylum seekers in Europe, compare the documentary film by Fernand Melgar, *La Forteresse*, 2008, cf. www.laforteresse.ch/fr/accueil; last accessed 9/27/2012.

106. Williams, *Playing the Racecard*, 9.

107. Louise du Toit, "Feminism and the ethics of reconciliation," in Eurozine, 3/17/2007, cf. www.eurozine.com/articles/2007-03-16-dutoit-en.html; last accessed 9/18/2014.

108. Brinkema, "A Tear that does not drop but folds," in *The Forms of the Affects.* (Durham, NC, London: Duke University Press, 2014), 2.

109. Sontag, *Regarding the Pain of Others*, 86.

100. As in a later filmic example "Man on Ground" in the chapter 3, *Burning Questions*, which re-tells the story of Ernesto Nhamuave under fictional auspices, it is stated again and again: "There are 3 sides to a story, mine, yours, and the truth."

111. Sontag, *Regarding the Pain of Others*, 89.

112. Yet I want to note that Fatima's role will change profoundly at the end of the film, although one sees her prominently in the beginning of the film as a "crying victim." Other aspects of this content-rich documentary film are discussed in part 5.1; here the focus lies on the testimony in tears.

113. As, for example, the documentary footage at the end of the otherwise completely animated film *Waltz with Bashir* by Ari Folmann 2008, which adds a strong "reality" effect in contrast to the animated film. In addition, it also shows women crying, see www.imdb.com/title/tt1185616/; last accessed 08/07/2010. Compare for the concept of "sincerity" also Jane Taylor, *Considering Forgiveness* (New York: Vera List Center for Art and Politics: 2009).

114. Cf. Emily Greenhouse, "Women in War Zones," in *The New Yorker.* 07/30/2014, www.newyorker.com/news/newsdeks/women-war-zones; last accessed 8/2/2014.

115. Jane Taylor, "Really?—On Sincerity in the context of the South African TRC—Commission," May 13, 2009, Lecture at New School.

116. Marie-Luise Angerer. *Vom Begehren nach dem Affekt* (Zurich, Berlin: Diaphanes, 2007), 14, translated by mk.

117. Patrick Sjoberg, in an email to the author, May 2011.

118. Linda Williams, *Hard Core: Power, Pleasure and the "Frenzy of the Visible"* (Berkeley, Los Angeles: University of California Press, 1989), 101.

119. In porn film, male ejaculation and orgasm are considered to be one and the same thing.

120. Patrick Sjoberg, unpublished paper given at Visible Evidence conference 2010 and quoted here from an email to the author, May 2011.

121. At the same time the slang term "to jerk off" means to masturbate, suggesting an action that was considered a neutralizing action by psychologists, where the subject pleases him-/herself instead of interacting with another.

122. Cf. Kimberly Christine Patton and John Stratton Hawley, eds., *Holy Tears: Weeping in the Religious Imagination* (Princeton, NJ: Princeton University Press, 2005).

123. In an excursion later, we will come across a response in popular culture on the topic of "violence against women." One can propose that Thandeka's daughter's story is the script of the "real" that Molekane's music video "Powa" is responding to.

124. *Martiné and Thandeka* directed by Xoliswa Sithole, 24 min. Filmmakers Against Racism, South Africa, 2008. Produced by Carolyn Carew. (Timecode of the scene discussed here: 5:36–9.34 min.)

125. Sithole won amongst others the prestigious Peabody Award, cf. halle institute.emory.edu/events/speakerseries/sithole.html; last accessed 8/2/2013.

126. Azoulay, 217.

127. Ibid., 253.

128. Ibid., 255.

129. Azoulay in footnote 13, *Civil Contract*, 528.

130. Roger Graef, "A Complaint of Rape," Episode 3 of the Series "Police," BBC I, originally screened, 1/4–3/15, 1982, cf. www.screenonline.org.uk/tv/id/464502/; last accessed 8/16/2014.

131. Pumla Gqola, *Rape: A South African Nightmare* (Johannesburg: Jacana Media 2015).

132. Cf. Project Unbreakable, projectunbreakable/tumblr/com; last accessed 9/20/2013. The artist Gillian Wearing already did a similar work with signs in 1992, cf. *Signs that say what you want them to say and not Signs that say what someone else wants you to say*, 1992–1993. Maureen Paley: London.

133. Project Unbreakable, projectunbreakable/tumblr/com, last accessed 9/20/2013.

134. Cf. Zanele Muholi. "Aftermath" 2004. For a detailed analysis of Muholi's photograph, cf. Gunkel, "Introduction," in *The Cultural Politics*, 1–2.

135. For a another thorough analysis of rape and the limits of representation, cf. Gillian Whitlock, "Remediating Gorilla Girl: Rape Warfare and the Limits of Humanitarian Storytelling," in *Biography 3.3,* 2010, 471–97.

136. See chapter 4, the discussion of the "Working the City" and the "Hotel Yeoville" Project.

137. Another destabilizing scene is the one "Telling Lies" with the girls refusing to talk in the camp, where Keniloe lies down on the floor, discussed in part 5.1.

138. Cf. Butler, *Frames of War.*

139. Butler, *Frames of War*, 12.

140. Cf. Johanna Schaffer, *Ambivalenzen der Sichtbarkeit. Visuelle Strukturen der Anerkennung* (Bielefeld: Transcript, 2008).

141. Steyerl, *Camera Austria*, 28.

142. Frantz Fanon, *Black Skin, White Masks* (London: Pluto Press, 1986), 231.

Chapter 3

1. Cf. the dissertation by Annett Schultz, *Unity in Diversity? Konstruktion von kulturellem Gedächtnis im Post-Apartheid-Südafrika*, Humboldt Universität Berlin, 2012.

2. Landsberg, *Prosthetic Memories*, 109.

3. Kathryn A. Manzo, *Creating Boundaries: The Politics of Race and Nation* (Boulder, CO: Lynne Riener, 1996), 71.

4. Surely it is no surprise that also the LGBT movement adopted the rainbow flag as its banner for an all-inclusive project of people no matter what sexual preference, lifestyle, skin color, or other category of difference

5. Cf. also Mbeki's famous speech on being African: Thabo Mbeki, "I am an African," www.soweto.co.za/html/i_iamafrican.htm; last accessed 6/9/2010; and on the African Renaissance, www.unu.edu/unupress/mbeki.html; last accessed 6/9/2010.

6. Compare Tom Lodge, *Politics in South Africa: From Mandela to Mbeki* (Bloomington, IN: Indiana University Press, 2003).

7. Wendy Brown, *States of Injury* (Princeton, NJ: Princeton University Press, 1995), 67.

8. Compare Ulrike Auga, *Intellektuelle zwischen Dissidenz und Legitimierung. Eine kulturkritische Theorie im Kontext Südafrikas* (Berlin: Lit, 2007), 130.

9. Achille Mbembe, "South Africa's Second Coming: The Nongquawuse Syndrome," published June 15, 2006, on the platform *open Democracy*, www.opendemocracy.net/democracy.africa_democracy/south-africa_succession_3649.jsp; last accessed 5/2/2014. *Nongquawuse* was a self-proclaimed Xhosa prophet who claimed that if people would kill all their cattle, the dead would arise from the ashes and the whites would be swept into the sea. This lead to the Xhosa cattle killing in 1856/57 that started a famine and effectively ended Xhosa independence and self-rule. Cf. J. B. Peires, *The Dead Will Arise: Nonquawuse and the Great Xhosa Cattle-Killing Movement of 1856/7* (Bloomington, IN: University of Indiana Press, 1989).

10. Achille Mbembe, "Black Nativism, White Melancholia," public lecture, University of Cape Town, South Africa, July 8, 2007; wiserweb.wits.ac.za; last accessed 7/6/2013.

11. Cf. Achille Mbembe, "Whiteness without Apartheid: the limits of racial freedom," 2007, opendemocracy.net/democracy_power/africa_democracy/south_apartheid; last accessed 9/1/2008 and Marjorie Jobson, *Arme gegen Arme*. Interview

in *medico-Rundschreiben* 02/2008, www.medico.de/material/rundschreiben/2008/02/suedafrika-arme-gegen-arme/; last accessed 9/1/2008.

12. Cf. e.g., the documentary films dealing with these issues: "Dear Mandela" by Dara Kell and Christopher Nizza, www.dearmandela.com; last accessed 8/1/2012 and "When the Mountain meets its Shadow" by Alexander Kleider, Daniela Michel, 2010, www.imdb.com/title/tt1590242/; last accessed 8/1/2012.

13. Cf. Jo Beall, ed., *Uniting a Divided City: Governance and Social Exclusion in Johannesburg* (London: Earthscan, 2002); Nathan Geffen, "Shattered Myths: The xenophobic violence in South Africa," 07/03/2008, www.pambazuka.org/en/category/comment/49179; last accessed 9/1/2008.

14. Cf. Loren Landau, Gayatri Sing, and Kaajal Ramjathan-Keogh, "Xenophobia in South Africa and Problems Relating to it," January 2005, Forced Migration Studies Program Wits University, Johannesburg, www.migration.org; last accessed 7/5/2011. "The criminal foreigner" is of course a global "image of the enemy" (Feindbild) or scapegoat.

15. See, for example: Auga, *Intellektuelle*, Neville Alexander, *Südafrika. Der Weg von der Apartheid zur Demokratie* (Munich: C. H. Beck 2001); Patrick Bond, *Elite Transition. From Apartheid to Neoliberalism in South Africa* (London/Sterling, Pietermaritzburg: Pluto Press and University of Natal Press, 2000). Kistner, *Commissioning and Contesting Post-Apartheid's Human Rights.*

16. The most extreme form of post-apartheid separation of poor and rich people is through the proliferation of gated communities. Cf. e.g., Derek Hook and Michelle Vrodjlak, "Gated communities, heterotopia and a "rights" of privilege: a 'heterotopology' of the South African security-park," in *Geoforum*, 33 (2) 2002, 195–219.

17. The "born-frees" is the generation of South African who were born after the end of apartheid. Cf. Jodi Matas and Phil Maynard, *The Guardian*, 05/26/2014, www.theguardian.com/world/video/2014/apr/25/born-free-generation-20-year-olds-south-africa-video; last accessed 9/9/2014.

18. Cf. article on violence and trauma in Libya: Michael Gleich, "Der Horror steckt noch in den Köpfen," in *Chrismon* 03, (Frankfurt a. M., 2013), 47. Again there are also many studies on this in the context of the Israeli-Palestine conflict.

19. The scope of the selected materials makes clear that there are also many everyday, mundane images of migration analyzed. But the catastrophic images produce a certain backdrop to all other images of migrants and migration. In part this is similar to the image production in the Israel-Palestine conflict.

20. Roland Barthes, *Die helle Kammer* (Frankfurt a. M.: Suhrkamp, 1985), 107. Translation mk.

21. Fred Moten, "Black Mo'ning," in *Loss: The Politics of Mourning*, 66.

22. As a female eye-witness recalls in the film *The Burning Man* by Adze Ugah, (FAR 2008 DVD). The film will be discussed in detail later.

23. The South African police force is known to use both rubber bullets and, at times, live ammunition against black protestors and groups pursuing violent acts. This is a continuity from apartheid policing practices, cf. for example, the shooting

of Marikana miners in 2012: Andiswe Makinana, "Marikana Tragedy. Who authorized the use of live ammunition?" in *Mail and Guardian*. 8/21/2012.

24. Sontag, *Regarding the Pain of Others.* Notably this book does not show any of the photographs it discusses. The book cover presents the reader with a drawing by Goya of a man hanging from the gallows and another man watching.

25. For example, Achille Mbembe discusses the photographic practice as "poverty pornography" together with Ayana Jackson, Gabi Ncgobo, Thembinkosi Goniwe, and Khwezi Gule at Momo Gallery, Johannesburg on Aug. 10, 2010, www.youtube.com/watch?v=csUW0T9vb-E; last accessed 4/15/2014.

26. Peter Geimer, "Fotos, die man nicht zeigt. Probleme mit Schockbildern," in Ludger Derenthal et al., ed., *Fotografische Leidenschaften* (Marburg: Jonas Verlag 2006), 250, translation mk. Peter Geimer is a protagonist of the German "Bildwissenchaft." These are visual culture studies with a slightly different focus than in the Anglo-American context. Cf. Horst Bredekamp, "A Neglected Tradition? Art History as *Bildwissenschaft*," in *Critical Inquiry*, Vol. 29, No. 3, Spring 2003, 418–428.

27. I follow here Christian Metz, who suggested, "It is impossible to *use* a theory to "apply it," while at the same time acknowledging that psychoanalytic models may be helpful to theorize photography and film. Cf. Metz, "Photography and Fetish," in *October*, Vol. 34, 1985, 89.

28. Trauma and compulsive repetition (Wiederholungszwang) are connected. Cf. Elisabeth Roudinesco and Michael Plon, *Wörterbuch der Psychoanalyse* (Vienna, New York: Springer 2004), 1028.

29. Cf. Torquato Tasso, "Jerusalem Delivered," (first published 1581). Or. *Gerusalemme liberata*, ed. Luca Caretti (Mondadori, 1983).

30. Sigmund Freud, "Beyond the Pleasure Principle," in *The Standard Edition of the Complete Psychological Works of Sigmund Freud.* Trans. from the German under the general editorship of James Strachey in collaboration with Anna Freud, assisted by Alix Strachey and Alan Tyson, 24 vols. (London: Hogarth, 1953–74), Vol. 18, Ch. 3.

31. Cathy Caruth, *Unclaimed Experience: Trauma, Narrative and History* (Baltimore, MD: John Hopkins University Press, 1996), 2.

32. For a detailed account on the visual politics of this image and its effects on white feminists in the United States, cf. Dietze, *Weiße Frauen in Bewegung*, 343–51.

33. Moten, "Black Mo'ning," 72.

34. Brian Massumi, "Chaos in the "Total Field" of Vision," in *Parables for the Virtual*, 145.

35. Cf. on the "problem of beauty of violence" in Indian documentary films Nicole Wolf, "Make it Real: Documentary and other cinematic experiments by Women Filmmakers in India," 10.

36. Audre Lorde, "Afterimages," in id.: *The Collected Poems of Audre Lorde* (W. W. Norton and Company Inc., 1997).

37. Hilton Als, "GWTW" in id.: *White Girls.* (San Francisco: McSweeney's, 2014), 135–43, here 137.

38. Christopher Saunders, "Lynching: The Southern African Case," in Manfred Berg and Simon Wend, eds., *Globalizing Lynching History: Vigilantism and Extralegal Punishment from an International Perspective* (Basingstoke, UK: Palgrave Macmillan, 2011), 87–100. For the American context, cf. Gabriele Dietze, *Weiße Frauen in Bewegung* (Bielefeld: Transcript, 2013), 191–211.

39. Saunders, "Lynching," 92. The mentioned photograph was printed only in the first edition of the novel, which took an anti-imperialist stance against Cecil Rhodes. Cf. Olive Schreiner, *Trooper Peter Halket of Mashonaland* (London: Unwin, 1905).

40. Cf. Hayes, "Power, Secrecy, Proximity: A Short History of African Photography," 150–51.

41. Saunders, "Lynching," 90–91.

42. Cf. Thelma Golden, ed., *Black Male: Representations of Masculinity in Contemporary American Art* (New York: Whitney Museum of American Art, 1994), 91–110.

43. In Germany a prominent example for a memorial with a Pietà scene is the sculpture of Käthe Kollwitz in the "Neue Wache" Memorial against the war. The Pietà scene has also been discussed in the context of the photograph of Hector Pietersen in "Affective Images I."

44. On the situation in Argentinia, see "History of Abuelas de Plaza de Mayo," www.abuelas.org.ar/english/history.htm; last accessed 4/15/2014. On Turkey see "Saturday Mothers," www.memorializeturkey.com/en/memorial/saturday-mothers/; last accessed 4/15/2014. In this context Judith Butler's *Antigone's Claim: Kinship between Life and Death* (New York: Columbia University, 2000) can be useful to explain how acts of mourning can become acts of dissidence.

45. Patricia Hayes, "Power, Secrecy, Proximity: A Short History of African Photography," in *Kronos* No. 33, 2007, 144. But one could even draw further parallels to the anti-slavery visual discourse in the United States that also concentrated on black suffering bodies, as I have also developed in chapter 2.

46. Cf. Bartholomäus Grill problematizes the catastrophic portrayal of Africa in the Western imagination, cf. *Ach, Afrika. Berichte aus dem Inneren eines Kontinents* (Munich: Goldmann, 2005).

47. Als, 138.

48. Achille Mbembe, "Necropolitics," in *Public Culture* 15(1), trans. L. Meintjes (Durham, NC, and London: Duke University Press 2003), 13.

49. For the question of the relationship of social and political memory, cf. Aleida Assmann and Linda Short, *Memory and Political Change* (Basingstoke, UK: Palgrave Macmillan, 2011).

50. Joanna Ball, "The Ritual of the Necklace," Centre for the Study of Violence and Reconciliation, 1994, www.csvr.org.za/index.php/publications/1632-the-ritual-of-the-necklace.html; last accessed 7/6/2014.

51. Mbembe, "Necropolitics," 17.

52. Pumla Gqola, "Brutal Inheritances: Echoes, Negrophobia and Masculinist Violence," 213.

53. Even though most countries prefer to receive only "highly skilled" migrants, they also benefit from the unskilled labor of migrants. Cf. Uri Dadush, "The Effect of Unskilled Migration on the Host Economy," www.knomad.org/powerpoints/Uri_Dadush_Paper_Unskilled_Migration_13Nov2013.pdf; last accessed 7/4/2014, Loren Landau, "Passage, profit, protection and the challenge of participation building and belonging in African cities," ANU-WIDER, Working paper No. 2010/49, World Institute for Development Economic Research, www.wider.unu.edu/publications/working-papers/2010/en_GB/-wp2010-49/; last accessed 6/2/2014.

54. Karl Marx, *The Eighteenth Brumaire of Louis Bonaparte*, 1852, Ch. V.

55. Gqola, "Brutal Inheritances: Echoes, Negrophobia and Masculinist Violence," 213.

56. Joanna Ball, "The Ritual of the Necklace," Centre for the Study of Violence and Reconciliation, 1994, www.csvr.org.za/index.php/publications/1632-the-ritual-of-the-necklace.html; last accessed 7/6/2014.

57. Cf. Mamdani, *Citizen and Subject.*

58. Landau, "Mobility and Metanarrative."

59. Bheki (name intentionally changed to protect his identity), Senior Councilor in ANC, quoted from Shmuckler, *The Line*, 7.

60. Mark Sanders, "Ambiguities of Mourning," in *Loss: The Politics of Mourning*, 79.

61. Yuval-Davis, *Gender & Nation* (London: Sage, 1997).

62. Ibid., 67.

63. Gqola, "Brutal Inheritances: Echoes, Negrophobia and Masculinist Violence," 218–19.

64. Ibid.

65. Arjun Appadurai "mediascapes" in: "Disjuncture and Difference in the Global Cultural Economy," in *Theory, Culture, Society*, 1990, (7), 296.

66. Mbembe, *Necropolitics.*

67. Mbembe, "South Africa's Second Coming: The Nongquawuse Syndrome."

68. Many shocking photographs are withheld from the public's view, especially in times of war, for example the photograph of Kenneth Jarecke of a burnt Iraqi soldier that was not published in the American press. Tori Rose DeGhett, "The War Photo No One Would Publish," in *The Atlantic,* 08/08/2014. Cf. www.theatlantic.com/features/archive/2014/08/the-war-photo-no-one-wouldpublish/37576; last accessed 9/20/2014.

69. Kylie Thomas argues in her article "Wounding Apertures" that in post-apartheid times a large number of self-vigilance acts of necklacing go unreported, because the understanding of what is "political" has changed and therefore photojournalists often do not cover post-apartheid violence in townships.

70. Similar arguments were held against Israel, "how can this country, intimately knowing the Holocaust, now repeat violence against Palestinians"? Or another example of this discursive pattern is the reproach of "homonationalism," how is it possible that formerly marginalized groups, once in power, do not act in accordance to their previous experience.

71. Cf. Libby Saxton, *Haunted Images: Film, Ethics, Testimony and the Holocaust* (London, New York: Wallflower Press, 2008), 2. Saxton analyzes images of the Holocaust; however, her findings are transferable to some of the violent images from South Africa.

72. Cf. Gina Shmuckler, *The Line*. Nadine Gordimer, *No Time Like the Present* (London: Picador, 2013).

73. Azoulay, *The Civil Contract of Photography*, 312.

74. Azoulay, 355. In Hebrew "rape" also has the meaning "to force someone to do something," cf. footnote 54 in Azoulay, 545.

75. Cf. Pierre Bourdieu on photography as social distinction, in *Distinction: A Social Critique of the Judgement of Taste* (Cambridge, MA: Harvard University Press, 1984).

76. *The Burning Man* (24 min.), South Africa, 2008, and *Man on Ground,* (80 min, Color, HDcam) South Africa, 2011.

77. The time code of these scenes is: 11.10 min.–14.19 min.

78. Cf. Hayes, "Power, Secrecy, Proximity: A Short History of African Photography."

79. Cf. Margie Orford, "A Foreigner in My Own Land," www.xenophobia.org.za/saspeakout.htm; last accessed 5/1/2010. Here, a white woman imagines a universal suffering beyond the color line as her own, or a black suffering as her own. Yet again, while in South Africa there were a lot of white people active in the anti-apartheid protest movement, and their role cannot be neglected; it still needs to be acknowledged that the "black man suffers differently than the white man," cf. Fanon, *Black Skin, White Masks*, 138.

80. The image of Nhamuave being burnt alive may indeed remind the viewer of other photographs and incidents of burning, of self-annihilation as forms of protest, as was the case in 1963 when Buddhist monk Thich Quang Duc set himself on fire in Saigon to protest the policies of the Vietnamese government. This act of self-immolation was photographed and won the World Press Award in 1963. President John F. Kennedy commented on the photograph, "no news picture in history has created so much emotion around the world as this one." Cf. Seth Jacobs, *Cold War Mandarin: Ngo Dinh Diem and the Origins of America's War in Vietnam, 1950–1963* (Lanham, MD: Rowman & Littlefield, 2006), 149. Even though the image of Ernesto resembled a figure of a martyr, it is important to keep in mind the obvious disparities, since he did not create this situation, he did not set himself on fire. He did not want to die but he unwillingly became a martyr figure through the visual records that showed how he was killed. This was due to the timing, since the photographers were not present or not ready to take photographs when the perpetrators set him on fire. There is no photograph of that moment.

81. The Sonke Gender Justice Network works specifically with men to create more gender justice. Cf. saynotoviolence.org/user/780; last accessed 9/24/2012, and www.genderjustice.org.za, last accessed 6/1/2012.

82. Unpublished interview with Adze Ugah by the author in Johannesburg 2010.

83. *Man on Ground* (80 min., color, HDcam), directed by Akin Omotoso, South Africa, 2011. Cf. www.imdb.com/title/tt2043914/; last accessed 8/5/2013. *Man on Ground* played at Berlinale Film Festival 2012 in the Panorama section. Cf. www.berlinale.de/en/archiv/jahresarchive/2012/02_programm_2012/02_Filmdatenblatt_2012_2012014.php; last accessed 8/12/2013.

84. Christian Metz, "Photography and Fetish," in *October*, Vol. 34, 1985, 88.

85. It may remind one of Max Frisch's play, *Biedermann und die Brandstifter* (Engl. *The Fire Raisers*) (1958) (Frankfurt a. M.: Suhrkamp, 2002).

86. John Maxwell Coetzee, *Disgrace* (London, New York: Penguin 2008), and Elahe Haschemi Yekani's discussion of Coetzee in *The Privilege of Crisis: Narratives of Masculinities in Colonial and Postcolonial Literature, Photography and Film* (Frankfurt, New York: Campus, 2011), 248–62.

87. Brown, *States of Injury*, 73.

88. Thomas, "Wounding Apertures," 206.

89. Cf. chapter 2.

90. Friedrich Nietzsche, *On the Genealogy of Morals* (New York: Vintage, 1969), 61, qtd. in Brown, *States of Injury*, 52.

91. Cf. Massumi, "The Autonomy of Affect," 25–28.

92. Wendy Brown, "Wounded Attachments," in *States of Injury*, 52.

93. Als, *White Girls*, 140.

94. South African black ANC-activist Steve Biko was killed while in prison for his political activities in 1977.

95. Peter Gabriel, "Biko" released in 1978, www.azlyrics.com/lyrics/petergabriel/biko.html; last accessed 12/1/2013. "Yihla Moja" is Xhosa, and means "Come Spirit." www.songfacts.com/detail.php?id=727; last accessed 12/1/2013.

96. For a discussion of Nollywood aesthetics, cf. Jeffrey Geiger, "Nollywood Style: Nigerian Movies and 'shifting perceptions of worth,'" in *Film International*, Issue 60, 2012, 58–69.

97. With "image space" I am referring to the Benjaminian "Bildraum."

98. As a character explains the events in "Man on Ground." One could read similar statements in *Chimurenga Chronic* May 2008.

99. The construction of "easy" and linear narratives of history with the master narrative of the "struggle and overcoming of apartheid" in South Africa has been widely criticized as being too simplistic and only working in retrospect.

100. Ungulani Ba Ka Khosa, "When History is Suspended. (In Memory of Ernesto Alfabeto Nhamuave)," in: *Chimurenga Chronic* 5/ 18–24 May 2008, Capetown.

101. The term "xenophobia" is contested, yet it is the one predominantly used in the South African context to describe the events.

102. "Powa" is hip-hop slang for "Power." At the same time there is also an organization by the same name: POWA: People Opposing Women Abuse. POWA http://www.powa.co.za/POWA/, last accessed 2/19/2017. The double meaning seems consciously intended. The video is available on YouTube, www.youtube.com/watch?v=BMdM03miCgo; last accessed 9/20/2012.

103. Tumi Molekane, "Powa," cf. www.mahala.co.za/culture/no-man-should-have-all-that-power/; last accessed 9/17/2012.

104. Cf. on this the illuminating text by artist and writer Thenjiwe Niki Nkosi, "Saying goodbye to a hero—and the idea of needing a hero," in the *Washington Post,* 12/13/2013.

105. Kgebetli Moele, *Untitled* (Cape Town: Kwela Books, 2013).

106. Moele, *Untitled,* 135.

107. Gunkel, *The Cultural Politics of Female Sexuality,* 90.

108. For instance, cf. Xolani Koyana on recent necklacings in Khayelitsha, "Justice Breakdown in Khayelitsha," in *Cape Times,* 03/26/2012, cf. www.iol.co.za/capetimes/justice-breakdown-in-khayelitsha-1.1263715#.VB6tH-c2ZyU; last accessed 9/2/2014. Khayelitsha is a large black township outside of Cape Town. In addition, for a more detailed analysis cf. Joanna Ball, "The Ritual of the Necklace," Centre for the Study of Violence and Reconciliation, 1994, www.csvr.org.za/index.php/publications/1632-the-ritual-of-the-necklace.html; last accessed 7/6/2014.

109. Cf. the section on photographs of necklacings in part 2.2. and chapter 3.

110. Gunkel, *The Cultural Politics of Female Sexuality,* 87–88.

111. Ibid., 90.

112. "SA-remains-world-rape-capital," SAPA 24H News, www.news24.com/SouthAfrica/News/SA-remains-world-rape-capital-20120921; last accessed 12/12/2012. For a problematization of the label of "rape capital" see Kate Wilkinson, "Why it is wrong to call SA (or any other country) 'the rape capital of the world,'" in *Mail and Guardian,* Johannesburg, South Africa, 1/29/2014.

113. Spivak wrote in "Can the Subaltern Speak" of "White men saving brown women from brown men," criticizing that privileged white males from Western countries claim to know what "the Third World Woman" wants and needs. Cf. Spivak, "Can the Subaltern Speak?" in Rosalind C. Morris, ed., *Can the Subaltern Speak? Reflections on the History of an Idea* (New York: Columbia University Press, 2010), 48.

114. Sandra Lee Bartky, *Femininity and Domination: Studies in the Phenomenology of Oppression* (New York, London: Routledge 1990).

115. For a closer analysis of hate crimes that include "corrective rape" in South Africa, cf. Pumla Gqola, *Rape: A South African Nightmare* (Auckland Park, SA: Jacana Media Ltd., 2015), and Gunkel, *The Cultural Politics,* 2 et seq.

116. Gunkel, *The Cultural Politics,* 85.

Chapter 4

1. Parts of chapter 4 have been published in the essay "Photographic portraits of migrants in South Africa," in *Social Dynamics. A Journal African Studies,* Vol. 40 (Cape Town: Routledge, 2014), 471–94.

2. I took this photograph when I was on a "photo walk" through Hillbrow as part of the "Wide Angle: Photography as Public Practice Conference," which took place March 23–26, 2011, at Wits University. The photo walks were organized by

the Johannesburg-based artist Dorothee Kreutzfeldt. I will analyze my own photograph using the same method as when looking at other people's images.

3. John Caputo, ed., *Deconstruction in a Nutshell: A Conversation with Jacques Derrida* (New York: Fordham University Press, 1997), 106–24. Georges Bataille used this expression originally but Derrida discussed the concept further. Cf. Marie-Eve Morin, "Putting Community Under Erasure," in *Culture Machine*, Vol. 8, 2006, www.culturemachine.net/index.php/cm/article/viewArticle/37/45; last accessed 12/3/2013.

4. Médecins Sans Frontières, International Website, www.msf.org/; last accessed 4/1/2013.

5. Nira Yuval-Davis, *Gender and Nation* (London: Sage, 1997).

6. Yet there are many photographers offering their services in Joubert Park in Johannesburg, some of whom also take ID photos. Many of these photographers are African migrants, as Terry Kurgan found in her Joubert Park Photo Project. Cf. Terry Kurgan and Louise Bethlehem, "Park Pictures: On the Work of Photography in Johannesburg," in Lynn Schler et al., eds., *Rethinking Labour in Africa, Past and Present.*(New York, London: Routledge, 2013), 128–43.

7. South African Passport Service, passportservice.co.za/2010/07/28/south-african-passport-photo-guidelines/; last accessed 9/2/2012.

8. Patricia Hayes. "Power, Secrecy, Proximity: A Short History of South African Photography," and Jens Schröter, "Das Zeitalter der technischen Nicht-Reproduzierbarkeit," in: idem et al., eds., *Navigationen.* No. 1 (Siegen: Universi, 2010), 9–36.

9. Cf. chapter 1.

10. Greg Marinovich and João Silva, *The Bang-Bang Club*, 81–82.

11. Azoulay, *The Civil Contract of Photography*, 68.

12. Ibid., 68.

13. Mbembe, *On the Postcolony.*

14. Photograph by Eli Weinberg (EW14-4-1. University of the Western Cape, Mayibuye Archives).

15. Cf. www.saha.org.

16. Newbury, *Defiant Images*, 5.

17. Papadopoulus and Tsianos, *The Autonomy of Migration.*

18. Édouard Glissant, *Philosophie de la Relation* (Philosophy of Relation) (excerpt), in *Frieze* Magazine, No. 7, Winter 2012, 73.

19. Barthes, *Camera Lucida*, 43–62.

20. SAHTT 2010, "Stop Human Trafficking in Southern Africa," saahtt.wordpress.com/; last accessed 2/3/2012.

21. At the same time, it can also be valuable to hide someone's identity, and there are many different ways to do it while at the same time maintaining that person's dignity. One example would be Tine Leisch's *Gangster Girls*, where female inmates wear theatrical makeup that obscures their faces, but their eyes are shown. Cf. Tine Leisch, *Gangster Girls*, 2008. Documentary Film, Online Movie Database, www.imdb.com/title/tt1399019/; last accessed: 9/4/2012.

22. International Organization of Migration, mission statement on their website, iom.org.za/; last accessed 4/21/2013.

23. Ingrid Palmary et al., eds., *Gender and Migration: Feminist Interventions* (London: Zed Books, 2010).

24. Médecins Sans Frontières, International Website, www.msf.org/; last accessed 4/1/2013.

25. Solidarity for Survival Website, www.solidarity4survival.org/; last accessed 5/15/2011.

26. E.g., Gayatri Chakravorty Spivak, "Can the Subaltern Speak?" in Rosalind C. Morris, ed., *Can the Subaltern Speak? Reflections on the History of an Idea* (New York: Columbia University Press, 2010),

Miriam Ticktin, *Casualties of Care: Immigration and the Politics of Humanitarianism in France* (Berkeley, Los Angeles: University of California Press, 2011).

27. Palmary et al., *Gender and Migration*, 13.

28. See the "Women's Charter," www.anc.org.za/ancdocs/history/women/wcharter.html; last accessed 5/6/2010.

29. South African History Archive, Saha, Struggle Poster Collection.

30. The nuclear family is in crisis everywhere, of course, and not only in South Africa.

31. Cf. e.g., the earlier discussed film *Martine and Thandeka* by Xoliswa Sithole, 2009, as well as *The Burning Man* by Adze Ugah, 2009.

32. Cf. Auga, *Intellektuelle—zwischen Dissidenz und Legitimierung*, 343, and McClintock, "No Longer in a Future Heaven," in *Imperial Leather*, 352–89.

33. Black South Africans from the metropolitan areas or townships referred to non-South African Blacks from other African countries as "Kwerekwere." Their various languages, which they did not understand, all seemed to sound the same to them, like "kwere-kwere." White foreigners in South Africa were usually not called Kwerekwere.

34. Médecins Sans Frontières, International Website, www.msf.org/; last accessed 4/1/2013. The other gallery mentioned above, of visitor portraits, was unfortunately not online anymore in 2013. Also, the AMCS distributed the same type of T-shirt in 2013, with its website address printed on the back side of the T-shirt: www.migration.org.za; last accessed 8/7/2014.

35. Richard Tomlinson et al., eds., *Emerging Johannesburg. Perspectives on the Post-apartheid City* (London, New York: Routledge, 2003).

36. There are several other photographers or NGOs working with images, as for example Guideon Mendel's work, documenting and facilitating the self-documentation of people living with HIV "Through Positive Eyes," or the "I was shot in Joburg" project that works with youth at risk, providing them with disposable cameras and generating income for them. Cf. Guideon Mendel's website, throughpositiveeyes.org/ and "I was shot in Joburg," cf. www.iwasshot.com/; both last accessed 9/17/2013.

37. Terry Kurgan, "Public Art/Private Lives A.K.A: Hotel Yeoville," in *Hotel Yeoville* (Johannesburg: Fourthwall Books, 2013).

38. Percy Zvomuya, "An outsider's Yeoville insight: Social responsibility meets mainstream art in this chronicle of public, private and mundane lives," in: *Mail and Guardian*, Johannesburg, SA, 8/3/2013.

39. Kurgan, "Public Art/Private Lives A.K.A: Hotel Yeoville."

40. Terry Kurgan is a Johannesburg-based artist, who has explored the idea of (self-)portraiture widely both in the medium of drawing and photography in several of her other projects. This study cannot address the complexity of the whole project and only looks at a few paradigmatic self-portraits that were produced there.

41. Kurgan, "Public Art/Private Lives A.K.A: Hotel Yeoville."

42. For a discussion of violence against black lesbians, cf. Gunkel, *The Cultural Politics of Female Sexuality*, 5–8.

43. Pumla Gqola, "Through Zanele Muholi's Eyes: Re/Imagining Ways of Seeing Black Lesbians," in Zanele Muholi, ed., *Only Half the Picture* (Cape Town: Stevenson & STE, 2006), 83.

44. Kurgan, "Public Art/Private Lives A.K.A: Hotel Yeoville."

45. Ibid.

46. Achille Mbembe, "The Aesthetics of Superfluidity," in idem, and Sarah Nuttal, eds., *Johannesburg, the Elusive Metropolis* (Johannesburg: Wits University Press, 2008).

47. Mbembe, *On the Postcolony*.

48. David Goldblatt, "Dear Christine," in *Camera Austria*, 2007, 14.

49. The project *Working the City* was presented at the *Wide Angle: Photography as Public Practice* conference, Wits University, Johannesburg, March 23–26, 2011, and several papers have been published on it, cf. e.g., Jo Veary et al., "Working the City: Experiences of migrant women in inner-city Johannesburg," in *Southern Africa Gender and Media and Diversity Journal* 9, 2011, 228–33. This chapter will only look at one specific poster of one participating woman in the context of photographic self-portraiture.

50. Market Photo Workshop, "Working the City Project Description," 2011, cf. www.marketphotoworkshop.co.za/; last accessed, 6/2/2011.

51. Ibid.

52. Cf. "Sexual Offenses Act, South African Government Information, www.info.gov.za/view/; last accessed 5/21/2011.

53. Compare Laura Agustin, "Migration, Feminism and the Sex Industry," Workshop at the University of Neuchatel, September 15–17, 2010. There are similar developments within Europe. The fear of unskilled migrants is also why in Europe the Schengen agreement is seen as such a threat, because it enhances the possibilities of migration in the informal sector.

54. Cf. Caroline Wanjiku Kihato " 'A Picture Speaks a Thousand Words': Understanding Women's Migration Through Visual Diaries," in *Scrutiny* 2, Vol. 15, Issue 1, 2010.

Cf. interview with Bishop Paul Verryn, 2011. The Bishop headed the United Methodist Church in Hillbrow where African migrants, predominantly from Zimbabwe, can sleep at night. Paul Verryn is a controversial figure, though. Cf. Faranaaz

Parker, "Paul Verryn, what went wrong?" 1/29/2010, *Mail and Guardian*, mg.co.za/article/2010-01-29-paul-verryn-what-went-wrong; last accessed 8/8/2013.

55. Market Photo Workshop Website 2011; last accessed 9/7/2011

56. Grant H. Kester, *The One and the Many: Contemporary Collaborative Art in a Global Context* (Durham, NC: Duke University Press, 2011), 1.

57. Hal Foster, "The Artist as Ethnographer?" in *The Return of the Real* (Cambridge, MA: MIT Press 1996), 171–204.

58. Nelson Goodmann, *Ways of Worldmaking* (Indianapolis, IN: Hackett, 1978).

59. Judith Butler, *The Psychic Life of Power: Theories in Subjection* (Stanford, CA: Stanford University Press, 1997), 20.

Chapter 5

1. Cf. for a discussion of post-representation and new types of media images. Hito Steyerl, "Politics of Post-Representation," cf. dismagazine.com/disillusioned-2/62143/hito-steyerl-politics-of-post-representation/; last accessed 9/7/2014. Post-representation can be connected to the question of post-blackness, but neither signifies a post-racism era. Cf. Nana Adusei-Poku, "The multiplicity of multiplicities. Post-Black Art and its Intricacies," in *darkmatter*, 11/29/2012, www.darkmatter101.org; last accessed 8/7/2014.

2. Cf. e.g., Étienne Balibar, *Sind wir Bürger Europas? Politische Integration, soziale Ausgrenzung und die Zukunft des Nationalen* (Hamburg: Hamburg Edition, 2003). Sandro Mezzadra, *Border as Method* (Durham, NC, London: Duke University Press, 2013).

3. Cf. e.g., Rom News: www.romnews.com/community/; last accessed 9/16/2011.

4. E.g., Vassilis Tsianos et al., *Escape Routes.* Tsianos and Dimitris Papadoupolus, "The Autonomy of Migration." And cf. Johanna Schaffer, *Ambivalenzen der Sichtbarkeit.*

5. Gqola, "Brutal Inheritences," 209–22. The term "Black on Black" racism needs to be criticized, though, as it seems to imply that this is a separate "ethnic" problem of "tribal" politics.

6. Fatima El-Tayeb, *European Others: Queering Ethnicity in Postnational Europe* (University of Minnesota Press, 2011).

7. Deleuze and Guattari, *A Thousand Plateaus: Capitalism and Schizophrenia.*

8. Vassilis and Papadopoulus, *The Autonomy of Migration.*

9. Cf. Mitchell, *What do Pictures Want?* 48–56. Cf. on another project on discarded, half-destroyed, found photos Arianna Arcara and Luca Santese, *Found Photos in Detroit* (Pienallo, Italy: Cesura, 2012) and Vince Leo's review of the project, cf. littlebrownmushroom.wordpress.com/2012/07/11/found-photos-in-detroit-reviewed-by-vince-leo/; last accessed 9/9/2014.

10. The head of the Center for African Society and Migration, Loren Landau, who co-financed the making of the film, commented: "We have this film, but it really is so violent—the statements that some people make in it, that one can't show it now without a facilitator. Or even better a facilitator's guide book and specifically trained people to do it, but unfortunately, we don't have the time and means to set this up, which means that the film isn't really shown" (Loren Landau, July 2012, Johannesburg). This statement attests to the difficulty of getting documentary films shown and distributed. The film has not been banned or censored, yet it is being kept in the drawer even by the academic institution that co-produced it for safety concerns, fearing that watching it could induce further violence.

11. Marietta Kesting, *Howzit? Migrant Life in Joburg* (ca. 20 min., HD & super 8, BW & color). Documentary Film, published on FOG platform, http://fog-platform.com/en/fragmented-city-en/; last acessed 8/25/2016.

12. Ibid.

13. Papadopoulous and Tsianos, *Autonomy of Migration.*

14. Deleuze and Guattari, *A Thousand Plateaus*, 279.

15. José Esteban *Muñoz, Disidentifications: Queers of Color and the Performance of Politics* (Minneapolis: University of Minnesota, 1999), 7.

16. Compare also Muñoz lecture: *With What Ass Does the Cockroach Sit?* at the Camp/AntiCamp conference, HAU Berlin, April 21, 2012. Muñoz borrowed the title for his lecture from a monologue written and performed by Carmelita Tropicana.

17. Sinethemba Twalo, "Into the Darkness, Black Subjectivities and Alternative Knowledge Production," Lecture at IFA, Berlin, July 17, 2014, cf. www.contemporaryand.com/de/exhibition/lecture-into-the-darkness-black-subjectivities-and-alternative-knowledge-production/; last accessed 7/25/2014.

18. Gayatri Chakravorty Spivak, *The Post-Colonial Critic. Interviews, Strategies, Dialogues* (New York, London: Routledge, 1990).

19. Needless to say, filming or visiting is usually not permitted in any detention camp, and Lindela is no exception to this rule, so this film manages to show images from an area that is usually invisible to the public.

20. While the viewer does not learn where the young women are from, they are not wearing the same type of clothes as the other women from Somalia, and the main character Fatima does, and they do not wear veils. Therefore, they do not seem to be hiding for religious reasons, e. g., because they are Muslim and do not want to show their faces to an unknown man. From the production settings of the film it is also clear that the filmmaker communicated with the people he filmed beyond what is seen in the film and got their permission to show the film and produce a DVD. He did not do a clandestine filming.

21. Cf. Toby Miller, *Technologies of Truth: Cultural Citizenship and the Popular Media* (Minneapolis: University of Minnesota Press, 1998), 4.

22. Hito Steyerl, "Können Zeugen sprechen?" in: *Die Farbe der Wahrheit.* (Vienna: Turia & Kant, 2008). An English translation is available at: eipcp.net/transversal/0408/steyerl/en; last accessed 8/5/2014.

23. Crenshaw, "Mapping the Margins: Intersectionality, Identity Politics, and Violence Against Women of Color."

24. Jean-Luc Godard and Jean-Pierre Gorin, "La Politique et le Bonheur," 1972; www.telerama.fr/cinema/films/vive-le-cinema-la-politique-et-le-bonheur-go-erges-kiejman-et-jean-luc-godard,262927.php; last accessed 10/01/2011.

25. For the idea of a certain self-reflexive potential in visual media, see also Cornelia Vismann, *Medien der Rechtsprechung* (Frankfurt a. M.: Fischer Verlag, 2011).

26. Jacques Rancière, "The Thinking of Dissensus," in Paul Bowman and Richard Stamp, eds., *Reading Rancière* (London, New York: Continuum, 2011), 2.

27. Bertolt Brecht, "Kleines Organon für das Theater," *Schriften zum Theater* (Frankfurt a. M.: Suhrkamp, 1957) 99 et seq.

28. Compare Brian Winston's lecture at "Visible Evidence," August 18, 2011, New York University, NY.

29. Khalo Matabane made this comment after the screening of Conversations at the Berlinale, Section International Forum of Young Cinema, 2006, where the film won the prize of the ecumenical jury. Cf. www.berlinale.de/en/archiv/jahresarchive/2006/02_programm_2006/02_Filmdatenblatt_2006_20060308.php; last accessed 6/6/2014.

30. *Border Farm* (HDV, 32 min., 2011), Thenjiwe Niki Nkosi and the Dublibadzimu Theatre Group of Musina, cf. borderfarm.blogspot.com/p/about-us.html; last accessed 7/1/2012. The film has been shown at various festivals and was screened on South African television.

31. De Wet Potgieter and Herbert Matimba, "Barbaric border activity during the 'hell run,'" in *The New Age*, South Africa 5/ 7/2012, www.thenewage.co.za; last accessed 7/1/2012.

32. Statement in *Border Farm*, timecode 08.59 min.

33. Jacques Rancière, *Film Fables* (London: Bloomsbury Academic, 2006), 161.

34. Vassilis Tsianos and Dimitris Papadopoulous, "The Autonomy of Migration," in Anna Hickey-Moody and Peta Malins, eds., *Deleuzian Encounters: Studies in Contemporary Social Issues* (Basingstoke, UK: Palgrave Macmillan, 2007).

35. *Border Farm*, time code: 15.23 min.

36. Tsianos et al., *Escape Routes*, 72–73.

37. Often documentary film shows the subjective, as for example a portrait of one or several individuals. Dialogues are shown face-to-face, filling the frame with one person at a time opposite the viewing audience—a very privileged position of communication.

38. Other scenes of *Conversations on a Sunday Afternoon* have already been discussed in chapter 2.

39. Walter Benjamin, "Der Sürrealismus—Die letzte Momentaufnahme der europäischen Intelligenz," in *Gesammelte Schriften, II, 1,* ed. R. v. Tiedemann and H. Schweppenhäuser (Frankfurt a. M.: Suhrkamp, 1977), 295–310.

40. Jürgen Habermas, *Strukturwandel der Öffentlichkeit* (Frankfurt a. M.: Suhrkamp, 1990).

41. Hito Steyerl, *The Wretched of the Screen* (Berlin: Sternberg Press, 2012), 82.

42. Frantz Fanon, *Black Skin, White Masks.* Trans. Charles Lam Markmann (London: Pluto Press, 1986).

43. Presentation at the seminar of the PhD-Research Group "Gender as a Category of Knowledge," Humboldt University, Berlin, 2010.

44. Fanon, *Black Skin, White Masks*, 138.

45. Ibid.

46. Compare the publication by the same title: Alan Read, ed., *The Fact of Blackness: Frantz Fanon and Visual Representation* (London, Seattle: Institute of Contemporary Arts and Institute of International Visual Arts London, Bay Press, 1996).

47. Fanon, *Black Skin, White Masks*, 135.

48. For a rigorous discussion of multiple blacknesses and post-black art, cf. Adusei-Poku, "The multiplicity of multiplicities: Post-Black Art and its Intricacies."

49. Clemens von Wedemeyer and Paolo Caffoni, eds., *First Contact* magazine, film material no. 4, information on the "fourth wall," January, 2010.

50. Such as the *hactivists'* group *Anonymous* and the *occupy* movements, whose members often use the Guy Fawkes mask. Guy Fawkes was part of the "Gunpowder Plot" to blow up the British House of Lords in 1605.

51. Jodi Dean, "Politics without Politics," in Paul Bowman and Richard Stamp, eds., *Reading Rancière* (London, New York: Continuum, 2011), 93.

52. Vladislavić, *Double Negative*, 13.

53. Vassilis Tsianos, Niamh Stephenson, and Dimitris Papadopoulos, *Escape Routes Control and Subversion in the 21st century* (London: Pluto, 2008).

54. Tsianos et al., *Escape Routes*, 72–73.

55. Tsianos and Papadopoulus, "The Autonomy of Migration."

56. Cf. Neill Blomkamp, *District 9*. (SA 2009, 112 min.), www.imdb.com/title/tt1136608/; last accessed 8/2/2012. Neill Blomkamp was born raised in Johannesburg, South Africa, and now resides in Canada, but frequently works on film projects in South Africa.

57. Mitchell, "Migrating Images—Totemism, Fetishism, Idolatry."

58. Mitchell. "Migrating Images—Totemism, Fetishism, Idolatry," 17.

59. Mitchell. *What Do Pictures Want? The Lives and Loves of Images.*

60. This link between visual politics and exclusion has been paradigmatically explored by comparing a gated community and Johannesburg's inner city "ghetto," in Kesting, *Politik und Sichtbarkeit in Johannesburg.*

61. Marguerite Waller, "Introduction," in Sandra Ponzanesi and Marguerite Waller, eds., *Postcolonial Cinema Studies* (London, New York: Routledge, 2012), 12–13.

62. Later in the film, however, the audience learns that the aliens are able to reproduce by hatching eggs factory-style in converted shacks. Their number is given with the enormous amount of 1.8 million aliens in District 9. Wikus and

his crew find the hatching place and set it into flames, burning thousands of eggs, basically performing a genocide.

63. While Wikus's infection and bodily change is not the main focus of my analysis, it could be explored further, for example with Isabell Lorey's notion of "whiteness" and "immunization." Cf. Isabell Lorey, "Weißsein und Immunisierung: Zur Unterscheidung zwischen Norm und Normalisierung," translate.eipcp.net/strands/03/lorey-strands01de; last accessed 9/9/2014.

64. For example the review by Jayna Brown: bullybloggers.wordpress.com/2009/09/19/on-becoming-alien-%E2%80%93-district/; last accessed 9/27/2009, and the review by Carina Ray, 2009, www.zeleza.com.symposium/494; last accessed 10/29/2009.

65. Yet these viewing conventions are always being experimented with, as for example in the American television series "House of Cards" where characters may also speak conspiratorially into the camera, addressing the viewers directly and thus breaking down the "fourth wall." An interesting work on the margins between documentary and art film installation was Clemens von Wedemeyer's piece "The Fourth Wall," shown at the Triennale de Paris, 2012. Intense Proximité, Palais de Tokio, available partly on YouTube: https://www.youtube.com/watch?v=0CdE2-iYkLI, last accessed 8/17/2014.

66. Curiously, an "angel" is strictly speaking—like the aliens—a non-human creature not from earth but from "heaven."

67. Cf. On family photos Gillian Rose, *Doing Family Photography: The Domestic, the Public and the Politics of Sentiment* (Farngate & Burlington: Ashgate, 2010).

68. Neill Blomkamp, quoted in Henriette Gunkel and Christiane König, " 'You are not welcome here,' post-apartheid negrophobia & real aliens in Blomkamp's *District 9*," in: *darkmatter* Journal, Issue 7, Feb. 2010, www.darkmatter101.org/site; last accessed 10/25/2013.

69. Henriette Gunkel and Christiane König, " 'You are not welcome here,' post-apartheid negrophobia & real aliens in Blomkamp's *District 9*."

70. Cf. Scott C. Johnson, "The Real District 9: Cape Town's District 6," in *Newsweek,* 8/27/09, www.newsweek.com/real-district-9-cape-towns-district-six-78939; last accessed 6/7/2014. Shamil Jeppie and Crain Soudien, *The Struggle for District Six: Past and Present* (Buchu Books 1990), Marco Bezzoli et al., "Texture and Memory The Urbanism of District Six," (Cape Town: Cape Technikon, 2002). See District 6 Museum, *www.districtsix.co.za/*, last accessed 08/01/2011.

71. Cf. Interview with Neill Blomkamp, "Five Things you didn't know about District 9," cf. io9.com/5341120/5-things-you-didnt-know-about-district-9; last accessed 9/5/2014. RDP stands for the "Restructuring and Development Program" of the South African post-apartheid government.

72. For the notion of the "historical uncanny," cf. W. J. T. Mitchell's lecture "The Historical Uncanny: Phantoms, Doubles, and Repetitions in the War on Terror," December 2, 2011, at C/O Berlin.

73. Cf. for example, John Fels and Denis Wood, *The Power of Maps.*

74. For this topic of *safe*, guarded living in South Africa, cf. Lindsay Bremner. "Crime and the Emerging Landscape of Post-Apartheid Johannesburg," in Judin and Vladislavić, eds., *Blank: Architecture, Apartheid and After*, 48–63. Sarah Nuttal and Liz McGregor, eds., *At Risk. Writing on and over the Edge of South Africa* (Johannesburg, Cape Town, SA: Jonathan Ball, 2007), and Richard Tomlinson et al. ed., *Emerging Johannesburg. Perspectives on the Post-apartheid City*.

75. See for example the photographs of Ernest Cole "For Whites Only," in *House of Bondage*, reproduced in Darren Newbury *Defiant Images*, 196.

76. The raised fist as a symbol of "black power" has been used in the United States, South Africa, and elsewhere in the transnational de-colonization movement since the 1960s. On the cultural history of the hand as transmitter of signs, cf. for example, Horst Wenzel, "Hand-Zeichen. Zur Mediengeschichte der Hand als Datenträger," in Moritz Csáky and Peter Stachel, eds., *Mehrdeutigkeit. Die Ambivalenz von Gedächtnis und Erinnerung* (Wien: Passagen, 2003), 179–202.

77. The APF, Anti-Privatization Forum, is a South African social movement for the economically disadvantaged, working with people in the townships around issues of access to water, electricity but also other issues. Cf. official website: apf.org.za/; last accessed 8/17/2014.

78. Cf. For "energetic images" Karl Sierek, *Foto, Kino und Computer. Aby Warburg als Medientheoretiker* (Berlin: Philo, 2007), 49.

79. Mark Dery, ed., *Flame Wars: The Discourse of Cyberculture* (Durham, NC: Duke University Press 1994), 180.

80. Cf. Tim Stuettgen, *In a Qu*a*re Time and Place* (Berlin: b_books 2014).

81. Sun Ra, quoted in Chardine Taylor-Stone, "Afrofuturism, where space, pyramids and politics collide," in *The Guardian*. 1/7/2014.

82. Besides Sun Ra, the musicians George Clinton and Lee Scratch Perry are prominent for their propagation of Afrofuturism. In literature Samuel Delaney and Octavia Butler were both writing Afrofuturist science fiction. Cf. also John F. Szwed, *Space is the Place: The Lives and Times of Sun Ra* (New York: Da Capo, 1998) and Kodwo Eshun, *More Brilliant Than The Sun: Adventures in Sonic Fiction* (London: Quartet Books, 1998).

83. Cf. Andries du Toit, "Becoming the alien, racism, apartheid and *District 9*." 0/4/2009, asubtleknife.wordpress.com/2009/09/04/science-fiction-in-the-ghetto-loving-the-alien/; last accessed 9/2/2014.

84. Mbembe. *On the Postcolony*.

85. Fanon, *The Wretched of the Earth*, 51.

86. The most famous example of this naming practice, of course, being "Nelson" Rohlihala Mandela.

87. Neill Blomkamp quoted in Henriette Gunkel and Christiane König, "You are not welcome here."

88. Gabeba Baderoon on "preferred silence" in "Primal Scenes, Forbidden Words," in Henriette Gunkel et al. eds., *Undutiful Daughters: New Directions in Feminist Thought and Practice* (Basingstoke, UK, New York: Palgrave Macmillan, 2012), 173.

89. Julia Kristeva, *Strangers to Ourselves* (New York: Columbia University Press, 1991).

90. Aurelia Segatti in collaboration with Olufemi Adeagbo and Samson Ogunyemi, "Nigerians in South Africa: Facts and Figures," Migration Issue Brief 8, June 2012, cf. www.migration.org.za/publication/issue-brief/9999/nigerians-south-africa-facts-and-figures; last accessed 8/28/2013.

91. "Muti" is derived from the Zulu word for tree and is a term for traditional medicine in South Africa.

92. Compare Neill Blomkamp, *Alive in Joburg*, cf. Youtube: www.youtube.com/watch?v=le3y0QlLjJE; last accessed 7/12/2010.

93. Kracauer has tried to show this in the context of the Weimar Republic. Siegfried Kracauer, *From Caligari to Hitler: A Psychological History of German Film* (Princeton, NJ: Princeton University Press, 1947).

94. E.g., Bashir Adigun, "Nigerian official rails against District 9," *Mail and Guardian*, 9/20/2011, www.mg.co.za; last accessed 9/25/2009. Yet the opposite opinion was also expressed: "Why District 9 isn't racist against Nigerians," cf. www.guardian.co.uk/film/filmblog/2009/sep/08/district-9-racism/print; last accessed 08/01/2011. There is also a Facebook group "Nigerians offended by District 9," www.facebook.com/group.php?gid=265942795001; last accessed 09/01/2011.

95. Homi Bhabha. *Nation and Narration* (New York, London: Routledge, 2000), 79.

96. See for example AbdouMalique Simone, "The narcotics enterprises that constitute an important component of the inner city economy are commonly seen as the purview of Igbo-dominated Nigerian networks," in "Spectral Selves. Practices in the Making of African Cities," Wiser Institute for Social and Economic Research & New School University. Cf. wiserweb.wits.ac.za/; last accessed 9/6/2011.

97. "Loving the Alien" has become a dictum in its own right since the 1980s in Afrofuturism, for example in Sun Ra's work. There has been a conference in Berlin in 1997 organized by the Rosa-Luxemburg Foundation by the same name, which also resulted in a book, Diedrich Diedrichsen, ed., *Loving the Alien. Science Fiction. Diaspora. Multikultur* (Berlin: ID, 1998).

98. Cf. on the notion of "savages" versus humans, Whitlock, "Remediating Gorilla Girl: Rape Warfare and the Limits of Humanitarian Storytelling," 475–76.

99. Partly *District 9* may work similarly to *Inglourious Basterds* by Quentin Tarantino, 2009, cf. www.imdb.com/title/tt0361748/; last accessed 9/9/2011. Cf. Frank Stern's discussion "Inglourious Basterds. Antifa-Movie als Feel Good Fantasy," in *Malmoe*, 47.

100. Neill Blomkamp, quoted in David Smith, "District 9/South Africa and Apartheid comes to the Movies," *Guardian*, 8/20/2009.

101. There exists a danger of unreflected nostalgia and too smooth portrayals of historic events in the current trend of film in historical settings, as for example in post WWII times, cf. Susan Vahabzadeh, "Touristen im Gestern," *Sueddeutsche Zeitung*, No. 68; March 22–23, 2014, 13.

Chapter 6

1. Cf. the Center for Historical Re-enactments, a Johannesburg based artists' and writers' collective, centerforhistoricalreenactments.blogspot.de/; last accessed 9/13/2012.

2. In South Africa *Nando's* has recently launched a "Diversity-Campaign" that aims at targeting xenophobia and promoting diversity as a positive element of society. This campaign included a new advertisement clip as well as funding for theater pieces, as for instance Gina Shmukler's "The Line," and other cultural events, and the printing of bags and hoodies with the *Nando's* slogan and the words: "Diversity is a good thing." Also *Nando's* started volunteer soup kitchens in communities affected by xenophobic violence, cf. www.souperstars.co.za/, last accessed 12/20/2012. *Nando's* official website is, www.nandos.co.za/; last accessed 8/1/2012. Other video examples include "Times are Tough," www.youtube.com/watch?v=93GhykXtd4Y; last accessed 9/24/2012. One may be reminded of Benetton's advertisement campaigns. However, Benetton seems to be more interested in shocking and provoking as such in a Western global context, whereas *Nando's* actually makes advertisement that is meaningful and critical in the local context of South Africa. Cf. on Benetton, Gianluca Mezzofiore, "Benetton, a history of shocking ad campaigns," in: *International Business Times,* 11/18/2011, www.ibtimes.co.uk/benetton-history-shocking-ad-campaigns-pictures-252087; last accessed 9/3/2014.

3. For a discussion of artistic strategies of re-imagining history, cf. Susanne Leeb, "Not Quite Embracing Failure: History in Contemporary Art," in Texte zur Kunst. December 2009, Vol. 19, No. 76, 100–08.

4. The predominant stereotype of "Nigerians as drug dealers" was discussed further in the analysis of *District 9* in part 5.2, where yet again Nigerians are portrayed as "the drug dealers."

5. The clip thus repeats apartheid terminology by labeling the white South Africans "Europeans" and the black South Africans in the ethnicized terms "Tsotos, Vendas. . . ."

6. The Khoi-San were the first people to settled in South Africa. They used to live as hunter-gatherers.

7. Current archaeological findings suggest that the Nguni and Sotho speaking groups had already arrived in the 1500s in what is now South Africa. In 1652, Jan v. Ribbeck and more Europeans followed. Cf. www.sahistory.org.za/article/1500s; last accessed 12/10/2011.

8. The official South African broadcasting committee banned the clip after it only screened for one week. Cf. South African Press Association (SAPA): "Nando's ad: Banned from TV . . . Goes to print," www.bizcommunity.com; last accessed 6/11/2012. The reason given was that it was violent in showing people "exploding" and therefore might lead to further aggression. The clip was not aired on television any more after the initial screening for a week in June 2012. A fate that many *Nando's* clips share, as for example the one on Robert Mugabe with the title

"Last Dictator Standing," www.youtube.com/watch?v=u1EX--vdxh4, last accessed 6/18/2012. This might even be part of the company's advertising strategy, since the banning may incite more interest. In addition the ads were moved from moving to still images that were shown as large printed banners.

9. Maria Hengeveld, "'Race Jokes' in South Africa." 12/20/12 cf. www.africasacountry.com/2012/12/20/the-race-joke/; last accessed 12/20/2012.

10. Interview with Kemang Wa Lehulere in Johannesburg 2012.

11. Frank Nxumalo, "South Africa remains one of the most unequal countries of the world," Cf. www.sabc.co.za/news/a/5975b6004c185051a3eaffa583a5af00/SA-remains-one-of-the-most-unequal-societies-in-the-world:-World-Bank-20122407; last accessed 9/5/2014.

12. Michelle Monareng, *Removal to Radium*, 2013. This piece was shown in the Group Exhibit at Brundyn Gallery Space in South Africa, with the title "Commute with Instinct," as well as at the Berlin Biennale Crashpad 2014. It was also featured in the Center for Historical Reenactments' magazine *Digging our Own Graves 101*. Published by the Center for Historical Reenactments based in Johannesburg, South Africa, in conjunction with the Berlin Biennale, Crash Pad, Kunstwerke 2014. The CHR staged its institutional suicide in 2012 with "We are absolutely ending this," but keeps on existing as a ghost. Cf. http://historicalreenactments.org/index3.html, last accessed 9/9/2016.

13. One video is called *Mist*, the other *A Grave in the Wind*, and the third consists of historical video footage.

14. Different accounts of what happened exist. It is certain, however, that the community was forced of their land continuously until they all were forced to leave in 1965.

15. Sonnyboy Abram Sikhwane, Memorandum: The Farm Rietspruit, No. 417, I. R. Woyenthin, District Heidelberg, Transvaal. Quoted in: Digging Our Own Graves, 101, 14.

16. This was in summer 2016 on a residency of the Zentrum für Kunst und Urbanistik (ZKU) in Berlin, where she also did a presentation on Aug. 25, 2016. Cf. http://www.zku-berlin.org/de/residencies/258/, last accessed 9/21/2016.

17. Norman Makhubu, "Visual Narratives of Dispossession in Michelle Monareng's Video art," interview with Michelle Monareng, quoted in: Digging our own Graves, 101, 14.

18. Ibid.

19. M. Blackmann, Review of "Commute with Instinct," Artthrob. 2014, cf. www.artthrob.co.za; last accessed 8/1/2014.

20. Advertisement images are part of the visual culture archive and often mirror or comment on certain trends in documentary works. The *Nando's* clip furthermore shares similar staging and aesthetics with the video work by Thenjiwe Nkosi, *Border Farm*, 2011, which has been analyzed and discussed in-depth in part 5.1.

21. Cf. Landsberg, *Prosthetic Memories*.

22. Lucilla Blankenberg, *Don't Shoot.* (HDV, 11:45 min.), South Africa, 2007. Released on DVD by "Why Democracy?" www.whydemocracy.net; last accessed

7/2/2014. For a thorough analysis of the relationship of the camera and the gun and the double meaning of "to shoot," cf. Alisa Lebow, "Shooting with Intent: Framing Conflict," in Joram Ten Brink and Joshua Oppenheimer, *Killer Images: Documentary Film, Memory and the Performance of Violence*. (New York: Wallflower Press, 2012), 41–62

23. Blankenberg, *Don't Shoot*.

24. As Mirzoeff proposed in his book, *The Right to Look*.

25. Khalo Matabane, *Mandela, the Myth and Me*. (Color, 85 min., 2013). Gebrüder Beetz film production. Trailer available on vimeo: vimeo.com/81181678; last accessed 5/16/2014.

26. Landsberg, *Prosthetic Memories*, 4.

27. Of course, one can never feel *exactly* what another has felt, still the question of empathy and how it may translate into political effects is highly important. Cf. on this for instance, Levinas. Emanuel. "Ethics and the Face."

28. This is often also caused by the architecture of apartheid urban planning that continues to exist up until today, since not all structures that were built have been torn down and rebuilt. These architectural structures still put low-income or unemployed black people at a disadvantage, as they may often have to live in locations built around the old townships, far away from services.

29. Cf. e.g., Mitchell, *What Do Pictures Want?*; Jacques Rancière, *The Emancipated Spectato*r.

30. In addition in the early modern age, people were not represented as having different skin colors. See for example in early religious cartography, Ham, representing the African continent, looking similar to Noah's other sons Shem and Japhet. Cf. Claudia Bruns, *Karten, Körper, Kollektive*. Forthcoming.

31. E.g. Hassim, *Go Home or Die Here*.

32. Hassim, *Go Home or Die Here*.

33. Michael Neocosmos, *From 'Foreign Natives' To 'Native Foreigners': Explaining Xenophobia in Post-apartheid South Africa* (Dakar: Codesira, 2010).

34. A similar process could be observed with "guest workers," also called Madgermanes from Mozambique in the GDR after the wall came down, who lost their permit to stay and were deported back to Mozambique. Cf. "The Fate of the Madgermanes" (Das Schicksal der Madgermanes) in ZDF heute Journal, screened on German television 11/9/2013, cf. www.zdf.de, last accessed 9/9/2014.

35. On these mechanisms in the German post-Holocaust context of perpetrator images, cf. Christina von Braun, "Die unterschiedlichen Geschlechtercodierungen," 261–65.

36. See also Kihato's work focusing specific on experiences of female African migration. Cf. Kihato, " 'A Picture Speaks a Thousand Words': Understanding Women's Migration Through Visual Diaries."

37. See the shooting of miners at Marikana in 2012.

38. Susie Linfield, "Advertisement for Death," *New York Times*, January 27, 2014, www.nytimes.com/2014/01/28/opinion/advertisements-for-death.html; last accessed 2/28/2014.

39. Cf. for example photographs from the armed forces from WWI, e.g., Agnes Matthias, *Die Kunst den Krieg zu fotografieren.* (Marburg: Jonas Verlag, 2005). Cf. also Andrian Kreye, "Terrorbilder . . . und man vergisst sie nie," in *Sueddeutsche Zeitung*, 9/24/2014.

40. Cf. international conference "Narrating War" at HKW, Berlin, 02/20-02/22 2014, www.hkw.de/en/programm/projekte/2014/krieg_erzaehlen/krieg_erzaehlen.php; last accessed 9/6/2014.

41. Cf. Arjun Appadurai "mediascapes," in "Disjuncture and Difference in the Global Cultural Economy."

42. Gabi Ngcobo. "Introduction," in *Digging our own Graves 101*, 2014, 2.

43. The notion of "wounding aperture" was developed in chapter 2 following both South African photo historian Kylie Thomas and American literary and trauma scholar Cathy Caruth. Cf. Thomas, "Wounding Apertures," and Caruth, "Introduction. The Wound and the Voice."

44. Cf. South Africa's Constitution, www.info.gov.za/documents/constitution/; last accessed 9/14/2012.

45. Cf. Andisiwe Makinana: "Marikana tragedy: Who authorised the use of live ammunition?" Marikana mine is operated by the British owned company Lonmin that extracts Platinum in South Africa, www.lonmin.com/; last accessed 9/7/2014. See also Aislinn Laing, "Striking Miners 'Were Shot in the Back," in *The Telegraph,* 8/27/2012; and Rehad Desai's documentary *Miners Shot Down.* (86 min, color) South Africa 2014, http://www.minersshotdown.co.za/, last accessed 9/9/201.6

46. Cf. among others, Ra'eesa Pather, "Students continue to march at UKZN, protesting against rape and police violence," *Mail and Guardian*, 9/7/2016; and Taschica Pillay, "Student shot in crossfire at KwaZulu-Natal varsity protest," *Herald Live*, 9/8/2016, http://www.heraldlive.co.za/tag/bongeka-mntaka/; last accessed 9/20/2016.

47. In Sharpeville, in 1976 police shot protesting school children. This event and the images it produced was discussed in part 2.1 on "Hector Pieterson—The South African Pietà."

48. As Rehad Desai argues in his documentary film *Miners Shot Down* (85 min., SA 2014), there was a method to the massacre, cf. Shaun de Waal, "Method to Marikana Massacre," in *Mail and Guardian,* 6/6/2014, cf. mg.co.za; last accessed 9/15/2014. For the film cf. www.minersshotdown.co.za/; last accessed 9/15/2014.

49. Norimitsu Onishi, "African National Congress Draws 62 Percent of the Vote in South Africa." www.nytimes.com/2014/05/10/world/africa/south-africa-vote.html; *New York Times*, 5/9/2014, last accessed 5/10/2014. This result is surprising when one considers the rising popular discontent with the ANC and its leader Jacob Zuma, but can only be attributed to the role the ANC and Nelson Mandela played in the fight for liberation of South Africa. It is therefore an inherited success.

50. Emma Graham-Harrison, "Voters Deliver Stinging Rebuke to ANC in South African Election," in *The Guardian,* Aug. 6. 2016, https://www.theguardian.com/world/2016/aug/04/south-africans-deliver-stinging-rebuke-to-anc; last accessed 9/17/2016.

51. Wendy Brown, *States of Injury*, 73.

52. Deleuze, *Foucault*. Trans. S. Hand. (Minneapolis: University of Minnesota Press, 1988), 59.

53. Simone Bignall and Paul Patton, eds., *Deleuze and the Postcolonial* (Edinburgh: Edinburgh University Press, 2010), 65–69.

54. Cf. John Peffer, "Gemeinsam im Bild," in *Chimurenga Chronic*. April 2014, special German edition, 16–18.

55. In German: "verrutschtes Klischeebild."

56. Judith Butler, "Gender is Burning. Questions of Appropriation and Subversion," in *Bodies That Matter*, 82.

57. Cf. *Paris is Burning*, by Jenny Livingstone, USA, 1991, cf. www.imdb.com/title/tt0100332/; last accessed 9/9/2014.

58. Cf. Tina Campt, *Image Matters: Archive, Photography and the African Diaspora in Europe* (Durham, NC, London: Duke University Press, 2012).

59. Cf. Sophie Feyer et al., "Photographic Traditions in South African Popular Modernities," www.materialworldblog.com/2011/04/photographic-traditions-in-south-african-popular-modernities/; last accessed 7/31/2014.

60. Cf. John Peffer, "Gemeinsam im Bild."

61. *Now-now* is South African English, meaning "exactly now" and "shortly," see also "Glossary." Cf. Jacob Dlamini, "South African English, No jive, my friend," July 6, 2009, www.mediaclubsouthafrica.com; last accessed 1/10/2013.

62. Von Braun, "Die unterschiedlichen Geschlechtercodierungen," 257–58. "Klischees . . . gewinnen immer dort an Macht, wo dem Selbst keine eigene Sprache zur Verfügung steht" [translation mk].

63. For a discussion of invisibilities and post-identitarian visual politics and the necessity to include the haptic realm, cf. Nana Adusei-Poku, "Enter and Exit the New Negro—Von Unsichtbaren Sichtbarkeiten," in *Feministische Studien*, Issue 2, Vol. 30, 2012, 212–27.

64. Rangoato Hlasane, "Making Space: Mediations on Encounters with Art," in Thenjiwe Nkosi and Pamela Phatsimo Sunstrum, eds., *Compendium* (Johannesburg: National Arts Council, 2014), 4–9.

65. José Esteban Muñoz, *Cruising Utopia: The Then and There of Queer Futurity* (New York: New York University Press, 2009). Similarly, Jennifer Wenzel writes of the importance to "acknowledge the past in the name of the future" in idem., "Remembering the Past's Future: Anti-Imperialist Nostalgia and some Versions of the Third World," in *Cultural Critique* 62, Winter 2006, 23.

66. Puar, *Terrorist Assemblages*, 215. Eve Kosofsky-Sedgewick explores a similar visionary political project in *Touching Feeling: Affect, Pedagogy, Performativity* (Durham, NC, London: Duke University Press, 2003).

67. Deleuze, *Cinema 1: The Movement Image*, 214–15. Deleuze is picking up this question about images and clichés back up again in *Cinema 2: The Time Image*, 20–22, claiming: "On the one hand, the image constantly sinks to the state of cliché . . . On the other hand, at the same time, the image constantly attempts to break through the cliché, to get out of the cliché."

Glossary

ACMS	African Centre for Migration and Society at the University of the Witwatersrand, the leading interdisciplinary research institute on migration in South Africa.
ANC	African National Congress, formed in 1912, banned under apartheid. The ANC has been the ruling party since 1994.
APF	Anti-Privatization Forum, established in 2000 by activists, fighting against the privatization of, e.g., water and electricity, working with economically deprived communities on a variety of issues.
Black Sash	A non-violent anti-apartheid organization of white women, founded in 1955.
Born-frees	The "born-frees" is the generation of South Africans who were born after the end of apartheid.
BSS	Black Students Society at the University of the Witwatersrand (Wits), Johannesburg, formed in the late 1970s.
Boer	Afrikaans and Dutch for "farmer," which denotes the white settlers in South Africa.
CHR	Center for Historical Reenactments, an artists and writers' collective in Johannesburg.
District 6	Historic innercity area with mixed inhabitants in Cape Town, declared a "whites-only" area in 1966 and demolished in the following years.
EEC	End Conscription Campaign, established in 1983, fought against the general conscription of all white men into the South African Defense Force, allied with the UDF.

FAR	Filmmakers Against Racism, established in 2008 after the xenophobic attacks in South Africa.
guma-guma	an outlaw who preys upon refugees crossing the South African border.
impimpi	*isi*Zulu: traitor, police informer.
Inkatha	"Inkatha" means "crown" in *isi*Zulu, name of the Inkatha Freedom Party (IFP). Founded in 1975 by Mangosuthu Buthulezi, the IFP was opposed to the ANC.
Kwerekwere	Derogatory term for black non-South Africans.
Marikana	A mining town, near Rustenberg in South Africa's north-west province, where 34 striking miners were shot by the police in 2012.
MSF	Médecins Sans Frontières (Doctors without Borders), globally operating medical relief organization.
MK/Umkonte we Sizwe	Armed wing of the ANC, *isi*Zulu for "Spear of the Nation," established in 1961.
muti	From the *isi*Zulu word "umuthi," traditional African medicine.
now-now	South African English, meaning "shortly," as compared to "just now—later," and "now—eventually, maybe."
PAC	Pan-African Congress, established in 1959 in Soweto and led by Robert Sobukwe, cooperating with the ANC, especially active in the campaigns against the pass laws.
RDP	The "Restructuring and Development Program" of the South African post-apartheid government.
SABC	South African Broadcasting Corporation.
SADF	South African Defense Force.
shebeen	Illegal bar, selling alcohol without a liquor license, often operating on private premises.
spaza shop	Also called tuck shop, is an informal small shop with household items that is usually run from home.
SUCA	Student Union for Christian Action, formed in 1980, opposed to apartheid.

SWAPO	South West Africa People's Organization, established in the early 1960s, operating as a national liberation army and political party in South West Africa—today Namibia.
TRC	Truth and Reconciliation Commission, which were set up in 1994 to uncover apartheid's crimes as well as to reconcile the "new" South African nation.
UDF	United Democratic Front, aligned with the ANC, formed in 1983, a non-racial anti-apartheid organization, with the slogan: "Apartheid divides, UDF unites."
Voortrekker	Afrikaans, literally meaning "the forerunners" or "pioneers."
Wits	University of the Witwatersrand in Johannesburg, established in 1922. Wits was non-segregated, even though black students formed a minority. In 1959, the apartheid government passed the *Extension of University Education Act*, which achieved the enforcement of university apartheid. Wits protested strongly and continued to uphold a consistent stand in opposition to apartheid.

Bibliography

Abolition Project, abolition.e2bn.org/campaign_14.html; last accessed 9/7/2014.

African Center for Migration and Society, *Mail and Guardian* and the individual writers. *Writing Invisibility: Conversations on the Hidden City*, 2013. Published online, mg.co.za; last accessed 12/20/2013.

Adigun, Bashir. "Nigerian official rails against District 9," *Mail and Guardian* online, 9/20/20 mg.co.za; last accessed 9/9/2014.

Adusei-Poku, Nana. "Enter and Exit the New Negro—Von Unsichtbaren Sichtbarkeiten." In *Feministische Studien*, edited by G. Dietze, E. Yekani, and B. Michaelis. "The Queerness of Things not Queer," special issue, 2, Vol. 30, 2012, 212–27.

Adusei-Poku, Nana. "The multiplicity of multiplicities: Post-Black Art and its Intricacies." In *darkmatter*, 11/29/2012, www.darkmatter101.org; last accessed 8/7/2014.

African Renaissance, www.unu.edu/unupress/mbeki.html; last accessed 6/9/2010.

Alexander, Neville. *Südafrika. Der Weg von der Apartheid zur Demokratie.* Munich: C. H. Beck, 2001.

Anderson, Benedict. *Imagined Communities.* London, New York: Verso, 2003 (1983).

Angerer, Marie-Luise. *Vom Begehren nach dem Affekt.* Zurich, Berlin: Diaphanes, 2007.

Appadurai, Arjun. "Disjuncture and Difference in the Global Cultural Economy." In *Theory, Culture, Society*, 1990, (7).

Appadurai, Arjun. *Modernity at Large.* Minneapolis: University of Minnesota Press, 1996.

Arcara, Arianna, and Luca Santese. *Found Photos in Detroit,* Pienallo. Milan, Italy: Cesura, 2012.

Arendt, Hannah. *On Violence.* New York: Harcourt, 1970, 1969.

Arndt, Susan, ed. *Mythen, Masken und Subjekte. Kritische Weißseinsforschung in Deutschland.* Münster: Unrast, 2005.

Assmann, Aleidan and Linda Short. *Memory and Political Change.* Basingstoke: Palgrave Macmillan, 2011.

Auga, Ulrike. *Intellektuelle—zwischen Dissidenz und Legitimierung, Eine kulturkritische Theorie im Kontext Südafrikas.* Berlin: LIT, 2005.

Azoulay, Ariella. *The Civil Contract of Photography*. Cambridge: MIT Press, 2012.

Baderoon, Gabeba. "Primal Scenes, Forbidden Words." In *Undutiful Daughters: New Directions in Feminist Thought and Practice*, edited by Henriette Gunkel et al., 169–81. Basingstoke, UK, New York: Palgrave Macmillan, 2012.

Bahl, Eva et al. "Unheimliche Arbeitsbündnisse. Zum Funktionieren des Anti-Trafficking-Diskurses auf lokaler und europäischer Ebene." In *Grenzregime. Diskurse. Praktiken. Institutionen in Europa*, edited by Sabine Hess et al., 161–78. Berlin, Hamburg: Assoziation A, 2010.

Baldwin, James. *The Evidence of Things not Seen*. New York: Owl Books, 1995.

Balibar, Étienne. *Sind wir Bürger Europas? Politische Integration, soziale Ausgrenzung und die Zukunft des Nationalen*. Hamburg: Hamburg Edition, 2003.

Balibar, Étienne. *Spinoza and Politics*. Translated by P. Snowdon. London, New York: Verso, 1998.

Ball, Joanna. "The Ritual of the Necklace," Centre for the Study of Violence and Reconciliation, 1994, www.csvr.org.za/index.php/publications/1632-the-ritual-of-the-necklace.html; last accessed 7/6/2014.

Barthes, Roland. *Mythen des Alltags* (Or. *Mythologies*). Frankfurt a. M.: Suhrkamp, 1964.

Barthes, Roland. *Mythologies*. New York: Farrar, Strauss and Giroux, 1972.

Barthes, Roland. *Die helle Kammer*. Frankfurt a. M.: Suhrkamp, 1985.

Barthes, Roland. *Camera Lucida: Reflections on Photography*. Translated by R. Howard. New York: Hill and Wang, 1982.

Barthes, Roland. *Camera Lucida*. London: Vintage Random House, 2000 (Seuill, 1980).

Bartky, Sandra Lee. *Femininity and Domination: Studies in the Phenomenology of Oppression*. New York, London: Routledge, 1990

Beall, Jo, ed. *Uniting a Divided City: Governance and Social Exclusion in Johannesburg*. London: Earthscan, 2002.

Benjamin, Walter. "Excavation and Memory," in: *Walter Benjamin: Selected Writings*, Vol. 2, 1927–1934. Cambridge, MA: Belknap Press of Harvard University Press 1999.

Benjamin, Walter. "Der Sürrealismus—Die letzte Momentaufnahme der europäischen Intelligenz." In *Gesammelte Schriften, II,1*, edited by R. v.Tiedemann, and H. Schweppenhäuser, 295–310. Frankfurt a. M.: Suhrkamp, 1977.

Bester, Rory. "City and Citzenship." In *The Short Century: Independence and Liberation Movements in Africa 1945–1994*, edited by Okwui Enwezor. New York, London: Prestel Publishing.

Bezzoli, Marco et al. "Texture and Memory: The Urbanism of District Six." Cape Town: Cape Technikon, 2002.

Bhabha, Homi. *Nation and Narration*. New York, London: Routledge, 2000.

Bignall, Simone, and Paul Patton, eds. *Deleuze and the Postcolonial*. Edingburgh: Edinburgh University Press, 2010.

Blackmann, M. Review on "Commute with Instinct," on Artthrob. 2014; www.artthrob.co.za/ last accessed 9/6/2014.

Blomkamp, Neill. Interview, "Five Things you didn't know about District 9," cf. io9.com/5341120/5-things-you-didnt-know-about-district-9; last accessed 9/5/2014.

Bond, Patrick. *Elite Transition: From Apartheid to Neoliberalism in South Africa.* London/Sterling and Pietermaritzburg: Pluto Press and University of Natal Press, 2000.

Bordieu, Pierre. *Distinction: A Social Critique of the Judgement of Taste.* Cambridge, MA: Harvard University Press, 1984.

Brandes, Kerstin. "Visuelle Migrationen—Bild-Bewegungen zwischen Zeiten, Medien und Kulturen." In *FKW, Zeitschrift für Geschlechterforschung und visuelle Kultur,* No 5, June. Jonas: Marburg, 2011.

Braun, Christina von. *Die schamlose Schönheit des Vergangenen: Zum Verhältnis von Geschlecht und Geschichte.* Frankfurt a. M.: Verlag Neue Kritik, 1989.

Braun, Christina von. "Zum Begriff der Reinheit." In *metis* 6, 1997.

Braun, Christina von. *Versuch über den Schwindel.* Zurich, München: Pendo, 2001.

Braun, Christina von. "Die unterschiedlichen Geschlechtercodierungen bei NS-Tätern und Täterinnen unter medienhistorischer Perspektive." In *"Bestien" und "Befehlsempfänger." Frauen und Männer in NS-Prozessen nach 1945,* edited by Ulrich Weckel and Edgar Wolfrum. Goettingen: Vandenhoeck & Ruprecht, 2003. 250–65.

Braun, Christina von, and Bettina Mathes. *Die verschleierte Wirklichkeit. Die Frau, der Islam und der Westen.* Berlin: Aufbau, 2007.

Braun, Christina von et al., eds. *Das Unbewusste. Krisis und Kapital in den Wissenschaften.* Bielefeld: Transcript, 2009.

Braun, Christina von. "Ceci n'est pas une femme. Betrachten, Begehren, Berühren—von der Macht des Blicks," *Lettre International* 25, 1994, 80–84.

Brecht, Bertolt. "Kleines Organon für das Theater." In *Schriften zum Theater.* Frankfurt a. M.: Suhrkamp, 1957.

Bredekamp, Horst. "A Neglected Tradition? Art History as *Bildwissenschaft,*" In *Critical Inquiry,* Vol. 29, No. 3, Spring 2003, 418–28.

Brink, Joram Ten, and Joshua Oppenheimer, eds. *Killer Images: Documentary Film, Memory and the Performance of Violence.* New York: Wallflower Press, 2012.

Brinkema, Eugenia. "A Tear that does not drop but folds." In *The Forms of the Affects.* Durham, NC, London: Duke University Press, 2014.

Britton, Hannah E. *Women in the South African Parliament: From Resistance to Governance.* Champaign, IL: University of Illinois Press, 2005.

Bronfen, Elisabeth. *Crossmapping. Essays zur visuellen Kultur.* Zurich: Scheidegger & Spiess, 2009.

Brown, Jayna. "District 9 Review," bullybloggers.wordpress.com/2009/09/19/on-becoming-alien-%E2%80%93-district/, last accessed 9/27/2009.

Brown, Wendy. *States of Injury: Power and Freedom in Late Modernity.* Princeton, NJ: Princeton University Press, 1995.

Brown, Wendy, and Janet E. Halley. "Suffering the Paradoxes of Rights." In *Left Legalism/Left Critique.* Durham, NC: Duke University Press, 2002.

Bruns, Claudia. *Karten, Körper, Kollektive.* Forthcoming.

Butler, Judith. *Bodies that Matter: On the Discursive Limits of "Sex."* New York: Routledge, 1993.

Butler, Judith. *The Psychic Life of Power: Theories in Subjection.* Stanford, CA: Stanford University Press, 1997.

Butler, Judith. *Antigone's Claim: Kinship between Life and Death.* New York: Columbia University, 2000

Butler, Judith. *Precarious Life: The Powers of Mourning and Violence.* London, Brooklyn, NY: Verso, 2004.

Butler, Judith. *Frames of War: When is Life Grievable.* Brooklyn, NY, London: Verso, 2009.

Butler, Judith. "Bodies in Alliance and the Politics of the Street," eipcp.net/transversal/1011/butler/en; last accessed 11/21/13.

Campt, Tina M. *Image Matters: Archive, Photography, and the African Diaspora in Europe.* Durham, NC, London: Duke University Press, 2012.

Caputo, John, ed. *Deconstruction in a Nutshell: A Conversation with Jacques Derrida,* 106–24. New York: Fordham University Press, 1997.

Carter, Donald Martin. *Navigating the African Diaspora.* Minneapolis: University of Minnesota Press, 2010.

Cartwright, Lisa. *Moral Spectatorship: Technologies of Voice and Affect in Postwar Representations of the Child.* Durham, NC, London: Duke University Press, 2008.

Caruth, Cathy. *Unclaimed Experience: Trauma, Narrative and History.* Baltimore: John Hopkins University Press, 1996.

Center for Historical Reenactments, centerforhistoricalreenactments.blogspot.de/; last accessed 9/13/2012.

Chapman, Audrey R., and Hugo van der Merve, eds. *Truth and Reconciliation in South Africa: Did the TRC Deliver?* Philadelphia: University of Pennsylvania Press, 2008.

Cioran, Emile M. *Tears and Saints.* Translated by I. Zarifopol-Johnston. Chicago: University of Chicago Press, 1995.

Clock, Jacklyn. "Gun Violence and Masculinity in Contemporary South Africa." In *Changing Men in Southern Africa,* edited by Robert Morrel, 43–55. London: Zed Books, 2001

Coetzee, John Maxwell. *Disgrace.* London and New York: Penguin, 2008.

Cole, Ernest. *House of Bondage.* New York: Random House, 1967.

Cook, John. "One-Man Truth Squad." In: *Mother Jones.* Issue May/June 1997, www.motherjones.com/politics/1997/05/one-man-truth-squad; last accessed 12/23/2012.

Copjec, Joan. "The Descent into Shame." In *Studio Art Magazine,* No. 168, February March 2007, 59–80.

Crenshaw, Kimberlé. "Mapping the Margins: Intersectionality, Identity Politics, and Violence Against Women of Color." In *Stanford Law Review* Vol. 43, No. 6, 1991, 1241–99.

Cvetkovic, Ann. *Depression: A Public Feeling.* Durham, NC, London: Duke University Press, 2012.

Dadush, Uri. "The Effect of Unskilled Migration on the Host Economy," www.knomad.org/; last accessed 7/4/2014.

Davenport, T. R. H. *South Africa: A Modern History.* London: Macmillan, 1991.

Dean, Jodi. "Politics without Politics." In *Reading Rancière*, edited by Paul Bowman and Richard Stamp, 73–94. London, New York: Continuum, 2011.

DeGhett, Tori Rose. "The War Photo No One would Publish." In *The Atlantic,* 08/08/2014, cf. www.theatlantic.com/features/archive/2014/08/the-war-photo-no-one-would-publish/37576; last accessed 9/20/2014.

Deleuze, Gilles, and Felix Guattar. *A Thousand Plateaus: Capitalism and Schizophrenia.* Translated by B. Massumi. London: Athlone, 1987.

Deleuze, Gilles. *Foucault.* Transslated by S. Hand. Minneapolis: University of Minnesota Press. 1988.

Deleuze, Gilles. *Spinoza und das Problem des Ausdrucks in der Philosophie.* Translated by U. J. Schneider. Munich: Fink, 1993.

Deleuze, Gilles, and Felix. *What is Philosophy?* Translated by H. Tomlinson and G. Burchell. New York: Columbia University Pres,s 1994.

Deleuze, Gilles. *Cinema 1: The Movement Image.* Translated by H. Tomlinson and B. Habberjam. Minneapolis: University of Minnesota Press, 1997.

Deleuze, Gilles. *Cinema 2: The Time Image.* Translated by. H. Tomlinson, and R. Galeta. Minneapolis: University of Minnesota Press, 1997.

Dery, Mark, ed. *Flame Wars: The Discourse of Cyberculture.* Durham, NC: Duke University Press, 1994.

Diedrichsen, Diedrich, ed. *Loving the Alien. Science Fiction. Diaspora. Multikultur.* Berlin: ID, 1998.

Dietze, Gabriele. *Weiße Frauen in Bewegung.* Bielefeld: Transcript, 2013.

Dietze, Gabriele et al., eds. *Kritik des Okzidentalismus, Transdisziplinäre Beiträge zu (Neo-) Orientalismus und Geschlecht.* Bielefeld: Transcript, 2009.

Dlamini, Jacob. "South African English, No jive, my friend," July 6, 2009, mediaclubsouthafrica.com; last accessed 1/10/2013.

Dovey, Lindiwe, and Angela Impey. " 'African Jim': Sound, politic and pleasure in early 'black' South African cinema." In: *Journal of African Cultural Studies.* Vol. 22, No. 1, June 2010, 57–73.

Du Bois, W. E. B. *The Souls of Black Folk*, (1903). New York: Signet, 1995.

Ebbrecht, Tobias. "Migrating Images: Iconic Images of the Holocaust and the Representation of War in Popular Film." In *Shofar, An Interdisciplinary Journal of Jewish Studies*, 2010, Vol. 28 (4), 86–103, 98.

Eckert, Andreas. "125 Jahre Berliner Afrika-Konferenz: Bedeutung für Geschichte und Gegenwart." Hamburg, 2009. GIGA German Institute of Global and Area Studies—Leibniz-Institut für Globale und Regionale Studien, Institut für Afrika-Studien ed., (GIGAFocus Afrika Nr. 12), nbn-resolving.de/urn:nbn:de:0168-ssoar-274593; last accessed 6/17/2014.

Els, Darryl, and Marie-Hélène Gutberlet. "B-Schemes," www.arsenal-berlin.de/en/living-archive/projects/visionary-archive/b-schemes.html; last accessed 6/13/2014.

Els, Darryl. "Shifting Grounds: Reflections on National Identity in the Archive." In *Living Archive: Archive Work as a Contemporary Artistic and Curatorial Practice*, edited by Arsenal, 69–75. Berlin: b_books, 2013.

El-Tayeb, Fatima. *European Other: Queering Ethnicity in Postnational Europe.* Minneapolis: University of Minnesota Press, 2011.

Eng, David L., and David Kazanjian, eds. *Loss: The Politics of Mourning.* Berkeley, Los Angeles: University of California Press, 2003.

Enwezor, Okwui. "A Critical Presence: *Drum* Magazine in Context." In *In/Sight: African Photographers 1940 to the Present*, edited by O. Enwezor, O. Obuibe, and O. Zaya. New York: Guggenheim Museum, 1996.

Enwezor, Okwui. *Snap Judgments, New Positions in Contemporary African Photography.* New York: International Center for Photography, 2006.

Eshun, Kodwo. *More Brilliant Than The Sun: Adventures in Sonic Fiction.* London: Quartet Books, 1998.

Esposito, Elena. *Soziales Vergessen. Formen und Medien des Gedächtnisses der Gesellschaft.* Frankfurt a. M.: Suhrkamp, 2002.

Fanon, Frantz. *Black Skin, White Masks.* Translated by C. Lam Markmann. London: Pluto Press, 1986.

Fanon, Frantz. *The Wretched of the Earth.* Translated by C. Farrington. New York: Grove Press, 1963.

Fels, John, and Denis Wood. *The Power of Maps.* New York: Guilford Press, 1992.

Feyer, Sophie et al. "Photographic Traditions in South African Popular Modernities," www.materialworldblog.com/2011/04/photographic-traditions-in-south-african-popular-modernities/; last accessed 7/31/2014.

Filmmakers Against Racism, *Reflecting on Xenophobia: Documentary Filmmakers respond to the violent attacks that hit South Africa in 2008.* Film Facilitator Guide, South Africa, 2009.

Foster, Hal. "The Artist as Ethnographer?" In: *The Return of the Real*, 171–204. Cambridge: MIT Press, 1996.

French, Howard W. "South Africa's Supreme Court Abolishes Death Penalty." In *New York Times*, 6/7/1995, www.nytimes.com; last accessed 6/16/2014.

Freud, Sigmund. "Five Lectures on Psychoanalysis" (1910). In *Standard Edition of the Complete Psychological Works of Sigmund Freud.* Translated by J. Strachey. London: Hogarth, 1953–74, vol. 11.

Freud, Sigmund. "Beyond the Pleasure Principle." In: *The Standard Edition of the Complete Psychological Works of Sigmund Freud.* Translated by James Strachey in collaboration with Anna Freud, assisted by Alix Strachey and Alan Tyson, 24 vols. London: Hogarth, 1953–74, vol. 18, ch. 3.

Frisch, Max. *Biedermann und die Brandstifter.* (Engl. *The Fire Raisers*) (1958). Frankfurt a. M.: Suhrkamp, 2002.

Fusco, Coco. "Racial Time, Racial Marks, Racial Metaphors." In *Only Skin Deep: Changing Visions of the American Self*, edited by idem., and Brian Wallis, 13–48. New York: ICP, 2003.

Geffen, Nathan. "Shattered Myths: The xenophobic violence in South Africa." 07/03/2008, www.pambazuka.org/en/category/comment/49179; last accessed 9/1/2008.

Geiger, Jeffrey. "Nollywood Style: Nigerian Movies and 'shifting perceptions of worth.'" In *Film International*, Issue 60, 2012, 58–69.

Geimer, Peter. "Fotos, die man nicht zeigt. Probleme mit Schockbildern." In *Fotografische Leidenschaften*, edited by Ludger Derentha et al., 245–57. Marburg: Jonas Verlag, 2006.

Gerhart, G. M. *Black Power in South Africa.* Berkeley: University of California Press, 1978.

Ghandi, Leela. *Affective Communities: Anticolonial Thought, Fin-de-Siècle Radicalism, and the Politics of Friendship.* Durham, NC: Duke University Press, 2006.

Gilroy, Paul. *Darker than Blue. On the Moral Economies of Black Atlantic Culture* (W. E. B. Du Bois lectures). Cambridge, MA, London: The Belknap Press of Harvard University Press, 2010.

Gilroy, Paul, and Luc Boltanksi. *Distant Suffering: Morality, Media, and Politics.* Translated by G. Burchell. Cambridge, UK: Cambridge University Press, 1999.

Gleich, Michael. "Der Horror steckt noch in den Köpfen." In *Chrismon* 03, Frankfurt a. M., 2013, 47.

Glissant, Édouard. *Philosophie de la Relation (Philosophy of Relation* 2009) (excerpt). In *Frieze* Magazine, No. 7, Winter 2012, 72–77.

Goldblatt, David. "Dear Christine." In "I am not afraid," *Camera Austria.* No. 100, Graz, 2007.

Golden, Thelma, ed. *Black Male: Representations of Masculinity in Contemporary American Art.* New York: Whitney Museum of American Art, 1994.

Goodmann, Nelson. *Ways of Worldmaking.* Indianapolis, IN: Hackett, 1978.

Gordimer, Nadine. *No Time Like the Present.* London: Picador, 2013.

Gould, Deborah. *Moving Politics: Emotions and ACT UP's Fight Against AIDS.* Chicago: University of Chicago Press, 2009.

Gqola, Pumla. "Brutal Inheritances: Echoes, Negrophobia and Masculinist Violence." In *Go Home or Die here: Violence, Xenophobia and the Reinvention of Difference in South Africa*, edited by Shireen Hassim et al., 209–22. Johannesburg: Wits University Press, 2008.

Gqola, Pumla. "Through Zanele Muholi's Eyes: Re/Imagining Ways of Seeing Black Lesbians,. In *Only Half the Picture*, edited by Zanele Muholi, 82–89. Cape Town: Stevenson & STE, 2006.

Gqola, Pumla. *What is Slavery to Me: Postcolonial/Slave Memory in Post-Apartheid South Africa.* Johannesburg: Wits University Press, 2010.

Gqola, Pumla. *Rape: A South African Nightmare.* Johannesburg: Jacana Media, 2015.

Gqubule, Thandeka. "Soweto Ungoverned." The article originally appeared in the *Weekly Mail*, 08/26/1988; mg.co.za; last accessed 6/6/2014.

Greenhouse, Emily. "Women in War Zones." In *The New Yorker*, 07/30/2014, www.newyorker.com/news/newsdeks/women-war-zones; last accessed 8/2/2014.

Grill, Bartholomäus. *Ach, Afrika. Berichte aus dem Inneren eines Kontinents.* Munich: Goldmann, 2005.

Gunkel, Henriette. *The Cultural Politics of Female Sexuality in South Africa.* New York, London: Routledge, 2010.

Gunkel, Henriette, and Christiane König. "'You are not welcome here,' post-apartheid negrophobia & real aliens in Blomkamp's *District 9.*" In: *darkmatter* Journal, Issue 7, Feb. 2010. www.darkmaater101.org/site; last accessed 10/25/2013.

Gutberlet, Marie-Hélène, and Cara Snyman, eds. *Shoe Shop.* Auckland Park, SA: Fanele, 2012.

Gutberlet, Marie-Hélène, and Sissy Helff. *Die Kunst der Migration. Aktuelle Positionen zum europäisch-afrikanischen Diskurs.* Bielefeld: Transcript, 2011.

Habermas, Jürgen. *Strukturwandel der Öffentlichkeit.* Frankfurt a. M.: Suhrkamp, 1990.

Habermas, Jürgen. *The Structural Transformation of the Public Sphere.* Cambridge, MA: MIT Press, 1991.

Halbwachs, Maurice. *Les Cadres Sociaux de la mémoire* (1925). German translation: *Das Gedächtnis und seine sozialen Bedingungen.* Frankfurt a. M.: Suhrkamp, 1985.

Hassim, Shireen et al., eds. *Go Home or Die here: Violence, Xenophobia and the Reinvention of Difference in South Africa.* Johannesburg: Wits University Press, 2008.

Hayes, Patricia. "Santu Mofokeng, Photographs: 'The Violence is in the Knowing.'" In *History and Theory,* 48, 2009, 34–51.

Hayes, Patricia. "Power, Secrecy, Proximity. A Short History of South African Photography." In *Kronos,* No. 33, November 2007, 139–62.

"Haysom, Nicholas. "Mabangalala: The Rise of Right-wing Vigilantes in South Africa." Occasional Paper No. 10, Centre for Applied Legal Studies, University of the Witwatersrand, Johannesburg, 1986.

Hector Pieterson Museum, cf. www.southafrica.net/za/en/articles/entry/article-south africa.net-the-hector-peterson-museum; last accessed 9/11/2014.

Hengeveld, Maria. "'Race Jokes' in South Africa." 12/20/12 cf. africasacountry.com/2012/12/20/the-race-joke/; last accessed 12/20/2012.

Hlasane, Rangoato. "Making Space: Mediations on Encounters with Art." In: *Compendium,* edited by Thenjiwe Nkose and Pamela Phatsimo Sunstrum, 4–9. Johannesburg: National Arts Council, 2014.

Hook, Derek, and Michelle Vrodjlak. "Gated communities, heterotopia and a "rights" of privilege: a 'heterotopology' of the South African security-park." In *Geoforum,* 33 (2) 2002, 195–19.

Hook, Derek. *(Post)apartheid Conditions: Psychoanalysis and Social Formation.* New York: Palgrave Macmillan, 2013.

Husmann, Jana. *Schwarz-Weiß-Symbolik. Dualistische Denktraditionen und die Imagination von "Rasse."* Bielefeld: Transcript, 2010.

International Organization of Migration 2013, IOM mission statement on their website iom.org.za/; last accessed 4/21/2013.

"I was shot in Joburg" cf. www.iwasshot.com/; last accessed 9/17/2013.

Jaar, Alfredo. *The Sound of Silence.* alfredojaar.net, last accessed 7/18/2014.

Jacobs, Seth. *Cold War Mandarin: Ngo Dinh Diem and the Origins of America's War in Vietnam, 1950–1963.* Lanham, MD: Rowman & Littlefield, 2006.

Jeppie, Shamil, and Crain Soudien. *The Struggle for District Six: Past and Present.* Buchu Books, 1990.

Judin, Hilton, and Ivan Vladislavić, eds. *Blank—Architecture, Apartheid, and After.* Rotterdam: NAi Publishers, 1999.

Jobson, Marjorie. *Arme gegen Arme.* Interview in *medico-Rundschreiben* 02/2008, Fehler! Linkverweis ungültig; last accessed 9/1/2008.

Johnson, Scott C. "The Real District 9: Cape Town's District 6." In *Newsweek,* 8/27/09, www.newsweek.com/real-district-9-cape-towns-district-six-78939, last accessed 6/7/2014.

Kappelhoff, Hermann. *Matrix der Gefühle.* Berlin: Vorwerk 8, 2004.

Karakayalı, Serhat. "Regime der Alterität. Affekt und Politik." In *Affekt und Geschlecht. Eine einführende Anthologie*, edited by Angelika Baier et al., 277–98 Wien: Zaglossus, 2014.

Kaußen, Stephan. *Von der Apartheid zur Demokratie.* Wiesbaden: Westdeutscher Verlag, 2003.

Kerner, Ina. *Differenzen der Macht. Zur Anatomie von Rassismus und Sexismus.* Frankfurt a. M.: Campus Verlag, 2009.

Kester, Grant H. *The One and the Many: Contemporary Collaborative Art in a Global Context.* Durham, NC: Duke University Press, 2011.

Kesting, Marietta. *Politik und Sichtbarkeit in Johannesburg.* Berlin, Vienna: LIT, 2009.

Khosa, Ungulani Ba Ka. "When History is Suspended. (In Memory of Ernesto Alfabeto Nhamuave)." In *Chimurenga Chronic*, May 18–24, 2008, Capetown.

Kihato, Caroline W. " 'A Picture Speaks a Thousand Words': Understanding Women's Migration through Visual Diaries." In *Scrutiny* 2, Vol. 15, Issue 1, 2010.

Kihato, Caroline W. *Migrant Women of Johannesburg: Everyday Life in an In-Between City.* Basingstoke, UK: Palgrave Macmillan, 2013.

Kistner, Ulrike. *Commissioning and Contesting Post-Apartheid's Human Rights: HIV/AIDS, Racism, Truth and Reconciliation.* Munster: LIT, 2003.

Köhne, Julia B. "Krieg Trauma Spiel. Einen britischen wissenschaftlichen Film (1918) und eine BBC-Documentary (2002) vergleichen." In *Filmische Gedächtnisse. Geschichte—Archiv—Riss*, edited by Frank Stern et al. Vienna: Mandelbaum 2007, 171-201.

Köppert, Katrin. "Contagious! The affective politics of AIDS scrapbooks!" In *Photography and the Album*, edited by Theresa Wilkie et al. Boston, Edingburgh: Museums etc., 2013.

Koyana, Xolani. "Justice Breakdown in Khayelitsha." In *Cape Times,* 03/26/2012, cf. www.iol.co.za/capetimes/justice-breakdown-in-khayelitsha-1.1263715#.VB6tH-c2ZyU; last accessed 9/2/2014.

Koivunen, Anu. "An affective turn? Reimagining the subject of feminist theory." In *Working with Affect in Feminist Readings: Disturbing Differences,* edited by Marianne Liljeström and Susanna Paasonen, 8–28. London, New York: Routledge, 2010.

Kracauer, Siegfried. *From Caligari to Hitler: A Psychological History of German Film.* Princeton, NJ: Princeton University Press, 1947.

Kreutzfeld Dorothee, and Bettina Malcomes, eds. *Not No Place, Johannesburg, Spaces and Fragments of Time*. Johannesburg: Jacana Media, 2013.

Kreye, Andrian. "Terrorbilder . . . und man vergisst sie nie." In *Sueddeutsche Zeitung,* 9/24/2014.

Kristeva, Julia. *Fremde sind wir uns selbst.* Frankfurt a. M.: Suhrkamp, 1990.

Kristeva, Julia. *Strangers to Ourselves.* New York: Columbia University Press, 1991.

Kurgan, Terry, and Louise Bethlehem. "Park pictures: on the work of photography in Johannesburg." In *Rethinking Labour in Africa, Past and Present,* edited by Lynn Schler et al., 128–43. New York, London: Routledge, 2013.

Kurgan, Terry. "Public Art/Private Lives A.K.A: Hotel Yeoville." In *Hotel Yeoville.* Idem., ed. Johannesburg: Fourthwall Books, 2013.

Laing, Aislinn. "Striking Miners 'Were Shot in the Back." In *The Telegraph,* 8/27/2012.

Lamuniere, Michelle. *You look beautiful like that: The Portrait Photographs of Seydou Keita and Malick Sidibé.* Harvard Art Museum, 2001.

Landau, Loren, Gayatri Sing, and Kaajal Ramjathan-Keogh. "Xenophobia in South Africa and Problems Relating to it." January 2005, Forced Migration Studies Program Wits University, Johannesburg, www.migration.org; last accessed 7/5/2011.

Landau Loren, and Tamlyn Monson. "Displacement, Estrangement and Sovereignty: Reconfiguring State Power in Urban South Africa." In *Government and Opposition*, Vol. 43, No. 2, 2008, 315–36.

Landau, Loren. "Pitfalls of a Language of Pity." In *The Star*, February 9, 2010, www.adf.org.za/; last accessed 8/6/2014.

Landau, Loren. "Passage, profit, protection and the challenge of participation building and belonging in African cities," ANU-WIDER, Working paper No. 2010/49, World Institute for Development Economic Research, www.wider.unu.edu/publications/working-papers/2010/en_GB/-wp2010-49/; last accessed 6/2/2014.

Landau, Loren. ed. *Exorcising the Demons Within: Xenophobia, Violence and Statecraft in Contemporary South Africa.* Johannesburg, SA: Wits University Press, 2011.

Landau, Loren. "Mobility and Metanarrative: Revisiting South African Social Science through Migration and Displacement," inaugural lecture, 6/18/2014. Wits University. Johannesburg. Cf. www.migration.org.za/; last accessed 6/20/2014.

Landsberg, Alison. *Prosthetic Memory. The Transformation of American Remembrance in the Age of Mass Culture.* New York: Columbia University Press, 2004.

Landy, Marcia. "Just an image. Godard, cinema, and philosophy." In *Critical Quarterly*, 43, 2001, 9–31.

Laurence, Patrick. "Twenty-one hanged in seventy-two hours." The article originally appeared in the *Weekly Mail*, 11/12/1987; mg.co.za, last accessed 6/6/2014.

Lebow, Alisa. "Shooting with Intent: Framing Conflict." in: Joram Ten Brink & Joshua Oppenheimer, *Killer Images: Documentary Film, Memory and the Performance of Violence*, edited by Joram Ten Brink and Joshua Oppenheimer, 41–62. New York: Wallflower Press, 2012.

Leeb, Susanne. "Not Quite Embracing Failure: History in Contemporary Art." In *Texte zur Kunst.* December 2009, Vol. 19, No. 76, 100–08.

Leo, Vince. "Review Found Photos in Detroit," cf. littlebrownmushroom.wordpress.com/2012/07/11/found-photos-in-detroit-reviewed-by-vince-leo/; last accessed 9/9/2014.

Levinas, Emanuel. "Ethics and the Face." In *Totality and Infinity,* translated by Alphonso Lingis. Pittsburgh, PA: Duquesne University Press, 1969.

Leys Ruth. "The Turn to Affect: A Critique." In *Critical Inquiry,* Vol. 37, No. 3 (Spring), 434–72.

Linfield, Susie. "Advertisement for Death," *New York Times*, January 27, 2014, www.nytimes.com/2014/01/28/opinion/advertisements-for-death.html; last accessed 2/28/2014.

Lodge, Tom. *Politics in South Africa: From Mandela to Mbeki.* Bloomington, IN: Indiana University Press, 2003.

Lorey, Isabell. "Weißsein und Immunisierung: Zur Unterscheidung zwischen Norm und Normalisierung," translate.eipcp.net/strands/03/lorey-strands01de; last accessed 9/9/2014.

Macleod, Scott. "The Life and Death of Kevin Carter," *Time Magazine*, Johannesburg, Sept. 12, 1994.

Mamdani, Mahmood. *Citizen and Subject: Contemporary Africa and the Legacy of Late Colonialism.* Princeton, NJ: University of Princeton Press, 1996.

Mamdani, Mahmood. "Teaching Africa at the Post-Apartheid University of Cape Town." In *Social Dynamics*, 24(2) 1998, 32.

Maingard, Jacqueline. *South African National Cinema*. New York: Routledge, 2007.

Makhubu, Norman. "Visual Narratives of Dispossession in Michelle Monareng's Video Art." In *Digging our Own Graves* 101, 14.

Makinana, Andisiwe. "Marikana tragedy: Who authorised the use of live ammunition?" 8/21/2012, *Mail and Guardian*, Johannesburg.

Manzo, Kathryn A. *Creating Boundaries: The Politics of Race and Nation.* Boulder, CO: Lynne Riener, 1996.

Marinovich, Greg, and João Silva. *The Bang-Bang Club.* London: Arrow Books, 2001.

Market Photo Workshop, Working the City Project Description 2011. www.marketphotoworkshop.co.za/; last accessed, 6/2/2011.

Marx, Karl. *The Eighteenth Brumaire of Louis Bonaparte.* 1852, Chpt. V.

Masilela, Ntongela. "*Come Back Africa* and South African film history." In *Jump Cut. Review for Contemporay Media.* No. 36, May 1991, 61–65. www.ejumpcut.org/archive/onlinessays/JC36folder/; last accessed 6/1/2014.

Massumi, Brian. *Parables for the Virtual: Movement, Affect, Sensation.* Durham, NC: Duke University Press, 2002.

Massumi, Brian. "Navigating Movements: An Interview with Brian Massumi," interview by Mary Zournazi, *21 C Magazine,* www.21cmagazine.com/issue2/massumi.html; last accessed 6/2/2014.

Matthias, Agnes. *Die Kunst den Krieg zu fotografieren.* Marburg: Jonas, 2005.

Mbeki, Thabo. "I am an African," www.soweto.co.za/html/i_iamafrican.htm; last accessed 6/9/2010.

Mbenga, Bernard, and Hermann Giliomee Hermann. *New History of South Africa* (1st ed.). Cape Town: Tafelberg Publishers, 2007.

Mbembe, Achille. *On the Post-Colony.* Berkeley, Los Angeles, London: University of California Press, 2001.

Mbembe, Achille. *Necropolitics.* Translated by L. Meintjes. In *Public Culture* 15 (1), 11–40. Durham, NC, London: Duke University Press, 2003.

Mbembe, Achille. "South Africa's Second Coming: The Nongquawuse Syndrome," published June 15th 2006 on the platform *open Democracy,* www.opendemocracy.net/democracy.africa_democracy/southafrica_succession_3649.jsp; last accessed 5/2/2014.

Mbembe, Achille. "Whiteness without Apartheid: the limits of racial freedom" 2007, www.opendemocracy.net/democracy_power/africa_democracy/south_apartheid, last accessed 9/1/2008;

Mbembe, Achille. "The Aesthetics of Superfluidity." In *Johannesburg, the Elusive Metropolis,* edited by idem. and Sarah Nuttal. Johannesburg: Wits University Press, 2008.

McClintock, Ann. *Imperial Leather.* New York, London: Routledge 1995.

McKernan, Luke. "Harald Shaw and de Voortreekers," thebioscope.net/2008/11/24/harold-shaw-and-de-voortrekkers/; last accessed 7/7/2014.

Mercer, Kobena. *Welcome to the Jungle: New Positions in Black Cultural Studies.* New York, London: Routledge, 1994.

Médecins Sans Frontières, International Website MSF 2013, http://www.msf.org/; last accessed 4/1/2013.

Mendel, Guideon. "Through Positive Eyes," throughpositiveeyes.org/; last accessed 9/17/2013.

Metz, Christian. "Photography and Fetish." In *October,* Vol. 34, 1985, 81–90.

Mezzadra, Sandro, and Federico Rahola. "The Postcolonial Condition: A Few Notes on the Quality of Time in the Historical Present." In *Postcolonial Text,* Vol 2, No. 1, 2006, postcolonial.org/index.php/pct/article/view/393/819; last accessed 9/8/2014.

Mezzadra, Sandro. *Border as Method.* Durham, NC, London: Duke University Press, 2013.

Mezzofiore, Gianluca. "Benetton, a history of shocking ad campaigns." In *International Business Times,* 11/18/2011, www.ibtimes.co.uk/benetton-history-shocking-ad-campaigns-pictures-252087; last accessed 9/3/2014.

Miller, Toby. *Technologies of Truth: Cultural Citizenship and the Popular Media.* Minneapolis: University of Minnesota Press, 1998.

Mills, Charles W. "White Ignorance." In *Race and Epistemologies of Ignorance*, edited by Shannon Sullivan and Nancy Tuana. Albany, NY: State University of New York Press, 2007.

Mirzoeff, Nicolas. *The Right to Look: A Counterhistory of Visuality*. Durham, NC, London: Duke University Press, 2011.

Mitchell. W. J. T. *Iconology: Image, Text, Ideology.* Chicago: University of Chicago Press, 1986.

Mitchell. W. J. T. "Migrating Images—Totemism, Fetishism, Idolatry." In *Migrating Images: Producing . . . Reading . . . Translating*, edited by Petra Stegmann and Peter C. Seel, 14–24. Berlin: HDKW, 2004.

Mitchell. W. J. T. *What do Pictures Want? The Lives and Loves of Images.* Chicago, London: University of Chicago Press, 2005.

Moele, Kgebetli. *Untitled.* Cape Town: Kwela Books, 2013.

Morin, Marie-Eve. "Putting Community Under Erasure." In: *Culture Machine*, Vol. 8, 2006. www.culturemachine.net/index.php/cm/article/viewArticle/37/45; last accessed 12/3/2013.

"Mourning Mothers in Argentina," "History of Abuelas de Plaza de Mayo," www.abuelas.org.ar/english/history.htm; last accessed 4/15/2014.

Muller, C. F. J., ed. *Five Hundred Years: A History of South Africa.* Pretoria: Academica. 1981.

Muñoz, José Esteban. *Cruising Utopia: The Then and There of Queer Futurity.* New York: New York University Press, 2009.

Nagl, Tobias. *Die unheimliche Maschine. Rasse und Repräsentation im Weimarer Kino.* Munich: Edition Text + Kritik, 2009.

Nando's, official website, www.nandos.co.za/; last accessed 6/11/2012.

"Nando's ad: Banned from TV . . . Goes to print," South African Press Association (SAPA): www.bizcommunity.com; last accessed 6/11/2012.

Natives' Land Act, 1913, www.polity.org.za/polity/govdocs/legislation/misc/nla1913.html; last accessed, 5/10/2014.

Neocosmos, Michael. *From 'Foreign Natives' To 'Native Foreigners.' Explaining Xenophobia in Post-apartheid South Africa.* Dakar: Codesira, 2010.

Newbury, Darren. *Defiant Images: Photography and Apartheid South Africa.* Pretoria: Unisa Press, 2009.

Ngcobo, Gabi. "Introduction," in *Digging our own Graves 101.* Published by the Center for Historical Reenactments based in Johannesburg, South Africa, in conjunction with the Berlin Biennale, Crash Pad, Kunstwerke, 2014.

Nkosi, Thenjiwe Niki. "Saying goodbye to a hero—and the idea of needing a hero." In *Washington Post*, 12/13/2013.

Nietzsche, Friedrich. *On the Genealogy of Morals.* New York: Vintage, 1969.

Ntsaluba, Gcina. "Alex killers are 'proud' of attacks on foreigners." In *Chimurenga Chronic* 5. May 18–24, 2008, Capetown.

Nxumalo, Frank. "South Africa remains one of the most unequal countries of the world." Cf. www.sabc.co.za/news/a/5975b6004c185051a3eaffa583a5af00/

SA-remains-one-of-the-most-unequal-societies-in-the-world:-World-Bank-20122407; last accessed 9/5/2014.

Onishi, Norimitsu. "African National Congress Draws 62 Percent of the Vote in South Africa," www.nytimes.com/2014/05/10/world/africa/south-africa-vote.html; *New York Times*, 5/9/2014; last accessed 5/10/2014.

O'Meara, Dan, Robert Davies, and Dlamini Sipho, *The Struggle for South Africa: A Reference Guide to Movements, Organisations and Institutions*. London: Zed Books, 1984.

Orford, Margie "A Foreigner in My Own Land," www.xenophobia.org.za/saspeak-out.htm; last accessed 5/1/2010.

Oxford Latin Dictionary. Oxford, UK: Oxford University Press, 1982.

Parker, Faranaaz. "Paul Verryn, what went wrong?" 1/29/2010, *Mail and Guardian,* mg.co.za/article/2010-01-29-paul-verryn-what-went-wrong; last accessed 8/8/2013.

Palmary, Ingrid et al., eds. *Gender and Migration: Feminist Interventions.* London: Zed Books, 2010.

Papadopoulous, Dimitris, and Vassilis Tsianos. "The Autonomy of Migration." In *Deleuzian Encounters: Studies in Contemporary Social Issues*, edited by Anna Hickey-Moody and Petra Malins. Basingstoke, UK: Palgrave Macmillan, 2007.

Passport Service, passportservice.co.za/2010/07/28/south-african-passport-photo-guidelines/; last accessed 9/2/2012.

Patton, Alan. *Cry, the Beloved Country.* New York: Charles Scribner's Sons, 1948.

Patton, Kimberly Christine, and John Stratton Hawley, eds. *Holy Tears: Weeping in the Religious Imagination.* Princeton, NJ: Princeton University Press, 2005.

Pedwell, Carolyn, and Anne Whitehead. "Affecting Feminism: Questions of Feeling in Feminist Theory." In *Feminist Theory* 13.2: Special Issue: Affecting Feminism (2012), 115–29.

Peffer, John. "Gemeinsam im Bild." In *Chimurenga Chronic*, April 2014.

Peires, J. B. *The Dead Will Arise: Nonquawuse and the Great Xhosa Cattle-Killing Movement of 1856/7.* Bloomington, IN: University of Indiana Press, 1989.

Peters, Kathrin. "History and Fiction." In *Texte zur Kunst,* December 2009, 19th edition, No. 76, 112–19.

Piper, Adrian. "Passing for White, Passing for Black," first published 1992, reprinted in *Out of Order, Out of Sight, Volume I: Selected Essays in Meta-Art 1968–1992.* Cambridge, MA: MIT Press, 1996.

Phelan, Peggy. *Unmarked: The Politics of Performance.* New York, London: Routledge, 1993.

Plaatje, Solomon Thsekisho. *Native Life in South Africa.* London: PS King and Son, 1916.

Ponzanesi, Sandra, and Marguerite Waller, eds. *Postcolonial Cinema Studies.* London, New York: Routledge, 2012.

Porter, Tim. "Covering War in a Free Society," February 18, 2003, www.timporter.com/firstdraft/archives/000071.html; last accessed 9/17/2012.

Potgieter, De Wet, and Herbert Matimba. "Barbaric border activity during the 'hell run.'" In: *The New Age*, South Africa 5/ 7/2012, thenewage.co.za; last accessed 7/1/2012.

Poulantzas, Nicos. *Staatstheorie,* Hamburg: VSA, 2002.

Puar, Jasbir. *Terrorist Assemblages.* Durham, NC, London: Duke University Press, 2007.

Rancière, Jacques. *The Emancipated Spectator.* Translated by G. Elliot. London, New York: Verso, 2011.

Rancière, Jacques. "The Thinking of Dissensus." In *Reading Rancière*, edited by Paul Bowman and Richard Stamp. London, New York: Continuum, 2011.

Rancière, Jacques. *Film Fables.* London: Bloomsbury Academic, 2006.

Rancière, Jacques. *The Politics of Aesthetics: The Distribution of the Sensible.* Translated by Gabriel Rockhill. London, New York: Continuum, 2004.

Rancière, Jacques, Fulvia Carnevale, and John Kelsey. "The Art of the Possible." In *Artforum*, 2007.

Ray, Carina. District 9 Review, 2009, www.zeleza.com.symposium/494; last accessed 10/29/2009.

Read, Alan, ed. *The Fact of Blackness: Frantz Fanon and Visual Representation.* London, Seattle: Institute of Contemporary Arts and Institute of International Visual Arts–London, Bay Press–Seattle, 1996.

Reynolds, Glenn, ed. *Images Out of Africa: The Virgina Garner Diaries of the African Motion Picture Project.* Lanham, MD: University of America Press, 2011.

Rogoff, Irit. "Studying Visual Culture." In *Visual Culture Reader*, edited by Nicolas Mirzoeff, 14–26. London: Routledge, 1999.

Rose, Gillian. *Doing Family Photography: The Domestic, the Public and the Politics of Sentiment.* Farngate & Burlington: Ashgate, 2010.

Rosler, Martha. "Bringing the War Home," theexposureproject.blogspot.de/2008/11/martha-roslers-bringing-war-home-1967.html; last accessed 8/2/2012.

Roudinesco, Elisabeth, and Michael Plon. *Wörterbuch der Psychoanalyse.* Vienna, New York: Springer, 2004.

"SA-remains-world-rape-capital," SAPA 24H News, www.news24.com/SouthAfrica/News/SA-remains-world-rape-capital-20120921; last accessed 12/12/2012.

Sanders, Mark. "Ambiguities of Mourning." In *Loss: The Politics of Mourning,* edited by Eng and Kazan, 77–98. Berkeley, Los Angeles: University of California Press, 2003.

"Saturday Mothers in Turkey," www.memorializeturkey.com/en/memorial/saturday-mothers/; last accessed 4/15/2014.

Saunders, Christopher. "Lynching: The Southern African Case." In *Globalizing Lynching History: Vigilantism and Extralegal Punishment from an International Perspective.* Edited by Manfred Berg and Simon Wend, 87–100. Basingstoke, UN: Palgrave Macmillan, 2011.

Saxton, Libby. *Haunted Images: Film, Ethics, Testimony, and the Holocaust.* London, New York: Wallflower Press, 2008.

Schaffer, Johanna. *Die Ambivalenzen der Sichtbarkeit. Visuelle Strukturen der Anerkennung*. Bielefeld: Transcript, 2008.

Scharf, Wilfried, and Baba Kgcokoto. "Images of Punishment in the People's Courts of Cape Town: 1985–7: From Prefigurative Justice to Populist Violence." In *Political Violence and the Struggle in South Africa*, edited by N. Manganyi and Andre du Toit. London: Macmillan, 1990.

Schmitt, Christian. *Kinopathos*. Berlin: Bertz&Fischer, 2009.

Schneider, Richard C. "Über Gaza berichten. Gegen die Bilder ist unser Text machtlos." In *FAZ*, August 4, 2014.

Schreiner, Olive. *Trooper Peter Halket of Mashonaland*. London: Unwin, 1905.

Schröter, Jens. "Das Zeitalter der technischen Nicht-Reproduzierbarkeit. In *Navigationen*. No. 1, edited by idem et al., 9–36. Siegen: universi, 2010.

Schultz, Annett. *Unity in Diversity? Konstruktion von kulturellem Gedächtnis im Post-Apartheid-Südafrika*. Humboldt Universität Berlin, 2012.

Sedgewick, Eve Kosofsky. *Touching Feeling: Affect, Pedagogy, Performativity*. Durham, NC, London: Duke University Press, 2003.

Segal, Lauren. "The Human Face of Violence: Hostel dwellers speak." In *The Journal of Southern African Studies*, Vol. 18, No. 1, March 1991, 190–231.

Segatti, Aurelia, Olufemi Adeagbo, and Samson Ogunyemi. "Nigerians in South Africa: Facts and Figures," Migration Issue Brief 8, June 2012, www.migration.org.za/publication/issue-brief/9999/nigerians-south-africa-facts-and-figures; last accessed 8/28/2013.

Shandler, David. Letter to Matt Meyer, War Resisters League, 18 September 18, 1986. Historical Papers, University of the Witwatersrand, AG1977–End Conscription Campaign, A4.2.2; www.historicalpapers.wits.ac.za/; last accessed 6/7/2014.

Shaviro, Steven. *Post-Cinematic Affect*. United Kingdom: O-Books, 2010.

Shmuckler, Gina. *The Line*, original play, (Johannesburg 2012) written and directed by Gina Shmukler, premiered July 18, 2012, at the Market Theatre in Johannesburg.

Sibande, Mary. "The work of South African Artist Mary Sibande," in *The Guardian*, 8/26/2012, www.theguardian.com/artanddesign/gallery/2012/aug/26/south-african-artist-mary-sibande; last accessed 8/12/2013.

Simone, AbdouMalique. "Spectral Selves: Practices in the Making of African Cities," Wiser Institute for Social and Economic Research & New School University. wiserweb.wits.ac.za/; last accessed 9/6/2011.

Sierek, Karl. *Foto, Kino und Computer. Aby Warburg als Medientheoretiker*. Berlin: Philo, 2007.

Smaill, Belinda. *The Documentary: Politics, Emotion, Culture*. Basingstoke, UK, New York: Palgrave Macmillan, 2010.

Smith, David. "'Racism' of early Colour Photography explored in art exhibition," in *Guardian*, January 25, 2013, www.theguardian.com/artanddesign/2013/jan/25/racism-colour-photography-exhibition/print; last accessed 7/20/2014.

Smith, Matthew Ryan. *Relational Viewing: Affect, Trauma and the Viewer in Contemporary Autobiographical Art.* Thesis in Philosophy. London, Ontario, Canada: The University of Western Ontario, 2012.

Smith, Roberta. "One Image of Agony Resonates in Two Lives," in *New York Times,* 4/15/2009, www.nytimes.com; last accessed 7/18/2014.

Smuts, Jan. *Native Policy in Africa* from *Towards a better World.* World Book Company, 1944, 322–27, quoted in *Captured in Time: Five Centuries of South African Writing,* edited by John Clare, 304–2. Johannesburg, Cape Town: Jonathan Ball Publishers, 2010.

Solomon-Godeau, Abigail. *Photography at the Dock: Essays on Photographic History, Institutions, and Practices.* Minneapolis: University of Minnesota Press, 1991.

Solidarity for Survival Website. (S4S) 2011, www.solidarity4survival.org/; last accessed 5/15/2011.

Solomon, Dan. "Steven van Zandt tells the story of "Sun City" and fighting apartheid," www.fastcocreate.com/3023454/steven-van-zandt-tells-the-story-of-sun-city-and-fighting-apartheid-in-south-africa; last accessed 8/10/2014.

Sonke Gender Justice Network, saynotoviolence.org/user/780; last accessed 9/24/2012 and www.genderjustice.org.za, last accessed 6/1/2012.

Sontag, Susan. *Regarding the Pain of Others.* New York: Picador/Farrar, Straus and Giroux, 2003.

South Africa's Constitution, www.info.gov.za/documents/constitution/; last accessed 9/14/2012.

South African Government Information, www.info.gov.za/view/; last accessed 5/21/2011.

South African History Archive, saha.org, last accessed 9/9/2014.

Spinoza, Baruch (Benedictus) de. *Die Ethik nach geometrischer Methode dargestellt.* Dt. Otto Baensch. Hamburg: F. Meiner, 1955.

Spivak, Gayatri Chakravorty. *The Post-Colonial Critic: Interviews, Strategies, Dialogues.* London, New York: Routledge, 1990.

Spivak, Gayatri Chakravorty. "Righting Wrongs." In *The South Atlantic Quarterly* 103 2/3, Spring/Summer 2004.

Spivak, Gayatri Chakravorty. "Can the Subaltern Speak?" In *Can the Subaltern Speak? Reflections on the History of an Idea,* edited by Rosalind C. Morris. New York: Columbia University Press, 2010.

Steffen, Therese. "Leben unter dem Schleier: Afroamerikanische Texte und Kontexte." In *Verschleierter Orient—Entschleierter Okzident. (Un-)Sichtbarkeit in Politik, Recht, Kunst und Kultur seit dem 19. Jahrhundert,* edited by Bettina Dennerlein et al., 181—202. Munich: Wilhelm Fink, 2012.

Stemberger, Claudia Marion. "Spot On South Africa: Women Photographers," an interview with Pam Warne, Curator of Photography and New Media at Iziko Museums (South African National Gallery) in Cape Town, *EIKON—International Magazine for Photography and Media Art,* No. 70, 2010.

Stern, Frank. "Inglourious Basterds. Antifa-Movie als Feel Good Fantasy," in *Malmoe,* 47.

Stuettgen, Tim. *In a Qu*a*re Time and Place.* Berlin, 2014.

Sturm, Herta. "Wahrnehmung und Fernsehen: die fehlende Halbsekunde," in *Media Perspektiven*, No. 1, 1984, 58–65.

Steyerl, Hito. "Documentary Practice Is Always Already an Action." Interview with Hito Steyerl by Reinhard Braun in *Camera Austria*, # 114, 2011, 27—28.

Steyerl, Hito. *The Wretched of the Screen*. Berlin: Sternberg Press, 2012.

Steyerl, Hito. "Politics of Post-Representation," dismagazine.com/disillusioned-2/62143/hito-steyerl-politics-of-post-representation/; last accessed 9/7/2014.

"Stop Human Trafficking in Southern Africa," SAHTT 2010, saahtt.wordpress.com/; last accessed 2/3/2012.

Strick, Simon. *American Dolorologies: Pain, Sentimentalism and Biopolitics.* Albany NY: State University of New York Press, 2014.

Sutton, Tony. *Drum 1976–1980: An Exhibition from the Pages of Drum Magazine.* 2006, www.coldtype.net/Assets.06/Essays.06/0606.DrumBook.pdf; last accessed 8/7/2014.

Szwed, John F. *Space is the Place: The Lives and Times of Sun Ra.* New York: Da Capo, 1998.

Taylor, Jane. "Really?—On Sincerity in the context of the South African TRC—Commission," May 13, 2009, Lecture at New School.

Taylor, Jane. *Considering Forgiveness.* New York: Vera List Center for Art and Politics, 2009.

Ticktin, Miriam. *Casualties of Care: Immigration and the Politics of Humanitarianism in France.* Berkeley, Los Angeles: University of California Press, 2011.

Trinh, Minh-ha T. "The Totalizing Quest of Meaning." In *Theorizing Documentary*, edited by Michael Renov, 90–107. London, New York: Routledge, 1993.

Trinh, Minh-ha T. "Speaking Nearby," Interview with Nancy Chen, in *Visual Anthropology Review*, Vol. 8, #1, Spring 1992, 82–91.

Thomas, Kylie. "Wounding Apertures: Violence, Affect and Photography during and after Apartheid," in *Kronos*, 38(1) (2012), 204–18. www.scielo.org.za/; last accessed 7/25/2014.

Toit, Andries du. "Becoming the alien, racism, apartheid and *District 9*," 0/4/2009, asubtleknife.wordpress.com/2009/09/04/science-fiction-in-the-ghetto-loving-the-alien/; last accessed 9/2/2014.

Toit, Louise du. "Feminism and the ethics of reconciliation," in *Eurozine,* 3/17/2007, www.eurozine.com/articles/2007-03-16-dutoit-en.html; last accessed 9/18/2014.

Tomaselli, Keyan. *The Cinema of Apartheid: Race and Class in South African Film.* Brooklyn, NY: Smyrna Press, 1988.

Tomlinson, Richard et al., eds. *Emerging Johannesburg: Perspectives on the Post-apartheid City.* London, New York: Routledge, 2003.

"Truth Commission Looks At First 'Necklace' Murder," SAPA. February 4, 1997; www.doj.gov.za/trc/media/1997/9702/s970204c.htm; last accessed 9/17/2012.

Tsianos, Vassilis, Niamh Stephenson, and Dimitris Papadopoulos. *Escape Routes: Control and Subversion in the 21st century.* London: Pluto, 2008.

Twalo, Sinethemba. "The Spectre of the Exception." In *Digging our Own Graves 101*, published by CHR and the 8th Berlin Biennale 2014, 11–13.

Twalo, Sinethemba. "Into the Darkness, Black Subjectivities and Alternative Knowledge Production." Lecture at ifa, Berlin, July 17, 2014, cf. www.contemporaryand.com/de/exhibition/lecture-into-the-darkness-black-subjectivities-and-alternative-knowledge-production/; last accessed 7/25/2014.

Vahabzadeh, Susan. "Touristen im Gestern," *Sueddeutsche Zeitung*, No. 68; March 22nd/23rd 2014, 13.

Veary, Jo et al. "Working the City: Experiences of Migrant Women in Inner-city Johannesburg." In *Southern Africa Gender and Media and Diversity Journal* # 9, 2011, 228–33.

Vismann, Cornelia. *Medien der Rechtsprechung*. Frankfurt a. M.: Fischer Verlag, 2011.

Vladislavić, Ivan. *Double Negative*. Cape Town: Random House/Umuzi, 2011.

Waal, Shaun de. "Method to Marikana Massacre." In *Mail and Guardian*, 6/6/2014, cf. mg.co.za; last accessed 9/15/2014.

Warnke, Martin, ed. *Aby Warburg, Der Bilderatlas Mnemosyne. Gesammelte Schriften, Band II.1*. Oldenbourg: Akademie Verlag, 2008.

Wedemeyer, Clemens von, and Paolo Caffoni, eds. "First Contact," magazine, film material no. 4, information on the 'fourth wall,' January 2010.

Wentzel, Marie. "Historical Origins of Hostels in South Africa: Migrant Labor and Compounds." In *Communities in Isolation: Perspectives on Hostels in South Africa*, edited by Anthony Minaar. Pretoria: Human Sciences Research Council, 1993.

Wenzel, Horst. "Hand-Zeichen. Zur Mediengeschichte der Hand als Datenträger." In*Mehrdeutigkeit. Die Ambivalenz von Gedächtnis und Erinnerung*, edited by Moritz Csáky, and Peter Stachel, 179–202. Wien: Passagen, 2003.

Wenzel, Jennifer. "Remembering the Past's Future: Anti-Imperialist Nostalgia and some Versions of the Third World," in *Cultural Critique* 62, Winter 2006, 1–32.

Weskott, Aljoscha, and Marietta Kesting, eds. *Sun Tropes: Sun City and (Post-) Apartheid Culture in South Africa*. Berlin: August Verlag, 2009.

Whitlock, Gillian. "Remediating Gorilla Girl: Rape Warfare and the Limits of Humanitarian Storytelling," in *Biography 3.3* 2010, 471–97.

Wilderson III, Frank. "Biko and Problematic of Presence." In *Biko Lives: Contesting the Legacies of Steve Biko*, edited by Amanda Alexander et al., 95–114. New York: Palgrave Macmillan, 2008.

Wilkinson, Kate. "Why it is wrong to call SA (or any other country) 'the rape capital of the world,'" in *Mail and Guardian*, Johannesburg, South Africa, 1/29/2014.

Williams, Linda. *Hard Core: Power, Pleasure and the "Frenzy of the Visible."* Berkeley, Los Angeles: University of California Press, 1989.

Williams, Linda. *Playing the Racecard: Melodramas of Black and White from Uncle Tom to O. J. Simpson*. Princeton, NJ: Princeton University Press, 2001.

Winston. Brian. *Claiming the Real: The Documentary Film Revisited.* London: British Film Institute, 1995.

Wilson, Richard A. *The Politics of Truth and Reconciliation in South Africa: Legitimizing the Post-Apartheid State.* Cambridge, UK: Cambridge University Press, 2001.

Witz, Leslie, and Noëleen Murray. *Hostels, Homes, Museums: Memorialising Migrant Labour Pasts in Lwandle, South Africa.* Cape Town: UCT Press, 2014.

Witz, Leslie. *Apartheid's Festival: Contesting South Africa's National Past.* Bloomington, IN: Indiana University Press, 2003.

Witz, Leslie. "Sun City and Lwandle: Making Apartheid Museums." In *Sun Tropes: Sun City and (Post-)Apartheid Culture in South Africa*, edited by A. Weskott and M. Kesting, 61–94. Berlin: August Verlag, 2009.

Wolf, Nicole. *Make it Real: Documentary and Other Cinematic Experiments by Women Filmmakers in India.* Dissertation, Frankfurt O., 2007.

"Women's Charter of the ANC," www.anc.org.za/ancdocs/history/women/wcharter.html; last accessed 5/6/2010.

Yekani, Elahe Haschemi. *The Privilege of Crisis: Narratives of Masculinities in Colonial and Postcolonial Literature, Photography and Film.* Frankfurt, New York: Campus, 2011.

Young, Robert. "Women, Gender and Anti-Colonialism." In *Postcolonialism: An Historical Introduction*, 360–82. Oxford: Blackwell, 2001.

Yuval-Davis, Nira. *Gender and Nation.* London: Sage, 1997.

Zvomuya, Percy. "An outsider's Yeoville insight: Social responsibility meets mainstream art in this chronicle of public, private and mundane lives." In *Mail and Guardian,* Johannesburg, SA, 8/3/2013.

Filmography

"A Complaint of Rape," by Roger Graef, Episode 3 of the Series *Police,* BBC I, originally screened, 4/01–15/03 1982, www.screenonline.org.uk/tv/id/464502/; last accessed 8/16/2014.

Alive in Joburg, by Neill Blomkamp, (6:24 min., South Africa, 2005), www.youtube.com/watch?v=le3y0QlLjJE; last accessed 7/12/2010.

Border Farm, by Thenjiwe Nkosi and the Dublibadzimu Theatre Group of Musina, (32 min., South Africa, 2011), cf. borderfarm.blogspot.com/p/about-us.html; last accessed 7/1/2012. Artist's website thenjiwenkosi.com/border-farm/; last accessed 9/4/2014.

"Born-Frees," by Jodi Matas and Phil Maynard, *The Guardian*, 05/26/2014, www.theguardian.com/world/video/2014/apr/25/born-free-generation-20-year-olds-south-africa-video; last accessed 9/9/2014.

Come Back, Africa, by Lionel Rogosin, (95 min., USA, 1959).

Conversations on a Sunday Afternoon, by Khalo Matabane, (80 min., South Africa, 2005).

Cry, the Beloved Country, by Zoltan Korda, (113 min., South Africa, 1951). Cf. www.imdb.com/title/tt0043436/; last accessed 9/17/2014.

Dear Mandela, by Dara Kell and Christopher Nizza, (90 min., USA, 2012).

De Voortrekkers/Winning a Continent, by Harold Shaw, (54 min., South Africa, 1916).

District 9, by Neill Blomkamp, (112 min., USA, South Africa, 2009), www.imdb.com/title/tt1136608/?ref_=nv_sr_1; last accessed 7/2/2014.

Don't Shoot, by Lucilla Blankenberg, (11:45 min., South Africa, 2007). Released on DVD by "Why Democracy?" www.whydemocracy.net; last accessed 7/2/2014.

Howzit? Migrant Life in Joburg, by Marietta Kesting, (20 min., HD & super 8, BW & color, 2015). Documentary film, published on FOG platform, http://fog-platform.com/en/fragmented-city-en/; last accessed 8/25/2016.

Drum, by Zola Maseko, (94 min., South Africa, 2004), www.imdb.com/title/tt0379765/?ref_=fn_al_tt_3; last accessed 9/9/2014.

Gangster Girls, by Tine Leisch, (79 min., Austria, 2008) www.imdb.com/title/tt1399019/; last accessed 9/4/2012.

"Got Till It's Gone," song by Janet Jackson, music video; last accessed 6/2/2013.

I am too sad to tell you, by Jan Bas Ader, (3.23 min., 1971). www.youtube.com/watch?v=vUzBCl6iVoc; last accessed 6/2/2013.

"I ain't gonna play Sun City," song by Artists United Against Apartheid, music video, www.youtube.com/watch?v=TlMdYpnVOGQ; last accessed 6/2/2013.

Inglourious Basterds, by Quentin Tarantino, (153 min., USA 2009), cf. www.imdb.com/title/tt0361748/; last accessed 9/9/2011.

Jim Comes to Jo'burg, by Donald Swanson, (50 min., B&W, South Africa, 1949), www.imdb.com/title/tt0211906/, cf. also www.villonfilms.ca/african-jim/; both last accessed 6/13/2014.

La Forteresse, by Fernand Melgar, (104 min., France, 2008), www.laforteresse.ch/fr/accueil; last accessed 9/27/2012.

La Politique et le Bonheur, by Jean-Luc Godard and Jean-Pierre Gorin, (18 min., France, 1972), www.telerama.fr/cinema/films/vive-le-cinema-la-politique-et-le-bonheur-goerges-kiejman-et-jean-luc-godard,262927.php; last accessed 10/01/2011.

Mandela, the Myth and Me, by Khalo Matabane, (85 min., South Africa, Germany, 2013). Beetz film productions, vimeo.com/81181678; last accessed 5/16/2014 and www.imdb.com/title/tt3451624/; last accessed 9/2/2014.

Man on Ground, by Akin Omotoso, (80 min., South Africa, 2011.)

Martine and Thandeka, by Xolishwa Sithole, (24 min., South Africa, 2008), Filmmakers Against Racism Collective. Produced by Carolyn Carew.

Meanwhile in Mamelodi, by Benjamin Kahlmeyer, (71 min., South Africa, Germany, 2011), www.imdb.com/title/tt2055675/; last accessed 5/14/2014.

Miners Shot Down, by Rehad Desai, (85 min., South Africa, 2014), www.minersshotdown.co.za/; last accessed 9/15/2014.

Nando's "Diversity Clip," (0:53 min., South Africa, 2012), www.youtube.com/watch?v=_R7vu9SuxaQ; last accessed 9/15/2014.

Paris is Burning, by Jenny Livingstone, (71 min., USA, 1991), www.imdb.com/title/tt0100332/; last accessed 9/9/2014.

"Powa," song by Tumi Molekwane, music video (4:10 min., South Africa, 2011), www.youtube.com/watch?v=BMdM03miCgo; last accessed 9/20/2012.

"Poverty Pornography," Achille Mbembe discusses the photographic practice as "poverty pornography" together with Ayana Jackson, Gabi Ncgobo, Thembinkosi Goniwe, and Khwezi Gule at Momo Gallery, Johannesburg on Aug. 10, 2010, www.youtube.com/watch?v=csUW0T9vb-E; last accessed 4/15/2014.

Removal to Radium, by Michelle Monareng, (3-channel video installation, South Africa, 2013).

Sandra Laing—A Spiritual Journey, by Karien van der Merve, (26 min., 2001), www.journeyman.tv; last accessed 9/2/2014.

State of Violence, by Khalo Matabane, (79 min., South Africa, 2010), www.imdb.com/title/tt1722517/; last accessed 9/25/2012.

The Bang-Bang Club, by Steven Silver, (106 min., South Africa, 2009), www.imdb.de/title/tt1173687/; last accessed 9/2/2012.

The Birth of a Nation, by D. W. Griffith, (190 min., USA, 1915), www.imdb.com/title/tt0004972/; last accessed 6/17/2014.

The Burning Man, by Adze Ugah, (24 min., South Africa, 2008), Filmmakers Against Racism Collective.

"The Fate of the Madgermanes," (Das Schicksal der Madgermanes) in ZDF heute Jounal, screened on German television 11/9/2013, cf. www.zdf.de; last accessed 9/9/2014.

Waltz with Bashir, by Ari Folmann, (90 min., Israel 2008), www.imdb.com/title/tt1185616/; last accessed 08/07/2010.

We Are Nowhere, by Andy Spitz, (South Africa, 2010).

When the Mountain Meets Its Shadow, by Alexander Klein and Daniela Michel, (93 min., Germany, 2010).

Index

A Complaint of Rape (film), 71, 220n130
Adusei-Poku, Nana, 232n1, 243n63
Affect, blocs of, 12; intensity, 11, 51, 85, 165, 198
affective, assemblage, 34, 49–50, 52, 100, 110, 165, 196; dispositive, 64; turn, 11, 207n50
African migrant worker, 8, 20–23, 34, 192–195; *see also* migration, migrant labor system
African Renaissance, 80, 144, 221n5
Afrofuturism, 163, 174, 237n81, 237n82, 238n97
aliens (*District 9*), 162, 194
Als, Hilton, 88–90, 108
ANC African National Congress, 92, 191, 197, 203n3, 214n23; defiance campaign, 124–125; Women Charter, 130
Angerer, Marie-Louise, 64
apartheid, government, 21, 32, 35, 38, 42–44, 53, 123; homeland, 20–23; native reserves, 20; native location 21; pass laws, 21, 31–32, 123–125; segregation, 19–26, 95, 171, 180, 199; *see also* Native Land Act, Natives Resettlement Act
archive, apartheid, 200; counter, 55, 73–74, 138; visual/image, 14, 18–24, 30, 40, 46, 88, 189, 200; colonial, 200; national, 19, 170–171; cultural, 21
Arendt, Hannah, 30
Appadurai, Arjun, 56
Auga, Ulrike, 80
Azoulay, Ariella, 9, 38, 56, 69–74, 96–97, 124, 207n43, 214n27

Baldwin, James, 55
Ball, Joanna, 91
Bang-Bang Club, 45–54, 89, 108, 116, 194, 216n55; *see also* Marinovich, Greg; Carter, Kevin
Barthes, Roland, 4–5, 84–85, 127
Bayley, Jim, 25
becoming (Deleuze), 144, 156
belonging, 183, 201
Benjamin, Walter, 18, 157
Berlin conference, 17
Berry, Ian, 1–2, 203n4
Bester, Rory, 20, 205n25
Bhaba, Homi, 180
Biko, Steve, 227n94, 227n95
Black Lives Matter, 143
Black Student Society, Women Group (poster), 131
blackness, representations of, 143, 158–159, 200; double-consciousness, 27
Blankenberg, Lucilla, 191
Blomkamp, Neill, 162, 176, 181

Boltanski, Luc, 9, 40
Bophutatswana, 35
Border Farm (film), 154–156, 162, 191, 194, 234n30; *see also* stills in color gallery K, L
borders, intimate, 94, 101; national, 17; South Africa's, 33–35; wars, 35
Braun, Christina von, 5, 10, 14, 30, 200
Brinkema, Eugenia, 60
Brown, Grace, 72
Brown, Wendy, 56, 108, 197
Burning Man, (photograph and film), 8–9, 79–118, 226n80; *see also* Nhamuave, Ernesto
Butler, Judith, 38, 48, 75–76, 199

Carter, Kevin, 47–49, 217n68, 217n69; see also *Bang-Bang* Club
Caruth, Cathy, 86
Center for Historical Reenactments, 7, 55, 183–184, 186, 190, 198, 240n12
Chimurenga (magazine), 5–6, 205n24
citizenship, 17, 110, 160–161, 166, 183, 187, 193; militarized, 34; flawed, 124
cliché, 144, 178, 180, 199–201, 243n67
Coetzee, J. M., 107
Cole, Ernest, 30–32, 52
colonialism, colonial neurosis, 176; colonial subject 57, 198
Come Back, Africa (film), 22–27, 211n31
Conversations on a Sunday Afternoon (film), 62–64, 74–75, 150–154
Crenshaw, Kimberlé, 153
crying, 63–66; public 76; victim, 219n112; crying woman 192, 219n113; *see also* tears
cyborg, 174

Dean, Jodi, 159–160
de-identification, 143–150
Deleuze, Gilles, 144, 149, 198, 201
Derida, Jacques, 119
Dery, Mark, 174
Dietze, Gabriele, 13, 207n45, 215n40, 223n32
discrimination, 130, 136–138, 175, 179
disidentification, 149–150
District 6, 170
District 9 (film), 162–181, 216–217n62
Dlamini, Jacob, 27
documentary, tradition, 3, 30, 47, 49, 61, 66, 96
domestic worker (female), 210n22
Don't Shoot (film), 191
Double Negative (novel), 160–161
Drum (magazine), 25–27; cover in color gallery A
Dublibadzimu Theatre Group, 154; stills in color gallery K, L
Du Bois, W.E.B., 27

Els, Darryl, 24
empathy, 39, 43, 48, 57, 75–76, 106, 201, 241n27
End Conscription Campaign 33–36; (poster), 33
Entertainment Act, 21
Enwezor, Okwui, 32, 205n25, 217n68

family portrait, 104, 132, 199
Fanon, Frantz, 13, 77, 158–159, 176
feelings, 10–13, 66, 103
Filmmakers Against Racism, 14, 67, 198
fingerprint, electronic, 121
Foster, Hal, 141
Foucault, Michel, 64, 152
Freud, Sigmund, 8, 86
futurity, 38, 51, 136, 181, 194, 198–199

Gabriel, Peter, 49, 108

Gama, Vasco da, 17
gated community, 8, 222n16, 235n60
Geimer, Peter, 85
gender, 13, 20, 22, 64, 91, 104, 114–117, 132, 159, 183, 193–194, 200, 203n2; gendered coding, 54, 59, 85, 192; gendered stereotypes, 94; gender studies, 10
Gilroy, Paul, 40
Glissant, Édouard, 126
Godard, Jean-Luc, 153, 158, 206n32
Goldblatt, David, 138
Gorin, Jean-Pierre, 153
Got Till It's Gone (music video), 26–27; figures 1.4 and 1.5 in color gallery B
Gqola, Pumla, 91–92, 136, 144
Great Trek, 18, 193; restaging of 19; Voortrekker, 210n9
Guattari, Félix, 10–13, 50, 145, 149
Gunkel, Henriette, 116, 118

Habermas, Jürgen, 56, 157
Halbwachs, Maurice, 14–15
Hayes, Patricia, 3, 90
Hersi, Fatima, 62–64, 74–75
Hillbrow, 119–120, 132, 157, 184
history, counter, 24, 156; visual, 17–19, 30, 33, 43, 54–58, 79, 88, 181, 190
Hlasane, Rangoato, 200
Holocaust, 177, 216–217n62, 226n71
Hotel Yeoville, 134–138, 199; *see also* Terry Kurgan

icon, documentary, 9, 105, 198; Christian 38, 89; hyper-icon 58, 63, 66, 74, 192; making, 97
identification, 2, 11, 56, 121–123, 136, 139, 147, 150; identity photos, 120–124
intervisuality, 5

Jaar, Alfredo, 48, 53
Jim Comes to Jo'burg (theme), 23, 100, 104, 211n24

Karakayalı, Serhat, 12
Kentridge, William, 88
Kester, Grant, 141
Kgoroge, Tony, 62–64, 74–75
Khoi-San, 185–186, 239n6
Khosa, Ungulani Ba Ba, 82, 112
Khumalo, Alfred, 26, 32
Khwezi, 72–74
Kihato, Caroline Wanjiku, 140, 241n36
King, Martin Luther, 132
Kracauer, Siegfried, 179
Kurgan, Terry, 134–138, 140, 229n6, 231n40
Kuria, Emily Ngubia, 158
kwerekwere, 132, 133, 230n33

Landau, Loren, 6, 93, 205n25
Landsberg, Alison, 79, 190
lesbians, black, 116, 136
Lorde, Audre, 87
lumpenproletariat, 92
Luthuli, Albert, 125, 203n3
lynching, USA, 224n38; South Africa, 224n38; memory of, 108

Magnum Photos, 2–3, 203n4, 204n6
Magubane, Peter, 26
Makeba, Miriam, 23, 52
Mamdani, Mahmoud, 22, 47
Man on Ground (film), 106–112; stills in color gallery E and F
Mandela, Nelson, 43, 80, 114, 125; (photo), 183, 19, 1971
Mandela, the Myth and Me (film), 191
Mandela, Winnie, 43–44
maps, 17, 18, 34, 170–171
Marikana mine, 196, 222–223n23, 242n45
Marinovich, Greg, 46; see also *Bang Bang* Club

Market Photo Workshop, 126, 138–142
Martine and Thandeka (film), 66–72
martyr, 38, 46, 90, 97, 104, 215n45, 226n80
Marx, Karl, 81, 92
masculinity, 36, 59, 81, 104, 113–114, 116–118, 193, 198; black, 36, 40, 81, 94, 104, 149, 214n22; hyper-, 179; white, 35, 45, 81, 104, 149, 180
mask, 126, 157–159
Massumi, Brian, 11, 51, 87
Matabane, Khalo, 61–64, 157, 191, 216n60, 234n29
Mbeki, Thabo, 80, 144, 221n5
Mbembe, Achille, 81, 92, 95, 124
McClintock, Ann, 20
memory, collective, 58; national, 15, 54, 58, 108, 170; prosthetic, 15, 190
meta-picture, 162, 196
Metz, Christian, 107, 223n27
migration, autonomy of, 144, 161; black, 14, 18; migrant labor system, 20–23; migrant worker, African, 8, 21–23, 92, 192–194; migrants from Mozambique, 112, 193; migrant women, 139–142, 194; photography and, 6, 30, 134, 138–141, 147, 205n25; white, 14, 17–20, 134, 185, 193
Minh-ha, Trinh T., 4–5
Mitchell, W. J. T., 146, 162, 198
mockumentary, 163
Moele, Kgebetli, 114
Mofokeng, Santu, 8
Molekane, Tumi, 113
Monareng, Michelle, 183, 186; see also *Removal to Radium*
Moten, Fred, 84, 86–87
mothership, 174
mourning, 39, 75, 81, 89, 103, 105; mournability, 75
Muholi, Zanele, 73–74, 198
Muñoz, José Esteban, 149
Musina, 154

Nando's "Diversity Clip" (video), 183–186
Native Land Act (also Black Land Act), 20–22, 186, 187, 190
Natives Resettlement Act, 170
necklacing, 43–45, 91, 215–216n51
Nhamuave, Ernesto, 8–9, 82–87, 90–112, 194, 226n80; figure 3.2.1; see also *Burning Man*
Nietzsche, Friedrich, 108
Nigerians, representations of, 6, 163, 177–180, 184, 205n23; *see also* stereotype
Nkosi, Lewis, 23–24
Nkosi, Thenjiwe Niki, 7, 114, 154–156, 162, 194, 198; see also *Border Farm*
Nkwali, Simphiwe, 83
Nyakudjara, Believe, *see* photo 4.1.4 in color gallery G
Nzima, Sam, 214n26

Omotoso, Akin, 106
opacity, opaqueness, 200; *see also* Édouard Glissant
Orford, Margie, 104

PAC Pan African Congress, 125
pain, 8, 9, 38, 56, 60, 66; painful memories, 79, 96, 103, 196; photographs of black bodies in pain, 30–34, 39, 40–43, 48, 51–54, 76, 84–88, 196, 198–200
Palmary, Ingrid, 13
Papadopoulus, Dimitris, 143, 149, 161
Paris is Burning (film), 199
Pass Burning (photo), 1
passport, 127; pass book, burning passes, 31; photo, 121–127, 141, 213n12

People in Pain (poster), 41
perpetrators (xenophobic attacks), 7, 91–93, 99, 105, 107, 109–111, 147, 194
photography, participatory, 74, 134–142, 193, 199
Pietà, 36, 38, 89, 192, 224n43
Pieterson, Hector, 36–39, 40, 51, 53; photograph, 37, 196, 214n26; museum, 215n34
post-representation, 200, 232n1
Powa (music video), 113–118
privilege, white, 3, 53, 79, 81, 85, 91, 95, 117, 180
Puar, Jasbir, 201
punctum (Barthes), 127

race, 13, 21, 29–30, 64, 89, 91–93, 117, 123, 141, 149, 159, 183, 192, 200, 203n2; and photography, 29, 212n2
racial, stereotypes, 27, 59, 144
racism, 91, 110; global, 112; apartheid and, 123; racialized subject, 3, 13, 85, 88, 90; post-racist, 197
Rancière, Jacques, 153, 155, 160, 206n32
rape, 66–74, 117, 140, 144, 226n74, 228n112; photographs of, 69, 226n74; *Remember Khwezi*, 72–74
reenactment, of apartheid images, 27; *see also* restaging
refugee, depiction of, 62–64
Removal to Radium (art installation), 183, 186–190; *see also* Michelle Monareng
Riebeeck, Jan van, 17, 18, 209n5
Rietspruit, 186–187
Robben Island, 191, 197
Robinson, Shayne, 103
Rogosin, Lionel, 22, 211n23
Rosler, Martha, 52–53

SABC South African Broadcasting Company, 191
Saunders, Christopher, 88, 102
Saxton, Libby, 96
self-portrait, 3, 73, 122, 132–134–142; figure 4.2.1 and 4.2.2 in color gallery H, I
shame, 10, 60, 63, 67–69, 139
Sharpeville, 26, 29, 39
Sibande, Mary, 210n22
Sidibé, Malick, 26
Sisonke Sex Worker Movement, 138, 140
Sithole, Xolishwa, 69, 220n125
Sjoberg, Patrick, 65
Smaill, Belinda, 38
Smuts, Jan, 21
Solomon-Godeau, Abigail, 4
Sonke Gender Justice Network, 105
Sontag, Susan, 60–61, 85
South West Africa People's Organization (SWAPO), 35
Soweto, 170, 183, 203n1; Uprising, 36, 171; freedom fighters, 44
Spinzoa, Baruch de, 10, 12
Spitz, Andy, 145, 198
Spivak, Gayatri Chakravorty, 57, 92, 150, 161, 198, 228n113
stagings, 156–160
state of emergency, 43–44
stereotype, 180; of Nigerians, 163, 184, 205n23; *see also* representations of Nigerians
Steyerl, Hito, 76, 152–153, 158, 232n1
suffering, individualized, 90, 105; viewing of, 9, 59–60
Sun City, protest video, 49–53, stills in color gallery C, D
Sun Ra (musician), 174

tears, 59–72; images of, 200; photograph of, 42; testimony in tears, 62–69; at the TRC, 57–59; visualizing of, 215n45
Thomas, Kylie, 39, 107

Till, Emmett, 86–87, 89
trafficking, 127–129; anti-, 120, 127–128, 144
trauma, 11, 15, 59, 64–69, 85–86, 91, 94, 111, 144, 191, 196, 208n53
Truth and Reconciliation Commission (TRC), 47, 57–59, 79
Tshabalala, Lindsaye, 46
Tsianos, Vassilis, 143, 149, 156, 161
Tutu, Desmond, 57, 80
Twalo, Sinethemba, 150, 159

Ugah, Adze, 100.

victimhood, 21, 59, 134; crying victim, 58, 62–74; victim tradition, 74
violence, 107–109; black on black, 45; colonial, 107; post-apartheid, 108–109; sexual, 66–74; *see also* rape, 111, 195
visibility, of black bodies, 14, 24; white bodies, 14, 27–28, 160; hypervisibility, 161, 200
Vladislavić, Ivan, 27, 160–161
voyeurism, 30, 60, 64, 66, 69, 89, 103, 200; voyeur, 42, 63
vulnerability, 9, 38, 62, 64, 66, 68, 118, 207n44

Wa Lehulere, Kemang, 186
Waller, Marguerite, 163
We are Nowhere (film), 144–147
Wedemeyer, Clemens von, 159
Weinberg, Eli, 125
Weza, Meza, 154–155
whiteness, 27, 91, 158, 200, 204n8, 207n45, 236n63; perspectives of, 200; white race, 36; white minority, 21, 88
Wilderson, Frank, 24
Williams, Linda, 39, 65
witnessing, 47, 70, 96, 103, 176, 194
Wolf, Nicole, 223n35
women, black, 21, 36; protest of, 3, 72–73
Working the City (poster), figure 4.2.3 in color gallery J; (project), 194, 199, 231n49
wound, images as, 12, 39, 56–57, 85, 96, 196, 198

xenophobia, 17, 81, 111–112, 141, 171, 173, 180, 198, 205n21
xenophobic attacks, 5–10, 44, 53–54, 67, 77–82, 99–113, 144–145, 168, 179, 181, 184–185, 193–196

Yuval-Davis, Nira, 94

Zimbabweans, stereotypes on, 144
Zuma, Jacob, 72, 73, 197, 242n49